D0590444

WHITE FLAG?

MICHAEL ASHCROFT & ISABEL OAKESHOTT

WHITE FLAG?

AN EXAMINATION OF THE UK'S DEFENCE CAPABILITY

Biteback Publishing

First published in Great Britain in 2018 by
Biteback Publishing Ltd
Westminster Tower
3 Albert Embankment
London SE1 7SP
Copyright © MAA Publishing Limited 2018

ISBN 978-1-78590-410-3

10 9 8 7 6 5 4 3 2 1

A CIP catalogue record for this book is available from the British Library.

Set in Minion Pro and Trade Gothic

Printed and bound in Great Britain by
CPI Group (UK) Ltd, Croydon CR0 4YY

CONTENTS

ACKNOWLEDGEMENTS

First and foremost we would like to thank the very many members of the armed forces who generously gave their time and consideration to this project.

Our investigation draws from interviews with several hundred military personnel of all ranks. Some of our most valuable sources were serving officers and talked to us on condition of anonymity. They know who they are and how very much their contributions were appreciated. We are particularly grateful to General Sir Mike Jackson GCB CBE DSO DL, former Chief of the General Staff, for his incisive and generous foreword.

As *White Flag?* is about the state of the armed forces today, we were especially keen to talk to individuals with current or very recent experience of the military. For this reason we did not interview all the very distinguished retired generals, air marshals and admirals whose passionate views on our subject are a matter of public record. This does not mean that their opinions were ignored. On the contrary, they were respectfully studied.

A number of military figures went to particular trouble to support our research. They did this because they care about defence, have concerns about the state of the armed forces, and believed in what we were trying to achieve. They are Lt General Sir David Capewell KCB OBE (former Chief of Operations at Permanent Joint Headquarters); General Sir Richard Barrons KCB CBE (former Commander Joint Forces Command); and Lord Richards of Herstmonceux, GCB CBE DSO DL (former Chief of the Defence Staff). We are very grateful to them. Lt General Sir Graeme Lamb KBE CMG DSO (former Director of Special Forces); Lord Houghton of Richmond GCB CBE DL (former Chief of

Defence Staff); General Sir Peter Wall GCB CBE DL (former Chief of the General Staff); Air Marshal Greg Bagwell CB CBE and Lt General Sir Simon Mayall KBE CB were also most supportive.

Rear Admiral Chris Parry CBE is a great communicator about the importance of sea power in the twenty-first century and was incredibly helpful with the naval sections of the book. Thanks are also due to Rear Admiral Roger Lane-Nott CB for his contribution to our section on submariners, and to Admiral Sir George Zambellas GCB DSC ADC DL. We would also like to mention James Glancy CGC, a Royal Marine, and Captain Anton Lin.

We were keen to explore how our armed forces are perceived by our allies and travelled widely for the project, attending defence conferences in Bahrain, Singapore and Germany and interviewing military figures in Brussels and Washington. We also went to Estonia and Lithuania. General David Petraeus AO, former director of the Central Intelligence Agency and former Commander of the International Security Assistance Force in Afghanistan, was among a number of distinguished Americans who kindly agreed to talk to us and we were very grateful for his time. Particular thanks are due to the Ministry of Defence of Ukraine, which facilitated our research trip to the Donbas. They offered interviews with serving military personnel at the highest level and arranged our trip to the frontline. Kevin Culwick, director of Lord Ashcroft Polls, arranged surveys in ten countries with characteristic efficiency and flair.

White Flag? is as much about the politics of defence as the military itself and we were extremely grateful to secure interviews with many former Defence Secretaries. The Rt Hon. the Lord Robertson of Port Ellen KT GCMG PC; Rt Hon. the Lord Hutton of Furness PC and the Rt Hon. the Lord Browne of Ladyton PC were all willing to go on record with their experiences and were very generous with time and insights. Several other Defence Secretaries spoke to us on background terms. Liberal Democrats Sir Nicholas Harvey, who was Minister of State for the Armed Forces between 2010 and 2012, a key period for this book; and the Rt Hon. Sir Vince Cable MP, who as Business Secretary during the coalition years was responsible for arms exports, also both kindly agreed to be interviewed. We talked to several former Ministry of Defence special advisers, among whom we would especially like to thank Michael Dugher, who worked for Labour Defence Secretary Geoff Hoon as well as in Downing Street during Gordon Brown's administration; and Rob Golledge.

Special thanks are due to a number of MPs who know a great deal about the armed forces and work tirelessly to promote the interests of our servicemen and women in the Houses of Parliament. Given the political focus of this book, their perspective was particularly important. Captain Johnny Mercer MP, who has led a determined and selfless campaign to end the pursuit of veterans over historic allegations of abuse, gave valuable advice throughout the project. His own book, *We Were Warriors*, about his tours of duty in Afghanistan, was a source of inspiration. The Rt Hon. Ben Wallace MP, James Cleverly MP TD VR, Kwasi Kwarteng MP and the Rt Hon. Tobias Ellwood MP were also very supportive. Lt Col Tom Tugendhat MP VR is an expert on war and the law and his exceptional work in this field was an important source for our chapter on 'lawfare'.

The Rt Hon. Gavin Williamson CBE MP, Defence Secretary at the time of writing, is keen to make the Ministry of Defence less risk-averse, and led by example by co-operating with this project. He did so unconditionally because he is keen to promote a greater understanding of the importance of defence to the UK and the value of our armed forces. His support for what we are attempting to achieve in this book made a very significant difference to the project and brought our understanding of the politics of defence right up to date.

A number of former Ministry of Defence officials talked to us off-record, and their contributions greatly enhanced our understanding of the inner workings of the department, particularly in relation to the complex procurement process. Though we are critical of some aspects of the department's record, we are clear that where there are shortcomings, they are generally institutional failures, not failures by individuals.

Defence academics were pivotal to our research. We spent a great deal of time listening to these specialists and attending conferences, lectures and seminars organised by defence and foreign affairs think tanks, especially the Royal United Services Institute. These academics sought nothing in return for assisting us. We would like to thank all of those who gave their time, including Professor Gwythian Prins; Dr Mark Galeotti; Dr Rob Johnson; the naval historian Eric Grove; Dr Patrick Bury; Dr Lee Rotherham; Dr Richard North; and everyone at Veterans for Britain. The ethnographer Dr Mark De Rond was another inspiration. We drew heavily from his powerful account of life and death in a field hospital in Afghanistan for our section on the ethics of modern warfare.

Among other valued contributors to the project were veteran defence correspondent Tim Ripley; Luke Skipper, former Chief of Staff to the Scottish National Party's Westminster Group; and Major General Mick Laurie CBE. We would also like to thank Peter Oborne.

We have tried extremely hard to avoid inaccuracies, but in a work of this length and detail, on a subject of such complexity, some mistakes are inevitable. Josh Dolder and Tony Diver worked very long hours towards the end of the project assisting with fact checking and referencing. Both were highly professional and committed, and helped us meet our publishing deadline. Any mistakes that have nonetheless slipped through the net are honest ones.

Finally, we are grateful to Angela Entwistle, corporate communications director to Lord Ashcroft, and her wonderful team; and to everybody at Biteback Publishing, for making this project possible.

FOREWORD BY GENERAL SIR MIKE JACKSON GCB CBE DSO DL

The Defence of the Realm does not preoccupy many voters, but nonetheless it affects us all. We are privileged that, unlike many in the world, our collective survival is not an issue that presents itself often in day-to-day life. The task of managing defence is trustingly delegated to those whom we elect to govern. We expect the state to fulfil the most basic function of government: the provision of armed forces trained, equipped and ready to protect us against those who seek to do us harm. The sharp end of this requirement is the provision of military forces with the capacity to close and destroy the Queen's enemies.

Far away from the bayonets and boot polish, it is ideological disagreements and budgetary constraints that consume the lives of those who work in the upper echelons of Parliament and the Ministry of Defence. Of course, it is right that decisions over how our country is to be defended are taken democratically, with advice from experts and intelligence from government agencies informing those who represent civilians at risk from foreign threats. But there are two grave errors that result from the political wrangling and horse-trading associated with the debate over defence in the UK, and they bear heavily on this country's safety.

First, the focus on funding the armed forces too often takes place at the beginning of the debate about defence rather than at the end. When Defence Secretary Gavin Williamson was appointed in November 2017, he was immediately asked to make a judgement on what capabilities to cut to ease the financial crisis engulfing the Ministry of Defence. In Whitehall, the priority seems to be improving the appearance of the departmental spending spreadsheet. At Westminster, there was much speculation over whether the new man could wrest more money from the Treasury than his predecessor. It is a metric by which many seem to assess the success of politicians who do his job. As this book is published, in autumn 2018, a major review of UK defence has been delayed indefinitely due to irreconcilable differences over finance.

This current obsession with the defence budget is a mistake. Rather than reflecting what is thought to be affordable, our armed forces should reflect the position we wish our country to hold in the world, and the threats to which we believe they may have to respond. Only then, when we have identified what we expect of our services, can we begin to assess what the necessary capabilities are going to cost. When governments alight on a relatively arbitrary figure (shaped by what is left in the public coffers after more popular causes like health and education have been given their lot) and ask defence chiefs to make the best of it, they are in danger of putting our security at risk.

Second, if we are to create a strategy that addresses threat, not thrift, then we must be realistic about how long it takes to construct a fighting force with the necessary software and hardware. We may look across Eastern Europe and into Asia, where future security challenges may lie, and conclude that nothing bad is going to happen any time soon; and if it does, it will be thousands of miles away. However, the wars of tomorrow will be fought with capability acquired today. What may be true now will not necessarily be true in ten or twenty years' time. It is impossible to know for sure what potential adversaries may be willing and able to do in the decades ahead. This is difficult for politicians, who instinctively operate on the five-year electoral timescale. They must, where they can, look beyond current challenges to future threat. It is often said that defence capability is an insurance policy against existential danger. The increasingly volatile world in which we find ourselves requires that we do not economise unduly on its protection.

In recent wars, the armed forces have employed superior technology in unfamiliar territory to destroy disparate enemies, some operating covertly. They have also been deployed on humanitarian missions and to combat pirates off the Horn of Africa. These are important and honourable roles that we should maintain the capability to perform. But politicians should not be so quick to dismiss the possibility of states, not terrorists, doing us real harm, especially where they have been blatant about their intentions. Asked what was the worst event of the twentieth century, Russian President Vladimir Putin once replied that it was the fall of the Soviet Union. Neither the Holocaust nor either of the two World Wars, in his mind, match the humiliation of the lowering of the hammer and sickle over Moscow in the early 1990s. That feeling of nostalgia for Russian imperium has powerful consequences for global security in the twenty-first century – as does the Chinese exceptionalism that is already finding expression in the aggressive militarisation of the South China Seas.

As the government considers its next move in terms of its defence strategy for the foreseeable future, Michael Ashcroft and Isabel Oakeshott's new book *White Flag?* is both highly topical and extremely relevant. Indeed, rarely could a book of this nature be better timed. *White Flag?* will be read and enjoyed by politicians and defence experts, but its key strength is that it is a book for everyone who cares about our country's security and their own family's safety. This is a salient, even an indispensable, work for the general reader, not just the military geek.

White Flag? takes a balanced, measured and analytical look at the UK's past, current and future defence capabilities. It is well written and well argued – it does not try to point the finger of blame at individuals or even a single political party for past failings, but it does provide a considered assessment of what the UK needs to do in future if it is to remain a respected and formidable power on the global stage.

White Flag? is thought-provoking and challenging too: when a reader puts this book down for the last time, I feel certain that he or she will be left with real concerns that the UK may not be sufficiently equipped at present to deal with the uncertain dangers that lie ahead.

I commend the two authors for producing a diligently researched, timely and important work that everyone who worries about our future security and safety should find the time to read.

AUTHORS' ROYALTIES

Lord Ashcroft is donating all authors' royalties from *White Flag?* to military charities.

LORD ASHCROFT AND
THE ARMED FORCES

Lord Ashcroft has a long-standing interest in defence and supports many charities relating to the armed forces.

Between 2012 and 2018, he was the UK government's special representative for veterans' transition. In this capacity, he worked with all departments to ensure military personnel receive the help they need when making the move to civilian life. In May 2011, he was appointed lead adviser to a government review of military bases on Cyprus.

A former treasurer and deputy chairman of the Conservative Party, Lord Ashcroft has written six books on gallantry. He is a trustee of Imperial War Museums, which display his collection of Victoria Crosses (VCs) and George Crosses (GCs) in the Lord Ashcroft Gallery along with other VCs and GCs in the museums' care. Over the past three decades, he has acquired more than 200 of these awards, the largest collection of such decorations in the world.

LordAshcroft.com | LordAshcroftPolls.com | LordAshcroftMedals.com
@LordAshcroft

SAXA VORD

A WARNING

Far away, where seagulls wheel and cry in graphite skies and the wind has been known to reach 197 miles per hour, lies the last outpost of the UK's air defence system.

The radar station of Saxa Vord clings to a barren hillock on Unst, the remotest tip of the Shetland Isles, battered by salt sea and winters that envelop it in darkness for up to eighteen hours a day. It is further north than St Petersburg.

Once upon a time, this desolate place was on a list of Russian nuclear targets. At the height of the Cold War, 300 military men were based there keeping watch for the Soviets. Sometimes Royal Air Force fighter jets would be scrambled to intercept Russian aircraft and escort them out of UK airspace. The radar system meant the stretch of sea between Greenland, Iceland and the UK known as the GIUK gap was under constant Ministry of Defence surveillance. Whoever controls this passageway controls Russia's access to the world's seas.

With the collapse of the Soviet Union, the threat to national security dissipated and the radar station was closed. When the last uniformed personnel left in 2005, the Ministry of Defence made a bit of money by selling off part of the site. The old buildings were converted into a hotel and bar for the remaining inhabitants of Unst and for tourists in search of shelter and refreshment after the odyssey from mainland Scotland.

Between 2006 and 2018, there was no routine surveillance of this area. Whether the Kremlin discovered that hundreds of miles of airspace were rendered invisible to the UK's armed forces after Saxa Vord closed, the Ministry of Defence cannot disclose. Under the Official

Secrets Act, Saxa Vord is defined as a 'prohibited place': such information is secret. A forbidding sign at the perimeter of the old radar station warns the curious to keep out – or risk arrest.

What *is* public knowledge is that the Royal Air Force now spends a lot of time and energy launching fighter jets to warn off approaching Russian military aircraft. For the past five years, it has happened approximately once every month.

In February 2018, Saxa Vord was officially re-opened.[1]

Some £10 million is being invested in new radar detection systems on Unst.

The Ministry of Defence has bestowed Saxa Vord with a motto: *Praemoneo de Periculis*. It means: 'I Give Advance Warning of Danger'.

THE GREENLAND, ICELAND AND UNITED KINGDOM (GIUK) GAP

WHOEVER CONTROLS THIS STRETCH OF WATER CONTROLS RUSSIA'S ACCESS TO THE WORLD'S SEAS.

INTRODUCTION

GREAT BRITAIN

Every Monday, British military chiefs file into a room on the fifth floor of the Ministry of Defence to discuss anything going on in the world that might affect the armed forces.

The meeting takes place in the sober surroundings of the Mountbatten Suite, the venue for the most sensitive official briefings in the department. The boardroom is dominated by a long, coffin-shaped table and a large map of the world.

Above the door, a set of digital clocks displays the time in London, Washington, Brussels, Moscow and Bahrain. At the far end of the room, a huge video screen patches in overseas commands, British representatives in NATO and Washington, and even US satellite imagery.

During the first part of the meeting, which is not attended by politicians, civil servants and military attendees like to play a game. After full and frank discussions among themselves about what is really going on, they discuss how little they can get away with telling the Secretary of State and his team.

One afternoon in 2017, after the politicians had settled themselves into the beige, faux-leather seats for the second part of the proceedings, the discussion took an unusual turn. At issue was whether British Commandos might be able to perform a daring operation to seize a port in Yemen, potentially allowing vital food and medical supplies to get through to starving civilians.

Around the table was the Director of Special Forces, heads of the army, navy and RAF, and various senior mandarins. They had been through the usual briefings on the position of Russian submarines

1

in British waters and the latest provocations from President Putin's bombers over the North Sea. Now they were on to the next item on the agenda: the long-running civil war in Yemen. There were reports that the former president had been murdered by Iranian militias angered by his close relationship with the Saudis. It looked like a humanitarian catastrophe that had already left 7 million civilians starving and 18 million in need of urgent aid was about to get much worse.[1] With the United Kingdom heading the UN Security Council group on Yemen, there was an onus on the British government to provide some leadership.

Pivotal to the success of any aid operation was access to the port of Al Hudaydah, a vital aid delivery point on the Red Sea, where the vast majority of Yemen's food imports arrive. The United Nations had been trying in vain to broker a deal between Iranian-backed Houthi groups controlling the port and the Saudi-led Arab coalition determined to crush them and establish dominance of the country at whatever cost. The challenge was to turn the port over to neutral parties.[2]

'How about this for an idea? We send in the Marines,' suggested junior defence minister Tobias Ellwood.

The exchange that followed between politicians, uniforms and officials in the Ministry of Defence illustrates how attitudes have changed towards Britain's role on the world stage. Ellwood, a former captain in the Royal Green Jackets who served in Kuwait, set out his vision for a carefully brokered intervention. Having worked on Yemen when he was a minister at the Foreign Office, he felt he understood the complexities.

'We have got to get everybody back to the negotiating table. There's a million people in Hudaydah. There's cholera; hunger; thousands of people are dying; and it's only going to get worse. The Saudi coalition is getting frustrated. There's a danger they will just charge in and try to take the port, and that will be a disaster,' he urged.

He reminded the room of the huge loss of life when the rest of the world turned a blind eye during a battle for the smaller Yemeni port of Mocha.

'This is much bigger than Mocha. It will be a bloodbath,' he warned.

Ellwood outlined the diplomatic and practical steps required before the UK could dispatch the Royal Marines. To his mind, the advantages of such an operation were obvious. Most importantly, securing the port could save many lives. Secondly, it would reassert the UK's status as an active player in international crises, reminding Gulf Nations and others that despite our refusal to enter the civil war in Syria, we are not ready to resign ourselves to the role of bystander in conflicts whose reverberations affect the wider world. Finally, as Treasury and Ministry of Defence budget-cutters question the relevance of amphibious capability in the twenty-first century, it could help secure the future of the Royal Marines.

For a painful ten seconds after Ellwood presented his case, nobody uttered a word. But their expressions said it all: the minister must be off his rocker. It wasn't just that Britain had no immediate skin in the game and that nobody was asking our armed forces to step forward. It was also the risk to the Marines. If this entirely discretionary rescue mission more than 4,000 miles away went wrong, by the minister's own reckoning, ten to fifteen British personnel could be killed. To the assembled group, this was unconscionable.

Eventually Ellwood broke the silence.

'Well, clearly nobody is taking me seriously. Let's move on to something else,' he said briskly, and that was the end of that. Perhaps that's a good thing. Even if the Marines had succeeded in seizing the port, how long could they have held it if things didn't go to plan?

What if the mission escalated, and more troops were required? What would taxpayers make of yet another disastrous foreign military adventure turning sour?

How different that discussion might have been under Tony Blair, however. When Labour swept to power in 1997, the new Prime Minister was quick to make clear where he saw Britain's place in the world. A year after taking office, he unveiled a defence review full of language and jargon from what now seems like a bygone age. It was the era of 'Cool Britannia', and his government was ready to get stuck into other people's wars.

With the bombast of an administration that had won the election by a landslide, Labour's Strategic Defence Review (SDR) of 1998 declared:

> The British are, by instinct, an internationalist people. We believe that as well as defending our rights, we should discharge our responsibilities in the world. We do not want to stand idly by and watch humanitarian disasters or the aggression of dictators go unchecked. We want to give a lead, we want to be a force for good.[3]

This gung-ho Strategic Defence Review received almost universal praise at the time. A UN intervention in Bosnia under the previous government, later passed to NATO, had been popular across the political spectrum in the UK. The failure of major powers and international organisations to intervene to prevent Rwanda's genocide in 1994 had added to the feeling that Britain, along with other Western powers, had a duty to help bring repressive foreign dictators to book; free the oppressed; and rescue those at risk from natural disasters or humanitarian crises. The road to Kosovo, East Timor, Sierra Leone, Afghanistan and Iraq was set.

Fast-forward twenty years, and we are in a very different place. The experiences of Iraq and Afghanistan have had a profound effect on public appetite for wars of choice.

We could not achieve decisive or lasting victories in either country, and the campaigns came at huge cost. Hundreds of brave men and women who set off to far-flung places on missions to make the world a better place returned from the deserts and mountains in Union Jack-draped coffins. Billions of pounds that could have been spent on hospitals, schools and roads were squandered. To critics of these operations, the sacrifices made without bringing peace and stability (never mind democracy) to those countries discredit the concept of using the British military as a force for good. Meanwhile, the furore over Blair's infamous 'Dodgy Dossier' about weapons of mass destruction in Iraq has left many voters deeply mistrustful of the motives of political leaders who choose to send our troops into conflict zones.[4]

The UK's ill-fated intervention in Libya in 2011, which rid the country of Muammar Gaddafi but ended up fuelling conflict across the region and strengthening ISIS and al-Qaeda, cemented a widespread view that we are better off keeping out.[5]

The grim determination among MPs of all political persuasions to avoid repeating such mistakes was exposed in the summer of 2013, when they refused to sanction UK involvement in US-led strikes on Syrian President Bashar al-Assad's regime. The majority of MPs did not want Britain to get involved, even when a tyrant crossed 'red lines' by using chemical weapons against his own people.[6] When it happened again in April 2018, Prime Minister Theresa May decided not to risk asking MPs for permission to join US strikes, and wisely so. It is entirely possible that she would have been defeated.[7]

When they oppose discretionary military action, MPs are largely reflecting the views of their constituents. In polling for this book, just 62 per cent of those questioned in June 2018* said they would support the deployment of UK forces to defend an ally that had been invaded by another country – the mutual defence that underpins the UK's relationship with other members of NATO. Only half would support 'pre-emptive action against foreign states believed to pose a threat to the UK'. The prospect of state-on-state warfare does not prey on the public mind.

All this has created the environment in which defence cuts are a political soft touch. Voters may not like reductions to the armed forces, but they do not take to the streets to protest. In so far as they give it any thought, many people imagine that drones and robots will soon be able to do the work of soldiers, sailors and airmen in any case. There is a sense that we can get by without much of an army or navy, because nobody is going to invade the UK, and wars of the future will probably be in cyberspace or outer space. It is widely taken for granted that any future military action will be with allies, who can fill our capability

---

* Note: 2,021 adults were interviewed online between 8 and 11 June 2018. Results were weighted to be representative of all adults in Great Britain. Full results are in the Appendix to this book, with detailed data at LordAshcroftPolls.com.

gaps. Preoccupied with getting through the day, successive Prime Ministers and their Chancellors have not lost sleep about cutting defence, reassuring themselves that any backlash will largely be confined to those they dismiss as 'the usual suspects': retired generals who suddenly find a voice after leaving office, and old boys harking back to the glory days of the Falklands in letters to the *Daily Telegraph*.

The downward trend in defence spending in the UK dates back to the so-called peace dividend following the end of the Cold War. The fall of the Berlin Wall was accompanied by a sense of triumphalism in the West and a feeling among intellectuals and policy-makers that the long struggle with the Soviet Union had come to a conclusion. With Communism in retreat, Francis Fukuyama, a young American intellectual, famously wrote that the world might be witnessing 'not just the end of the Cold War, or the passing of a particular period of post war history, but the end of history as such: that is, the end point of mankind's ideological evolution and the universalization of Western liberal democracy as the final form of human government'.[8] His intervention reflected widespread optimism among Western policy-makers that the last redoubts of dictatorship would eventually succumb to the march of capitalism, and state-on-state warfare driven by diverging political ideologies would become a thing of the past.

The new world order had a dramatic impact on the balance between 'guns and butter', setting the scene for decades of defence cuts. In 2010, the coalition government went further than any previous administration dared. Declaring there was no 'conventional military threat' to the 'territorial integrity of the United Kingdom', they proposed such brutal reductions to the armed forces that parts of the service felt they were in danger of going extinct.[9]

Those who are content with the status quo have a peacetime mentality, shaped by decades of life in a stable, secure, rules-based environment. They see no reason to think any differently. But can policy-makers be so confident that tomorrow will be like yesterday?

In recent months, military leaders, politicians and academics have begun voicing increasing concerns about the nature and scale of new threats and our ability to counter them. As we shall see, in Ukraine, Russia disdains the rules-based international order that acts as a restraining influence on the ambitions of unscrupulous political leaders and has underpinned global security for decades. A resurgent China is busy militarising the South China Seas, aggressively asserting its sovereignty over disputed territory and transforming rocks into military outposts that could be used to disrupt global free trade. Meanwhile, in North Korea, a dictator in a country where most people earn just a few dollars a month and have no access to gas or electricity threatens to hold the world to ransom with a growing arsenal of nuclear weapons. All this at a time when ISIS may be weakened but has not yet packed away the black flag, and any oddball or extremist with exceptional computer skills can hack into sensitive IT systems and disrupt or cut off vital services. There is no evidence that any of these dangers are receding.

Against this backdrop, there is deepening disquiet at every level within the armed forces, and within wider defence circles, at what looks like a terrible mismatch between defence resourcing and a growing likelihood that we may soon be at war again. As the defence cliché goes: 'We may not be interested in the enemy; but they sure as hell are interested in us.' Moreover, as Chief of the Defence Staff General Sir Nick Carter has warned: 'The threats we face are not thousands of miles away but now on Britain's doorstep.' Carter went on to declare: 'The time to address those threats is now – we cannot sit back.'

The chorus of distinguished voices highlighting the perils of complacency is becoming difficult to ignore.[10] [11]

Our polling suggests that a great majority of people in Britain think the country now faces bigger dangers than it did during the final years of the Cold War. Three quarters of British adults said they thought the overall threat to the UK's national security is higher today than it was thirty years ago – and more than four in ten thought it much higher. Perhaps surprisingly, those with the longest memories were the most likely to think the peril had increased: among those aged sixty-five or over, 85 per cent thought the current threat was greater, compared to just under two thirds of those aged eighteen to twenty-four.

Under Defence Secretaries Philip Hammond and Sir Michael Fallon, the Ministry of Defence adopted a brilliant catchword as a cover for diminishing strength. Ministers and officials would insist the debate was not about numbers, but *capability*.

On the face of it, it was a fantastic way to neutralise arguments about vanishing regiments and mothballed ships. The same rhetoric has been used to justify cuts to other public services during the austerity years.

Sometimes it is indeed possible to do more with less. There are compelling examples of super-efficient NHS Trusts treating more patients and police forces catching more criminals despite slimmed-down budgets. More often, having less results in doing less, as doctors and detectives know.

After years of dissembling, government ministers are beginning to admit that defence cuts have gone too far. This is not the fault of any one political party. As we shall see, the state of our armed forces today is the product of multi-billion-pound procurement decisions whose origins stretch back decades. It is a consequence of both Labour and Conservative policies, devised by politicians grappling with limited public funds and no crystal ball. No party occupies the moral high ground.

Politicians aren't the only ones responsible for confusing voters in this debate. There are many vested interests. Heads of the army, navy and RAF compete for resources, and have to justify their budgets while rivals question their value. The defence industry, which has a turnover of £23 billion and contributes £8.7 billion in Gross Value Added to the UK economy, needs to peddle new kit.[12] Some retired air marshals, admirals and generals need to maintain a public profile to keep them in work. This doesn't make their views any less valid, but they are not necessarily objective.

Think tanks produce brilliant reports about the state of defence, but the sheer volume of jargon, acronyms and assumed knowledge often renders the subject impenetrable to those with no background in defence. The manner in which the issues are discussed and reported elsewhere (typically by specialists for specialists) can be off-putting.

This book does not attempt to compete with the experts, but to complement their work. It is designed for a general audience. It is for people who sense that the UK may not be fully prepared for a conflict we cannot avoid, and would like a better understanding of what's going on, particularly at the top. It is as much about the politics of defence as the military itself.

In our polling for this book, we presented people with a list of potential hazards and asked them to give each one a score out of 100, according to the danger they thought it currently posed. Top of the list across the board was 'terror attacks in the UK carried out by terrorist groups' (p. 393). Detecting and preventing possible extremist threats, mainly from radical Islam but also from cyber terrorism, organised criminals and the far right, is chiefly the job of the UK's intelligence services, not the armed forces, so will not be given detailed treatment in this book.

We have not attempted to re-write the Chilcot Report on the UK's role in the Iraq War, or trawl over the mistakes of Afghanistan and the notorious era of 'bad kit'. We do not start from the premise that efficiency savings are bad per se, or that Britain necessarily needs a huge field army or a certain number of ships and planes.

We have simply asked questions about whether we still need a well-resourced military; what range of capabilities they require; and what shape they're really in. We have explored whether the armed forces are equipped to deal with the threats we might face later today or tomorrow; the extent to which we can rely on allies to fill gaps in our capabilities; and how well the Ministry of Defence works.

These are huge subjects, and each of the chapters that follows is worth a book in itself. Indeed, hundreds of highly specialised tomes and journals have been written by distinguished individuals about specific strands of the subject. This book tries to bring it all together, to give the lay reader an overview.

There are many good reasons why nobody has attempted anything similar to date, not least that the subject is so vast that covering it in the depth that would satisfy defence experts would take years – and necessitate a work longer than the Bible. By the time it was complete, it would be hopelessly out of date. So we have had to be pragmatic. We acknowledge that the intelligence agencies play a huge role in defence and recognise that soft power and international aid are vital parts of the picture. However, the work of spies, diplomats, charities and NGOs is beyond the scope of this project. Our focus is the British military, as it is today.

We do not intend to paint a picture that is all doom and gloom. The UK still has the sixth largest military budget in the world.[13] It is one of only a handful of countries with fully functional expeditionary capabilities that allow us to launch some operations on our own on faraway shores.[14]

As we shall see, there are certain things our armed forces do that nobody else does better. Our Special Forces, our anti-submarine warfare capabilities and our ability to fight on all terrains in extreme weather are the envy of armed forces across the globe.[15]

When we started this project, in late 2016, there was less cause for optimism. In political circles, few were talking about the importance of defence. The Ministry of Defence was institutionally secretive and deeply risk-averse.

Two years on, there are signs that political and public opinion is starting to change – and so is the Ministry of Defence. Under an energetic and committed new Secretary of State, Gavin Williamson, the department is cautiously opening up – and defence has shot up the political agenda.

As we prepare to leave the European Union, this country is at a crossroads. We must forge a new identity on the world stage. The shape and size of our armed forces, and our expectations of them, will be pivotal to our new international status. Our hope is that this book contributes to the debate about what happens next.

PART ONE

THE THREAT

'SI VIS PACEM – PARA BELLUM'
If you want peace, be ready for war

VLAD'S BOYS

A NOTE ON THE SOFT UNDERBELLY OF RUSSIAN AGGRESSION

One November evening, a stocky businessman from Bristol strolled up to the gates of a London embassy, announced his arrival through the intercom, and slipped into the heavily guarded confines of the building.

What happened next perfectly illustrates the dilemma facing the British armed forces today: do they tool up with conventional military hardware for the mother of all battles with a powerful nation state, or switch their focus to cyber and robotics, quietly accepting subordination to the intelligence services?

It was 16 November 2015, and Arron Banks was on a high. He had recently started bankrolling a Brexit campaign and was putting the finishing touches to plans for the official launch. It would take place later that week in a grand auditorium a few streets from the Palace of Westminster, with a respected American pollster called Gerry Gunster and a representative from the data mining firm Cambridge Analytica lined up to deliver speeches. His new movement was beginning to attract serious political attention.

As he made his way along Kensington Palace Gardens, Banks must have been reflecting on the challenges that lay ahead. His determination to take on the establishment over the relationship between Britain and Brussels was going to thrust him into the media spotlight, a position in which he was not always comfortable. It was also going to require serious capital. Luckily, new business opportunities were always coming his way – which was why he was off to the Russian Embassy again.

Banks was getting to know the place, having already spent some time there. His growing relationship with the Ambassador, Dr Alexander Yakovenko, had begun with a chance encounter on Doncaster racecourse a few weeks earlier. There, he'd bumped into a senior Russian Embassy official, who'd followed up with an invitation to lunch with his boss.

The meal had been a tremendous success. What might have been a rather stiff and formal event turned into a riotous social occasion. Over a marathon six-hour lunch, Banks had briefed the Ambassador about his plans for the referendum, gushing about his friend and hero Nigel Farage. He explained his conviction that the controversial leader of the UK Independence Party should play a key role in the campaign.

The Ambassador was impressed. He was beginning to see just how useful this maverick character could be. As the vodka flowed and tongues loosened, the conversation shifted from politics to money. It was then that the Ambassador dangled a tantalising business opportunity in front of his English guest: a stake in a major consolidation of Russian gold mining companies.

For Banks, such an investment was not unnatural territory. Though he had made his fortune in car insurance, he already had significant interests in precious metals and gemstones in Africa. He kept a close eye on the gold market and believed it was on the rise. When he and the Ambassador finally parted ways, more than a little merry, they exchanged mobile phone numbers, promising to catch up again very soon.

Yakovenko lost no time following up. The following day, 7 November 2015, he texted Banks inviting him for a drink. He wanted to introduce him to an associate who could explain more about the Russian gold opportunity. The date he suggested was 16 November.

'1800 at my place. He will come to London. Is it good for you?' he messaged.

'The 16th will be fine,' Banks replied eagerly, offering an invitation of his own.

'I would like to reciprocate your hospitality and invite you and your wife to my home in the countryside. Maybe December?'

The Ambassador accepted 'with pleasure'.

Over drinks at the Ambassador's Residence on 16 November, Banks was introduced to a wealthy Russian businessman named Siman Povarenkin. A key player in the potential gold speculation, he too was keen to get Banks involved. After some small talk, he gave an informal presentation on the business proposal they had been discussing. It involved the possible acquisition and amalgamation of six gold mining companies, three of which were listed on the London Stock Exchange. All had something important in common: they depended on loans from Sberbank, a state-owned Russian banking and financial services company headquartered in Moscow.

Banks liked what he heard. Eager to take the project forward, the following day, he messaged Povarenkin suggesting next steps. 'Very nice to meet yesterday with the Russian Ambassador,' he wrote, in an email with the subject line 'Gold Play'. 'I'm very bullish on gold so keen to have a look.'

It was just the beginning of an extraordinary relationship between the Kremlin's political and diplomatic emissaries in London and the individual who donated the most money to Brexit. This relationship would involve the discussion of further potentially lucrative business opportunities; intelligence-sharing about the Brexit campaign; and numerous invitations to social and cultural events. During this period, Banks pushed the Kremlin's point of view in various political debates, including during a diplomatic spat between Russia and the UK government over migration.

In the aftermath of the EU referendum, Banks found himself under mounting public pressure over his Russian links. Quite how he raised several million pounds for his referendum campaign, becoming the single most generous supporter of the cause, was the subject of intense speculation in the UK. He had initially told friends he was ready to put up £250,000. In the end, he spent some twenty times that amount on the campaign, in cash and services in kind. Friends say that had Leave. eu become the official Brexit campaign, he would have recouped some of his outlay, which he had hoped would only have to be loaned. That did not happen. Such was the suspicion surrounding his huge loans and donations that a formal investigation was launched into the source of his funds.

Certainly, the outcome of the referendum suited the Kremlin: disarray in the European Union, hampering its ability to react to Russian aggression, and turmoil in the UK, temporarily weakening its position on the world stage. Much better conditions, in other words, for Putin to pursue his geopolitical aims. And all without a single shot fired!

Banks just laughed it all off, rubbishing the notion that any 'dark money' from the Kremlin was involved. 'The allegations of Brexit being funded by the Russians … are complete bollocks from beginning to end,' he has said. 'My sole involvement with "the Russians" was a boozy six-hour lunch with the Ambassador where we drank the place dry (they have some cracking vodka and brandy!) and then wrote the account of the lunch in my book … Hardly top secret stuff!'

It is now clear that this was far from the full story. Almost by accident, the Kremlin had managed to forge a very useful relationship with one of the most powerful players in the Brexit campaign.

Why were they so keen to cultivate this self-styled anti-establishment figure? Perhaps they are incredibly generous and regularly offer relative strangers big business opportunities that require the support of the Russian state. Perhaps it's because Banks just struck lucky, and the Ambassador was feeling friendless around the time they met.

More likely, however, the astute Russians identified the Bristol-based businessman as an extraordinarily valuable political asset. Not only did he provide an entrée into the Brexit campaign, with its delicious potential to upend the EU; he also offered a direct line to Farage, one of the most influential political figures in the UK.

That Farage had close links to figures close to Donald Trump, who was running for the White House, must have been the icing on the cake. Clausewitz famously described war as the 'continuation of politics by other means' – but for the Kremlin in the twenty-first century, *politics* is the continuation of war by other means.

What has this got to do with the state of the British armed forces?

To some, it is evidence that we are already at war…

BLOSSOM AND BLOOD

A NOTE ON THE HARD EDGE OF RUSSIAN AGGRESSION

The trenches on the frontline of the war the West forgot are not deep enough for tall men. 'That is the frontline of Europe right there,' Ukrainian Colonel Vitali Krasovsky says as he points at the five-foot-high dugout fortified with scraps of timber and a few sandbags.[1] These soldiers see themselves as the bulwark against Russian aggression towards the West.

The enemy has yet to pinpoint where the Ukrainian army is positioned outside the abandoned village of Novogorodsky in the Donbas, but the platoon based at the Forward Observation Post know to keep their heads down: snipers are always a threat.

It is not immediately obvious that this is a war zone. There are no bodies lying in the rubble or fighter jets roaring overhead. In the small town a kilometre or so from the frontline, where the former community centre has been turned into an army base, civilian life just about goes on. The roads are lined with pretty apricot and apple trees in blossom. A small child plays in a dilapidated playground; an old woman totters to a faded grocery store; stray dogs skitter in the dust.

But the birdsong is mixed with a more ominous sound: the faint thud of mortar attacks in the distance. The Ukrainian armed forces in this town and at the Observation Post beyond do not spend every day fighting for their lives – but the zip and smack of bullets somewhere not far off is a dark reminder that, in the surrounding area, their comrades are under fire.[2]

What is happening in this part of the former Soviet Union matters not just to the people of Ukraine but to everyone who would prefer to contain President Putin's regime. It is a showcase for the fate that can befall places he considers weak. It exposes the vulnerability of parts of Russia's 'near abroad' that have neither the protection of NATO nor the military capability to make short work of Russian aggression. The UK and its allies could shrug and let it go, but that would risk emboldening Putin's administration, which is why our armed forces are involved.

Putin has already appropriated chunks of Ukraine, creating a series of Russian-controlled enclaves in sovereign territory over which he had no legitimate claim. The number of ethnic Russians in Ukraine who were prepared to tolerate or help the operation made it relatively easy. As the Kremlin continues a low-key campaign to seize more ground, Ukraine's Ministry of Defence is determined to resist.

The soldiers charged with holding the line against Russian-backed separatists bear a grave responsibility. The loss of Crimea after it was illegally annexed by the Russian Federation in 2014 underlines what is at stake.[3] At the time, the world stood by, leaving the region to its fate. Now NATO allies have come to recognise the potential price to be paid for turning a blind eye and are helping prop up Ukraine's armed forces. Some would say that this assistance has come much too late.

The UK has contributed at least £5 million to the effort.[4] In an initiative called Operation Orbital, British troops have been training thousands of members of Ukraine's armed forces in fourteen locations outside the contested Donbas region. More than 1,300 British servicemen and women have been deployed since 2015. Ministers say the UK stands 'side by side' with the Ukrainians 'in the face of Russian belligerence and aggression'.[5]

Along with a £200 million contribution from America this year,[6] the help has been very gratefully received, but it is not enough. Since April 2014, Russian-backed separatists have been in control of Donetsk, the fifth largest city in Ukraine. They show no sign of stopping there. Almost every day, Ukrainian soldiers lose their lives to the fight. To date, over 4,000 have been killed in action; a further 11,000 have been wounded. Morale is holding up, but only just.[7]

On the frontline, what they really want is drones. The enemy has more than enough, allowing them to scope out Ukrainian positions and launch well-targeted attacks. Ukraine's determined but overstretched armed forces cannot compete with this very modern capability.

The platoon at the Forward Observation Post spends long days hanging around waiting for sporadic contact with the enemy. In recent weeks they have lost comrades and were shaken when a popular commander lost a leg in a mortar attack on a village a few kilometres away. He keeps in touch with his men, sending video messages of encouragement from hospital.

Until a few years ago, what is now their base was someone's home: a small house with a nice garden on the outskirts of the village. Apparently, the owner offered it to Ukrainian troops as the local population fled. Now it is somewhere for soldiers to eat, sleep and monitor opposition forces.

Boredom is a problem. On quiet days, the men while away the hours as best they can. In an outdoor area protected by sandbags and other makeshift fortifications, they try to keep fit, keeping an eye out for unmanned aerial vehicles as they exercise. When darkness falls, those who are not keeping watch outside sit around the grubby kitchen chatting about home and family. Their rations are surprisingly tasty. 'We believe that if you don't feed your army well, you'll soon feed someone else's,' their commander observes wryly.

Some men get closer to the action. One beady-eyed Special Forces operative has just returned from a sabotage mission behind enemy lines. He has a skull-and-crossbones insignia and his blood type sewn onto the shoulder of his military fatigues.

But for most it is a long, hard grind, and the end is nowhere in sight. In several months, the 26 km section of frontline that is the responsibility of this platoon has only moved a few metres. In some ways it would be less painful for the platoon if there was more drama – they would relish the adrenalin of a fight – but the Kremlin is loath to use its mighty firepower to bring this mission to a swift, bloody end, knowing it would attract too much international attention. Putin plays a long game, and while the evidence that his forces are helping local rebels is incontrovertible, he is careful to keep their efforts below the threshold that would trigger too much outside interest. Both sides expect to be here for years.[8]

*   *   *

The gregarious senior Ukrainian general is a bear of a man. He is tall and imposing, with a thatch of white hair and thick glasses. But his voice, after four years of commanding a war with no end in sight, is low and tinged with sorrow. He still can't believe how quickly the rules-based international order has broken down.

'No one could have imagined that in the twenty-first century someone could just grab territory. It was Russia, a permanent member of the UN Security Council. But Putin was sure that no one would stop him!' he says. The Russian President was half right. Ukraine was advised by Western allies not to fight for Crimea militarily, a decision that some in Ukraine bitterly regret. At least they blocked what they expected to be Russia's next move. The general looks proud as he declares, 'We messed up all their plans.' On a piece of scrap paper, he draws a line cutting Ukraine in half diagonally, from Kharkiv in the north-east to Odessa in the south-west. 'They wanted all of this to be part of Novorossiya, new Russia! But they didn't expect us Ukrainians to fight back.'[9]

Now, the country is on a permanent war footing. The general illustrates this by flicking open his notepad and scribbling a crude map of the country and its neighbours. He draws arrows pointing to Kiev from every direction. He sees threats from Russia and Belarus to the north, annexed Crimea and the Russian Black Sea fleet to the south, Transnistria* to the west and the occupied Donetsk and Luhansk regions to the east. The Ukrainian government believes that, in total, the Russians have nearly 60,000 soldiers along the borders, and are ready to invade.[10] When Russia conducted large-scale military exercises in Belarus in late 2017, Western analysts watched with academic

---

*   A Russian aligned breakaway state whose territory the international community considers part of Moldova.

20

detachment. It was different for the Ukrainians: their eyes were not only on Russian military capability, but what troops left behind. They believe Russia deposited stockpiles of equipment and weapons in strategic positions at the end of the exercise in preparation for a potential future assault.[*]

RUSSIAN MILITARY ASSETS IN ITS 'NEAR-ABROAD'

THESE FORMER SOVIET UNION BREAKAWAY STATES ARE LARGELY PRO-RUSSIAN.

The extensive military operation, along with the condemnation of the international community and crippling economic sanctions, has cost Russia dear. But for the Kremlin, it is a small price to pay for what is seen as a step towards restoring Russia's prestige as a great power. The 1990s were a catastrophe for Russia. Overnight it lost an empire, along with the associated political and economic clout. Living standards fell dramatically. The humiliation was compounded by the Russian army's shocking military defeat at the hands of a rag-tag band of freedom

---

[*]   Ministry of Defence observers doubt this analysis.

fighters in Chechnya. Putin came to power in 2000 determined to turn things around.

He started softly. Senior Western officials saw no cause for alarm during his early years in power. (Lord) George Robertson, NATO Secretary General from 1999 to 2004, recalls constructive meetings with the Russian President. He says:

> I met Vladimir Putin nine times during my years at NATO. He said in my first meeting with him, 'I want Russia to be part of Western Europe. That's what I believe our destiny is.' For the first time in its history, Russia had a stable Western border. There was the prospect of prosperity and stability, in a way they had never experienced before.[11]

In his London office, Robertson points to a photo of the two of them sitting down at a table, smiling for the camera and looking cordial. Contrary to the Kremlin's subsequent claims of 'NATO encroachment', Robertson says that 'at no point did he object to the Baltic States becoming members of NATO.'[12]

The first sign of how Putin's geopolitical strategy might play out came with the crushing of the Chechen rebels who were fighting for independence from the Russian Federation. Then, in 2008, Russian troops invaded Georgia in support of a pro-Russian breakaway government in the disputed territory of South Ossetia.[13] When pro-European demonstrators toppled the Russian-oriented President Viktor Yanukovych in Kiev, Putin feared both that Ukraine would join NATO and that he would lose control over Russia's only warm-water naval base in Sevastopol, which was on lease from Ukraine.[14] So he moved in.

The Kremlin's device was to send 'little green men' – Russian Special Forces dressed in civilian garb, many of whom entered Ukraine as tourists. Once inside Crimea, in unmarked uniforms, they seized control of key strategic positions. Shortly afterwards, pro-Russian separatists took control of government buildings in the major cities of Donetsk and Luhansk and declared 'independence', prompting civil war.[15] In August of 2014, when it looked as if the rebels were losing the fight, the Kremlin sent in regular troops, disguised as humanitarian assistance.[16] The next six months saw the heaviest fighting in Europe since the Yugoslav wars.

The British government condemned Russian actions in the strongest terms and sent soldiers and military aid. But ministers stopped short of supplying lethal weapons to the Ukrainian armed forces.[17] It was only in 2018 that the US finally agreed to provide Javelin missiles, designed to destroy tanks, to counter the rebels' advantage in heavy armour.[18]

In February 2015, all parties signed the Minsk Protocol, which was supposed to herald a ceasefire.[19] It cooled, but failed to end, the conflict. Since then, it has been stalemate. Fighting resembles First World War trench combat, with each side measuring gains in metres.

By April 2018, the battle lines had barely moved in three years. The army has turned a former leisure centre in the frontline town of Novogorodsky into the Brigade HQ. An upright piano gathers dust; there are still disco balls suspended from the ceiling, a reminder of happier times. Just seven kilometres away, a gun fight ravages the town of Zaitseve.

In a dusty briefing room, a Ukrainian commander explains the 'hybrid warfare' that is being orchestrated by the Kremlin. Regular ground combat is augmented by political meddling and propaganda. Every day the rebels bombard Ukrainian forces with machine guns, armoured vehicles, mortar systems and 152mm artillery weapons.[20] When the operation began, the Russians tried to hide their officers within separatist units. They no longer bother. Ukrainian soldiers estimate that one in ten of the opposition forces are Russian fighters, the rest being locals. That would make around 8,000 Russian regular troops, which they believe are supported by 600 tanks and 3,000 artillery pieces.[21]

The Ukraine government has just enough resources for armoured vehicles and hand machine guns. Thanks to Russia's support, the rebels have the technological edge. They are better at co-ordinating Unmanned Aerial Vehicles (UAVs) and artillery fires. Ukrainian UAVs only last two or three launches before they're disabled or brought down. The rebels can also use theirs at night; Ukraine doesn't have any with thermal imaging. The devices make a big difference: they are used to target observation posts, trench systems and to find targets for snipers. Russian UAVs often have a type of electronic buffer, making them very difficult to neutralise.[22]

Yet there is no sense of defeat here. The local population is resilient, and proud of an identity that has nothing to do with politics. For decades, they have seen themselves as the workers who feed and fuel Ukraine. Average earnings are a modest £199 a month in Luhansk and £287 a month in Donetsk; coal miners receive a little more.[23] They aren't wealthy, but the cost of living is low. They live decently – at least they did, until all this started.

*   *   *

In rebel-controlled Donetsk, the situation is much worse. Joel Gallagher, an international security consultant who specialises in post-Soviet conflict zones, has seen what happens to a town when it is taken over by Russian-backed forces.

When I first visited Donetsk in the summer of 2013, it was known as the city of roses! Public parks were full of life and colour, restaurants and bars were full of clamour and excitement. On my last evening my friend Igor took me to see Shakhtar Donetsk, the top Ukrainian football team, play in the newly built stadium. My flight back to Kiev was from the ultra-modern and brand-new Donetsk airport. I had fallen in love with the city and its people.

But when I returned to Donetsk in the winter of 2016, the road was lined with military checkpoints and filled with refugees. The streets were mostly empty. The currency exchange bureau was now manned by a sinister-looking guy with suitcases of cash flanked by three armed men. I stayed in the same hotel I had used during my first visit. The family who owned it had fled. It was now loosely run by rebels and seemed to be being used as a rest stop by all sorts of armed groups. The curtains had blood stains and there were screams down the halls during the night.

On my first day in the city, I discovered Igor had been dead for a year. He was non-political when I knew him. However, after an artillery shell landed on his parents' house, killing them both, he took up arms and fought in Donetsk airport where he was killed in a grenade blast. So I walked around Donetsk alone. Billboards that once advertised sim cards and laptops now featured Soviet-style propaganda to take up arms and defend against what was represented as a 'Western conquest' designed to dominate Russia. Donetsk Stadium, which I last saw bustling with happy crowds, was now deserted and abandoned. The souvenir stalls were shredded with shrapnel. The rebels were proposing that the banners of the players, viewed as traitors for leaving the Republic, should be replaced with images of fighters and heroes of the Republic. The late-night vibrant culture was replaced with a 10 p.m. curfew. Elderly women huddled together under faded propaganda of the Red Army on the walls as shells pounded in the distance.[24]

*　*　*

In Kiev, the palace of the ousted President, Viktor Yanukovych, now lies empty. It is an extraordinary temple of profligacy; an eye-popping modern-day Versailles, more extravagant and less tasteful than the worst flights of fantasy of overpaid international footballers or African dictators. It has a private zoo; a Thai massage parlour; a nail and beauty salon complete with a cryotherapy tank; a lavishly equipped gym with a full-size professional boxing ring (never used). Everything is hand-crafted, from the crystal-encrusted doors to the his-and-hers reclining leather home cinema seats. There are huge houseplant pots made of mother of pearl; vases made of dried snake skins; a stuffed lion; a crocodile skin stretched the length of a dining table, teeth bared. A custom-made gold-leaf chandelier is reputed to have cost €1.5 million. The only decorative theme is ludicrous excess: a gleaming life-sized sculpture of a jaguar that would not look out of place in a nightclub sitting alongside reproduction Classical bas reliefs and replicas of medieval knights in shining armour.

These days it is a visitor attraction, managed in haphazard style by local volunteers who unlock the doors when it suits them to show people round. Small groups of tourists troop through the rooms wearing compulsory disposable overshoes to protect the shagpile carpets and mosaic floors. The majority of visitors are local, gasping at what has come to be seen as a symbol of Russian corruption.[25]

As for Yanukovych, he fled to Russia, where he still lurks, blaming the West for turning Ukraine into a 'wild' place, and complaining that he is much misunderstood.[26]

In the UK, while there is growing concern about social media trolling and Russian meddling in Western democracies, few are aware of the way Russia treats more vulnerable nations. The perception among other EU member states is very different. For people in Poland and the Baltic states, Ukraine's fate underlines the fragility of their newfound security and freedom. Major Tomas Balkus, a director at NATO's Strategic Communications Headquarters in Riga, says:

> Most observers say that Russia is not ready for a big conflict with NATO. I agree. But Russians are crazy, so even though they are not ready, it doesn't mean they won't do anything. In the world wars, men didn't have anything to eat and would attack with one rifle per ten soldiers. That's OK for them.[27]

One former Polish Special Forces commander who led NATO troops in Afghanistan says they ignore intelligence from the West that tells them not to worry about a Russian invasion. 'They don't understand how Russia thinks. We've been occupied by them, so we know. Russia is not a country – it is a state of mind. They don't care about their economy or society. They want to be a great nation that is feared and respected.'[28]

The government of Ukraine now sees itself firmly allied with the West and has its sights set on joining the EU and NATO. The General's briefing room in the International Cooperation Directorate of the Ukrainian General Staff is decorated with the national flag of Ukraine, flanked by the EU and NATO flags. On the wall is a photo of NATO Secretary General Jens Stoltenberg. There is also a framed handwritten letter from George Robertson, sent in November 2001, congratulating Ukraine on opening its new liaison office and underlining the 'strength and quality of the NATO–Ukraine relationship'.

They won't be able to join NATO while the conflict rages in the Donbas. The problem is that it would immediately drag the Alliance into war with Russia: under Article 5 of the NATO Treaty, an armed attack against one member is considered an armed attack against all. Georgia is in a similar position, unable to join because of ongoing conflicts in South Ossetia and Abkhazia. Some suspect that the Kremlin continues these military operations to stop them doing just that.

Ukraine illustrates the hard edge of Russian aggression. The military element means there is no hiding the malign intent. In this case, the Kremlin's aim is nothing short of seizing physical ground in a long, slow campaign to expand Russia's sphere of influence. But Putin's ambitions are not limited to places he regards as easy targets. When it comes to NATO member states, including Britain, he simply pursues his geopolitical ambitions in more subtle ways.

RED ALERT

RUSSIA'S GREAT GAME

In 1981, Margaret Thatcher's government thought that the only real threat faced by the UK was from the Soviet Union. The defence review that year suggested the armed forces prepare for land-based war in Germany or anti-submarine warfare in the North Atlantic. It imagined all this taking place within NATO structures, and assumed the UK would no longer need to project force independently.

Within a year, Argentina invaded the Falkland Islands, making a nonsense of all the Ministry of Defence's predictions. The ruling junta was reportedly satisfied that because of Britain's declining global ambitions, it wouldn't put up a fight.

There are two lessons here. The first is that the British armed forces can be called upon at any moment to undertake precisely the tasks it least expects. The second is that the more the UK signals its readiness to raise the white flag, the likelier potential adversaries are to make us pay.

At the height of the Cold War, voters did not need to be convinced of the potential threat posed by Russia. Today, it is harder to believe that the UK could be drawn into war with such a great power – depending on what is meant by 'war'.

When politicians and defence chiefs talk about the threat posed by President Putin's regime, they're not suggesting this country is about to be invaded. They are referring to other scenarios that could require a military response. The short-term fear is that Putin will launch another military campaign in what he considers Russia's 'near abroad'. If his target is a NATO member state, the UK will automatically be drawn in.

Another possibility is that this country is attacked in a way that stops short of full-on confrontation, but nonetheless does so much damage that the armed forces have to get involved. Defence chiefs believe both are realistic scenarios.

Armed forces need enemies. It is hard to train for a fight without a notional adversary, and even harder to make decisions about what weapons you need if you have no idea who you might be up against. With the end of the campaign in Afghanistan and the gradual disarming of Daesh, Russia fills a hole in the market for a bogeyman – but the fact that the Russian threat is useful for politicians, the military and the defence industry does not make it any less real.

In March 2018, the imaginative leap required to envisage a conflict between the UK and Russia became a little easier when the deadly nerve agent Novichok was used to poison Sergei Skripal, a former Russian military intelligence officer who acted as a double agent for the UK's intelligence services, on British soil. His daughter Yulia and a British policeman who rushed to their aid were also affected.

For defence analysts who have been struggling to convince politicians to take the Russian threat seriously, the silver lining to this appalling episode was that people finally sat up. Just six weeks earlier, Defence Secretary Gavin Williamson had been lampooned for suggesting that Russia could cause 'thousands and thousands and thousands' of deaths in the UK by attacking critical infrastructure.[1] What happened to the Skripals was hardly vindication, but it certainly made him look less silly. Here was shocking evidence of what the Russian regime can do in this country. It catapulted the long-running debate over Putin's capability and intent towards the West out of academic and military circles to the top of the political agenda.

'It showed the Russian threat isn't theoretical. It is real,' Williamson says. 'The truth is that we have pretended and hoped for so long that the world will go on becoming safer, that we have been blinded to the dangers.'[2]

The mini chemical attack in the genteel English town of Salisbury highlighted Russia's flagrant disregard for the rules-based international order. The way the Kremlin handled the political and diplomatic fallout was almost as telling. It was a reminder that the regime has no qualms about peddling half-truths and lies. Experience has taught the Kremlin that almost all countries have a ready supply of citizens willing to believe the worst of their government. All that is required to undermine an administration is to tap into this sentiment at sensitive moments.

In this case, the Kremlin skilfully set about suggesting that the UK's esteemed intelligence services might have got it all wrong, just like they did over weapons of mass destruction in Iraq. Putin must have been delighted to hear various opposition MPs making this spurious case.

Against the odds, the Skripals survived, but there is disturbing evidence that the attack was not limited to the poisoning. As the victims lay in a critical condition in hospital and public attention switched to the political and diplomatic repercussions, another sinister sequence of events was unfolding in Salisbury.

According to the leader of Salisbury City Council, Matthew Dean, three curious things happened.

First, the local radio station broadcast erroneous claims that a newly installed CCTV system was not working in the city at the time of the attack – a story Dean claims was prompted by a tip-off they received from a Russian news agency called RTVI News.

'It seemed an astonishing thing for an outside agency to do. They had no interest in the listenership of a local radio station. I think they were trying to spread a bit of worry and discontent, in the battle for public opinion,' Dean says.[3]

Next, the council's computers came under what Dean describes as a sustained cyberattack.

I was told that I personally shouldn't be sending any emails on Wiltshire Council's Outlook system, because they had reason to believe that my account could be hacked; and that anything I put on the system could be compromised. It went on to be explained to me that GCHQ [Government Communications Headquarters] were providing support to Wiltshire Council, because there had been a huge number of invasive incidents. I was told that there had been 90,000 attempts to try to hack the system over three days.[4]

Finally, iPads and smartphones issued to Wiltshire Council staff for work lost access to the council's servers. It was later explained that this was for 'security reasons'. Dean says:

I had been a Wiltshire councillor now for over a year, and those systems had worked perfectly the whole time I'd been here. I'm told by more long-standing colleagues that in the eight years Wiltshire Council has been there, the systems had never been down even for one day. For significant numbers of us, for three or four days, we couldn't send email.

It is interesting to note Wiltshire Council is the only local authority to share IT infrastructure with the police.[5]

Quite who or what was behind these strange events will probably never be known. Perhaps they were entirely coincidental. However, the apparent attack on Wiltshire Council's IT infrastructure and attempts to unsettle the local population via fake news are typical of the Kremlin's modus operandi. Those who have long been warning of the dangers posed to the UK by Russia see the entire episode as a dark warning of worse to come if the UK assumes there will never be a serious clash with Russia and lowers its defences.

For the armed forces, this situation is relatively new. For the past two decades, they have been immersed in combating international terrorism in Asia, the Middle East and Africa. The focus has been on extremists armed with Kalashnikovs and improvised explosive devices, not hostile states with professional armies and sophisticated air defences.

Jihadis could do a lot of harm, but they did not pose an existential threat.

Defence chiefs in Britain and America believe we have now entered a new era, in which hostile states are the gravest danger.

'Great power competition – not terrorism – is now the primary focus of US national security,' US Defense Secretary Jim Mattis has said,[6] while

General Sir Nick Carter, now Chief of the Defence Staff, has singled out Russia as the most pressing state-based threat to the UK.[7]

Just how far Putin is prepared to go is a matter for debate. Some believe he is locked into nothing less than a 'political and civilisational struggle with the West'.[8] The Russian President has openly admitted that he regrets the collapse of the Soviet Union, calling it the 'greatest geopolitical catastrophe' of the twentieth century.[9] Equally important-ly, he has made no secret of his bitter resentment over the expansion of NATO, which he has called a 'serious provocation'.[10] Analysts gener-ally agree that he wants to restore what he believes is Russia's rightful position in the world, and ensure his country is not encircled (as he would see it) by NATO member states. Events in Georgia, Crimea and Ukraine show what this can mean in practice, and there is no evidence that he has finished. Perhaps he has no grand plan and it is more a question of seizing opportunities. That does not make him any less dangerous. At home, his voters support Russian aggrandisement. Poll-ing work conducted for this book shows that Russians have a unique view of the global hierarchy. While people from Britain, Australia, Estonia, France, Germany, Israel, Italy, South Korea, Poland and the United States all ranked the USA as the most powerful and influential of the states we asked about, the Russians believed the distinction be-longed to their own country.

Many defence analysts believe that Putin is eager to exploit what he sees as a window of opportunity to take on liberal democracy because Russia is politically strong and the West (in his view) is politically weak. 'If Russia is to take its place in the world as he sees it, he has to change the world order; destroy our capacity to dominate it,' according to one academic.[11]

General Sir Richard Barrons, former Commander of Joint Forces Command and one of the leading military thinkers of his time, believes the Russian regime 'understands the weakness of the West very well'.

It can see the lack of will. It can see the strategic failure after Iraq and Afghanistan. It can see the battle with austerity. It can see that NATO is divided. Under President Obama, a President determined to end wars, not to start them, it sensed a shift towards greater American isolationism.[12]

The suggestion that the Kremlin is determined to change the world order might seem melodramatic were it not for the fact that President Putin's posturing has been accompanied by a sweeping programme of rearmament and, as we have seen in Ukraine, military aggression. Since 2004, he has presided over the wholesale modernisation of his country's ground, air and maritime forces, investing billions in state-of-the-art hardware and new electronic, cyber, satellite and nuclear capabilities.[13] Top brass in NATO member states where leaders refuse to spend the Alliance's recommended 2 per cent of GDP on defence can only look on in envy.

To ensure everybody knows about Russia's new military prowess, it is showcased in annual war games known as the 'Zapad' exercises. These displays of what academic Dr Mark Galeotti calls 'heavy metal diplomacy' are designed as much to impress their international audience as they are to test capability.[14]

They involve land, sea and air components, and thousands of personnel. In 2017, the drills were staged across a vast expanse of land in Russia's west, as well as in Belarus, the Baltic Sea and the strategically important Russian enclave of Kaliningrad. Putin talks down Zapad to his domestic audience, making a great show of scoffing at what he depicts as the exaggerated response of the West. He likes to present the exercises as 'counter-terror drills'.[15] However, international observers were left in no doubt that the exercises were designed to rehearse a full-on clash with NATO forces.[16]

Ministry of Defence observers were impressed, and worried. They concluded that the Russian military is now quick and capable, having invested 'heavily and cleverly' to neutralise NATO advantages.[17]

'The exercise absolutely wasn't a counter-terror exercise, it was very much a state threat they were responding to,' the official noted.

Russia used it to practise Command and Control and as far as we're aware, did so extremely well. Russia doesn't seem to have a bandwidth problem – it conducted operations in Syria at a high tempo at this [same] period; and in Ukraine – it did not seem to struggle to do that. Our analysis is that they are increasingly capable. I don't think they're a paper tiger – they're a credible threat. It's quite a concerning situation.

Politicians and defence chiefs have been ramping up the rhetoric about what Russia's capabilities – and intent – might mean for the UK. General Sir Nick Carter likened the Russian threat to a 'chronic contagious disease' which, if left untreated, could 'creep up on us, and our ability to act will be markedly constrained – and we'll be the losers of this competition'.[18]

This was too much for some defence and foreign policy experts, who dismiss the notion that Putin would risk a conventional match off with NATO. ('Completely for the birds' is how General Sir Nick Houghton, former Chief of the Defence Staff from 2013 to 2016, puts it.) Houghton and others point out that Russia is an economic 'basket case', highly dependent on the price of oil, and struggling to recover from Western economic sanctions placed on it after the invasion of Crimea.[19] Corruption is rampant, the state still controls many key industries and economic inequality is so extreme that leading banks say it should be placed 'in a separate category' to other countries.[20]

Others stress that Russia's new ground forces have many flaws. Units are stuffed with reluctant conscripts; dogged by low morale; and struggle with widely varying kit, a good deal of which they're not trained to use. The lack of standardisation is a throwback to the Soviet era, when preserving equipment of all generations was the only way to maintain stocks large enough for a mass mobilisation in the event of general war. In practice, what it means is that soldiers that are moved to new bases may very well find they are issued with weapons they don't know how to fire.[21]

Galeotti, who has spent a decade cultivating sources within the Russian armed forces, doubts Putin would risk invading a Baltic state, never mind mess with the UK to the point that it necessitated a military response.[22]

He recounts a frank exchange with a contact about the likelihood of an offensive in the Baltics:

> It was a lengthy and boozy conversation, as the best ones are. I said: 'You must have operational plans for an operation in the Baltics?' Eventually he said: 'We have to have them in the drawer just in case the Kremlin says "Go!" but you know, the real problem with the Baltic States is that they're full of Balts! [as opposed to Russians]' And that is the point. Why would the Russians want to occupy countries full of people who are recalcitrant; don't want to be occupied; and would fight?[23]

Yet Russia's military activities are already a significant drain on the UK's armed forces: land, sea, and air. At the time of writing, some 800 British troops are stationed in Estonia as part of NATO's so-called Enhanced Forward Presence – an effort to show that the Alliance is ready if Putin crosses the line.[24] Meanwhile, British Typhoon jets from RAF Coningsby spent summer 2017 based in Romania defending NATO airspace over the Black Sea.[25]

For the already stretched RAF, Russia's periodic threatened incursion into UK airspace is a further pressure. Approximately once every six weeks, an alarm goes off at RAF Lossiemouth or RAF Coningsby and two fighter pilots from the so-called Quick Reaction Alert crew dash to a fully fuelled and armed Typhoon for a high-altitude face-off at a cost of around £50,000 to British taxpayers.[26] The armed forces could simply abandon this tiresome and costly routine, but if they did, Russian jets would probably come a little closer each time. Finally, they would enter UK sovereign airspace, at which point it would be clear that we had given up bothering to defend our skies.

These games are also played out in the North Atlantic, where there has been an 'extraordinary increase' in Russian submarine activity, according to a former UK Defence Secretary.[27]

In December 2017, the then Chief of the Defence Staff Air Chief Marshal Sir Stuart Peach admitted there was also a 'new risk' from Russia 'to the cables that criss-cross our seabeds, disruption to which through cable-cuts or destruction would immediately – and cata-strophically – fracture both international trade and the internet'.[28] Russian submarines have even reportedly been caught lurking near Faslane, where the UK's nuclear deterrent is based. Some experts believe they may have been attempting to identify the acoustic 'signature' of the UK's Vanguard submarines, information that would make the position of our so-called Continuous At-Sea Deterrent (CASD) detectable.[29]

However, it is Russia's so-called hybrid activities that many analysts believe are the greatest threat. The fostering of a relationship with Arron Banks, who hoped to run the official Brexit campaign, is a classic example of a multi-layered approach to achieving geopolitical objectives. The dalliance was probably a greater source of excitement to the Bristol businessman and his associates than it was to the Russian regime, but as the Englishmen fell in with Donald Trump, what appears to have started as casual opportunism on the Russian side turned into a much more valuable connection than they originally envisaged.

In this very modern approach to warfare, everything is a potential weapon, from the media to energy supplies. Culture and language; money as investment; bribes; organised crime; deception and so-called psyops (psychological operations); subversion; dirty tricks; espionage: all are marshalled to the cause of undermining liberal democracy.

Crucially, the Kremlin's 'sub warfare' is a continual process, executed with varying degrees of aggression both in conflict zones like eastern Ukraine and in countries and regions with which the Kremlin has no ostensible or immediate quarrel. It blurs the distinction between war and peace, making it extremely difficult for the target to know when and how to respond. Some call it 'threshold warfare', a reference to hostile behaviour calculated to fall just short of what is required to trigger a formal response.

Lieutenant General Sir Graeme Lamb, former Director of UK Special Forces, believes what he calls 'Phase Zero' warfare – what happens before conventional conflict begins – poses a serious challenge for the UK's armed forces. He says:

The trick is to keep it *below the threshold of what you would consider to be warfare*. By doing that, you can get away with all sorts of shit! You know, 'Fancy a cup of radioactive tea, downtown London?'* Do you want to just smack the Estonian banking system?† Just do it! If you want to use chemical weapons … *[do it] just below what we are somehow looking to be that trigger point.*[30]

General Sir Richard Barrons says that Russia senses that it could easily be overwhelmed by the West, 'if the West put its mind to it'. So the regime has found other ways to achieve its geopolitical goals.

Is there a Russian plan to conquer Europe? Absolutely not. Although they maintain astonishingly large and capable conventional forces, these are primarily for the traditional defence of a very, very large country. They have invested heavily in keeping us out. Their Armata tank is better than any Western tank, and they make it themselves.

They have also made very thoughtful investments in disruption to weaken the West. Most of that happens in the information space, whether that's the TV channel Russia Today, or cyber, or social media, or spending money to bankroll rather strange political parties. I don't believe there's any greater thought behind that, than keeping the West off balance. It suits Russia's purposes to keep the West disunited and internally focused on its own squabbles.

'And there is scope for opportunism,' he says.[31]

Barrons points out that in hybrid warfare, the Russians have a significant advantage over Western democracies, because they are not bothered by the truth.

'The truth isn't necessary. It's only necessary to shift things in your favour,' he says.[32]

This is a very different type of threat from physical invasion or

---

* A reference to the infamous fatal poisoning of former KGB officer Alexander Litvinenko in central London.
† http://www.bbc.co.uk/news/39655415

bombardment, but the running of this country is fragile. A relatively minor computer outage brings air travel to a halt, while the Wanna-Cry ransomware attack on the NHS in spring 2017 had an immediate and devastating effect on the health service, leading to thousands of cancelled appointments and operations.[33] The impact of a co-ordinated and comprehensive attack, involving cyber, misinformation and sabotage of underwater cables, all individually below the threshold, but deadly in combination, would be crippling.

Of course, hard power is not the obvious or only answer to hybrid war. It is no use pointing a gun at computer viruses, Facebook or Twitter. But without hard power, hybrid can swiftly become conventional – as the Ukrainians have found – and a country unable to mount a credible military response to a co-ordinated and comprehensive hybrid attack is a country unable to defend itself.

General David Petraeus, former Director of the CIA and former Commander of US Central Command, believes that Russia's new way of pursuing its geopolitical aims has 'profound implications' for Western armed forces.

'This is qualitatively and quantitatively *very* different ... this is a level of intrusion and disruption and attempted influence that is way beyond the pale. You're in a whole new realm, a new battlefield domain ... How you organise your forces; train them; develop leaders; even how you provide facilities for them,' he says.[34]

Across the armed forces, it is the Russian threat they have in mind as they exercise and equip. But Putin's regime is only one among many growing dangers.

CHOPPY WATERS

CHINA, NORTH KOREA AND THE ASIAN CENTURY

THE ASSASSIN'S MACE

If persuading voters that the UK could find itself at war with Russia is difficult, armed conflict with China is an even greater stretch. However, military planners look at China's attitude towards the rules-based international order; they look at Chinese military might; and they can easily envisage a scenario in which it all blows up. History shows that major confrontations often begin over minor things.

As an indication of just how seriously some in government take the Chinese threat, you only have to look at what happened when Boris Johnson casually suggested that the UK's new aircraft carriers take a trip through the South China Sea. Dispatching a colossal warship with multiple frigates and destroyers on a peaceful voyage through these fiercely contested waters would, the then Foreign Secretary thought, send a powerful message to the world about the UK's commitment to the freedom of navigation.[1]

Unfortunately, he had omitted to run the idea past the then Defence Secretary Sir Michael Fallon, who was aghast. Fallon had visions of an ugly and unpredictable row with the Chinese. His private view was that provoking the Chinese in this way was a very bad idea indeed.[2] According to one insider, the Defence Secretary 'went ballistic'. Others deny that he lost his cool, but in any case, he got his way: Johnson was forced to backtrack.[3] The UK would not risk annoying the People's Republic by sending an aircraft carrier on an entirely legitimate voyage in this region.

In 2018, Fallon's successor, Gavin Williamson, felt a similar urge to show the Chinese what the UK is made of. He decided to dispatch a number of Royal Navy warships to Japan and other ports in the region to take part in various Allied training drills and freedom-of-navigation operations. They would exercise their right to navigate the South China Sea.[4]

This time it was the Treasury that was horrified. When officials discovered that the navy would be sailing close to some of the uninhabited atolls that have been commandeered by Beijing and turned into islands with extensive military fortifications, all hell broke loose. Fearing it could harm Anglo-Sino business relations, the Treasury told the Defence Secretary he should not do it. Williamson refused to bow to what he saw as 'Operation Kow Tow'[5] and HMS *Sutherland* duly set sail, to be joined by HMS *Albion* and HMS *Argyll* later the same year.[6] The voyage passed off uneventfully. Williamson sees this as a point of principle, and agrees with Johnson that our aircraft carriers should exercise their right to freedom of navigation, whether or not it irritates the Chinese.

'We absolutely should send *Queen Elizabeth* through the South China Seas! Imagine the story if we did not. We are entitled to do that,' he says.[7]

However, the alarm with which various individuals have viewed these proposals shows just how nervous the government has become about China's growing power.

Sooner or later, defence chiefs believe there is every prospect that a local or regional dispute or a clash between the Chinese and the Americans could escalate to war.

'There's no script to this,' according to General Sir Richard Barrons, former Chief of Joint Forces Command.

If sensible counsel prevails, we'll all be fine. But given the fiercely opposing narratives, and the Chinese concept of 'face', a really clumsy thing could happen in the South China Sea, which will result in a ship sunk or an aeroplane shot down, and then you're in a wholly different place.[8]

It may take time to convince voters of the need to prepare for this threat – time the Chinese will be using to accelerate their advantage.

Their intelligence-gathering operation about our own armed forces is meticulous and tireless. While much of it is covert, some of their research is on open display at major defence conferences in the UK. On a sunny afternoon outside Westminster Abbey in June 2017, for example, Zhang Yang, Director-General of the Political Department of the People's Liberation Army, could be found busily taking photographs of everything and everyone. He and his assistant were at the annual Land Warfare Conference of the Royal United Services Institute think tank. They spent their time lurking at the fringes, taking snaps of the assembled delegates and top brass. During lunch breaks, they headed outside, where their attention to detail was such that they could be seen capturing images of woodwork, plants and pottery in nearby gardens.

A puzzled General Sir Nick Carter, then Chief of the General Staff, wondered aloud what they were doing.

'Just tourism, I suppose,' he muttered to an aide.[9]

More likely, they were busy creating an image bank of our defence establishment for facial recognition purposes.

While the head of the army was bemused, experienced China watchers are all too familiar with such behaviour. The Chinese military does not have a strong culture of innovation (though this is rapidly changing). What it does very effectively is watch the West; figure out what we do well; and attempt to do it better. As a liberal democracy, we let them snap away with their cameras, but the indulgence only goes one way. British officials caught doing the same at a Chinese defence conference would probably find themselves in a police cell.

Should the worst happen, we have few permanent military assets in that part of the world. Before the Second World War, the UK's influence in the Asia Pacific region was immense. This country controlled global trade routes through bases in Hong Kong, the Philippines and Malaysia, and most importantly Singapore. For the British Empire, Singapore was regarded as a 'fortress', towering over major trade routes in the area, protecting them from Japanese aggression and upholding the international order. In the period between the humiliating surrender of Singapore to the Japanese in 1941 and the return of Hong

Kong to the Chinese in 1997, our foothold in the region has all but slipped away.

Post-Brexit, the government touted a new 'military base' in Singapore to illustrate that the UK has returned 'East of Suez'.[10] At the time of writing, it was just a lonely colonel in a modest office at the back of the British High Commission, whose arrival was accompanied by sniggering from our allies.[11]

The 2015 Strategic Defence and Security Review painted a sunny picture of collaboration between China and the UK. Ministers waxed lyrical about how new partnerships could combat everything from climate change, North Korean nuclear ambitions and Middle Eastern terrorism.[12] Nowhere was China listed as a current or even potential threat. This was a serious error, according to an expert cross-party group of MPs and peers, which castigated the government's failure to recognise the potential danger posed by the regime. They listed a catalogue of concerns, including China's woeful record of human rights abuses, state-sponsored cyber espionage, and aggressive militarisation of the South and East China seas.[13]

They questioned why ministers had allowed Chinese investors to secure stakes in Critical National Infrastructure like the nuclear reactor at Hinckley Point[14] and Chinese telecommunication giant Huawei's contract to improve British Telecom's copper broadband service.[15] As the report pointed out, putting the levers of vital public services into the hands of potentially hostile regimes means they could be turned into weapons.[16]

American politicians are less blasé. They know China has set its sights on replacing the US as the most powerful force in east Asia.

'They essentially want the US out,' General Mark Milley, the US Army's Chief of Staff, has said.[17]

US defence chiefs still shudder at the memory of a Chinese submarine surfacing in the middle of an American aircraft carrier group near the island of Okinawa in the Pacific in October 2006: 'the equivalent to Pepsi-Cola's management popping up in a Coca-Cola board meeting after listening under the table for an hour.'[18]

'The Americans were amazed and angry in equal measure,' according to Tim Marshall in his book, *Prisoners of Geography*. 'Amazed because they had no idea a Chinese sub could do that without being noticed, angry because they hadn't noticed and because they regarded the move as provocative, especially as the sub was within torpedo range...'[19]

The Chinese Song-Class sub surfaced to give America the diplomatic middle finger. The message was clear: China is now a naval power to be reckoned with.

Unlike Russia, China has the financial and human resources to match its geopolitical ambition. The regime has the second largest military budget in the world: around £110 billion per year.[20] Like Russia, it is in the middle of a formidable defence modernisation and procurement programme.[21]

Defence chiefs on both sides of the Atlantic believe it would be naïve not to take this seriously. Since 2014, China has launched more submarines, warships, principal amphibious vessels and auxiliaries than the total number of ships currently serving in the navies of Germany, India, Spain, Taiwan and the United Kingdom. The combined tonnage of new warships and auxiliaries launched by the People's Republic in the past four years alone also significantly outweighs that of the entire French Navy.[22] Meanwhile, the regime has the largest commercial shipping fleet in the world – vessels which are all state-owned and could potentially be refitted for military purposes. Fifteen years ago, China could fire missiles, but the weapons missed their targets. Now they're accurate within one square metre.[23]

Most concerning of all is the suggestion that the regime may have developed cyber and missile technology capable of crippling the United States' command and control structures, including its satellite communications and targeting procedures, during a war.[24] The Chinese call this mix of technology, asymmetric warfare and the fusion of space, cyber and electronic warfare the 'Assassin's Mace'.[25]

In its latest assessment of the regime's military capability and assets, the International Institute of Strategic Studies describes China's progress in defence aerospace as 'remarkable'. The think tank singles out its acquisition of low-observable combat aircraft (robbing the US of its monopoly on operational stealthy combat jets) and a series of advanced guided-weapons projects as a particular challenge to Western military hegemony.

'For the past three decades, air dominance has been a key advantage for the US and its allies. This can no longer be assumed,' they say.[26]

Meanwhile, the modernisation of the ground forces of the People's Liberation Army – the world's largest, numbering nearly one million – continues apace.[27]

The fear among Western defence experts is that China's formidable new hard power might come to be deployed in a dispute over maritime free passage or underwater resources. In the South China Sea, the regime's brazen disregard for international maritime law has already resulted in numerous clashes with neighbouring countries. In 2016, an international arbitration case brought by the Philippines judged that China's policy in the South China Sea was violating other nations' use of their exclusive economic zone. The Chinese shrugged and carried on.[28]

Why does any of this matter for the British armed forces? In the short term, perhaps it doesn't. As with Russia, it is important not to exaggerate China's military prowess. The regime's ability to conduct a ground war is completely untested – its last serious ground combat experience was in 1979, against the Vietnamese. Its naval commanders are excellent at following orders, but are not encouraged to think on their feet. However, as General Sir Richard Barrons points out, the Chinese regime sees the South China Sea as 'existential':

> For them, it's where the raw materials come through, and exports go out. And these waters are a means to keep the US out. And the US, because of the UN Convention on the Law of the Sea, and its own sense of freedom of navigation, has now got an aircraft carrier group in the South China Sea. So these positions are irreconcilable, unless either politicians or diplomats sort it out, or we have a fight.

He believes the Chinese regime's aggressive behaviour in these waters is a clear warning of what may be to come.

We live in the Asian century. Power is transiting east. China has this view of the world that it has been the strongest in the world for twenty out of twenty-two centuries. It has no doubt that it's the coming global super-power. The assertion of control over the eastern South China Sea is a clear example of China saying, 'We are China, and we believe in peaceful coop-erative development' – by which they mean, 'We are China, and this is how it's going to go, and you agree with us!'

'They don't mean it any other way,' he says.[29]

In the event of a dispute in the region, the US will expect the British armed forces to be in a position to contribute.

Complicating all these calculations is another regime the UK armed forces may be called upon to fight, thanks to the highly unpredictable behaviour of a man the Chinese call 'Fatty Kim'.[30]

ROCKET MEN

Deep in the mountains of North Korea are some of the world's dead-liest weapons. In caves and tunnels dug by political prisoners lie mul-tiple production and storage sites for chemical, biological, nuclear and radioactive materials that could be used against South Korea and the West.[31]

As Theresa May grappled with Brexit negotiations in early 2018, the diplomatic row between Kim Jong-un and President Trump over this terrifying arsenal may not have felt like a British problem. In London, however, defence chiefs were quietly making contingency plans for war.

Unusually, the armed forces were in a position to offer the Amer-icans a capability the Pentagon felt it lacked: Special Forces trained and equipped to work in mountain ranges at very low temperatures for long periods. While America's elite operatives, Seal Team 6, are re-nowned for their expertise at short, sharp missions in hot jungles and deserts, UK Special Forces undertake brutal Arctic training and are arguably more skilled than their American counterparts at operating in sub-zero conditions.[32] Had the mutual chest-beating and trading of insults between Trump and Kim ended in military action, the plan was for UK Special Forces teams supported by Royal Marines to play a key role in an operation to neutralise dozens of weapons' sites.

'The Americans didn't fancy it, so we were going to take the lead,' according to a well-placed Special Forces source.[33]

In a sign of how seriously the Ministry of Defence took the possibility of the UK playing a supporting role in a US strike against the regime, in spring 2018, Defence Secretary Gavin Williamson ordered a stockpile of anthrax vaccines for troops that could be sent to the Korean peninsula.[34]

In 2017, Kim Jong-un carried out sixteen tests of nuclear-capable missiles, culminating in the launch of what appeared to be an intercontinental ballistic missile. This went beyond any previous test. The speed with which North Korea had developed its arsenal shocked international observers. President Trump is determined it goes no further.[35]

Following his historic summit with the Supreme Leader in Singapore in June 2018, there is new hope that Pyongyang will concede to a denuclearisation programme. Nobody is holding their breath, however. If, as many fear, 'little rocket man' (as Trump once called him) returns to his 'suicide mission',[36] and the Trump administration decides a military response is necessary, our armed forces will probably be involved in some shape or form, with all the associated risks to UK national security. As Fallon himself pointed out last September, London is closer to Pyongyang than Los Angeles.[37]

At this stage, nobody is standing down.

DARWIN

Perhaps 'state-based' threats from Russia, China and North Korea are being exaggerated, or will recede. Even so, defence analysts believe seismic global changes mean the armed forces should be ready for a major conflict soon.

The Ministry of Defence has a 'Futures Team' tasked with looking at the way the world is changing and assessing what it might mean for UK defence.[38] It does not predict world peace.

This type of crystal-ball gazing is fiendishly difficult, and politics often get in the way. A source involved in one of the recent reports ('The Future Operating Environment 2035') says it was an agonising process requiring twenty-nine drafts. He described the final version as 'bloody awful', claiming it was neutered by mandarins determined to play down the nature and scale of potential threats to the UK for fear of putting defence ministers in an awkward position. By the time it was published, he claims, it was so watered down it had 'lost all value'.[39] The imperative not to upset the political and diplomatic applecart apparently resulted in an entire section, called 'Global Powers', being cut, and long passages on the potential dangers posed by a resurgent Russia and China reduced to a few lines on a map.[40]

'We tried to go much further, but that's when you outstrip the imaginations of senior officers and mandarins,' says the source. 'They were even uncomfortable over any mention of nuclear weapons, saying they "couldn't envisage a scenario" where nuclear weapons would be used.'[41]

The Futures Team failed to predict Brexit or the appetite of US voters for an 'America First' champion like Donald Trump.

However, it highlighted huge demographic and environmental shifts that are making the world less stable.* If defence chiefs did not have to worry about the threat posed by Russia, China, North Korea and other rogue states, these changes would keep them awake at night.

In the next thirty years, global population is expected to soar by two billion, creating intense competition for resources.[42] Ageing populations in the first world and a youth bulge in developing countries will add to the pressure, with rising migration likely to generate tension between nation states.[43] By 2045, most people are expected to live in cities, some 280 of which could have more than 20 million inhabitants.[44] In cramped conditions, natural disasters, pandemics and epidemics are likely to result in higher death tolls. Increased interconnectivity

---

* 'Global Strategic Trends – Out to 2045', June 2014, lists thirteen. They are: population growth; urbanisation; competition for resources; climate change; disease; transport; information technology; education; automation and robotics; corruption and money; changes in gender equality; the role of the state; and defence spending and capabilities.

between cities could mean that communicable diseases travel faster, and the fight against disease-resistant bacteria could become much more difficult if outbreaks are harder to quarantine.[45] Meanwhile, fresh water is likely to become a source of intense competition, with supplies already running out in some parts of the world. Over the next few decades, demand is likely to grow by 55 per cent, making shared river basins and aquifers potential flashpoints.[46] Energy supplies will be crucial to meeting growing demand for water and food, but dwindling fossil fuels could lead to resource protectionism from big energy producers and create conflict with states reliant on imports.[47] In the next thirty years, the annual tonnage of both air and sea travel is likely to double, potentially creating major maritime choke points that become significant areas of international conflict, particularly as the law of the sea is much vaguer than the law of the land.[48] Meanwhile, climate change could cause harvest failures and floods that unleash unprecedented waves of migration.[49]

In the longer term, automation could create mass unemployment, as many manual or information processing jobs are taken over by computers.[50] All this has profound implications for the armed forces.

Barrons says:

The world we've known for the past twenty-five years is changing very rapidly – and not to our advantage. A combination of hubris, complacency and a preoccupation with our own internal business, like Brexit, or austerity, means we haven't faced up to these things.

Many of the Western powers, particularly in Europe, are running on assumptions that reflect all our adult experiences from the end of the Cold War where we didn't feel any existential risk to our homeland. We felt that the Western way was always going to hold primacy. That is eroding very quickly. We have to acknowledge that there is a new range of risks out there and the way conflict and confrontation is prosecuted, in terms of both method and thinking and ideas and capability, has changed.[51]

It is easy to see how such shifts could combine to create local or regional trouble. What worries defence chiefs and academics is the potential for conflict to spread as a result of a growing disregard for international laws and norms on the part of some regimes.

All this is focusing attention on how the UK's armed forces would perform if there is a war soon.

In the UK and the US, military figures are increasingly frank about the scale of the challenge.

Potential adversaries are rapidly acquiring military assets that match or even outperform our own. Many unfriendly regimes can draw from hundreds of thousands of conscripts to complement increasingly professional regular troops.

This is a profound strategic shift. The US and its allies have enjoyed military supremacy in every conflict in which they have engaged since the 1991 Gulf War. Western technology offered the impression of what was dubbed 'full spectrum dominance'.[52] Stealth planes appeared able to avoid enemy defences;[53] Cruise missiles and laser-guided bombs hit targets with pin-point accuracy;[54] depleted uranium shells penetrated any known tank around;[55] and drones provided continuous surveillance of targets while controlled by satellite from the other side of the world.[56] Insurgents in Iraq and Afghanistan were only able to challenge this technological superiority by using snipers and improvised roadside bombs. These low-tech weapons inflicted a drip, drip of casualties designed to sap the democratic consent in Britain and America required to continue the war, but Western troops were not defeated in straight-up battles.[57]

The Russian invasion of Crimea in 2014 and subsequent intervention in Syria showed that the terms of military trade had changed. Western powers are now up against opponents with conventional weapons and capabilities on a par with their own. Some of the latest Russian, Chinese, Indian and Iranian weapons are now believed to rival our kit, much of which was designed in the Cold War.[58] To make matters worse, as we shall see, our armed forces must now be ready for battle in multiple domains, using information, robotics, electronics and magnetics; in space, underwater and in cyberspace.

GAVIN

All this is what was going on in the world when a former fireplace salesman from Scarborough suddenly became Britain's youngest ever Secretary of State for Defence.[59]

Gavin Williamson, a man best known at Westminster for his pet tarantula Cronus, had never run a Whitehall department. Now he had one of the most challenging ministerial briefs.

The circumstances in which he arrived in the post in November 2017 were highly unusual, not least because in the eyes of many of his colleagues, he appointed himself.[60] As Chief Whip, it had fallen to him to propose an appropriate successor to Sir Michael Fallon, who had suddenly lost his job in a bizarre sex scandal known as 'knee-gate'.[61] Williamson did not recommend himself for the job, but that did not stop colleagues sniping that, as Chief Whip, he had arranged his own promotion.

His appointment triggered a vicious backlash among colleagues. Tory MPs questioned how a man with no experience as a Secretary of State or in the military could be better suited to the role than others with more relevant credentials. He had never even spoken in the Commons from the dispatch box. 'Unbelievable', 'ludicrous' and 'astonishing' were among the politer reactions.[62]

Within the Ministry of Defence and armed forces, his appointment was no less of a surprise. Many had never heard of him. Yet the sudden change at the top was also a source of optimism. Williamson had been at Prime Minister Theresa May's side since June 2016, when he decided to back her in the Tory leadership campaign prompted by David Cameron's resignation.[63] He acted as her parliamentary campaign manager, and when she won, she made him Chief Whip, an exceptionally difficult position when a Prime Minister has no parliamentary majority. His performance impressed. As one of May's most trusted acolytes, perhaps he could succeed where others had failed and finally secure a sustainable defence budget?

To the delight of the armed forces, the new Defence Secretary immediately made it clear he was on a mission to do just that. Within weeks, he showed he meant business, taking the extraordinary step of barring the Chancellor from using RAF jets in a row over an unpaid invoice to the Treasury.[64]

It was a high-risk way to start his new job, antagonising the very department he would need on side if he wanted to leave the armed forces in better shape at the end of his tenure than at the start. Soon his unconventional style and apocalyptic warnings about threats to the UK sent defence rocketing up the political agenda.

Like other Defence Secretaries before him, his first challenge was not the politics, however, but figuring out how to handle the strangest department in Whitehall: the Ministry of Defence.

PART TWO

THE POLITICS

GUNFIRE

THE MINISTRY OF DEFENCE

RUM

Back in the days when hardware was more important than software, the Ministry of Defence used to check how our kit compared to the competition by getting hold of foreign stuff and taking it apart. All sorts of weapons used by allies and adversaries would be meticulously dismantled to inspect components and mechanics and figure out how they were put together.

Often the MoD would have to be highly resourceful to lay its hands on the materiel for this process of 'reverse engineering'. At one point during the Cold War, a MiG-25 Soviet fighter aircraft was flown out of Russia by a defector – a very valuable present for the British.[1] The job of taking materiel to pieces fell to the Ministry of Defence's weapons design team, which would spend days unpicking it all to see what was worth copying and what was flawed.

If anyone tried to carry out the same process on the MoD itself today, they would quickly become overwhelmed by the sheer size and complexity of the machine. This is a government department like no other, as one seasoned Whitehall operator realised on his first day as Permanent Under Secretary. Stephen Lovegrove had barely taken off his coat when a charming fellow handed him a cocktail called Gunfire made of cold black tea and rum. It is traditionally served by army officers to lower ranks before a morning attack. Lovegrove gamely downed the drink and says he was rather disappointed when he wasn't offered another the following day.[2]

Whether the alcohol eased his initiation into his bewildering new environment is unclear – even for the most experienced bureaucrats, it's a culture shock. The health department isn't stuffed with doctors; the education department isn't full of teachers; but the Ministry of Defence is a baffling hybrid of civilians and military personnel. Confusingly, members of the armed forces on secondment to the department, often referred to by colleagues as 'the uniforms', don't always wear uniform, leaving one new minister trying to identify them by the state of their shoes. ('I would look down at their boots. If they were shiny, they were usually military,' Sir Malcolm Rifkind, Secretary of State for Defence between 1992 and 1995, recalls.)[3]

The complex relationship between military top brass ('uniforms'), senior civil servants ('mandarins') and politicians ('suits') shapes decision-making, and is an important determinant of the UK's military capabilities.

In all, some 7,750 civil servants are based in the Ministry of Defence's Main Building on Whitehall, and 49,150 more are dispersed across multiple MoD sites elsewhere in the UK.[4]

At the top of the food chain is the Secretary of State (SoS), who is based on the fifth floor. He (to date, no woman has ever held the job) is the political head of the department, representing the Ministry of Defence in Cabinet, on the National Security Council and in the House of Commons. He represents the MoD at meetings with counterparts at NATO, the EU and in bilateral meetings with Allied defence ministers.

In theory, the Secretary of State has a great deal of power, playing a key role in devising defence policy at the highest level, including negotiating with the Prime Minister and Chancellor over the armed forces' budget. He signs off rules of engagement for military operations and has significant powers of patronage, recommending senior military figures for top jobs.

However, he can't declare war and can't make alliances with foreign governments or armed forces, though he can advise the Prime Minister to do so.

As in other Whitehall departments, the shock for many new Secretaries of State is just how little power they have to drive this mighty machine in the direction they want to go. They soon realise that whatever they do, the department trundles on in much the same way as ever – especially if there's no money.

For political veterans like Labour's John Reid or Sir Michael Fallon, who have run other Whitehall departments and are pragmatic about what it is possible to achieve, this matters less. They are more likely to see their job as primarily to keep the show on the road; minimise conflict with Treasury; and ensure Downing Street is happy. Incremental improvements to the state of the armed forces are a bonus.

For Cabinet newcomers like Williamson, however, the limited room for manoeuvre is harder to accept. The legacy of decisions taken by predecessors, limited interest in defence policy in Downing Street and the sheer length of time it takes to change anything all conspire against implementing any 'big visions' for the armed forces.

As they walk into the Ministry of Defence for the first time, many new Defence Secretaries feel overwhelmed by the magnitude of their responsibilities. What they do not generally realise is how little their arrival means to others in the department. One very high-ranking former MoD mandarin, now working for the private sector, went so far as to describe defence ministers and other politicians as 'irrelevant' to the functioning of the MoD, claiming everything works at least as well, if not better, without them.

'Politicians cause trouble and they cause more dysfunction, but they are not really that important,' he says.

I had a parliamentary pass for four years and I used it once to see somebody because he couldn't get into his office in the MoD. I had no engagement with Parliament and the only time they intruded on my visage – and I wasn't a minor person in the scheme of things – was when there was a Defence Select Committee report which one of the ministers got upset about because it put a finger on him. They are irrelevant, these people.[5]

59

According to the source, civil servants and defence chiefs regularly conspire to freeze politicians out of sensitive discussions. As we have seen, ahead of their weekly meeting with politicians about ongoing operations, defence chiefs and mandarins 'decide how little they are going to tell ministers'.

'That is how it works,' he says.

> The meeting goes from lunchtime until about six or seven in the evening. You get beamed in to American intelligence for that meeting and you get parties coming in from, say, Kabul or NATO. It's where everyone is frank about what the scenarios are. There are no politicians in the first section, and that's where we have the candid discussions of the strategic military implications of what is going on.[6]

Ministerial pet subjects are a particular source of frustration for mandarins. The source recalled one former junior minister being 'obsessed with the Lebanon', prompting much rolling of eyes among bureaucrats less excited by the subject.

> What you don't want is 'hobbyism' from ministers. That is the danger. They come in with particular bees in their bonnet. With one, every fucking meeting was about the Lebanese, and the answer was 'We don't want to talk about their border arrangements, minister, because actually they want to keep it secret.'[7]

The rationale behind installing thousands of military personnel within the Ministry of Defence is straightforward: committing the armed forces to war or other high-risk operations is an extremely serious decision, and defence ministers need authoritative military advice close to hand. In recent years, very few Defence Secretaries have had any military experience, leaving them heavily reliant on the heads of the army, navy and RAF for guidance as to what can and cannot be done.

Often this doesn't matter: as Defence Secretary during the Labour years, John (now Lord) Hutton took the view that he could not hope to understand more than about a fifth of what was going on in the department, and that it was not his job to do so.

> The Secretary of State is there to provide leadership and direction for as long as he or she is in that department. It's not to understand every aspect of every bit of policy about outsourcing or logistics or fleet support. Your job is to be the person with the direction and strategy.

'It's not operations,' he says.[8]

The system is specifically designed to accommodate the military ignorance of the political masters. However, the mix of civilian and military personnel makes for confusing parallel chains of command. In theory, politicians – advised by civil servants – set policy, but they have no power of discipline over service personnel. If military personnel work in an organisation headed by a civil servant, then the civilian boss can tell the soldier, sailor or airman what to do, within his job description; but the civilian has no power to discipline his military staff and he or she does not write the annual review determining whether those military staff will be promoted. The situation is reversed for civil servants working for military bosses.

If the politicians matter less than they'd like to think, the 'sofa-style government' of recent Prime Ministers and associated expansion in the power of the Cabinet Office has diminished the influence of senior defence mandarins. Once upon a time, top civil servants like the late Sir Michael Quinlan (Permanent Under Secretary of State at the Ministry of Defence from 1988 to 1992) were defence experts, sometimes amassing more specialist knowledge in certain areas (in Quinlan's case, nuclear deterrence) than the 'uniforms'.[9] Now the Cabinet Office has captured top-level policy creation across Whitehall, they do not need this expertise. They are far more likely to be elite management types than policy specialists, and after a few years in the department, they generally move on. Today, some complain that the emphasis is on running the Ministry of Defence like a business, rather than an organisation whose primary objective is to promote defence and security. This approach has significant implications for the armed forces.

As one defence analyst points out, running a business and serving the national interest are two very different things.

> The 'fitness function' of the MoD is now assessed on the basis of business criteria of efficiency rather than on the department's effectiveness at providing for the country's defence and security. This is not to paint the former MoD system as perfect, nor to deny that a lot can be learned from business, just as business has learned a lot from the military in recent years. But business function and culture now dominate at the top of the MoD.

'Their annual reports are now company reports, not defence and security reports,' he observes.[10]

The top civil servant in the MoD is the Permanent Under Secretary of State – or 'Perm Sec' – who has little profile outside the department. He or she is the professional head of all civil servants within the MoD; is the MoD's chief accounting officer; and is responsible for ensuring all spending by the MoD is properly managed. The Perm Sec is the Secretary of State's senior adviser on all non-military matters, such as budgets, legal issues, international agreements and property. He or she signs the cheques; issues orders to mandarins; and approves appointments, but has no power over military personnel.

'Uniforms' arrive at the MoD as junior officers and can return several times on their way up the career ladder. Little prepares them for the tribal agendas of other military personnel in the department, or the Machiavellian manoeuvres of the mandarins and suits. Conflicting priorities are a particular problem. Military people are focused on achieving missions; the armed forces honour those who win the day by being imaginative, brave and different. Civil servants, with their focus on process and order, are much more nervous of novel behaviour.

At the top of the pecking order is the Chief of the Defence Staff (CDS), the professional head of the armed forces. He and colleagues who head the army, navy, RAF and joint forces are known as the 'service chiefs'. His role is to provide 'politically aware military advice' to the Prime Minister, Secretary of State and other parts of the government. He does this at the highest level in his capacity as a member of the National Security Council and via government committees. When military operations are being considered or are under way, it is the CDS's job to present the proposed plans to the Prime Minister and Secretary of State and to make recommendations. It is up to politicians whether to approve or reject the suggestions.

With most critical decisions made in Downing Street, the Treasury or the Cabinet Office, the authority of the four service chiefs and their ability to advise and influence the politicians is limited to operations. Their task is simply to manage their services as they carry out the orders of the CDS. They can offer ideas and feedback to the CDS, but no more.

For the chiefs, the Ministry of Defence is a particularly alien environment. Suddenly they find themselves at the political interface, managing multiple conflicts of interest. On the one hand, they are the head of their service – army, navy or RAF – and thousands of service personnel look to them for leadership. They are expected to protect their own tribe and ensure their people are not committed to operations that can't succeed. At the same time, they are expected to form part of a collegiate group planning and managing military operations, advising ministers and contributing to – if not determining – strategic direction for defence. Meanwhile, they have to deal with politicians who abhor precision and commitment – precisely the traits that are encouraged by the military. Highly complex operational language has to be reduced to sound bites and they find themselves being asked to formulate plans for vague missions, all the while ensuring that whatever they recommend does not return to haunt the government.

All this adds up to a machine that is sub-optimal when it comes to producing the right advice up the chain to senior officers and ministers: cold comfort for Gavin Williamson, when within days of starting his new job in November 2017, he was asked to make decisions that would have profound consequences for the armed forces.

WOLVERHAMPTON

Surveying the contents of his ministerial red box at his home in Wolverhampton, Williamson felt slightly dizzy. It was the weekend, and he was being asked to consider no lesser question than what role the armed forces should aspire to play in the world. Should they continue to be a global expeditionary force, ready to send soldiers, sailors and ships overseas to topple tyrants and make life better for the oppressed? Or should they just focus on being a good NATO ally, developing capabilities other members of the Alliance do not have?

The answers he gave could change the armed forces for ever. He had just two weeks to decide. He had been in the job less than forty-eight hours.

In front of him were various briefing notes about the National Security Capability Review that had prompted the dilemma. Announced that summer, the assessment was a response to a growing clamour for the government to update defence planning in the light of Brexit and dramatic changes to the nature of threats the UK might face. Yet none of what was being suggested tallied with Williamson's vision for the armed forces. In his early twenties, he had lapped up books about great admirals like Nelson and Mountbatten. In their own way, he felt these historical figures embodied what today's government calls 'global Britain'. What, Williamson wondered, does that catchphrase mean, if the UK no longer has real hard power and ministers give up offering any international leadership? He admired the way Trump and French President Emmanuel Macron articulated a confident view on their country's place in the world. He hated the creeping sense that the UK was in retreat. So far from withdrawing from the world stage, he had visions of the armed forces opening new outposts in far-flung places, re-establishing a presence in regions they left long ago. He was realistic enough to recognise that all this was a pipe dream, but he was certainly not going to give up before he had started.

PART TWO: THE POLITICS

MAP OF THE UK'S OVERSEAS DEFENCE BASES

Ascension Island – RAF Ascension and site of joint UK US signals intelligence facility.
Bahrain – New Naval Support Facility opened in 2018. Also home to the UK Maritime Component Command.
Belize – British Army Training and Support Unit Belize (BATSUB).
Bermuda – Base of the Royal Bermuda Regiment.
British Indian Ocean Territory – A Permanent Joint Operating Base. The Naval Support Facility and airbase on Diego Garcia are leased to the United States.
Brunei – A battalion from the Royal Gurkha Rifles and an Army Air Corps.
Canada – British Army Training Unit Suffield (BATUS).
Cyprus – There is a Permanent Joint Operating Base with garrisons at Akrotiri and Dhekelia. This includes RAF Akrotiri.
Falkland Islands – There is a Permanent Joint Operating Base. The British garrison is centred around RAF Mount Pleasant.
Germany – 20th Armoured Infantry Brigade is stationed in Germany.
Gibraltar – There is a Permanent Joint Operating Base. Facilities include RAF Gibraltar and the Port of Gibraltar.
Kenya – British Army Training Unit Kenya (BATUK).
Montserrat – Base of the Royal Montserrat Defence Force.
Nepal – Small outpost for recruitment purposes to the Brigade of Gurkhas.
Oman – UK Joint Logistics Support Base is under construction.
Qatar – RAF Al Udeid is shared between the UK, US and Qatar.
Singapore – Royal Navy Repair and Logistics Support Facility at Sembawang Wharf.

DEFENCE SECRETARY GAVIN WILLIAMSON WOULD LIKE TO EXTEND THIS NETWORK.

And so the Defence Secretary's first big decision was not to make any decision. He knew he could not meet the two-week deadline. The National Security Capability Review would have to wait while he figured out the challenges he had inherited.

GHOSTS

THE DEFENCE LEGACY

PULVERISED

The ghosts of Defence Secretaries past haunt their successors for decades.

Williamson's immediate predecessor had spent much of his tenure at the Ministry of Defence in a funk over money. Sir Michael Fallon had found himself under constant attack* about the seemingly remorseless efficiency savings top brass were having to make to avoid plunging further into the red.

The Secretary of State's dogged mantra, repeated at every opportunity – 'the defence budget is growing' – was theoretically true, following an increase of £800 million in 2016,[1] but the spending decline in preceding years had been so steep that critics saw the statement as little more than weasel words from a career politician. Many in defence circles longed for some honesty to be injected into the debate.

The dire state of affairs was not Fallon's fault. Many of the problems dated as far back as 1990, when, following the fall of the Berlin Wall, the Thatcher government announced a so-called peace dividend. A document called *Options for Change* paved the way for dramatic reductions to the defence budget. It fell by 6 per cent in 1992, setting a pattern that continued for the next half-decade. Cuts were made of 4 per cent in 1993, 5 per cent in 1994, 7 per cent in 1995, 2 per cent in 1996 and 7 per cent in 1997. Spending as a proportion of GDP fell from 4.1 per cent in 1991/92 to 2.4 per cent by 2000.[2]

---

* From politicians, the media, defence experts and commentators as well as members of the armed forces themselves.

Williamson, who would have been just fourteen years old at the time, says he remembers his heart sinking as he listened to a news item about *Options for Change*.

'I was hanging out with my mates in Gilly's Amusement Arcade in Scarborough, and it came on the radio. I was thinking, even back then, "This is going to mean a smaller armed forces, and this is going to be bad,"' he says.[3]

The downward trend continued during Labour's administration from 1997 to 2010. However, it is summer 2010 that many in defence circles see as the watershed. The tumultuous weeks after the Conservatives failed to win a majority in the general election, and the decisions taken about defence in that period, are widely seen as a turning point in the state of the armed forces, accounting for the many challenges they face today.

In the MoD's Main Building on Horse Guards Avenue, service chiefs and senior civil service mandarins had enjoyed a ringside seat of the coming and goings in Whitehall as attempts were made to form a government. Every day, from their windows, they could see the scrum of journalists outside the Cabinet Office as Conservative and Liberal Democrat politicians trooped in to thrash out the coalition agreement. For all the drama unfolding across the street, however, they had precious little intelligence about what the new political landscape would mean for the military. All they knew was that it wouldn't be good. The new coalition was preparing to conduct the first defence review in more than a decade, and the Treasury was looking to impose huge spending cuts across government. There was no suggestion defence would escape.

In May 2010, the pieces began to fall into place. Delivering a commitment made in opposition, the incoming premier, David Cameron, announced the creation of a new government body called the National Security Council (NSC).[4] Its first task was to oversee what the government called a Strategic Defence and Security Review (SDSR) – the first since 1998. That summer, ministers and senior officials held several NSC meetings in the Cabinet Office building off Whitehall to thrash out the general direction of British defence policy. Their conclusions were not radical: Britain was to continue to fight the war in Afghanistan until the Americans pulled out; stay in NATO; and retain the USA as our major ally. International terrorism was seen as the immediate threat. The replacement of the nuclear deterrent would remain the country's number-one defence priority (though under the coalition agreement, the Lib Dems, long-standing opponents of Trident, would have special dispensation to vote against it).[5]

Everyone knew that, at the end of the process, the armed forces would have less money, troops and kit. Throughout the summer, defence chiefs argued about whether they needed more or fewer tanks, ships, planes and troops, but little was decided.

Over in the Treasury, a separate and more important exercise was taking place. The newly installed Chancellor of the Exchequer, George Osborne, was working out what every government department could spend for the next decade. His so-called Comprehensive Spending Review (CSR) was designed to achieve an ambitious goal: abolish the financial deficit by 2015.[6] The idea was that the government should no longer spend more than it was collecting in tax each year. A delegation of senior Ministry of Defence officials was dispatched to find out what this meant for their department.

The news was a shock: Osborne was looking at real-terms cuts of between 10 and 20 per cent.[7]

'It felt as if the armed forces were effectively being put out of business,' said a senior Ministry of Defence civil servant who was in the thick of it. 'We were practically going extinct.'[8] Some politicians feared it would turn the UK into 'Belgium with nukes'.[9]

In the weeks that followed, mandarins and senior military officers tried to work out how to achieve what the Chancellor wanted, putting together a 'CSR scorecard' listing military spending priorities. Despite the huge potential long-term repercussions for national security, it was all a massive rush.

'This was about preserving as much as possible, not looking at radical changes or being innovative. There was just not time as the Treasury clock was ticking,' according to a source involved in the process.[10]

The new Defence Secretary, Liam Fox, had been an effective and energetic operator in opposition, but power brought a cold dose of reality. He had devoted five years to working out how the Ministry of Defence and armed forces could be strengthened and was eager to put his ideas into practice. His party had spent the long Labour years emphasising stewardship of national security as the first duty of government. Now they were in charge, and it was all about *dismantling* capabilities.

Fox found the process brutal. The single biggest problem was the amount of money already tied up in contracts that could not be cancelled. Other legal obligations, such as the £3 billion a year on pensions to retired service personnel[11] and the huge clean-up cost of redundant nuclear submarines, were also inescapable.[12] Crucially, though Osborne had talked about eliminating the deficit by 2015, he had warned that budgets were unlikely to rise after that date, so deferring costs and hoping for more cash later wasn't an option.

Looking at the MoD's legal obligations, Fox could not see any quick economies. Instead, civil servants worked on longer-term plans. The commitment to maintain the Trident nuclear deterrent left little flexibility over the submarine fleet. A delayed and over-budget project to build Astute-class nuclear hunter-killer submarines could not be cancelled[13] because the shipyards would be needed to build Trident's replacement and had to be kept in work.[14] In turn this meant that the Faslane submarine base and the Aldermaston nuclear bomb re-processing site had to stay open. Civil servants suggested 'deleting' amphibious shipping (landing docks, helicopter platforms and support ships) and axing a new maritime patrol aircraft or 'spy plane' called Nimrod. This would also help the RAF, which was sharing the cost of the programme.[15]

For the air force, there was no nuclear cushion. A large chunk of the RAF budget was tied up in multi-billion-pound contracts for new planes, as well as for refits and spare parts. These deals were too expensive to cancel. Some aircraft were heavily committed to the war in Afghanistan so could not be mothballed until British troops were withdrawn after 2014. The easiest target was the programme to procure 138 American-made F-35B Lightning II Joint Strike Fighter jets.[16] Nimrod could be scrapped altogether – it was well behind schedule – and delaying the Joint Strike Force programme would save billions.[17]

For the army, the commitment of 10,000 troops to Afghanistan provided some protection.[18] While the war dragged on, around a third of the force was tied up. Any dramatic cuts to troop numbers would mean extending tours of duty for service personnel or deploying them more often, neither of which was good for morale or public opinion. Contracts with US defence giants General Dynamics (for a new reconnaissance vehicle called Scout)[19] and Lockheed Martin (for an upgrade to the Warrior troop carrier)[20] would have been too awkward to cancel for diplomatic reasons. The only viable option would be to cut troops as soon as it was possible.

After much agonising, mandarins finally came up with a list of capabilities that could be axed to meet Osborne's target of 20 per cent cuts. The combined effect was devastating: the armed forces would be pulverised.

Looking at what would have to be done, Fox was appalled. He knew he could not preside over such a reduction in capabilities. In a letter leaked to the *Daily Telegraph*, he warned David Cameron of the 'grave political consequences' of pressing ahead, saying it could 'destroy' the Prime Minister's reputation.

'Party, media, military and international reaction will be brutal if we do not recognise the dangers and continue to push for such draconian cuts at a time when we are at war,' he wrote.

'Our decisions today will severely limit the options available to this and all future governments. The range of operations that we can do today we will simply not be able to do in the future.'[21]

The letter worked. Cameron pulled back. The amount of money involved was not enormous in the Chancellor's overall deficit reduction plan, so the Ministry of Defence budget was given a degree of protection. There would be no cash cuts, but nor would there be any automatic increases in the budget to cover rising wage bills, currency fluctuations and any cost overruns. This amounted to an 8 per cent cut in real terms.[22] Just over £40 billion in cuts – around half from military hardware – would have to be made over the decade.*[23]

Nearly every equipment procurement would take a hit. More than £5 billion was sliced off the budget for new fighter planes, mostly by delaying the bulk of the F-35 contract until 2020. Other cuts involved £3 billion from spy and transport planes; £2 billion from armoured vehicles; £2 billion from logistic shipping; and £1 billion from guided weapons.[24] £4.1 billion would be clawed back by sacking 42,000 service personnel and civil servants between 2010 and 2015.†[25] The detail would be unveiled in the Strategic Defence and Security Review, to be published that October.

On the Friday before the announcement, Cameron summoned Fox; the then Chief of the Defence Staff Air Chief Marshal Sir Jock Stirrup; and a couple of other senior military officers to Chequers to finalise decisions. According to one of those present, the Prime Minister effectively engaged in a 'pick and mix' approach to capabilities.

'It was pretty brutal – things were taken in and out in the course of the meeting,' he said.

> There was nothing coherent or joined up about this – there just wasn't time. Cameron also wanted to make some political statements. So, the Nimrod was to be canned and not stored for use later. HMS *Ark Royal* and her Harrier jump jets would go too – this was a way of sharing the pain across three armed services.[26]

The navy got to keep its new aircraft carriers as well as all its Astute nuclear subs. To find savings it would have to retire four Type 22 frigates and lose two of its seven amphibious landing ships. Some 5,000 sailors would have to be made redundant.[27]

---

* Approximately £20 billion would be saved from military hardware, £10 billion through personnel cuts and £11 billion as a result of bureaucratic cuts.

† In spring 2011, the number of service personnel and civil servants that were being sacked increased to 54,000.

The RAF escaped with most of its projects intact but the delivery of new aircraft would be delayed, leaving what were euphemistically referred to as 'capability gaps'. To generate savings, they would have to eliminate duplicate types of aircraft – C-130 transports, Sentinel spy planes, Tornado bombers and Merlin helicopters – though some of these cuts were postponed until the end of the Afghan commitment. This 'rationalisation' of the aircraft fleet would allow the RAF to lose 5,000 people and close several air bases.[28]

The army was given enough money to ensure it could continue to fight the Afghan war, and the annual £4 billion of additional war funding from the Treasury reserve would remain until 2014, cushioning the service in the short term.[29] However, they would lose 7,000 soldiers;[30] a slew of bases would be closed; and they were instructed to move the last troops home from Germany by the end of the decade.[31] Around a third of Challenger tanks and AS-90 field guns would be placed in storage.[32]

Meanwhile, Ministry of Defence civilian staff took a big hit. The department was asked to shed 25,000 people from its 85,000 headcount[33] as part of a drive to save £4.3 billion through cuts to bureaucracy.[34] The army's network of repair depots, the MoD military port and a section of radio frequency spectrum would be sold to raise £500 million for the Treasury.[35]

Cameron announced the Strategic Defence and Security Review on Tuesday 19 October. In a statement to the House of Commons, he did his best to put a positive spin on it, insisting it was 'not simply a cost-saving exercise' but about 'taking the right decisions' to protect future national security. He stressed that the UK would continue to spend NATO's recommended 2 per cent of GDP on defence and would still have one of the biggest military budgets in the world.

Before listing all the bad stuff, he did what every new government does and blamed the last lot, claiming Labour had left an 'appalling legacy' on defence.[36]

The 2010 Strategic Defence and Security Review was a perilous experiment. Politically, Cameron got away with it. No ministers or generals resigned in protest; there was no backbench rebellion; voters did not march on Downing Street. The armed forces did what they had to do, and just got on with it.

Little did they know it would not be enough: the Strategic Defence and Security Review quickly unravelled. The figures simply didn't stack up. Some of the cost projections were hopelessly optimistic and others were rapidly overtaken by events, such as the rise of Islamic State and a resurgent Russia. In the years that followed, coalition politicians constantly talked about a '£38 billion black hole' in the defence budget – the gap between the MoD's plans for future spending and the available money from the Treasury. The Tories constantly reiterated that it was all Labour's fault.[37]

In 2012 and 2013, the Treasury returned to the Ministry of Defence for more cash, clawing back more than £1.2 billion from the department in two consecutive autumn statements.[38] Once again, the savings drive was unsuccessful, and by the time the 2015 Strategic Defence and Security Review and Comprehensive Spending Review were under way, the unpaid bill for savings was still being presented to the Ministry of Defence by the Treasury.

VIDEO TAPE

All this was a sea change from Labour's approach to defence. Just as Conservatives remain terrified of any suggestion they are running down the National Health Service (a policy area in which they are less trusted by voters), New Labour under Tony Blair had been determined to show it had moved on from any pacifist, nuclear-disarming tendencies of the past.

'We certainly didn't want to be accused of running down defence. We were very clear on that,' recalls Lord Hutton, who was Defence Secretary between 2008 and 2009.

On taking power, Blair signalled that he wanted Britain to follow a more assertive foreign and defence policy. One of his first initiatives was to reverse orders to British troops in Bosnia not to seize war crimes suspects. A programme of arrest operations was launched by the SAS to bring senior Bosnian Serbia army officers to justice at the International Criminal Tribunal for the former Yugoslavia (ICTY). The Prime Minister was widely applauded for his new robust approach.[39]

The ministerial line-up at the Ministry of Defence – George Robertson, John Reid and John Spellar – had reflected the Labour leader's interventionist instincts.

'The joke at the time was that Blair's first defence team was the most right-wing collection of ministers ever assembled – by *any* government,' recalls Michael Dugher, a Labour apparatchik who went on to become a special adviser in the department.[40]

On arrival at the MoD, Robertson had embarked on a sweeping defence review. Though there would be no extra money, the positive mood music and direction from No. 10 could not have been more different to the negativity that would surround the same process under the Tories in 2010.

Over dinner with Foreign Secretary Robin Cook, Robertson had agreed that the starting point should be making the armed forces more 'useable' and 'deployable' in service of New Labour's new 'ethical foreign policy'. For the first time ever in a defence review, members of the public, academics, parliamentarians, defence industry figures, community groups, retired service chiefs, non-governmental organisations, the media and even serving junior members of the armed services were asked to make contributions and suggestions. Robertson wanted to generate excitement about what was going on. As he recalls:

> We agreed to have the biggest consultation ever, meeting every conceivable expert: ex-ministers; Parliamentarians; pressure groups; critics and so on. We set up an advisory committee which included a lot of people like [the journalist] Simon Jenkins who were highly critical of the military. We went out on a road show in Manchester; we went up North; we had a big round table [meeting] in the Foreign Office with three permanent secretaries; all the junior ministers; all the pressure groups. We had the CND; trade unions; the whole thing. We had people saying, 'This is a waste of time. Hardly any new ideas are coming out!' and I said, 'Well there are a few, but

the idea is we are buying people into the process. Nobody, at the end of the day, is going to be able to say, "Nobody asked us."[41]

At the end of the consultation, Robertson gathered his ministers and chiefs of staff round a table to reach some decisions. Such was the enthusiasm that the government even allowed some of the discussion to be filmed. The footage was later turned into a documentary.

In a decision that would have huge repercussions long after Labour left power, the navy was granted two new aircraft carriers.[42] Robertson's team had nicknamed the ships 'Gordon Brown 1' and 'Gordon Brown 2', reflecting the Chancellor's enthusiasm for the shipyard jobs they would create. The quid pro quo was the loss of some attack submarines and frigates. The navy went through the motions of putting up a fight but knew they'd secured a big win.

Robertson recalls:

> Sir Jock Slater was First Sea Lord at the time and wanted to make the case for more frigates. He went through all the reasons. He was a very methodical guy, and the final reason was 'You cannot have a cocktail party in a Tornado!' Though I have to say I put that to the RAF pilots in Saudi Arabia when I went down there shortly afterwards, and they said, 'Yes, you can, and we've done it!'[43]

It was all going remarkably smoothly until the Treasury stepped in. During the 1997 election campaign, Brown had pledged to follow Conservative spending plans for the next two years.[44] Determined to show New Labour could be trusted with the economy, he was championing what he called financial 'prudence', and made a sudden lunge at the defence budget.

Robertson was incandescent. He had been told to reshape the armed forces so they could go out and make the world a better place. Nobody had said it had to be done with less cash. He and his ministers threatened to quit.

> The Treasury said, 'We want two billion out of your plan.' John Spellar,

John Reid and I went to see the Prime Minister late at night and said, 'If this budget is going to be cut by two billion, we're going to resign.' We'd given our word that this was all going to be foreign-policy-led, and [our recommendations] were the conclusion we'd come to.[45]

Faced with the prospect of a mass ministerial walk-out, Blair and Brown blinked first. Shortly afterwards, Robertson's Strategic Defence Review was published, to near-universal acclaim. The document was filled with colour photographs of smiling soldiers, data tables and maps[46] and, unlike many previous defence white papers, it had a coherent political and strategic narrative. The 'force for good' concept, highlighted in Robertson's introduction, caught the national mood. The aircraft carriers (which, at 40,000 tonnes,[47] would be the largest warships ever built for the Royal Navy') symbolised Labour's wholehearted commitment to defence and the surge in national confidence accompanying the end of the long Tory years and the arrival of Blair and 'Cool Britannia'. Labour left-wingers may have felt a little queasy, but they could still feel good about commitments to support United Nations peacekeeping operations and plans to scrap the RAF's aircraft-dropped WE177 nuclear bombs[48] as well as a reduction in the number of warheads fitted to the missiles of the Royal Navy's Trident deterrent submarines.[49] The Royal United Services Institute, a think tank, subsequently published a study titled *The Strategic Defence Review: A Good Job*.

This proved the high point of defence policy under Labour. Brown had made it clear that there would be no money for new programmes until after 2000 because they were not in the Tories' spending plans. Though he subsequently gave the Ministry of Defence more cash – the budget increased from 25.1 billion in 1997 to 32.4 billion by 2004 – the usual cost overruns, coupled with wars in Iraq and Afghanistan, rapidly gobbled up the budget.[50]

By Brown's Spending Review in 2004, the balance sheet was in crisis. In what has been a repeating pattern for Defence Secretaries over the

---

* The aircraft carriers would increase to 65,000 tonnes by the time they were completed.

last two decades, Robertson's successor as Defence Secretary, Geoff Hoon, had to battle the Treasury to secure a realistic budget. When negotiations broke down, Hoon played his ace, and sent the Chief of the Defence Staff to appeal to Blair personally. Less than forty-eight hours before the review was due to be published, General Sir Mike Walker pitched up at Chequers, Blair's weekend retreat, and successfully argued the case.

'He made an absolute point of wearing his uniform. Full regalia. He had this quiet authority, and it worked. Geoff got the settlement he wanted,' Dugher recalls.

> I remember that we were holding up the entire process. It all came to a head that weekend. We found out that the review had to go to the printers that Sunday night. So, the Treasury absolutely had to wrap up the negotiations by then. We just held out. We were holding up the entire spending review. Once we'd got the settlement, I remember Geoff calling me, and telling me to call off the dogs. We had got what we wanted, and now we had to play nice.[51]

Hoon may have won that tussle, but the years that followed were characterised by remorseless hostile media coverage about procurement cock-ups and 'crap kit'. Shortcomings in everything from army-issue boots and rucksacks to radios and ammunition were exposed in the heat of battle in Iraq and Afghanistan.[52] There were RAF bombs that missed their targets;[53] Chinook helicopters that could not fly in cloud;[54] Snatch Land Rovers dubbed 'mobile coffins';[55] and Destroyers that doubled in price.[56]

Behind the damning headlines and media rebuttal, the truth was that the MoD equipment programme was sinking under the weight of extortionate new hardware programmes and urgent requirements for wars on two fronts. This chaos was dubbed the 'bow wave' by insiders.[57] To grieving families of young servicemen killed in Afghanistan due to shoddy equipment, it looked more like culpable negligence.[58]

It was not all the government's fault. There were service chiefs who were unwilling to cancel pet programmes; civil servants who bungled contracts; overconfident defence contractors who promised things they couldn't deliver. While some of the problems were made in White-hall, others involved genuine technical challenges and events outside anyone's control. In the dying days of the Labour administration, the Ministry of Defence's financial woes deepened.

Lord Hutton now admits he preferred to run the department further into the red than cut holes in the nation's defences. He recalls coming under pressure to cancel the Harrier aircraft and point-blank refusing.

> I said, 'I'm only going to do that if there is a strategic case for it. I'm not going to cut it [just] because we don't have the money! I'm going to con-tinue with my overdraft until the world situation has changed and we don't need these aircraft.' We did need those aircraft and the idea that we didn't was ridiculous! We couldn't afford them, and the Tories did the deed [and cancelled them] in the end.[59]

Looking back, he feels he did the right thing.

> It was clear to me that we weren't in a good place. We had money problems, and were being asked to cut capabilities, without any strategic analysis of what that meant. I refused to do those things, because there wasn't a specif-ic strategic case made. I didn't want to make those cuts.[60]

When Labour left government in 2010, much of the new headline equipment announced in the Strategic Defence Review 1998 had still not been brought into service due to technical delays, cost overruns or cash shortages, and the defence budget remained in deep trouble.

Liam Fox and his successor Philip Hammond bore the brunt of the coalition's cuts programme. By the time Fallon arrived, the worst was over. In 2015, the Treasury signed off a 0.5 per cent annual real-terms increase in defence spending until 2020/21.[61]

To Fallon, it was symbolic, but the armed forces were under-whelmed. Many felt that he was just a time-server at the Ministry of

Defence, primarily concerned with avoiding controversy and burnishing his political reputation as 'a safe pair of hands'.[62]

In fact, though he never went public about his battle, Fallon *had* been trying to secure a better deal for defence. In early 2017, he secretly appealed to Prime Minister Theresa May for up to £2 billion more for the MoD.

In a tense meeting in Downing Street, he warned that his department's budget was in crisis, and asked for help meeting the huge cost of renewing Trident. In return, he offered to put more pressure on top brass to bring their budgets into line. He was rebuffed.[63] And so, like every other Defence Secretary in the past two decades, Fallon's successor, Gavin Williamson, found himself in charge of some amazing people and capabilities – without the resources to do what they do best.

ULAN BATOR

None of this was on Gavin Williamson's mind as he walked into the Ministry of Defence for the very first time on 2 November 2017. Earlier that day, the Prime Minister had warned him that his new role would be difficult because of the department's perennial money problems, but as he headed through the grandiose North Door, past Permanent Secretary Stephen Lovegrove and Vice-Chief of the Defence Staff General Sir Gordon Messenger, who were waiting to greet him, he was reflecting on less material things.

'It was only coming up those steps and coming through the North Door, that you realise the enormous sense of responsibility; the sense of duty, and it is so humbling,' he recalls. 'There are people who are literally willing to give everything to their country, when a politician deems that is the right thing to do.'[64]

In any case, there were reasons to be positive. Depending how it is measured, the UK still has the fifth or sixth most powerful armed forces in the world, after the US, Russia, China, India and France.[65] The defence budget is stretched, but, at £38 billion a year, it is still the sixth biggest in the world and accounts for 3.2 per cent of global defence spending.[66]

UK defence spending compares to £113.4 billion spent by China;

£45.6 billion by Russia; £36.6 billion by France, £31.5 billion by Germany and £14.0 billion by Israel. All of these are dwarfed by the United States' defence budget, which stands at £454.3 billion. This is almost 40 per cent of the entire military spend in the world.[67]

At the time of writing, the UK has 146,560 active serving personnel. Some 81,120 (3,150 of which are Nepalese Gurkhas) are in the army, while the navy has 32,480 servicemen and women; the air force 32,960.[68]

SIZE OF THE UK ARMED FORCES

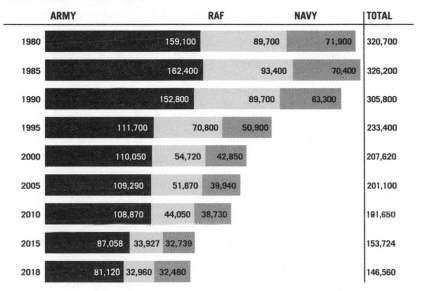

	ARMY	RAF	NAVY	TOTAL
1980	159,100	89,700	71,900	320,700
1985	162,400	93,400	70,400	326,200
1990	152,800	89,700	63,300	305,800
1995	111,700	70,800	50,900	233,400
2000	110,050	54,720	42,850	207,620
2005	109,290	51,870	39,940	201,100
2010	108,870	44,050	38,730	191,650
2015	87,058	33,927	32,739	153,724
2018	81,120	32,960	32,480	146,560

THE UK ARMED FORCES HAVE SHRUNK, BUT ARE STILL AMONG THE MOST POWERFUL IN THE WORLD.

These are backed up by 86,872 Reservists across all the services. This includes both the volunteer reserve, civilians who have signed on for part-time military service, and the regular reserve, which is formed of ex-personnel who can still be called up.[69]

The UK armed forces are dwarfed by the armed forces of China and Russia, which stand at 2,035,000 and 900,000 respectively.[70] Even the Germans and the French have larger armed forces than our own at 178,600[71] and 202,700 respectively.[72] Israel, with a population of under

9 million, but surrounded by potential enemies, has 176,500 men and women under arms.[73]

All the same, the UK is one of only five internationally recognised Nuclear Weapons States, along with the US, Russia, China and France. Four other states have either declared or are known to have a nuclear deterrent: India, Pakistan, Israel and North Korea.[74] Moreover, on paper at least, we retain a 'full spectrum capability'. In theory, this means we could take part in combat operations in the three traditional battlegrounds of land, sea and air. In the modern world, it also means that we are keeping up to speed in new domains such as space and cyber.

These figures tell only a fraction of the story. A serious judgement about relative military strength would have to consider many factors that are hard to measure, like readiness to fight, calibre of training and popular support for the military. It would not be complete without ascertaining a nation's willingness to defend itself if necessary. The Swiss have only 20,000 active troops across all services,[75] but with a compulsory military service programme that gives a total fighting force of more than 150,000 and one in four owning a gun, an invasion would not be a pushover.[76]

Since 1959, the International Institute of Strategic Studies (IISS) has undertaken an annual audit of the military assets of almost every country in the world, an exercise that gives at least part of the picture. The results are published in an enormous tome called *Military Balance*.

The book provides an impressive level of detail about every conceivable state and its military hardware, from Afghanistan to Zimbabwe. (Planning a raid on Baku and want to know how many artillery pieces the Azerbaijani army has in stock? They've got you covered: 575.[77] Sleepless nights worrying about a new Genghis Khan launching a bombing run from Ulan Bator? Fear not: modern Mongolia only has three planes in its air force – to be precise, two creaky old An-24 Coke planes and one lonely An-26 Curl.)[78]

For Britain, two reasonable comparisons are with the French, a country with a similarly sized population, defence budget and expeditionary capability; and the Russians, currently considered the most likely state threat. The UK has 227 Challenger 2 Main Battle Tanks[79] and an air attack of 139 Typhoons and 46 Tornados, soon to be phased out by a consignment of F-35Bs.[80] By contrast, the French have 273 tactical aircraft[81] but only 200 Leclerc Main Battle Tanks.[82] The Russians are far ahead on both measures, with 3,090 Main Battle Tanks[83] and 1,160 tactical aircraft.[84] However, 'like for like' comparisons are extraordinarily difficult with military kit. China's tally of 7,000 ZTZ tanks may sound impressive, but 2,850 date back to the 1950s and would be useless in a modern war.[85]

Following the 'gapping' of maritime patrol capability, the UK currently has no spy planes. However, the RAF will take possession of nine 'P8' Poseidon aircraft in 2019.[86] Few other nations can boast two aircraft carriers – although the USA has ten Nimitz-class 'supercarriers'[87] – but HMS *Queen Elizabeth* and HMS *Prince of Wales* will not be ready to operate at full capability ('carrier strike') until at least 2020.[88] There are currently just fourteen F-35Bs for the carriers, the first four of which arrived in the UK in June 2018. The MoD is contractually committed to buying a total of forty-eight by 2024, though plans to buy as many as 138 in the long term. This figure may well be reduced.[89] The navy has thirteen frigates and six destroyers – just enough for a carrier group.[90] Under the National Shipbuilding Strategy, the MoD will buy an additional five 'Type 31e' general-purpose frigates to bolster the fleet, with the first one expected to enter service in 2023.[91]

The army has been cut to the bone by numbers, but states looking to modernise their forces still consider it a 'reference army', to be analysed and emulated. On paper, the numbers look as if they compare poorly to Russia's 280,000[92] and France's 112,500,[93] but the figures reveal nothing about combat experience, training quality and weapon strength. Many in the Russian Army, for example, are bored conscripts waiting out their year of service in a vodka-fuelled haze.

In any case, most voters only care about the big picture: whether the armed forces could stave off a threat to the UK. Williamson's instinct was that the government needed to be more honest with voters about this question. He was willing to be more open than some of his predecessors about his concerns over the UK's diminishing defence capability and the risk of being drawn into another war. Should the worst happen, however, at least there would be a safety net: NATO and other allies.

OPERATION TETHERED GOAT

A NOTE ON ALLIES

Deep within part of Poland known as 'the land of a thousand lakes' lies the town of Orzysz. It is a three-hour drive north of Warsaw in a deeply Catholic part of the country. The gardens of houses here feature elaborately decorated crosses and icons of Jesus and the Virgin Mary. Orzysz has a population of about 7,500. The only hint that this very ordinary-looking Eastern European agricultural town has any particular military significance is a rusting T-34 tank from the Second World War lying abandoned in the middle of the field. Next to it is a similarly decrepit field artillery gun. A small sign in Polish, written on a grubby A4 piece of laminated paper, explains that it was used by the Germans before being captured by the Soviets in a great battle around these lakes.

Despite outward appearances, this is one of the most important strategic regions in Europe. Just sixty kilometres away is the 'Wolf's Lair', a decrepit bunker that was Hitler's personal headquarters during much of the Second World War. If World War Three were to break out in Eastern Europe, this sleepy town would probably become the epicentre of NATO's response. Already, there are 4,000 troops based in the area as part of the US-led NATO 'Enhanced Forward Presence'.[1] They are only a few kilometres shy of an area known to NATO's military planners as the Suwalki gap, the 65-mile Polish–Lithuanian border straddled ominously by Kaliningrad to the west and the Russian satrapy of Belarus on the east. American defence chiefs regard this flat piece of land as the most vulnerable location in the entire Alliance. The fear is that it could be caught in a pincer movement, as troops from the so-called CIS states – a pro-Russian grouping of former Soviet countries – join forces to cut the Baltics off from the rest of Europe.[2]

THE SUWALKI GAP, WHICH IS WITHIN THE EUROPEAN UNION

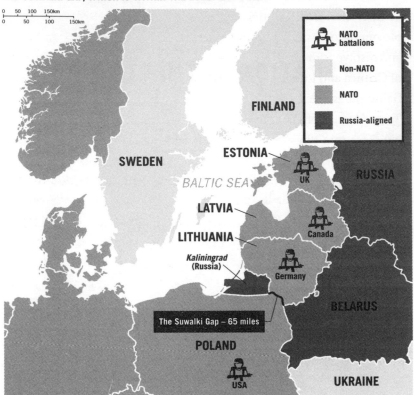

NATO MILITARY PLANNERS SEE THIS THIN STRIP OF LAND AS
A POTENTIAL FLASHPOINT BETWEEN RUSSIA AND THE ALLIANCE.

If Russia were to attempt to close the gap, NATO's only option would be to punch north with the US-led brigade based here. Until then, it would be up to the Baltic states to hold their ground, supported by small detachments of NATO forces stationed inside their borders. One of those forces would be headed by a small but fierce battalion of UK troops stationed in Tapa, Estonia.

Some 800 troops from the 1st Battalion The Royal Welsh are here, supported by smaller deployments from other member states – the French until November 2017, and subsequently the Danes. NATO has designated the UK the 'Framework Nation' in Tapa, meaning other forces fit around the British deployment, following British command.

The system seems to work well. Colonel Giles Harris, the Commander of Operation CABRIT, the official codename for the British Army's deployment to Eastern Europe, describes it as a demonstration of 'unity and resolve with our NATO allies'. He explains that after the annexation of Crimea and Russia's aggressive manoeuvring in eastern Ukraine, the Baltic states – Lithuania, Latvia and Estonia – felt extremely exposed. They pressed NATO for a tangible security guarantee. At the 2016 NATO summit in Warsaw, the Alliance agreed to station a permanent force in the region. Now there are so-called Enhanced Forward Presence (EFP) units in Poland, Estonia, Latvia and Lithuania, as well as a multinational brigade in Romania.[3]

NATO TROOPS IN THE BALTICS/EASTERN EUROPE

ESTONIA
800 TROOPS
UK-led battalion and troops from Denmark and France.
Baltic Air Policing with 4 German Typhoon jets.

LATVIA
1,200 TROOPS
Canadian-led battalion and troops from
Albania, Italy, Poland, Spain and Slovenia.

LITHUANIA
1,200 TROOPS
German-led battalion with troops from
Belgium, Croatia, France, Luxembourg,
Netherlands and Norway.
Baltic Air Policing with 4 Dutch F-16 jets.

POLAND
4,000 US TROOPS*
US-led battalion with heavy armour including
250 tanks, Bradley Fighting Vehicles and
Paladin howitzers.

ROMANIA
Southern Air Policing with 4 RAF Typhoon jets.**

BULGARIA
The US is conducting rotated training drills at Novo Selo
Training Area (NSTA) with troops from the 3rd Armored
Brigade Combat Team, 4th Infantry Division.

RUSSIA

BELARUS

UKRAINE

* Estonia, Latvia, Lithuania, Poland, Bulgaria and Romania
  will all receive US troop and hardware rotations.
** Four months from summer 2018.

DESIGNED TO DETER RUSSIAN AGGRESSION, BUT CRITICS SAY THEY'RE JUST A 'TRIPWIRE'.

In the case of the UK deployment, 'unity and resolve' got off to a frosty start. When British units arrived, Estonian troops were unceremoniously ejected from their comfortable barracks to make way for the newcomers. They had to pitch tents on the plains outside the base. Apparently there was much grumbling that NATO and UK forces thought they could push the locals around because they were coming to bail them out.

Colonel Harris looks slightly embarrassed but doesn't deny it was a bumpy start.

'Yes, when we first moved here, we were overcrowded, and this unfortunately meant the local soldiers were moved into... tented accommodation,' he says carefully – though he maintains that the arrangements were made at the behest of the Estonian government, which was anxious to give the visitors a proper welcome.[4] In any case, the minor diplomatic incident was soon forgotten and today both sides agree the relationship is flourishing. Polling for this book suggests that the UK's efforts in the Baltics are at least having a positive diplomatic effect: people in Estonia were the most likely among the countries we surveyed to see the UK as a close ally, followed by the Australians, the Americans, the French and the Israelis.

The encampment, spread over about two square miles, is at the end of a dusty road an hour's drive from the Estonian capital of Tallinn. Accommodation for soldiers, in twelve-bed dormitories, is clean and comfortable. The bunks are decorated in time-honoured style with letters from home and photos of girlfriends. One squaddie has even managed to score a TV and an Xbox. The lads spend much of their time training on the base or in the surrounding countryside. Several cite a 'cold-weather environment' course they undergo in Estonia as the hardest bit of training they've experienced in their army careers. In one exercise, in the depths of Baltic winter, they say they were thrown into a hole that had been pickaxed into a frozen lake and forced to talk sense. Gasping for breath in the sub-zero temperatures, they had to answer a barrage of questions from a bellowing sergeant.

'Soldier, tell me how to shine your shoes!' he demanded. 'Soldier, tell me how to load and unload a gun!'

The lads recount this trial by ice with pride. It is designed to train them to keep a clear head when their adrenalin is pumping in the harshest of conditions. In quieter moments, they undertake community outreach projects designed to develop a rapport with the local population. In October 2017, they joined a local automobile association's 'vehicle day', delighting the community by bringing some tanks. A photo shows a dozen wide-eyed Estonian kids clambering happily over a Challenger.[5] The Royal Welsh have also been training the Estonian national rugby team, a relatively inexperienced side keen to gain international status.[6]

Aspects of day-to-day life may sound relaxed, but troops never forget where they are, or why. They are expected to be on their guard at all times, scouring the horizon for anything suspicious. Posters with images of drones remind them to look up as well as out. If they spot anything untoward overhead, they can call an 'Unmanned Aerial Vehicle hotline'.[7]

These men and women are fit, sharp and well-trained. They are provided with some of the best kit available to the armed forces, and both they and their commanders maintain that they are ready to fight. Inside a vast metal hanger is a fleet of Challengers. The army originally wanted to send eighteen, but the Ministry of Defence decided that only ten were needed. At least two of the vehicles were taken apart for repairs, leaving them minus turrets or compartments.[8]

The soldiers view these fearsome machines with comical affection, claiming they each have distinct personalities. A suave Canadian tank mechanic attached to the British deployment named the vehicles after his ex-girlfriends. One called 'Betsy' is regarded as the least temperamental, supposedly functioning well come rain or shine.

Asked if the fleet would be enough if the Russians came over the border, the men shrug and laugh. 'If the Russians invaded, I'd want fifty!' says one – though 500 would probably only be a start. They are far too professional to admit it, but troops are under no illusion about the extent to which the odds would be stacked against them if that happened.

Doubtless they would cope admirably if the Kremlin followed its tried-and-tested modus operandi of initiating an annexation attempt using unaccountable 'little green men' to foment unrest. A serious operation involving Russian ground forces would be an entirely different matter. A report by the RAND Corporation, a think tank, war-gamed a potential Russian invasion and estimated the Russians could muster twenty-two tank battalions for an invasion. Calling the NATO forces 'woefully inadequate', the report said that in every way they tried the exercise, Russian forces reached Tallinn and Riga within sixty hours.[9] This is why some in the armed forces privately call the EFP in Estonia 'Operation Tethered Goat' – a light-hearted reference to the vulnerability of the base should a predator attack.

There is similar muttering within RAF circles about the limitations of a NATO air patrol mission they are undertaking in Romania. In the event of a Russian incursion, they would have no automatic power to act, because they are not operating in UK sovereign airspace. In all cases, NATO's hope is that the mere presence of Allied forces will minimise the prospect of ever having to put their military capability to the test. If that proves wishful thinking, the question is whether NATO is ready.

SECURITY BLANKET

NATO

SHOWBOATING

When politicians need to reassure voters they've got defence covered, the first word they pluck from their trusty rhetorical toolbox is 'NATO'. In two syllables, they can argue that if the UK finds itself in a sticky situation, there's no need to worry, because twenty-eight nations will rush to our side.

The principle of collective security that brought the Alliance into existence in 1949, enshrined in Article 5 of the North Atlantic Treaty, is the ultimate guarantor of our defences, and is a wonderful comfort blanket for countries with diminishing military power. It commits each member state to treat an armed attack against one member as an armed attack against them all.[1] Underpinned by America's formidable military might, NATO is routinely described as 'the most successful alliance in history'.[2]

'There is nothing else like it and there never has been,' according to George Robertson, former Secretary General of the organisation. 'It is hugely successful at what it does. Every four or five years, someone says, "NATO's out of time; it needs modernising; it's finished; it's gone." Then they realise the value of twenty-eight automatic allies.'[3]

For a brief period, the election of Donald Trump as US President in 2016 raised questions over NATO's future after he labelled it 'obsolete' and refused to commit to upholding the collective security guarantee.[4] In office, it became clear he didn't really mean it. Though he continued to complain about 'chronic underpayments' by some allies towards collective defence,[5] after eighty-one days in the White House, he declared the organisation rehabilitated ('I said NATO was obsolete. NATO is not obsolete.').[6]

Along with the US, Greece, Poland, Romania and Estonia, the UK is one of just six countries that spend the Alliance's recommended 2 per cent of GDP on defence[7] – or at least not far off that figure.* The UK is frequently described as a 'second leader' of the organisation. In a sign of this country's status within the Alliance, the role of Deputy Supreme Allied Commander has been in British hands since 1951.[8]

UK DEFENCE SPENDING AS PERCENTAGE OF GDP, RELATIVE TO NATO ALLIES AND POTENTIAL ADVERSARIES*

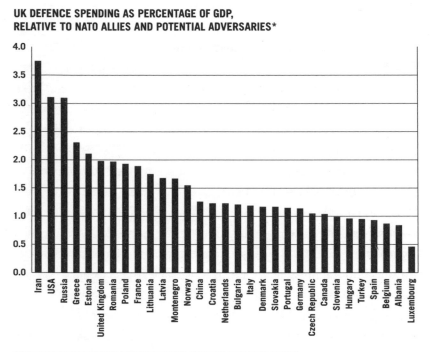

NATO WOULD LIKE MEMBER STATES TO SPEND AT LEAST 2 PER CENT OF GDP. OFFICIALLY THE UK MEETS THIS TARGET. CRITICS SAY THE REAL FIGURE IS SLIGHTLY LESS.

*SOURCE: MILITARY BALANCE 2018, IISS

Key to the Alliance's credibility is the appearance of unity. NATO summits are an opportunity to show it – though President Trump's unusual style has upended this tradition. The July 2018 summit was a

---

* There have been question marks over the way the MoD calculates the figure. See, for instance, Deborah Haynes, 'MoD accused of cooking books to hit Nato defence spending target', *The Times*, 26 September 2017.

case in point: he began his trip to Europe by insulting the Germans, accusing them of being 'captive' to Russia over an energy pipeline; continued with an attack on other NATO allies over the scale of their defence spending; and rounded it all off with a spurious claim that thanks to his efforts, the Alliance was now 'strong and rich'.[9] There was further confusion when, having agreed that all member states would reach the 2 per cent recommended defence spending threshold within six years, Trump suddenly tweeted that the ruling should in fact be immediate.[10]

NATO officials are still struggling to adapt to the uncertainty the President brings to what has, for years, been a very set routine. Twice a year, the leaders of the twenty-nine member states, accompanied by swarms of military advisers, officials and spin doctors, descend on some random town for two days of ostentatious handshaking and shoulder-to-shoulder body language. Roads are cleared, shops are closed, and locals are swept out of the way while a steel cordon is erected around the whole pantomime. Journalists from all over the world are corralled into a hangar, where they are grudgingly fed occasional pre-prepared lines. Tanked up on cheap instant coffee, they watch keynote speeches via video link and pounce on anyone official who ventures into the press centre in the vain hope of securing a real story off the record.

The ceremonial 'family photos' taken at these summits, featuring leaders of each member state posing with sombre expressions and arms rigidly at their sides, are the ultimate signal to potential adversaries that the organisation sings as one. The meticulously choreographed image taken at the May 2017 event in Brussels, with Trump centre stage, was typical of the genre. That particular summit marked the opening of the Alliance's gleaming new headquarters – and Trump's first visit to Brussels.

Embarrassingly, the US$1.1 billion building (designed to look like 'interlocking fingers' but disturbingly reminiscent of a giant nit comb) wasn't quite ready, so most of the meetings were held in the old building.[11] Throughout the proceedings, UN Secretary General Jens

Stoltenberg looked as if he would rather be anywhere else. At his 9 a.m. press conference, he appeared anxious and pale, reading from a script in a shaky monotone while constantly fiddling with his pen. His trepidation was understandable: a highly unpredictable US President was about to give a speech about an organisation whose continuing value he had publicly questioned, in a city he had previously described as a 'hellhole'.[12]

The entire event was apparently designed with Trump's interests and eccentricities in mind. The two items on the agenda – international terrorism and burden- and cost-sharing among member states – were his personal bugbears, and other heads of state were reportedly told to limit their contributions at the working dinner to between two and four minutes, to keep him interested. One insider grumbled that it was 'like preparing to deal with a child – someone with a short attention span and mood who has no knowledge of NATO, no interest in in-depth policy-making, nothing.'[13]

In the eyes of his many critics, the President treated the occasion as an extended opportunity for peacocking. One much-circulated video shows him thrusting out his chest after shoving Montenegrin President Filip Vujanović out of the way to position himself in front of the cameras.[14] There was also a farcical handshake with French President Emmanuel Macron, in which both men grimaced as they crushed the other's hand.[15]

What the assembled leaders really wanted from the US President they did not get. Stoltenberg dropped desperate hints to encourage a declaration of commitment to Article 5, but it flew over the President's head. Instead, Trump rebuked 'twenty-three out of twenty-eight'* allies over their financial contributions, accusing many of owing 'massive amounts of money from past years'. As German Chancellor Angela Merkel scowled in the background and Stoltenberg looked dejected, the US President conspicuously failed to endorse Article 5 and barely

---

* At the time of the conference there were twenty-eight members; Montenegro joined in summer 2017.

mentioned Russia. (The magazine *Foreign Policy* later scored it as a 'Win for Putin.')[16]

Nonetheless, the summit concluded on the note NATO choreographers wanted, with a series of rousing speeches about transatlantic unity in uncertain times and a symbolic flag-raising ceremony. The finale was a spectacular display of air power. As a series of F-16s; Gripens; Eurofighter Typhoons; A400 Ms; Rafale and Belgium French Alpha Jets roared overhead, the twenty-eight leaders resisted the temptation to block their ears, gazed at the sky looking suitably impressed and then swept off to their waiting limousines, from which point they could forget about the whole thing for another few months.

These theatrical displays of unity mask deep divisions within the organisation and the inevitable dysfunction associated with attempting to co-ordinate twenty-nine countries with different languages, histories, economies and political priorities. The dynamics between individual member states are in constant flux, and each has an agenda. Those with similar concerns naturally coalesce, creating informal 'northern' and 'central' and 'southern' groupings dominated by the three countries with the most powerful militaries: America, the UK and France. According to one former Chief of the Defence Staff, these three act as 'puppet masters', while 'the Turks can only think about Syria; the Poles, Estonians, Lithuanians and Latvians can only think about Russia; and the Italians can only think about mass migration.'[17] Difficult business is thrashed out far away from the cameras during regular meetings of the North Atlantic Council. This ensures nobody goes off-message; smooth joint statements can be issued and (Trump's periodic admonishments notwithstanding) they can all look like one big military family. Each member state has permanent representatives on the council, which is the principal political decision-making arm of NATO. If they agree that there is a defence threat that NATO should start getting ready to meet, defence chiefs at SHAPE (the Supreme Headquarters of Allied Powers Europe), NATO's military headquarters in Mons, are instructed to come up with a plan. The problem is that there is no voting or decision by majority, so unless representatives from all twenty-nine countries agree there is a problem, nothing much gets done. In practice, what that means is that contingency plans for a military crisis are worryingly threadbare.

JOBSWORTHS

Bremerhaven, northern Germany, January 2017. Some 3,500 American troops; 87 tanks and 144 other military vehicles bound for Poland began rolling off giant transport ships in a statement of NATO's intent to deter Russian aggression on its eastern flank. It was the largest shipment of US brigades since the fall of the Soviet Union, and marked a new phase of Operation Atlantic Resolve, involving the establishment of a semi-permanent American armoured brigade team in Europe.[18]

If the arrival was designed to impress the Kremlin, however, it probably fell short, because three days later, parts of the brigade were still stuck in port. Embarrassingly, they were delayed by limited capacity on German trains capable of carrying heavy military equipment across Europe. As if this were not frustrating enough for military commanders, they had also had to endure what one defence analyst described as 'a farcical trial by paperwork'[19] ahead of the operation – which is what always happens in advance of any troop manoeuvre through Europe.

This encapsulates the fears of generals and NATO figures responsible for devising plans for 'worst-case scenarios' for conflict in Europe. Geography means German bureaucracy is critical. Unfortunately, it is simply not designed for military emergencies. The red tape involved in securing permission to deploy soldiers, tanks and ammunition across borders can tie commanders and officials in knots for up to forty days.

According to an insider, the Germans insist on at least ten days' notice for any military movements of more than four vehicles.

'Even then, they must have regular breaks every two hours and travel not more than six hours per day. Furthermore, no more than ten to twenty vehicles are allowed to form a convoy. There are special rules for vehicles over 30 tonnes,' according to the source.[20] The worry is that if President Putin attempts an incursion in the Baltics, the mind-boggling morass of peacetime rules and regulations designed to stop funfair operators clogging up the German Autobahn with Ferris wheels on wobbly lorries will thwart a NATO response.

Lieutenant General Ben Hodges, recently retired head of the US Army in Europe, believes that the Alliance will have just five to seven days of 'unambiguous warning' that Russia is preparing to carry out an illegal act of aggression, and that a new system to allow military personnel and kit to move more freely across Europe in an emergency is vital.

> Everything we're going to do, up short of Article 5 … is going to be done under peacetime conditions. In other words, nobody is going to say, 'Don't worry about that border stuff; don't worry, you can move your ammo wherever you want to go – you can have all the *Deutschbahn*! [German railway]' None of that is going to happen! Because our political leaders, understandably, are going to do everything they can to preserve maximum flexibility, to avoid being seen as provocative.

'So, they're going to wait until the very last second,' he says.[21]

At the time of writing, the US is spending millions of dollars adapting its military vehicles to comply with European regulations on the movement of 'dangerous goods' by road. They are also buying eighteen HETS (Heavy Equipment Transporters) from the UK for American tanks because American HETs do not have enough axles to meet EU road restrictions.[22]

Hodges has described the diplomatic clearance required to move from Germany to Poland as 'eye-watering' and 'unbelievable'.

> You have to have a roster naming who is driving every vehicle, and what's in every vehicle. I don't know who's driving me tomorrow! I am pretty sure that Alpha Company [of the US Infantry] will not know, three weeks from now, when they turn the paperwork in, who's going to be driving what vehicle, or what the hell's even going to be in that vehicle. But that's the process we're still having to deal with.
>
> I [recently] went to the German [military] logistics centre and talked to

the excellent group of officers who are responsible for every military move-ment in the Federal Republic of Germany. And they said, 'Don't worry, sir! If there is a crisis, you'll be able to do all those things you want to do!' I said, 'Great. Who determines if there is a crisis?' And they said, 'Well of course, the Bundestag. The Parliament.' I'm fairly sure they won't get it done inside five days.[23]

During his time as head of the US Army in Europe, Hodges lobbied for what he called a 'military Schengen zone' allowing NATO forces to move at least as fast as a migrant across central Europe.[24] He was not successful. However, in a sign of how seriously NATO is begin-ning to consider the potential for a major conflict involving Russia, in early 2018, it announced the establishment of a new logistics command centre in Germany, charged with handling the logistics associated with moving troops quickly across Europe.[25] In the first expansion of NATO structures in two decades, a second new NATO HQ is to be set up in the US, focused on securing air and sea routes between North America and Europe.[26]

It will be some time before these organisations (and all the politicians and mandarins who will have to rubber-stamp any plans they devise) get their act together. Meanwhile, British defence chiefs privately admit NATO's so-called Enhanced Forward Presence – what it describes as an Allied 'defence and deterrence posture' in Eastern Europe – is just that: posturing. They acknowledge that, in the absence of detailed de-ployment plans, the multinational battalion battle groups in Estonia, Latvia, Lithuania and Poland, led by the UK, Canada, Germany and the US, are really just 2,000 or so poorly armed and ill-equipped sol-diers, without supply lines, maintaining a symbolic presence.[27]

Speaking about the 800 British troops currently stationed in Esto-nia, General Sir Richard Barrons says:

They're not part of a joined-up force. There's no air force above them to fight; no stocks, hospitals or reinforcements lined up to come. In any case, Russia so controls things in that region that we'd never get anything through. So it is what it is: just some people living in Estonia, who happen to be soldiers, doing some training, showing we're concerned about this. It's no more than a signal. It's better than nothing, because it complicates Russian opportunistic calculations about the Baltic states, but what it's *not* is a Cold War-level response, where you had a joined-up force, and stocks, with a plan, and you were ready to fight. This is ready to train – that's all.[28]

Privately, nobody in the Ministry of Defence seems to disagree.

'If they were actually *needed*, they wouldn't be able to do much,' concedes a senior figure in the department.[29] A military source went further, describing the British troops as 'hostages, not a deterrent'.[30]

Since leaving office in 2016, Barrons has repeatedly warned of NATO's shortcomings.

'NATO was once just a military alliance; it was quite good like that. It would train and exercise and was dealing with a Russia that it genuinely feared. Now it's really a political alliance with a de-mobilised military arm,' he says, adding that 'the things that make an alliance ready – planning, training, worked-up command and control – are absent in many cases, or in a state of disrepair.'

There is no NATO general deployment plan for dealing with the problem of Russia, because opinion in NATO is divided; some [members] don't see it as necessary, and some see it as provocative. Without a consensus in the North Atlantic Council, SHAPE is not allowed to produce plans that it might like to. So there is no longer a plan, at Alliance or national level, for mobilisation.

I went to the Baltics to see the heads of the armed forces in Lithuania, Latvia and Estonia and they just give it to you with both barrels. 'What don't you get about Russia?' These are people who know Russia well and have good intelligence operations across their borders. They were absolutely clear. What they wanted [from NATO] was a permanent presence of a joined-up force. A force that doesn't go home at Christmas, because the Russians will invade at Christmas, because their Christmas is at a different time. A permanent force; planning, training, and with a mobilisation plan, so that Russia knows that it doesn't own the airspace – as it does now – and that there is a credible NATO reinforcement plan.[31]

Privately, a senior NATO adviser admits the organisation has 'no common policy' on deterrence; whereas 'the Russians have a unified plan and know exactly what they are doing'.[32]

In an illustration of the scale of the challenge NATO will face if Article 5 is invoked, it currently has no joint cyber capability. Though there is a NATO Co-operative Cyber Defence Centre of Excellence in Estonia, designed to encourage the pooling of expertise, it has no chain of command or rules of engagement; and insiders say it is neutered by the reluctance of individual member states to contribute talent, partly because of fears of leaks to the Russians. According to a recently retired British general, 'NATO is a heavily penetrated thing. Russia walks all over it. If you have a North Atlantic Council meeting, you might as well put the minutes on the internet.'[33] This is a wider anxiety in NATO. Barrons thinks NATO members will not volunteer their finest brains or share offensive cyber capability until the Alliance is 'Russia-proofed'.[34]

While some defence analysts fret about NATO's military capability, others are more preoccupied with the politics. Article 5 has only ever been invoked once, following the 9/11 attacks in America. Even in the face of the worst terror attack in US history, whipping nineteen governments into a swift collective response was not straightforward. George Robertson says he had to use all his 'political wiles and back-street tactics' to make it happen after the September 11th attacks on the Twin Towers and Pentagon.

One Prime Minister wouldn't speak to me because there was a 9/11 memorial service, and I had to get him hauled out of that. One foreign minister said, 'We don't like the wording of the statement; can we have twenty-four hours to look at it?' I told them they were part of a treaty and had treaty commitments. Another foreign minister worried that if they signed up to this [response] they were also signing up to attacking Baghdad. There were honest feelings about how this was a big, big thing.[35]

Though the 9/11 attacks did not constitute the conventional act of aggression authors of Article 5 envisaged, member states did pull together. Robertson believes Putin is in no doubt that Article 5 would be enacted again if he 'crossed a line'.

'Would you invoke Article 5 over some little island off the Estonian coast? Yes, you would, and Russia knows that. There is a very, very bright red line down the borders of NATO that the Russians respect and understand,' he says.[36]

Others with more recent experience of the inner workings of the Alliance are less confident, fearing that if NATO is tested by Russia in the near future, it will fall short.

'NATO is a political cabal. To get consensus is hugely difficult. Right now we are being tested on the periphery and we can't get consensus. NATO will fail when the Russian hordes are at the gate,' says one grimly.[37]

Some defence analysts and military planners would like to see amendments to Article 5 itself, allowing individual members to opt out in some cases. The thinking is that this could speed up a collective response by other member states willing to engage.

At the closing ceremony of the May 2017 summit, Stoltenberg repeatedly stressed NATO's ability to adapt.* The attempted murder of former Russian double agent Sergei Skripal and his daughter Yulia in Salisbury, using a military-grade nerve agent produced by the Russian state, was a reminder that illegal acts of aggression can take many forms. There is a growing feeling in defence circles that the clause may need to be updated to ensure it remains fit for purpose as the character of warfare changes.

Lieutenant General Sir David Capewell, former Chief of Joint Operations, says, 'Article 5 is a very difficult threshold tool. It used to work well when you were sitting under the umbrella of mutually assured destruction – a peer-on-peer enemy – and we all played by the rules. It is designed around rules-based reactions to escalation. But life isn't like that anymore.'[38]

---

* 'We have constantly adapted as security challenges have evolved,' he claimed.

At the time of writing, this country is widely seen as one of the most committed NATO member states. That may not last. Labour leader Jeremy Corbyn has repeatedly cast doubt on his support for the Alliance, a position which prompted a very public fall-out with his shadow Defence Secretary Nia Griffith in January 2017.[39] His long-standing reluctance to criticise the Russian regime was exposed during the Skripal affair, when he suggested overwhelming evidence linking the nerve agent to Putin's regime might be incorrect.[40]

All this suggests that UK ministers and defence chiefs cannot afford to take NATO for granted. The security blanket is not as comfortable as it seems.

BROOMSTICKS

Just south of the equator in the central Indian Ocean lies one of the last bastions of the British Empire. With whispers of CIA operations, human rights abuses and Foreign Office skulduggery, the island of Diego Garcia is one of the most controversial places on earth.

Once known as 'Fantasy Island' because it is so cut off, this part of the Chagos Archipelago has an extraordinary history, marked by the expulsion of the entire local population in the late 1960s. They were kicked out by the British Army to make way for a military base and have never been allowed back.[41]

Today, endangered green and leatherback turtles and whales swim freely in the emerald waters, but journalists and tourists are barred. The only people who live on the island are military personnel and contractors. All food arrives by sea and air; all waste is shipped off. Precious little information about everyday life slips out.

What is known is that this 30 km sq. piece of real estate is very important to the United States. Though it still belongs to the UK, it is on a long lease to America, and has become one of their largest overseas airbases. Along with Guam, it is one of two critical US military outposts in the Asia Pacific region, offering access to East Africa, the Middle East and Southeast Asia.

Under a deal struck via an 'Exchange of Notes' in 1966, the United

States has permission to use the island for defence until 2036.[42] No money has ever changed hands. Instead, according to a de-classified document, the UK was given a US$14 million discount on the purchase of a submarine-launched ballistic missile system called Polaris.[43]

For much of the Cold War, the island was used as a low-profile staging post and storage site.

Since 1990, however, it has become a take-off point for US heavy bombers,[44] including the B-2 Spirit stealth bombers used to attack Iraq, Afghanistan and other targets in the Middle East.[45] At any one time, four United States Air Force Units and around a dozen naval ships are stationed there, along with global satellite and naval computer communication systems.[46]

The island is still nominally under British control, with a naval captain and a handful of token Royal Marines and sailors deployed to stake British sovereignty over the American service personnel. According to a Royal Navy admiral, 'They have little to do but make sure the grass is cut properly.'[47] Now and again, however, the Americans are reminded who owns the place. Under the Exchange of Letters between London and Washington that governs use of the island, when the US wants to launch combat aircraft from Diego Garcia, theoretically the President must obtain the explicit approval of the British Prime Minister. In practice, the protocol is only observed in relation to very high-profile or politically sensitive operations, such as the B52-launched Cruise missile attacks on Iraq and Afghanistan in the 1990s and immediately after the 9/11 attacks. When the invasion of Afghanistan was well and truly under way in late 2001, the US was launching so many bombing sorties it was impractical to secure such high level sign-off every time. Instead, the RAF sent an air marshal (Jock Stirrup) to US Central Command (CENTCOM) to give authority on behalf of the PM.

For America, Diego Garcia is a very tangible benefit of the so-called Special Relationship. Despite the imbalance in the relationship linked to US military superiority, the long history of defence co-operation between the two countries still matters to the Americans. British expertise in counter-terrorism, honed through the long years of the

Troubles; British intelligence; and British Special Forces – widely considered to be as good as their US equivalents, Delta Force and the Navy Seals – are particularly valued. Most US ministers and top brass remain effusive about the UK's contribution to collective defence and joint operations.

General David Petraeus, former Director of the CIA and former Commander of US Forces in Afghanistan, describes the relationship as 'quite extraordinary'.

'Our best military partner, our best intelligence partner, our best signals partner, always was, and still is, the United Kingdom,' he says simply.[48]

During operations in Iraq and Afghanistan, Petraeus served along-side a total of seven British deputies. He says there is 'no question' that the UK was America's most valuable ally in joint operations in Iraq, Bosnia, Kosovo, Iraq, Afghanistan, Yemen – 'you name it.'

'The UK punches in a weight class above virtually any other country,' he adds.[49]

This country's traditional willingness to deploy a significant portion of our armed forces to reinforce US-led campaigns, and share casualties, has been at the heart of the relationship. The ability to use other kinds of power – political, economic, technical expertise or 'soft' power – to achieve an effect which supports US policy or interests has also long been valued by Washington, as has our support in areas in which we excel, such as naval mine-sweeping.

However, at the highest level in the British government, and among top brass, there is now growing concern that the steady decline in UK military capability over the past two decades is beginning to affect the nature of the defence relationship.

Towards the end of his stint as head of the US Army in Europe, Hodges revealed a series of further frustrations with the UK, including a decision not to participate in certain joint (simulated) exercises designed to improve the ability of different militaries to work together and ensure kit is compatible. He also questioned the British Army's continuing attachment to training at BATUS in Canada, pointing out that part of the purpose of training exercises is to put on a show of strength for potential adversaries who might be watching, something that Putin, with his Zapad theatrics, understands very well.

'I'm pretty sure the British Army is not going to fight the Canadians. Training in Europe is where your allies are; it's where the terrain is where you're most likely to fight; it's where you get the chance to practise what you're most likely to do. Training in Canada has zero deterrence effect,' Hodges has said.[50]

Amid the resurgent threat from Russia, the Americans are also frustrated by long-standing plans to withdraw British troops from Germany. As Hodges put it bluntly:

> You've just added a couple of minor obstacles to get back into the fight: the Channel; moving through France; moving through the Netherlands, when of course if there's a crisis, the Russians are not just going to sit on their guns in Kaliningrad and allow you to sail up into the Baltic Sea.[51]

Carter is taking these concerns seriously, and has indicated that a forward base may be retained in Germany after all.[52]

In June 2018, ahead of a NATO summit in Brussels, the UK Defence Select Committee published a damning report of British defence capability and urged the government to increase Ministry of Defence funding. Describing NATO as the 'cornerstone of UK defence', it argued that a 'military-to-military relationship' with the United States was central to political and diplomatic ties between our two countries. It also warned that if the UK was to maintain its leadership position in NATO and its 'fruitful defence relations' with the US, then the Exchequer must invest heavily in the UK's armed forces.[53]

'Analysis we commissioned has demonstrated that at current spending levels, the Ministry of Defence will not be able to maintain UK military capacity and capability,' it read.[54]

This echoes the view of Gavin Williamson. Privately, the Defence Secretary is deeply concerned that without a significant boost to defence spending, the UK could lose its long-standing status as America's greatest ally to the other great military power in Europe: France. The language barrier and some lingering historic mistrust between the two countries will buy the UK extra time, but as Macron positions himself to inherit German Chancellor Angela Merkel's crown as the most powerful EU national leader and prepares to boost defence spending by 40 per cent to meet the NATO target by 2025, the idea that France could eventually replace the UK as America's premier defence ally is not entirely far-fetched.[55] The Americans have been particularly alarmed by cuts to UK land forces, and are beginning to speak out. On his retirement in late 2017, Hodges issued a blunt warning that the UK 'risks going into a different sort of category' if the trend continues. He refused to deny that further cuts would be a 'disaster'.

'The UK is a global leader. It's a leader in NATO. But NATO won't always be the most successful alliance in the history of the world if all its leaders don't invest and do the work that's needed to keep it that way,' he said pointedly.[56]

He stressed the importance of the UK maintaining the ability to field a division (a large military unit of between 10,000 and 20,000 soldiers, made of up regiments and brigades) to slot into an American Corps for joint operations. Speaking about the UK's 'very good' deployable divisional headquarters, 3rd Division at Bulford in Wiltshire, he said:

> It doesn't just come in a box, you know. It has got to be manned; it's got to have training opportunities; it's got to have modern equipment; it has to exercise … You have commitments everywhere! I don't see how the UK could maintain those commitments if it got any smaller. I'm talking about British land forces. It's not just the size and structure; it's also the investment for modernisation and what we call readiness. You have to train, you have to do maintenance, you have to have the stuff.[57]

Hodges's intervention, in an interview for BBC News, didn't make headlines but was certainly noted at the Ministry of Defence. When US Defense Secretary Jim Mattis came to the UK shortly afterwards, Williamson feigned offence.

'Tell your generals to stay out of British politics!' he admonished.[58]

Privately, he agreed with the American and recognised that the comments were helpful in his ongoing battle to secure more cash for defence.[59]

Of course, the strength of the special relationship is not just about capability, but willingness to use it. Here, too, Washington has concerns. The Americans are under no illusions about the diminished political appetite in the UK for discretionary military 'away games', underlined when the Commons refused to back Cameron's plans to intervene in Syria in August 2013.[60] Indeed, Petraeus describes the 'most significant challenge' to NATO as political risk aversion, a lesson he learned the hard way at the hands of the British.

'Virtually no country except the US deploys its forces without caveats,' he says. He thought Britain was the exception until, during the US surge in Afghanistan in 2011, a nervous Downing Street vetoed his request to move British forces to a slightly different position in Helmand Province for fear of incurring more casualties.

'I just wanted to move them three villages over,' he recalls – a tactical manoeuvre he thought could easily have been signed off 'by a two-star general or below'. Instead 'the force that we *thought* had no caveats – because they said so repeatedly – at the very highest level, would not allow a tactical movement of British forces … The UK was the country that we thought had no caveats; or at least minimal caveats. But they were not allowed to move.'

He describes 'a pretty long screwdriver from London to Basra; and from London to Helmand Province' controlled by successive British Prime Ministers.

Initially it was Gordon Brown; then later on it was David Cameron. And to be fair, and we should be fair, at the end of the day, only the political leader knows what his country will bear in terms of additional casualties. And again, the UK had fewer caveats than any other country; but as we found out, it did have caveats; sometimes unstated until you tried to do something and found out that there are limits.[61]

Politicians who set great store by the special relationship may need reminding that it never overrides US interests. A defence academic points out that, during the Cold War, America was 'happy' that the British-made TSR-2 strike and reconnaissance aircraft was cancelled in favour of an American-made F-111; just as today they will not give the UK essential computer codes for the F-35 fighter jets.

He says the US is disappointed in a wide range of UK defence decisions over the past fifteen years or so, including our diminishing enthusiasm for inventing new ways to beat the enemy. In the old days, between 10 and 20 per cent of the Ministry of Defence budget went on research and development. Now it's less than 5 per cent.

'At that level, we are just not credible players in the field,' he says, adding that Israel currently spends a fifth of its budget on research and development, 'something the US really values'.

His fear is that if the UK does not contribute to the relationship 'from a position of self-reliance and intellectual equality', the relationship will falter. If the most we can offer is expertise in a few specific capabilities, he believes it could descend into that between customer and supplier – and suppliers that become uncompetitive are easily replaced:

> If the UK simply provides troops for the US to command without an independent command capability, or if the UK commits to procuring US-built aircraft but cannot persuade the US to release the computer codes which will allow the UK to develop the aircraft independently, then the UK is in a subservient role, with no freedom to deploy independently – and the 'Special Relationship' is changed fundamentally as a consequence.[62]

The nature of the relationship changes, too, according to the tenant of the White House. In a poll conducted for this book, British respondents rated Donald Trump's actions as the fourth highest threat to UK national security, after terrorism, terrorist cyberattacks and cyberattacks by foreign states. Russian expansionism and intervention in Eastern Europe was seen as less of a threat than the behaviour of the

President. His highly unconventional manner stops short of flouting the rules-based international order, but his aggressive approach to diplomacy; extraordinary unpredictability; casual U-turns; and habit of policy-making on the hoof all make the security landscape more complex and potentially dangerous.

America watches the shrivelling of other European armed forces with consternation too. A farcical episode in which German troops resorted to using painted broomsticks instead of machine guns in a training exercise because of equipment shortfalls was the source of more than just schadenfreude.[63] The episode was highlighted in a damning essay by a prominent US academic called Hal Brands, entitled 'Dealing with Allies in Decline'. He cites the UK as a 'particularly stark example' of the overall European trend. He concludes that the British military has 'largely divested itself of the capabilities needed' to act as America's most important partner in conflicts.[64]

This is not a new theme for the US. In January 2014, former US Defense Secretary Robert Gates warned that this country cannot continue to be 'full partner' to America if it does not retain 'full-spectrum' capabilities.[65]

Expressed in more or less diplomatic terms, the overall message is clear: America's patience with allies who fail to devote sufficient resources to protecting themselves is not infinite – even if those allies have long been considered 'special'.

EU ARMIES

If there is one subject guaranteed to anaesthetise all but the most die-hard defence geeks, it's EU military co-operation. The spectre of joint armies marching to a Brussels brass band is so over-hyped by jittery Brexiteers, and sensible suggestions of constructive co-operation so ineffectually communicated by their proponents, that normal eyes instantly glaze over. Few voters and even fewer MPs understand what the EU really wants to do in this sphere.

Dr Nathalie Tocci is all too familiar with what she calls 'the look'. As a senior adviser to the EU's Defence Cooperation Project, she knows her job title is no aphrodisiac. Yet she makes a compelling case for why it matters to the British armed forces and how our closest geographical allies are likely to change in shape and strength.

The EU looms over more than two dozen sovereign armed forces, each of which is too modest individually to make much difference to world peace, but combined can produce much greater effect. Every year, these countries spend tens of billions of euros on tanks, missiles and communication systems that look roughly the same but have slight variations, which means they are impossible to link. They commit very large sums to researching and procuring small numbers of items when collectively they would have more bargaining power with defence companies. To those without a principled aversion to the EU playing a more active role in defence, the solution is glaringly obvious.

'Essentially the EU has twenty-eight bonsai armies. Some of these bonsais are slightly bigger than others, but they are all pretty small,' Tocci explains. Her vision is to turn this coppice of bonsais into a veritable arboretum.

> The EU have something like 127 different weapons systems, when the United States has something like twenty-eight. Those 127 weapons systems are not interoperable. So, what the EU is trying to do is to encourage member states to work together. It is not about everyone doing everything at the same time. We are talking about five or six member states here, seven or eight member states there, working together on certain projects.[66]

Proponents of greater EU defence co-operation believe somewhere between £25 billion and £100 billion is 'wasted' on duplication by member states.[67] The EU's plan to reduce all this doubling up, which goes by a characteristically dreary name – 'Permanent European Security Co-operation' or 'PESCO' for short – involves joint defence procurement and research projects between small groups of nations.[68]

A total of twenty-five EU member states are involved and will pay into a European Defence Fund.[69] Crucially, despite what the more alarmist Eurosceptics would have voters believe, each country will retain sovereignty over its share of assets bought together.

'Co-operation, not integration,' is how Tocci describes it.[70]

There will be no tanks bearing the EU flag rolling across the European plain any time soon.

'Let's say an armoured vehicle is produced by six member states, all of whom are NATO members. It's not as if the EU will own this thing. It doesn't mean it will only be used in an EU operation. That would be an absolute nightmare – it would never be used!' Tocci concedes.[71]

In theory it sounds very reasonable. To those with a keen interest in the issue, the question is how it might affect NATO. Perhaps understandably, given how the EU has evolved from its origins as a common trade agreement to a mighty political project, the worry is mission creep. Opponents of the project fear that, little by little, it will start to undermine or duplicate NATO structures. The difficulty is that some Brussels zealots really do dream of going much further, and Eurosceptics are conditioned to fear the worst.

For all their anxiety, however, there is no sign that the UK armed forces will deal with the EU as a single military entity in the foreseeable future. For the time being, the UK will contribute to PESCO as a 'third-party signatory' and the Prime Minister has been at pains to stress that Brexit will have no impact on existing defence relationships with European allies.[72] Speaking to British troops in Estonia, Theresa May said that the UK remained 'unconditionally committed' to maintaining Europe's security.[73]

Macron's visit to the UK in January 2018, during which he toured Sandhurst, underlined the continuing importance of our defence relationship with the French, the UK's second most valued ally after the US.[74] The Lancaster House Treaties between the two countries, signed by the then Prime Minister David Cameron and the then French President Nicolas Sarkozy, paved the way for the pooling of equipment and collaboration on the development of nuclear technologies, but could also form the basis of a bilateral defence partnership with France after the UK's departure from EU projects.[75] A joint force created in the 2010 treaty was expanded in 2018 to form an expeditionary force of 10,000 troops.[76]

Although the UK competes with France for the attention of the United States, the Sandhurst summit showed a desire of both leaders to emphasise similarities rather than differences. As Europe's foremost military powers, and the only European members to enjoy the dual status of permanent membership of the UN Security Council and the G7 club, they share common experience. In recognition of the countries' historic military opposition, Macron agreed to loan Britain the 950-year-old Bayeux Tapestry, which commemorates the Norman Conquest.[77] Theresa May took him for lunch in a gastropub in her Maidenhead constituency.[78]

The importance of the UK's relationship with France in the lead-up to its departure from the EU showcases the delicate diplomatic ties that leaders must cultivate in order to sleep easily under the principle of collective security. The EU is 'not a primary defence organisation', as a former Chief of the Defence Staff has acknowledged,[79] but it is one that affects the UK's place in the world and the delicate balance of power between Western allies. In the context of Brexit and while Trump is in the White House, that balance matters more than ever.

BUNKERS

A NOTE ON THE NUCLEAR THREAT

In the event of a nuclear attack on London, a few lucky politicians and civil servants will have a better chance of survival than most.

In Downing Street, they're known as the Red Team: a handful of individuals who automatically qualify for entrance to the bunker deep beneath the Ministry of Defence, where it should be possible to live and govern what remains of the nation until it is safe to emerge. Prime Minister Theresa May and her husband Philip are on the list, as is her Chief of Staff, Gavin Barwell, and Downing Street's Director of Communications. The bunker is manned and kept in reasonable condition – though a source who toured the facility in 2017 was surprised to see it still contained clothes and toys for David Cameron's children, some eighteen months after he had left office.[1] Named the Pindar Bunker after a Greek poet whose house was spared when Alexander the Great sacked Thebes in 335 BC,[2] the subterranean bolthole is stocked with enough food, toiletries and medical supplies for three months.[3] Built on the instruction of Margaret Thatcher during the Cold War at a reported cost of £126 million, it can accommodate around 100 people.[4] As well as the Red Team, others would join the Prime Minister underneath Whitehall, but not all Cabinet ministers qualify. Priority is given to defence chiefs and various senior government officials whose expertise would be particularly valuable in a crisis of this magnitude.

On appointment to a job that carries entitlement to entry, individuals are weighed and measured, and the details are recorded for the allocation of food rations according to what they are deemed to need.

There are not enough beds for everyone, so occupants would sleep in shifts.[5]

In 2008, a photographer managed to persuade the Ministry of Defence to grant access to the space for an art project. The small selection of pictures he was authorised to release reveal that the bunker contains very little in the way of creature comforts. There are spartan single bedrooms for the most senior personnel; utilitarian changing facilities; communal washrooms; and piles of toothbrushes, bottles of mouthwash and shower gel.[6] The bunker has its own ventilation system to keep out contaminated air, stockpiles of breathing apparatus and a simple medical bay.[7]

Equipped with a state-of-the-art broadcasting suite and communications systems, it also has command and control offices for military leaders, from where they might orchestrate retaliatory strikes, negotiate terms of surrender or desperately liaise with allies.[8]

During the Cold War, the Soviet Union also built extensive underground refuges in the event of a nuclear holocaust. Under the streets of the Ukrainian capital of Kiev, for example, are more than 400 bunkers, 80 per cent of which have been abandoned. The government has neither the money nor the inclination to keep the Soviet Civil Defence system functioning, so they have been left to gather rust and dust.[9]

In recent years, a band of self-styled 'urban explorers' has been on a mission to re-discover these facilities. Finding a way in is dirty and sometimes dangerous work, but for those with an interest in the history of the Cold War, the rewards are considerable.

'We break into such lost places through ventilation shafts or emergency exits,' explains a youth called 'Max' who makes a living on the black market escorting small groups of backpackers to the tunnels.[10]

'They are usually located under big Soviet buildings such as hospitals, factories and government buildings.'[11] These expeditions aren't entirely legal, but police turn a blind eye.

In a rundown courtyard just outside the Kiev centre is the entrance to one of these lairs. The huge reinforced steel door to the fallout shelter wouldn't budge, but urban explorers found another way in. Armed with a pickaxe and a blowtorch, they made a huge hole in a wall leading to a ventilation system. There they found perfectly preserved relics of a bygone era. By the light of headtorches, they were able to make their way through a labyrinth of rooms designed to accommodate a small community in the event of Armageddon, exploring artefacts that had lain untouched for decades.[12] There were bedrooms, small kitchens, rusting toilet facilities and even a classroom. Everywhere they turned were boxes and crates crammed with emergency supplies – dusty old gas masks, small medical kits, bags of flour and sugar. In drawers and stacked on shelves were reams of economic documents; old production records; and Soviet-era propaganda tabloids. A yellowed newspaper cutting from the early 1970s celebrated the visit of a Turkish poet to the Soviet Union. Lying on the ground in the classroom was a bright-red cardboard certificate, an image of Lenin and various Communist symbols such as the hammer and sickle on the cover. It was awarded to a boy called 'Vladimir'. Dated 1986, the certificate congratulates him on being 'the best worker!' of his class. Since this bunker was discovered, tourists have taken the odd memento, but by and large urban explorers say the scene is much the same today as it was when they first saw it. It is difficult to know what might have gone missing: no one has bothered to make an inventory, and it seems no one ever will.[13]

What lies beneath Kiev may be nothing relative to what is underneath Moscow, which is reputed to have the biggest underground complex in the world. The most colourful reports talk of an entire subterranean town capable of housing up to 15,000 people in the event of a nuclear war; as well as a secret railway network dubbed 'Metro-2'.[14]

Russian officials have never confirmed its existence, but a former adviser to Soviet leader Gorbachev and Russian president Yeltsin has suggested it was built to give Stalin a straight line from his country *dacha* (residence) to the Kremlin.[15] The Russian police take a rather less relaxed view of urban explorers than the authorities in Kiev.

'I only knew one guy crazy enough to try and break in. We believe he made it inside – but he's been sitting in a Russian prison ever since,' according to 'Max'.[16]

Back in the UK, the Pindar Bunker is just one of many old Cold War bunkers, some of which have been maintained for key figures, including the royal family, in the event that disaster strikes. Others, like the Burlington Bunker beneath Corsham in Wiltshire, have fallen into disrepair. It was declassified in 2004 and is now completely dilapidated.[17]

It is more than half a century since the moment two superpowers teetered on the brink of nuclear conflict in the Cuban Missile Crisis. As the year 2020 approaches, the threat of nuclear war still lingers. As we shall see, insuring against this possibility is one of the most expensive functions of the UK's armed forces.

THE BOMB

TRIDENT

RAGGLE TAGGLE

Iona Soper leans forward, pulling on a Marlboro Red with a cheek-hollowing drag.

Her hair is greasy and she is wearing a scuffed black leather jacket and battered jeans which she has customised with the words 'Power To The Planet'. Around her neck is a chain with an anarchist symbol. Strikingly beautiful, in another life she might have made it as a model. Instead, she is sitting on a grubby couch in a cabin next to a misty Scottish loch, explaining why she spends every day protesting about the UK's nuclear weapons programme.

'They cost billions; we'll never use them; and if we do, we'll be monstrous excuses for human beings,' she says. 'I've never understood the point of a deterrent. Either you use it first and it's not a deterrent, or you use it second and it hasn't worked!'[1]

She doesn't have a job, she says, because 'most employers wouldn't take people turning up smelling like fire, sweat and dog'.

This is the Peace Camp at Faslane, a few minutes' walk from HM Naval Base, Clyde. It is here, on a remote stretch of the west coast of Scotland, that the UK's weapons of last resort, known as Trident, are based. If all else fails, the government believes they could prevent a catastrophic attack on the UK.

At any one time, at least one of four Vanguard-class submarines carrying sixteen Trident II D5 long-range ballistic missiles, each armed with eight warheads, lurks somewhere beneath the ocean, poised to blast entire nations into radioactive oblivion should the order to fire ever come. Capable of hitting targets within a range of 7,500 miles, supposedly within a few feet accuracy, this is what the MoD calls the UK's 'Continuous At-Sea Deterrent' (CAS-D). Each warhead is believed to be eight times as powerful as the atomic bomb that killed 140,000 people in Hiroshima in 1945.[2]

Quite when – or if – these weapons would ever be used is another matter. Assuming they work as intended, they would unleash so much death and destruction that it is almost impossible to imagine the scenario. In theory, as Soper described, the weapons system is a 'deterrent', the idea being that its mere existence is enough to dissuade adversaries from doing anything that might result in its use – though a handful of politicians, including former Defence Secretaries Sir Michael Fallon and Geoff Hoon, have suggested that in the most extreme circumstance it could even be used to strike first.[3]

In this sense, defence chiefs argue that it is used 'every second of every minute of every day'. As General Sir Nick Houghton put it when he was Chief of the Defence Staff, 'The purpose of the deterrent is that you don't have to use it because you successfully deterred.'[4]

To the raggle-taggle posse of protestors who have set up home near the base, this makes no sense. Their position is that Trident is a moral outrage.

Soper says:

I started off believing these weapons are part of our lives, so what are we going to do about it? But I came to hate the way that the public are patronised into believing politicians who say they're essential for our safety … I suppose it must be easy when you're a politician living in Westminster, but when you're living right next to them as we do in Scotland, these weapons are much harder to ignore. I remember sitting down next to the loch one day. It's so picturesque and beautiful, with clear blue water and a thin film of mist. As I was sitting there, one of the Vanguards came in, surrounded by its escort of police boats. It's terrifying to watch – this huge dark beast. What's most eerie about it is that it's completely silent. It looks evil.

The Peace Camp is made up of brightly painted campervans and a few beaten up cabins. It claims to be the oldest continuously running protest site in the world: the protestors reason that if the deterrent is continuous, so too must be their dissent. Some feel so strongly about it that they are prepared to risk criminal charges.

In summer 2017, they managed to block the road on which the warheads are transported to and from the base, getting themselves arrested in the process. It resulted in a court appearance, but they relish testing the authorities. On this occasion, the charges were dismissed, with the judge agreeing they were engaged in legal peaceful protest.[5]

One of their favourite pastimes is tracking trucks carrying munitions from the nuclear weapons factory where they are assembled in Burghfield, Berkshire, up to the submarine base. Naturally, there are no markings on the vehicles advertising their radioactive load, but the protestors have learned how to identify them. They like to position themselves in front of the vehicles and force the drivers to a standstill.

'These things carry up to 8 kg of active plutonium. And they break down all the time!' according to one of the group. In his late forties, he is a walking, talking, peace protestor cliché, complete with dirty dreadlocks.[6]

'They've had over seventy mechanical failures in the past five years. If a bunch of crusty hippies can track them and stop them, imagine what people with seriously bad intentions could do. It doesn't bear thinking about!' he exclaims.[7]

On the face of it, Faslane is impenetrable; its forbidding perimeter a tangle of barbed wire and high fences. In reality, the protestors say, the base is fairly easily infiltrated.

In summer 2016, a young man named Tjaadrk Siemssen from Bremerhaven near Hamburg managed to kayak his way around the loch to the heart of the base before being arrested and thrown out.

'It was a spontaneous thing. He was going for a paddle, realised the entrance to the base was unguarded, and just went for it. Of course, he was eventually caught. Initially, he was charged with trespass, but the MoD quietly dropped the case and he left the country,' according to one of his friends at the camp.[8]

The protestors say this wasn't even their best effort. A few years ago, they claim they were able to break into the base itself and clamber on top of an Astute-class submarine.[9] A Faslane Peace Camp blog details another incident they describe as a 'daring moonlit amphibious assault'.

> Two boats made it under the first jetty and under the radar, allowing one camper to make a landing at berth 7 near the sub pen. Staff were again caught napping, with no-one seemingly concerned by our man's soaking wet clothes, boots and dreadlocks. Having marched along the road unimpeded by several manned checkpoints, the intrepid trespasser was finally huckled by a singularly conscientious Ministry guard on entering the Trident area.[10]

In 2017, the US Navy docked some of its Ohio-class boats in Faslane.[11] The protestors say the visit prompted some good-humoured warnings about the attitude of the US authorities to security breaches.

'A couple of MoD officials turned up at the Peace Camp and warned protestors to keep a low profile while the visitors were around,' a protester says. 'They said: "Just letting you know the Americans are in town this week. Don't try anything; don't block the road. Please don't embarrass us. They won't be nice to you like we are. The Americans don't fuck around. Cause too much of a fuss, and they'll just shoot you."'[12]

Such is the rough end of the campaign against Trident. However, objections to the nuclear weapons system are far from limited to idealists. Indeed, many respected figures in politics and the armed forces believe that plans to renew the weapons system when it reaches the end of its official lifespan in 2030 – at a cost of at least £31 billion – are a ruinously expensive mistake.[13]

The government's position is that Trident is a vital component of national security. Ministers argue that nuclear capability on this scale not only keeps this country safe but also maintains the UK's status as a leading military power, underpinning the UK's position as a permanent member of the UN Security Council. All five permanent members have nuclear weapons.

However, the staggering cost of maintaining the weapons and submarines, and the ethical questions about deploying something so apocalyptic, make these Doomsday Machines the single most controversial feature of UK defence. Perhaps surprisingly, the higher up the military hierarchy, the easier it is to find voices questioning whether the continuous at-sea deterrent represents value for money.

YES, PRIME MINISTER

Back in 1986, an episode of *Yes, Prime Minister* portrayed an over-enthusiastic new premier attempting to cancel Trident. In farcical scenes, the sitcom shows scheming Cabinet Secretary 'Sir Humphrey' thwarting the proposal on the basis that the nuclear weapons system is the best that money can buy, and that ditching it will upset the Americans.

'If you walked into a nuclear missile showroom, you would buy Trident! It's lovely, it's elegant, it's beautiful, it's quite simply the best, and Britain should have the best!' he wheedles. 'In the world of the nuclear missile, it is the Savile Row suit! The Rolls-Royce Corniche; the Château Lafite 1945! It is the nuclear missile *Harrods* would sell you! What more can I say?'

'Only that it cost £15 billion and we don't need it?' replies the Prime Minister doubtfully, wondering aloud whether he would ever actually 'press the button' anyway. He muses that he could spend the cash on conventional forces instead. Meanwhile, his Chief Scientific Officer suggests they use the funds to invest in 'emergent technology; smart missiles; target finding; infrared'.

More than three decades later, that script is as pertinent as it was in 1986. Indeed, in one uncannily prescient scene, the scriptwriters appear to anticipate exactly the sort of 'salami tactics' the Kremlin employs against state targets now, suggesting that by 2020, Russia's 'little by little', 'accidental' invasions could trigger a major confrontation with the West. The *Yes, Prime Minister* episode also points to scepticism about the nuclear deterrent in the highest ranks of the armed forces, depicting the head of the army backing the Prime Minister's plan to jettison the weapons.

'Good idea. We don't need it. Complete waste of money,' says the general – a view that is privately shared by a number of senior military figures – particularly in the army – today.[14]

At the time the episode was filmed, the UK's original submarine-based nuclear weapons system, Polaris, was approaching the end of its lifespan. Bought from the Americans in the early 1960s, and entering service in 1968, Polaris kept going until 1996, when, after considerable political debate, it was replaced by Trident. Though the new system (submarines, missiles and warheads) was built to last several decades, the strength of feeling among some voters and politicians about the morality of nuclear weapons, coupled with the length of time taken to build a replacement (around seventeen years), has ensured the issue has never been off the political agenda for long.

Newly elected Prime Ministers who enter 10 Downing Street having given the subject little thought have to form a quick opinion. One of their first tasks on entering office is to sit down and write four 'letters of last resort', one for each of the nuclear submarines, setting out what the Royal Navy Commander should do if the UK is hit by a devastating nuclear attack and the government is destroyed. For any new Prime Minister, it is a sobering moment.*[15]

Instructions could range from launching a retaliatory strike to doing nothing at all. To date, no Prime Minister has revealed the content of his or her letter. The secret missives are kept in a safe on board each vessel and destroyed unopened when the premier leaves office.

Were the content to be made public – which would obviously make a nonsense of the process – taxpayers might find it easier to judge whether Trident is worth having. Jeremy Corbyn has repeatedly indicated that he would never order a nuclear attack, which suggests the continuous at-sea deterrent would be redundant in his hands.[16]

His position is not unusual within the Labour Party, though it is not shared by his shadow Defence Secretary Nia Griffith, who has said she would be prepared to authorise the use of the UK's nuclear weapons.[17]

---

* A Radio 4 documentary on letters of last resort tells how Tony Blair 'went white' at the enormity of the responsibility.

In March 2007, Blair successfully overcame a massive Labour backbench rebellion over proposals to begin planning the so-called Successor programme to Trident. Four members of his government resigned. At the time, his Defence Secretary, Des (now Lord) Browne, fully supported plans to renew the weapons system, arguing that the nuclear deterrent was essential for the UK's security in an uncertain world.[18]

However, he now believes he was hoodwinked by the Ministry of Defence into supporting renewal and says he would not do so again today. He feels officials were not entirely honest, either about the likely costs or the lifespan of the current programme, which he believes could be far longer than the MoD claims.

> In 2006, as the white paper on Trident makes clear, all the advice I received from technical and engineering experts was unequivocally that the service life of the first Trident boat could be extended safely only to the mid-2020s and would, therefore, have to be replaced by then. I tested this advice as robustly as possible, in the absence of truly independent evidence. History has shown that that deadline for renewal was clearly wrong, as it has now been moved, without explanation, to the mid-2030s.

'I am not surprised that there is some scepticism about the value of the expertise upon which these judgements are being made,' he says now.[19]

At the time of the Blair vote in 2007, the government claimed a replacement for Trident would be needed by 2024; a deadline that was extended to 2028 in the 2010 Strategic Defence and Security Review and has since been pushed back again to the 'early 2030s'. The timeframe is based on a set of assumptions about the service life of the current submarines, the rationale for which has never been made fully public. A cross-party inquiry headed by Browne, former Tory Defence Secretary Sir Malcolm Rifkind and former Liberal Democrat leader Sir Menzies Campbell pointed out that the nearest equivalent to the Vanguards – the US Ohio-class submarines – have had their planned life extended to forty-four years, a full decade longer than what is proposed in the UK, suggesting that the current weapons system could last much longer.[20]

Browne recalls a conversation with a senior naval engineer who claimed that, with the necessary repairs, the boats could last indefinitely. Ministers have dismissed this suggestion, citing differences in safety standards and specific components of the Vanguard,[21] but Browne is unconvinced.

The debate over the nuclear deterrent was reignited in 2010 when the Conservatives failed to win a majority at the general election, forcing them into coalition with the Liberal Democrats – the most sceptical of the major parties south of the border towards Trident renewal. The two parties committed to maintaining Trident but agreed that plans for renewal should be scrutinised 'to ensure value for money'. As part of the coalition arrangements, the Lib Dems were allowed to oversee a government-commissioned review into alternative nuclear-weapon delivery systems.[22] The study was initially overseen by armed forces minister Nick Harvey, whose experience led him to believe that Trident is a monstrous folly.

'Essentially there is no point to us sailing the high seas 24/7, armed to the eyeballs with a deadly level of nuclear forces when we have no known nuclear adversary … It is a quite unnecessary gargantuan effort, greedy on consumption of resources, and the corollary is that we are much less ready for the type of conflict we might be facing,' he says now.

He is frustrated by what he sees as the absence of intelligent political debate about Trident, which he condemns as a 'national phallic symbol'.[23]

Much to his chagrin, Harvey was forced to leave the Ministry of Defence before the review was complete. ('Nick Clegg seemed to think that we would do better by swapping my job for that of farming minister,' he recalls gloomily.)

The role of overseeing the study was passed to Danny Alexander, who was Chief Secretary to the Treasury at the time and was fully occupied overseeing the coalition's austerity programme. To the disappointment of Trident critics, the eventual report pulled its punches, suggesting that alternative systems would be too expensive.

Harvey believes that if he had remained in post, the conclusions would have been different. He reflects:

> Danny was very competent, but a formidably busy man, overseeing expenditure across the entire waterfront of government. Although I believe he interrogated the team who did the review very well over the finances, I don't think he had enough background in defence to call their bluff over the frankly absurd proposition that it would take until the 2030s to adapt a warhead to go on a Cruise missile, which is what the credible alternative was.

He claims that before embarking on the review, the Ministry of Defence's Chief Science Officer at the time had told him that a Cruise missile was a perfectly valid alternative.

Looking back, he feels the review was just a sop from the Conservatives during the coalition negotiations and that it was never designed to produce a credible alternative. His research into Trident left him no less sceptical about its value, especially for a retaliatory strike.

> If I was ever to write the letter of last resort, I would say, 'Head to Australia, get a cold beer', and I would make sure the Ambassador's got a pension fund! I mean, it can't possibly improve the state of the world after the strike for there to be a second strike. It would just be the most criminal lunacy in the history of mankind.[24]

Clegg himself remains mystified by what he calls 'the British establishment's fetish' about the continuous at-sea deterrence 'orthodoxy'.[25]

Divisions over the issue within the Labour Party resurfaced in 2016 when MPs were asked to rubber-stamp the renewal programme. A total of forty-seven Labour MPs followed Corbyn through the No lobby. They were joined by all fifty-two members of the Scottish Nationalist Party.[26]

Bitter opposition to Trident north of the border will be one of the government's biggest headaches in the event of future Scottish independence, potentially requiring the construction of an entire new naval base in England to accommodate the weapons system. While it is possible to imagine a scenario in which Scottish ministers allow Vanguards to remain on the Clyde till the end of their lifespan, there seems little prospect that an independent Scotland with an SNP administration would contemplate extending that offer to the Successor programme. The cost of building new facilities would run to billions and place a huge strain on the defence budget at a time when the Ministry of Defence would be in turmoil over the loss of up to a fifth of the armed forces, as Scottish regiments broke away from the union.

One former Defence Secretary, a supporter of renewal, says he believes Scottish independence would mean the end of Trident.

'Before the referendum, the government said they would just "relocate" the Trident base, but to do so would be either physically near impossible and certainly prohibitively expensive. It would cost so much money that no British Prime Minister would sign it off,' he says.

According to a well-placed SNP source, in the run-up to the referendum campaign, the MoD privately floated the idea of basing the submarines at the US nuclear submarine base in Kings Bay, Georgia. This would have been a temporary solution, while a new English base was constructed.[*]

As the prospect of a second referendum north of the border in the short to medium term recedes, this debate is no longer pressing.[27]

However, nationalist fervour has not gone away, and another plebiscite could easily take place within the next decade. Some MPs believe it is another reason to re-think the Successor programme.

Crispin Blunt MP, former chairman of the Foreign Affairs Select Committee and one of a handful of senior Tories to question the

---

[*] The MoD has done little contingency planning for Scottish independence. However, an SNP plan for the establishment of a new Scottish defence force, published before the 2014 independence referendum, demanded 18 per cent of the army's manpower; RAF Lossiemouth and at least twelve Typhoon fighter jets plus some spy planes; transport aircraft and transport helicopters; and Faslane naval base, along with 18 per cent of the navy's frigates and patrol boats.

case for renewal, fears pressing ahead could hasten the break-up of the union.

'Let us not forget the risks that this weapons system presents to the United Kingdom. Basing it in Scotland reinforces the nationalist narrative, and, ironically, for a system justified on the basis that it protects the United Kingdom, it could prove instrumental in the Union's undoing,' he has said.[28]

The exact cost of renewal is unclear. In 2006, the government put it at £20 billion, a figure Des Browne now describes as a 'back of a fag packet' calculation. A decade on, the official projection has soared to £31 billion, with a further £10 billion set aside for 'contingencies'. Blunt estimates the 'lifetime' running costs of the new programme at £179 billion and says it 'does not pass any rational cost-effectiveness test'. He believes Trident has become more of a 'political weapon' against the Labour Party than a genuine instrument of defence.

'Britain's independent possession of nuclear weapons has turned into a political touchstone for commitment to national defence, but this is an illusion,' he has said.[29]

In a decision with profound long-term consequences for the defence budget, in July 2010, the government quietly announced that the Ministry of Defence would have to foot the bill for renewal. Behind the scenes, Liam Fox had been trying to persuade the Chancellor to take up the burden, knowing it would cripple the departmental budget for decades.

At the time, the MoD was battling to stave off cuts of up to 20 per cent, and nobody took much notice of what seemed a rather technical debate in Whitehall over how the Successor programme would be funded. At the flick of the Chancellor's pen, the MoD was lumbered with a huge long-term liability.

A former MoD civil servant who worked at the highest level in the department says the Treasury 'did the MoD up like a kipper'.

They pulled a blinder. The MoD was so ecstatic about the idea that the Treasury was going to help them out that they didn't really read the small print. When the Treasury said, 'Here's the deal: we're going to save your skin, but in doing so, Successor will go under the MoD,' nobody said, 'Forget it! That's a crap deal! We'd rather have it the other way around!' They were completely hoodwinked. I distinctly remember being told by MoD [colleagues] at the time that it was really good news. I remember them saying, 'It's amazing! We've just got a great settlement out of the Treasury.' I was like, 'Is there a downside?' And they were like, 'Oh, not really. The only thing is that the Successor programme is going to be in our budget.' I said, 'Are you serious?!' And they replied that it was fine; they'd budgeted it well. But at the time, I knew, because I'd been doing a lot of work on it, that the budget was wholly inadequate. I said, 'Hang on. You've just signed your next death warrant.' It was an extraordinary miscalculation, drawn out of desperation. They'd been offered a deal which got them out of today's jail.

And this is where human nature comes in, in a not very edifying way. Human nature says, 'It's not going to be on my watch [that it goes wrong], is it? That will be someone else's watch.'[30]

Today this little-noticed decision is consistently cited by those concerned by the state of the armed forces as a critical factor in the MoD's financial struggles.[31] Successive Defence Secretaries have fought in vain to persuade the Treasury to reverse the move.

Supporters of Trident say the huge headline costs should be kept in perspective. A £200 billion 'lifetime' cost for the Successor programme is about one fiftieth of what will be spent on the NHS in the same period. As the pressure group 'Save the Royal Navy' puts it, 'Other government expenditure is rarely discussed in this way. No one talks in terms of the £5 trillion NHS or the £7 trillion welfare bill we face if we attempted to estimate their cost over the next thirty years.'[32]

On one matter, all sides can probably agree: if taxpayers are going to spend billions of pounds a year on this system, it had better live up to Sir Humphrey's glowing description, and function properly.

SPACED OUT

One evening in May 2015, a young submariner sat down to what he feared might be his last supper with his family. William McNeilly was not long home from a three-month draft on HMS *Victorious*, one of the Royal Navy's four Vanguard-class ballistic submarines.

During his stint as a Trident weapons engineer at Faslane, the 25-year-old had become increasingly concerned by safety and security standards at the base. He had decided to chronicle everything he observed.

According to his own account, Able Seaman McNeilly initially followed official protocols, diligently flagging up his concerns to his chain of command. Not once did anyone even attempt to make a change, he claims. Eventually he decided to go public 'for the safety of the people'.[33]

By exposing serious alleged defects in the UK's nuclear weapons programme, he knew he could lose everything. However, he was convinced he was doing the right thing for his country.

'This is bigger than me; it's bigger than all of us. We are so close to a nuclear disaster it's shocking,' he wrote in the dossier he was about to release.

That night his mother 'cooked a little too much food for dinner' and they tried not to think about the momentous personal and political implications of the step he was about to take. Then he cast a final eye over the 11,000-word document he had written, took a deep breath, and pressed 'send' to WikiLeaks, along with a photo of his naval ID card to prove his authenticity. He had broken the Official Secrets Act.[34]

'If I die, it wasn't suicide,' he declared dramatically, in the final section of his expose.

Published on 17 May 2015, McNeilly's claims sparked a furore. Labelling Trident a 'broken system', he detailed thirty alleged safety and security breaches arising from what he depicted as a culture of casual corner-cutting and recklessness on board the submarine. His aim, he said, was to 'break down the false images of a perfect system that most people envisage exists'.

He claimed it was 'harder getting into most nightclubs' than accessing top-secret control rooms and listed various alarming-sounding practices and risks, including the routine flouting of rules about use of personal electronic devices on board the boat as well as multiple fire and electrical hazards.

If you've never seen a missile compartment before you probably have a picture of a glistening high tech piece of equipment ... Before Captain's round or a VIP visit it is pretty glistening, but during most of the patrol it's far from it. Missile Compartment 4 turns into a gym. There are people sweating their arses of [*sic*] between the missiles, people rowing between a blanket of s**t because the sewage system is defective, sometimes the s**t sprays onto the fwd [*sic*] starboard missile tubes and there's also a lot of rubbish stored near the missile tubes.

'Not an image you would expect of the "most advanced weapons system on the planet," he wrote in one of many colourful passages.

Finally, and most devastatingly, he claimed that on a number of occasions, when tested, the so-called weapon of last resort simply didn't work.

'At the end of a patrol tests are done to see if the weapons system could have performed a successful launch. These tests let us know if we really were providing the UK's strategic nuclear deterrent ... The test was carried out 3 times and it failed 3 times,' he claimed, supplying some technical detail about the alleged faults.

Naturally, the MoD was swift to dismiss his evidence, labelling it 'subjective and unsubstantiated'. McNeilly makes no secret of his fundamental opposition to nuclear weapons, and it is evident from his testimony that he set out to find fault. Doubtless some of his account is exaggerated or lacks context, but reading it in full, to an outsider at least, it has the ring of truth.

Significantly, he did not face any criminal charges. Having handed himself in to police, McNeilly simply left the navy with a dishonourable discharge. For the MoD, no good could come of protracted debate about his claims, especially when others might come forward to back his case. Indeed, some of his allegations have been reiterated by another whistle-blower.[35]

There are other question marks over whether Trident is what Sir Humphrey described as the 'Rolls-Royce Corniche' of weapons systems. In 2017, it emerged that a test fire of an unarmed Trident ballistic missile veered several thousand miles off course. Detonated off the coast of Florida, it had been targeted at the southern Atlantic off the coast of west Africa. Instead, it headed in the opposite direction, and would have hit America had the test been live. The malfunction happened just a month before the 2016 Commons vote on renewal, but did not come to light until 2017, when it was revealed by a newspaper.[36]

Once again, the MoD played down the incident, arguing that previous tests were successful and that such exercises are designed to expose flaws in the system so that they can be rectified. Many independent defence analysts agree, pointing out that the US frequently tests its nuclear weapons system, which shares the same underlying technology, and is considered entirely fit for purpose. All the same, if the weapons system is designed to be a deterrent, what matters most is that potential adversaries believe it works. Any doubt undermines the whole concept.

There are further concerns relating to the technology. In interviews for this project, two senior military sources have privately suggested that the continuous at-sea deterrent can be seen from space in certain locations and conditions. Neither source would provide more detail: such information is classified.

A third source, former Chief of the General Staff General Sir Peter Wall, admitted that even if it is not currently visible via satellite, 'it soon will be'.

He is not in favour of jettisoning Trident, but believes it makes no sense in conjunction with cutting conventional forces:

My opinion is not that it's a waste of money; it's just not something we should spend disproportionate amounts on. My definition of disproportionate is 'that which erodes conventional deterrence' ... Deterrence theology is about a series of steps on the escalatory ladder ... if some of those rungs go missing, it's not credible to rely on nuclear capability. There is a profound theological reason why you should not spend more on the top end of the ladder and take out the lower rungs, because it's not credible in the escalatory chain.[37]

In 2015, General Sir Nick Houghton, then Chief of the Defence Staff, suggested Corbyn's stance on Trident undermined the credibility of the deterrent.[38] He now says he has 'some sympathy' with the Labour leader's moral position on using nuclear weapons. He too stops short of suggesting Trident should be abandoned in the short term, but believes that in the medium term there will be more ethical and effective deterrents than nuclear weapons.

> To me we can't be that far short of being able to threaten something in the cyber domain against the critical national infrastructure of a country, which is a more credible deterrent than a nuclear one, and a lot cheaper. If we can come up with a credible way of holding the critical national infrastructure of the country at risk by 2035 then, by Jove, that would be a far better deterrent.
>
> It makes no sense that for the rest of human history, the way in which the peoples of the world live in peace is by the perpetual threat of mutual destruction. That just can't be right.

'If that is the best hope for mankind, if the only way we can live together in peace is by perpetually threatening to mutually destroy ourselves, then we are all basket cases,' he says.

Perhaps the most important and frequently voiced concern over the system is its potential vulnerability to a cyberattack. A report called 'Hacking UK Trident', compiled by the British American Security Information Council (BASIC) think tank, describes the scope for infiltration as 'significant', detailing multiple ways in which the system could theoretically be compromised. The authors acknowledge that neither a 'lone wolf teenager in a basement' nor terrorists would have the resources to penetrate the system. However, they believe hostile states might one day be able to do it. As construction of the new Dreadnought-class submarines gets under way, they urge the MoD to attach the highest level of importance to cyber protection across the whole supply chain, warning that this will have major implications for the programme budget, 'with uncertain success'.

Once again, these concerns are not limited to dreamy peaceniks. The report is officially endorsed by Browne, who warns, in the conclusion, that it would be 'irresponsibly complacent' to imagine that the system is 'somehow immune' to cyberattack.

'When states invest hundreds of billions of dollars in offensive nuclear weapons systems, the incentives are there amongst adversaries to develop capabilities that could neutralise that threat,' he writes.[39]

The MoD rejects these concerns, stressing that Vanguard submarines are not connected to any civilian computer network and are surrounded by an electronic buffer zone known as an 'air gap'. They argue that this cannot be circumvented.

The extent to which Trident is truly 'independent' is a geeky debate. Critics claim that so many aspects of the deterrent – from the technology to maintenance and testing – are reliant on the Americans that it could never be used without Washington's say-so.[40]

In reality, the UK maintains full operational control over the system,[41] so if Doomsday ever comes, no permission will be required from any foreign state to fire.

As Brexit approaches, now would be a dangerous time for a new approach to nuclear weapons. Abandoning Trident – even for an alternative – could have a devastating impact on the UK's international status, creating an impression of diminishing ambition and power on the world stage. However, the deterrent is particularly vulnerable to a series of political shocks. Scottish independence, the election of a pacifist premier, or developments in satellite or cyber technology could render it anywhere on the spectrum from less effective to completely redundant. Trident worked brilliantly for the twentieth century, but it is far from clear it will do the same in the twenty-first. It is questionable whether the government has seriously considered these risks in making the case for renewal.

For the armed forces, there is one encouraging recent development in the debate. In December 2017, the government announced that it was considering shifting the cost of renewal to the Treasury.[42]

That would be a huge relief to the navy in particular, which – as we shall see – has quite enough problems without the nuclear millstone.

TO THE RIGHT

A NOTE ON MONEY

It is impossible to have a discussion with anyone about the state of the armed forces without the word 'money' coming up within a few seconds. With the exception of the NHS, other public services seem to tick along without endless reports of 'black holes' in their budgets. So why is the Ministry of Defence always in such trouble?

Whitehall is strewn with the unmarked graves of heroes who have tried and failed to answer this question. Many, like Aston Martin-driving entrepreneur Lord (Paul) Drayson, are drafted in from the business world and arrive full of hope, vowing to turn everything around.[1] A few years later they slope back to corporate life, having concluded it's a lost cause.

Countless investigations, reviews and reports on how and why things are always so tight have made little obvious impact. The department seems locked in an eternal cycle of hiring and firing; ordering and cancelling; staggering along from one day to the next in the hope of a magical Treasury bailout. Secretaries of State agonise over cutting capabilities, while pumped-up defence chiefs dream of Trafalgar and Waterloo and continue to add kit to their shopping carts, telling themselves they must put defence of the realm ahead of the tedious demands of the bean-counters. Civil servants employed to deal with the never-ending crisis devise spreadsheets that suggest it will all be OK if projects and payments are simply delayed. In Whitehall, they call this trick 'pushing to the right' – a reference to where figures appear on a spreadsheet if they are deferred for a few years. Everyone has the best intentions, but still the MoD cannot make ends meet. A minister can declare with a flourish that the mysterious black hole has vanished (as Defence Secretary Philip Hammond did in relation to a £38 billion problem in 2013),[2] only for the dastardly dark void to reappear a few years later (as Fallon found in 2017, when the MoD developed another black hole to the tune of £20 billion).[3] All this is so normal that nobody at Westminster ever bats an eyelid. How come nobody seems able to get a grip?

Few understand the scenario better than Sir Bernard Gray, who risked driving himself and some more sensitive MoD colleagues loopy in a heroic campaign to end this endless cycle of despair. As Chief of Defence Materiel, he was relentless in his quest to hammer sense into the procurement process and extract better value for taxpayers. Pinned to the wall of Gray's office during his 2005–10 tenure at the MoD was a picture of two boats: a small tender tied to the back of a super yacht. The modest little vessel was called 'Original Order'. The super yacht was called 'Change Request'.[4] It was a pictorial dig at the military's unfortunate habit of adding bells and whistles to everything they buy – which is just one part of the money problem.

Five years after his appointment as Chief of Defence Materiel in 2010 – seventeen years after he first started working on the issue under Labour Defence Secretary George Robertson – Gray gave a speech to a think tank summarising everything he had learned. As he acknowledged, his conclusion was remarkably obvious: the Ministry of Defence should not order what it can't afford.

> It sounds self-evident, doesn't it? I mean, how hard can it be to realise that you can only buy what you can afford? It sounds patronising to even suggest such an idea. But it is absolutely central to the issue, and it is so often ignored or underestimated by defence systems around the world.

When it comes to defence procurement, he says, the fundamental question – can the department afford to buy this thing? – is easy to ignore, *because they never have to pay for it straight away*. So ministers sign off big orders, secretly hoping that they will magically turn out to be cheaper than they know in their hearts will be the case. They are comforted by the knowledge that the day of reckoning won't be for many years. By the time it all goes pear-shaped, with luck it will be someone else's problem.[5] A procurement programme can take decades, but most people in the MoD move jobs every two years. With such rapid staff turnover, accountability is a real problem. There are no obvious penalties for screwing up, and no individual is given responsibility for delivery.

'The vast committee system means every poor decision can be blamed on everyone and no one. Also every decision can be reversed at any stage by simply convening another meeting, with no one person ever taking the hit for a shoddy programme or suboptimal capability,' says a former navy chief wearily.

Gray was bewildered by the apparent inability of ministers and mandarins to grasp simple truths about what he calls the 'curse' of defence procurement. He vividly remembers someone at the MoD producing a spreadsheet showing that, by extending the deadline for delivery of a new electronics system for the Eurofighter jet, it would be possible to transform the project balance sheet from a multi-million-pound negative figure to zero. MoD officials presented the move as if it would be free and were a no-brainer. In fact, it would have cost the public purse up to £100 million, leaving large numbers of people underemployed; factories used less efficiently; and taxpayers picking up the tab for an awful lot of long lunches and corporate away days while everyone twiddled their thumbs waiting for the MoD to press 'Go' on the project again.

'Put another way, we were proposing to delay a programme that was costing the UK around £20 billion by eighteen months [in order] to *defer*, not cancel, just *defer* 0.01 per cent of the programme cost, in a move that would cost five times as much as it deferred. And the MoD thought this was free,' Gray has explained incredulously.[6]

He likes to compare what can happen with defence procurement to what can happen when people buy a new car or house. They fall in love with something they can't really afford; scrape together just enough deposit to persuade a bank to lend them the cash; then belatedly realise they have no cash left to furnish and maintain their new asset – especially if something goes wrong.

When it comes to why the MoD budget always tanks, there are many other factors, of course, including the strange way in which prices for anything related to defence supposedly shoot up automatically. 'Normal' inflation for consumer goods like food, energy and clothes hovers between 2 and 3 per cent. Defence inflation is generally said to stand at around 8 per cent.*

Politicians and civil servants cite this economic curiosity as if it's like the weather and there's nothing they can do about it. It would certainly explain a lot. After all, against annual equipment cost inflation on this scale, a 0.5 per cent increase to the defence budget (grudgingly extracted from the Treasury in 2015)[7] is only ever going to buy a few extra bullets.

During Gray's time at the MoD, he had a comrade-in-arms, who also made gargantuan – and ultimately doomed – efforts to turn things around. His name was (Lord) Peter Levene, and he was parachuted in from the City by the Tories in 2010, having previously worked in the MoD in the 1980s.[8] Cameron's government wanted to show they were serious about changing the way the MoD buys materiel, having spent years accusing the previous administration of giving the military substandard kit. They appointed a 'brains trust' of business leaders and management consultants headed by Levene to come up with a plan. In 2011, the group produced a series of recommendations now known as the 'Levene Reforms'.

Levene's big idea was to make the heads of the navy, army and RAF responsible for their own budgets. The upside for the three so-called chiefs was that they would now hold the purse strings for their own service. Instead of having to defer to ministers and mandarins, they could decide how the cash should be divided between kit, personnel, training and logistics support.[9] This was new: up until 2011, when the

---

* There is no official measure of defence inflation. It is regularly cited by defence industry and MoD figures as falling anywhere between 8 per cent and 15 per cent a year.

reforms came in, the hardware budget had been controlled by staff in the MoD Main Building. The chiefs only had to worry about spare parts and running costs. It had led to 'left hand/right hand' problems. Levene hoped that ending the division of responsibilities would ensure people only bought things they could afford to maintain. The downside was that they would be evicted from their grand offices in the MoD's Main Building in London and banished to their respective service headquarters in Portsmouth, Andover and High Wycombe respectively.[10] Levene and his team felt they were an unhelpful presence at the MoD, where he felt they were wasting time getting involved in debates that were none of their business. The thinking was that they should spend more time with their soldiers, sailors and airmen and women. Not only were they exiled from Whitehall – they were also kicked off the MoD's highest policy-making body, the Defence Board, and replaced with business executives, management consultants and other technocrats.[11]

Inside the Ministry of Defence, all this was seen as quite revolutionary, shifting the balance of power and accountability across the department.

A senior MoD official, now retired, says:

When I first heard about the Levene reforms, I thought it was a smart move. What had happened before was that each of the three services absolutely bet the ranch that they would be bailed out by the other two. One hundred per cent bet the ranch on it. Now they could say to the navy, 'There's your money. You ain't getting a penny more. So don't think you're going to go over there and raid the army, because that's not going to happen. Your money is your money; the only rule is that that is all you're getting.

At first, the chiefs were keen on the changes. As Professor Peter Roberts, Director of Military Sciences at the Royal United Services Institute, later told the Defence Select Committee:

Those chiefs were the ones who agreed to the Levene reforms. In fact, they wanted them. They wanted their own money. They didn't want central government – the Cabinet Office or the Treasury – deciding what capabilities they had. They are the ones who said, 'Give us our money and we'll decide how to spend it.'[12]

The enthusiasm didn't last. The trouble was that they were now liable to get the blame when things went wrong. This had an upside for politicians: as the chairman of the committee, Julian Lewis MP, put it, ministers could 'offload the guilt'.[13]

Meanwhile, neither politicians nor top brass really wanted to cut their coats according to their cloth. First Sea Lord Admiral Sir George Zambellas was particularly resistant to the diminution of naval capability on his watch – and often got his way. This irritated less persuasive figures in the other two services. They would grumble about being forced to pay what they called the 'navy tax'.

According to a senior MoD insider:

Zambellas effectively refused to reduce his spending to fit the cash available, and persistently spent about £500 million more per year than the navy budget allowed. The MoD was too weak to force him to comply. As a result, the navy overspend was always being clawed back out of the budget for the other forces. He basically took a stand that said, 'This is the size of navy that I think is appropriate, so to hell with the available budget.' Zambellas's supporters would say he was simply doing what he believed was right. Ships, unlike soldiers, are fantastically expensive. And what is a maritime nation without ships?[14]

PART THREE

THE SERVICES

THE NAVY

CATS AND TRAPS

THE AIRCRAFT CARRIERS

SEA SALTS

Six months into his new job, Gavin Williamson was still trying to get his head around aspects of the brief, which was not unreasonable. Though he had two close relatives in the armed forces, one serving in the Royal Navy, the other a former RAF man, the world of defence was as much of a mystery to him as it is to most politicians without a background in the military. For any new Defence Secretary, the endless acronyms peppering every verbal and written communication are a particular challenge. It is like learning a foreign language without the benefit of a dictionary, because there are multiple potential definitions. The terminology makes it even harder to develop a quick understanding of key weapons, surveillance systems and so-called platforms (tanks, planes and ships); especially when some, like the F-35 (AKA Lightning II or Joint Strike Fighter; not to be confused with the Eurofighter), have multiple names, none of which offer any clue as to whether they sail or have wings. As to which government ordered what kit; when the contract was originally signed; and when the goods are finally supposed to be delivered, only those who have been immersed in the subject for some time have any hope of keeping up.

Williamson's political inexperience made it all much more difficult. In his first few weeks in the job, he was all over the media, highlighting threats to national security and proactively making the case for defence.[1] To those who had become disillusioned by the reluctance of his predecessor Sir Michael Fallon to upset Treasury and Cabinet colleagues with public demands for more money, it was a refreshing change. Initially, the small but energetic group of Conservative MPs for whom defence is a priority were cautiously optimistic about the influence he might have, particularly on 10 Downing Street. After a while, however, even those eager to see him succeed became nervous about the way he was courting the media, fearing it would backfire. Less generous colleagues muttered that he was more interested in becoming Prime Minister than in the defence of the realm.[2] A round-robin email in spring 2018, announcing his availability for photo opportunities with fellow Tory MPs, was a source of some derision among fellow MPs. It elicited a snooty response from Tory grandee Sir Nicholas Soames, who replied to the effect that he too was available for pictures in his House of Commons office should the Secretary of State wish.[3] Meanwhile, an unfortunate choice of words directed at the Kremlin following the Skripal affair, that 'Russia should go away and shut up', was much parodied,[4] fuelling whispers that he was 'not up to the job'.[5] The Defence Secretary was so bruised by this episode that he summarily 'disinvited' broadcast journalists from accompanying him on an official visit to British troops in Estonia, fearing more hostile media coverage. In his first few weeks in his job, the gangly Defence Secretary had got away with an embarrassing episode involving a fall from a tank on Salisbury Plain, fortunately not captured on camera. Invited by army officers to inspect the vehicle, he had gamely clambered aboard, but somehow lost his footing and tumbled off. Those present spared his blushes. Meanwhile, a visit to Sandhurst where officer cadets were so immaculately turned out they could see their own reflections in their buttons was privately dubbed '#amateurhour' by some of those present after the Secretary of State arrived with a blob of what appeared to be shaving foam on his chin.[6]

Perhaps Williamson was reflecting on these troubles as he lolloped into Admiralty House on Whitehall for the Royal Navy's annual board meeting in March 2018. How much time he had found to prepare for the dull deliberations over the budget is unclear. According to a source at the meeting, there were some raised eyebrows round the table over his understanding of some aspects of the agenda. His novel take on plans for the Type 26 warship particularly startled the old sea salts.

These new ships will be the backbone of the Royal Navy, and have been in the pipeline for years. A fortune has been ploughed into the design; binding contracts with industry were signed long ago; and construction of the hull of the first vessel, HMS *Glasgow*, has already begun. Without Type 26, there will be nothing to replace the navy's thirteen ageing Type 23 frigates in their anti-submarine role. In the MoD's endless struggle to find cash down the back of the sofa, however, nothing is assured, even if construction is under way.

'Why don't we just cancel them?' Williamson offered brightly.

The First Sea Lord blanched. If the minister was serious, by 2035, the navy would not have a single frigate, except the planned Type-31E, a much less capable vessel.

'Secretary of State,' the Admiral replied firmly, 'when you took office, you told me you wanted me to speak frankly to you. I am doing that now. We cannot cancel the Type 26.'[7]

In fairness to Williamson, it was far from the most radical proposed solution to the navy's ongoing financial problems. According to a highly distinguished former civil servant, during the fraught budget discussions immediately after the coalition came to power, a Treasury official casually suggested abolishing the navy altogether.

'At that point, the navy was already at such a low point that significant further reductions would have raised questions about its future viability,' according to the source.[8]

Fortunately, the idea met with the derision it deserved and the navy lived to fight another day. However, as Williamson's surprising intervention at the Royal Navy's annual board meeting suggests, what remains of the fleet is constantly under threat.

To those conscious of the UK's proud history and status as a maritime nation, its diminished capability is a deepening concern. Under Cromwell in 1650, it had 46 powerful 'ships of the line,'* supported by

---

* A sailing warship of the largest size, used in the line of battle.

twenty-six medium-sized but nevertheless powerful warships. Those ships swelled in number to 127 and forty-nine respectively by 1700, making it the strongest maritime force in the world and laying the foundations for the British Empire. At its peak in 1810, the navy boasted 152 ships of the line and 182 other significant fighting vessels, plus an array of smaller warships, bringing the total fleet to some 1,000 vessels.[9]

Successive governments have been chipping away at the fleet since the early 1980s, when the navy had fourteen destroyers and forty-six frigates.[10] Today, it has just nineteen of those warships, slightly more than European allies, except France, which has twenty-two[11] – a shadow of America's mighty fleet of ninety-six frigates, destroyers and cruisers and China's rapidly expanding fleet of eighty-two.[12] All three of the UK's amphibious ships – HMS *Ocean*,[13] HMS *Bulwark*, and HMS *Albion*[14] – have been decommissioned or have a question mark hanging over their future, while the submarine fleet is massively outnumbered by those of Russia and China.

Numbers can of course distort comparisons, with no consideration given to professionalism, geopolitical constraints and pressures, or quality of leadership. A better measure is whether the navy can at least reliably perform its basic functions, which sadly is no longer always the case. With critical manpower shortages;[15] a fleet of destroyers with notorious engine troubles;[16] and the financial burden of ambitious construction projects which won't produce operational ships for years, it struggles to carry out routine patrols, never mind counter potential threats.

In a damning report in 2016, the Defence Select Committee described this state of affairs as a 'dangerous and historic low'.[17]

The decline of the navy has been accompanied by remarkably little noise, perhaps because the service is short of political advocates. With the exception of International Development Secretary Penny Mordaunt (a Naval Reserve), barely any MPs or peers have a naval background. Few outside the defence committee regularly make the case for robust naval forces. As retired Rear Admiral Chris Parry puts it, Parliament has become 'sea blind' and fails to recognise that peace at sea does not keep itself. He recalls an MP telling him that it was good to see a naval officer visiting the Commons, as the army seemed to be there on an almost daily basis.[18]

The army is indeed well represented by politicians who were once officers or have served in the Reserves. Several are vocal champions of their former service, speaking out against cuts to personnel and equipment and finding opportunities to remind voters why it matters. Highly visible military campaigns in Iraq, Afghanistan, Libya and Syria have continually showcased what the army and RAF do, but while many naval personnel were involved in these missions, their role was not particularly broadcast to the electorate. Voters under the age of forty-five cannot remember the Falklands and struggle to envisage future battles at sea.

All this may be about to change, as the navy prepares to take possession of some spectacular new toys. The long-awaited arrival of two gleaming aircraft carriers will transform the fleet. If deployed imaginatively, they could herald the renaissance of the entire British armed forces.

The question is whether they will prove assets or liabilities.

GRAND DESIGNS

The tale of the two carriers is so extraordinary that it is hard to know where to begin. It involves pride and humiliation; power and profiteering; skulduggery and lies; but it is also a story of hope, as well as laudable political vision and ambition. It has been the source of so much political trauma, and is so pivotal to the state of the navy and wider armed forces today, that it is worth examining how it came about.

Back in 1998, when the project began under the Labour government, aircraft carriers were still the undisputed empresses of the sea. They played a key role in the Falklands, and would go on to be critical to the Allied operation in Afghanistan, providing a platform for airstrikes. No piece of military hardware was more emblematic of hard power. America's fleet of aircraft carriers has been projecting military might to the far corners of the globe since the Second World War.[19]

Fast-forward twenty years, and carriers are still magnificent assets for humanitarian, defensive or offensive operations. They are chunks of sovereign territory that can be positioned just about anywhere in the world. Very few countries can afford them, making them powerful international status symbols. Assuming they are not condemned to languish 'alongside', they signal that a nation is interested in what is going on overseas and willing to get involved. But as we shall see, the march of technology threatens their utility.

Labour originally envisaged two vessels weighing around 30,000 to 40,000 tonnes each.[20] They were designed to replace HMS *Invincible*, HMS *Illustrious* and HMS *Ark Royal*, the UK's ageing light aircraft carriers, which were going out of service.[21]

No sooner had the government given the go-ahead to the project, however, than the navy began pushing for something bigger and better. By 2003, the potential designs were double the original planned size.[22]

This metamorphosis was down to pork-barrel politics, heady idealism and a desire to please the US. For the then Chancellor, Gordon Brown, the appeal of building two huge ships was obvious: the project would create as many as 10,000 jobs, many of them in Scotland, including at the Rosyth dockyards bordering his constituency of Dunfermline East (now known as Kirkcaldy and Cowdenbeath).[23] With a majority of 15,063 he did not need to worry about his own seat,[24] but the project would cement Labour's stronghold north of the border and burnish his image as a future Prime Minister. The work generated by the carriers would become so vital to the British defence industry that at one point ministers deliberately strung out the timetable, at a cost of around £1.6 billion to taxpayers, to keep the shipyards in business.[25]

For Tony Blair, the attraction was different: the project symbolised how he saw the UK's place in the world. The carriers would show that this country was ready to commit hard power to geopolitics. For admirals, jubilation at having talked the government into the carrier project soon gave way to a lust for enhanced specifications. The then First Sea Lord Admiral Sir Alan West would later tell the Commons Defence Select Committee that the ships needed to be much bigger than originally proposed so they could support more intense military operations. He thought the navy and RAF would want to be able to conduct 'something like seventy-five sorties per day' over a five-day campaign from the carriers, 'or something like that.'[26]

Quite where he thought all these raids would be taking place ten to fifteen years down the line when the carriers finally materialised, nobody asked. The navy also wanted to ensure that whatever they ended up with would enable closer co-operation with the Americans. They told ministers that the US wanted the UK to develop a carrier that could 'mix and match' with American vessels.

'I have talked with the CNO [Chief of Naval Operations] in America. He is very keen for us to get these because he sees us slotting in with his carrier groups. For example, in Afghanistan last year they had to call on the French to bail them out with their carrier,' Lord West told MPs on the Defence Select Committee at the time.[27] In a policy that would later acquire great significance, the navy wanted to keep its options open regarding the type of plane that could be used from the platform, meaning the new ships had to be long enough to support aircraft that took off and landed using a catapult and arrestor system (a bit like a rubber band, that 'pings' the planes into the air and traps them into position as they land), as well as aircraft that took off in a more conventional fashion.

And so it was that, in 2007, Labour confirmed orders for the largest ships ever operated by the Royal Navy.[28] They would initially be designed for jump jets (so-called 'short take off and vertical landing' or 'STOVL') rather than the more sophisticated 'cats and traps'. This was the cheaper option and involved F-35B Harrier-style planes from America's Joint Strike Fighter programme. The government indicated that it would buy up to 138 of these jets.[29]

By the time Labour left office, the project was in crisis. Some believed it should be abandoned altogether, though there was a recognition that the navy's artful decision to name the ships after the monarch and heir to the throne made such a move even less politically palatable. The coalition spent months exploring all options, including cancelling one of the ships. Cameron was dismayed to discover that getting out of the contract would be more expensive than pressing ahead.[30] The government was stuck.

Instead, the new Prime Minister decided to soup up one of the carriers, fitting it with the more sophisticated take-off and landing system, and relegate the other to what he called 'extended readiness' – a euphemism for mothballing. Sooner or later, he conceded, it 'might' be sold off.[31]

Announcing the decision in the 2010 Strategic Defence and Security Review, the Prime Minister laid the blame for this mess squarely on his predecessors.

'There's only one thing worse than spending money you don't have. And that's buying the wrong things with it – and doing so in the wrong way. The carriers they ordered are unable to work effectively with our key defence partners, the United States or France,' he said, adding that carriers using jump jets were 'less capable'.[32]

It was an intervention he would come to regret. In the months that followed, it became increasingly clear that changing the design would be far more expensive than anticipated and risked giving the consortium of defence companies building the ships an excuse for other price hikes. The Chief of the Defence Staff, General Sir David Richards, was becoming increasingly uneasy.

According to an MoD source:

David Richards thought changing to cats and traps was insane. His view was that it would have to be changed back. However, he wasn't under any illusion about the politics. Cameron had stood up in the Commons and pissed from a great height on what he depicted as the Labour Party's stupid decision to have jump-jet carriers. It wasn't going to be comfortable climbing down from that.[33]

The MoD had originally estimated the cost of conversion to cats and traps at £950 million. Technical problems with the F-35C were now pushing the bill towards the £2 billion mark.[34] The MoD was acutely aware of the discomfort a reversal would cause the Prime Minister.

Cameron had stood before MPs and personally taken command of what he called 'difficult decisions' about the carriers. It was going to be hugely embarrassing.

'We would not just be asking the government to do a U-turn. We would be asking the government to do a 360-degree *doughnut* in the middle of Whitehall, where the Prime Minister himself had stood up and criticised the original decision as part of his first U-turn. We'd be asking him to stand up and U-turn on his U-turn!' says a former MoD official who was involved in the debacle.

The situation was equally painful for Liam Fox, who had, he thought rightly, pushed the case for cats and traps. He knew it would raise serious questions over his judgement, and was furious with the navy, which had lobbied hard for the fancier take-off and landing system. Privately, he told friends they 'lied' to him about the likely costs of conversion. It was not Fox's problem for much longer, however. In October 2011, he was forced to resign from the Cabinet over his working relationship with his former flatmate and self-styled adviser Adam Werritty, admitting he had broken the ministerial code by allowing his friend to accompany him on multiple overseas trips.[35] It was left to Fox's successor, Philip Hammond, to sort out the mess. With the forensic attention to detail that would earn him the moniker 'Spreadsheet Phil', Hammond set about doing the maths. After an exhaustive review, and some lobbying by Richards, he agreed that conversion to cats and traps was no longer viable.

'I said that we must go back to the V/STOL version – we could not afford two cats and traps carriers and the cost was escalating daily,' Richards recalls. 'Hammond said to me, "Why are you the only person in this building telling me this?"

'I had one more conversation with Hammond where I got a bit more muscular, and he changed it. Cameron had to eat his words because the inexorable logic came through. We could already see it was having a hugely distorting effect, not only on defence but on the Royal Navy.'[36]

It was left to the Defence Secretary to tell an incredulous Commons that the MoD was reverting to the original plan. He admitted the U-turn on the U-turn would cost about £100 million.[37]

For the navy, there was one big consolation: they would get their two new ships. In another volte face, the government had decided both carriers could become operational after all. By 2020, Hammond promised, they would have their amazing new vessels.[38]

FISH AND SHIPS

The fiasco over cats and traps was mortifying for all concerned, but a bitter wrangle with the defence industry (largely suppressed at the time) over the price would be a source of longer-term pain.

The Ministry of Defence had originally estimated that the ships would cost £2.14 billion, a figure that proved hopelessly optimistic. As the specification became ever more ambitious, so the bill escalated, until before too long the projected price had almost doubled.[39] There was no price cap, so nobody knew where it would end.

A bizarre deal with the consortium of defence companies building the ships – known as the Aircraft Carrier Alliance – locked taxpayers into the vast majority of any cost overruns.[40] A battle between ministers and industry to change the terms of business came perilously close to ending, Russia-style, with one half-built carrier rotting in a dry dock.

Backed by Gordon Brown, the MoD signed an initial £3.9 billion contract with the ACA in 2008.[41] By 2010, taxpayers would meet 90 per cent of any costs over and above a £5.2 billion 'target price'.[42] For a Chancellor who prided himself on 'prudence', this was an extraordinarily reckless way to approach a project of this nature, giving the consortium very little incentive to keep the price down. When Labour lost power in 2010, it did not take the coalition long to work out the horrible mathematical reality: the final bill for the carriers could rocket to £8 billion before the ACA started making a loss.[43] It would have to be renegotiated.

MoD civil servants spent months attempting to extract concessions from the industry, to no avail. Simmering tensions between the two sides eventually boiled over at an excruciating dinner at the corporate headquarters of BAE Systems in London, where they met to thrash it out.[44]

It was summer 2011 and the MoD's 'ships team' had been invited to a presentation by the Aircraft Carrier Alliance. The ACA was feeling the heat, and hoped a convivial evening would get the department off its back. Members of the consortium aimed to convince the MoD they could develop the ships for around £5.2 billion.

As they tucked into fish suppers, the businessmen had good reason to be nervous: glowering at them across the salt and vinegar was the MoD's Chief of Defence Materiel, Sir Bernard Gray. Charged with wresting the spiralling cost of the carriers under control, the former investment banker and journalist turned Whitehall fixer had a formidable reputation for holding the defence industry to account. Over his long years as a civil servant and in the business world, he had developed a finely honed bullshit detector and was not known to take prisoners. To make matters worse, he was teetotal, so there was no question of plying him with drink.

According to an insider, Gray immediately made it clear he did not believe their figures, pointing out that they had already used up two thirds of their contingency funds welding steel for the first of the two ships, HMS *Queen Elizabeth*. They had yet to begin the more complicated phase of installing electronics.

'This thing will hit the wall!' he told them bluntly.[45]

For the next two hours, the ACA tried to bamboozle Gray and his officials with facts and figures, claiming the final bill was unlikely to exceed £5.4 billion, and could even hit the target price.

A lengthy PowerPoint presentation designed to hammer home the message did little to improve the mood of the MoD team. Gray was convinced defence companies knew the carriers would be far more expensive than they were admitting and was determined to smoke them out.

The atmosphere remained cordial enough until after coffee, when Gray finally snapped, challenging the industry to accept a fixed price. According to a source familiar with what happened, he turned to the industry representatives and told them he would write them a contract for £5.8 billion that very day.

'We'll do that contract right now. Because if you're so convinced you can do this for £5.4 billion, and maybe £5.2 billion; I'm giving you £400 million extra taxpayers' money!' he is said to have told them.

This was a bold move: in theory, Gray had no authority to make such an offer. However, he was confident he would get Hammond's backing.

The businessmen shifted uncomfortably in their seats, while Gray eyeballed them. Finally, one broke the silence, decrying the offer as 'juvenile'. The meeting broke up in acrimony.

The MoD was now certain the industry was trying to pull a fast one. In the days that followed, Gray stood his ground. The industry doggedly refused to come up with a figure, preferring to let taxpayers take the risk. Eventually, under relentless pressure, they suggested a fee of £7.4 billion – a full £2 billion more than the number they'd given over the fish and chips. Incensed, Gray rejected the offer outright.

It was just the start of a long war of attrition between the MoD and the ACA which came to a head in 2013, when the consortium finally suggested a £6.8 billion 'maximum price'. To Gray, this was proof of what he'd always suspected: they had known all along that the final bill would be far higher than their original suggestion of 'around £5.2 billion'.

According to the same source: 'Bernard was furious. He felt they had lied. Not only had they lied, but they also made the mistake of taking him for a fool. There was a lot of swearing.'[46]

Gray and Hammond met to decide what to do. The nuclear option was to fire the consortium and start again with a new team. Gray wanted the industry to know the MoD was not afraid to pull the plug, however dire the political consequences. Still furious, he told Hammond he was revving up the tanks for war.[47] Lawyers were called in to begin exploring how to break the contracts.

In truth, both Hammond and Gray knew this was a desperate proposition. Taxpayers would be left with half a ship languishing in Babcock's dry dock. In theory, it could be handed to another consortium to complete, but extracting it from the yard would be a nightmare. Visions of an abandoned vessel carrying the monarch's name splashed across newspaper front pages were not appealing.

Plan B was to meet the industry half way. Unbeknown to the industry, the MoD had already set aside £6.2 billion as a contingency. Hammond thought they could find another £300 million somewhere. It was agreed to offer the ACA £6.5 billion.

'Bernard phoned the Alliance and said, "Here's the thing. We'll split the difference. £6.5 billion." He was about to go on holiday for three weeks and told them they would need to talk about it among themselves while he was away, and come back to him with an answer in September,' according to an MoD source.

Returning from his break, Gray was astounded to find a letter on his desk that, in the words of one MoD insider, 'just said "No."'

'Basically, it said, "Dear Bernard. Piss off." We were amazed. Were they *insane*? Tactically, it was awful, from their point of view.'

There was now a Mexican stand-off. For the MoD, there was no easy way out. They decided not to reply to the letter, and let the ACA sweat it out. Meanwhile, they would make sure the industry knew that lawyers were on the case.

The ruse worked: a few weeks later, the ACA sheepishly returned to the negotiating table. The MoD now had the upper hand. More than two years after the row began, a fixed price of £6.2 billion was finally agreed. The ACA's 'No' letter had cost them a cool £300 million.

The bill for construction and timetable for delivery of the ships was finally fixed. By 2023, the UK would be proud owners of two gleaming carriers, built to last fifty years.[48]

Running them would cost £130 million a year.[49] Attention began to turn to how they should be used.

THE HIGH SEAS

No hair was out of place, no jaw at the wrong angle, as 12,000 Chinese military personnel goose-stepped their way through Tiananmen Square.[50] It was China's 2015 Victory Parade, and the attention to detail was meticulous, from the operation to make the sky a clearer shade of blue by shutting factories and banning barbecues; to the fixed smiles the all-female unit had practised by gripping chopsticks between their teeth. Across China, normal television schedules were suspended to make way for wall-to-wall coverage of a display by the world's largest military marking the 70th anniversary of the end of the Second World War in Asia.

With 2.3 million personnel, the People's Liberation Army had no trouble filling the stage.[51] Resplendent in a Mao suit, President Xi Jinping stood in the sunroof of a Chinese-made Red Flag limousine, inspecting the rigid formations with a poker face.

'Greetings, comrades!' he shouted.

'Greetings, chief,' chorused the military personnel.

'Comrades, you've worked hard!' he declared.

'Serve the people,' they replied.

Overhead, dozens of military helicopters formed the number 70 while tanks and trucks showcasing China's latest weaponry trundled through the square. A huge drone, remarkably similar to *Predator*, used by the CIA to hunt and kill terrorists, attracted gasps of admiration from spectators. Then came the planes, roaring across the old city, rattling buildings and windows. In a final flourish, 70,000 doves were released, a nod to the regime's spin that the event was really all about peace.[52]

The parade was scrutinised by defence chiefs around the world. In the UK, one exhibit was of particular interest to military figures: a fearsome anti-ship missile. For years, its development had been shrouded in secrecy. Finally, it was being unveiled in public.

Called Dongfeng-21D, the ballistic missile is said to be able to close in on its target at ten times the speed of sound, making it almost impossible to intercept. China can make about 1,200 units for the price of a single aircraft carrier, meaning the missiles could easily overwhelm mechanisms put in place to neutralise their effect. The weapon has become known as a 'carrier killer'[53] – and the fear is that it will consign carriers to history, just as aircraft from aircraft carriers themselves did to battleships with Japan's 1941 attack on Pearl Harbor.

There is nothing new about the march of technology rendering so-called 'exquisite platforms' obsolete. Once upon a time, the main battle tank saw off the horse. Later, tanks became much easier to target thanks to aerial surveillance and reconnaissance techniques, making them highly vulnerable in some settings. Now, high-precision long-range missiles are shifting the economies and practicalities of blowing up big bits of military kit in favour of the aggressor. Militaries determined to stay ahead of the game must continually find new ways to offset advantages accrued by the enemy.

For the West, the first major 'offset' was nuclear weapons. When the Russians acquired these too, the second offset involved computers, electronics and satellites. High-end technology allowed the US and the UK to re-establish military dominance for several decades. It worked very well until recently, when potential adversaries caught up, developing munitions like Dongfeng that threaten to make a nonsense of our biggest defence investments.

Carriers as far as 2,000 km from the enemy could be vulnerable in future, according to General Sir David Richards:

> The Chinese and others – they will develop these technologies. So, you've got to keep further away, keep more ships to protect it, so ironically [it] can't use the air power which it is all about. It is a bizarre development. We did anticipate it, but not that it would happen quite so quickly.

In typically provocative language, Russia has openly taunted the UK that the carriers are now just very large sitting ducks.[54]

If this is really the case, it begs the question why Russia and China are investing in carriers themselves. The answer is that carriers do not have to enter conflict zones to be useful. Indeed, Rear Admiral Chris Parry points out that US naval carriers have never been put directly in harm's way.

'Like nuclear-powered ballistic missile submarines, if you have to use them in anger, you have probably failed,' he says. 'Carriers spend most of their time in service keeping the peace, so that they will not have to fight close-up, as in the Falklands, when the two British carriers stayed well to the east of the combat zone and provided aircraft at range to support combat air patrol and land attack missions.'[55]

Privately, ministers admit HMS *Queen Elizabeth* and HMS *Prince of Wales* will have to be kept a long way from trouble. Indeed, Sir Mark Sedwill, the National Security Adviser, has said that Britain's new aircraft carriers will not be sent into a conflict zone unless they are escorted by Allied (most likely American) aircraft and warships.[56] This effectively undermines Britain's ability to undertake a national operation in its own interests at a time and place of strategic choice and limits the sovereign use of the military instrument of power. It implies that the Royal Navy is no longer capable of dealing with high-end threats on its own, especially in dealing with the highly sophisticated and numerous weapons systems associated with what has come to be known as 'Anti-Access Area Denial' or 'A2AD'.

In the past, creating an A2AD zone was tricky. New weapons-detection systems have made it much easier. For aircraft carriers, the consequence is what one defence expert calls the 'Dalek problem'. If a carrier has to be kept a long way back from a coastline, because it is vulnerable to Dongfeng or some other nasty weapon, combat aircraft may have to fly such a long distance to drop munitions that they could run out of fuel during the mission. Positioning a tanker somewhere nearer the coast to allow the jet to refuel simply creates a new and much closer target for the enemy. It means hostile forces only have to down the tanker to doom the fighter jets as well. In a contested space, this dramatically reduces the ability of our armed forces to show up on a big ship, at a time and place of their choosing, and launch effective bombing sorties.

As the defence expert puts it: 'You might have an extremely effective weapons system called a Dalek, but when it gets to a set of stairs, if it can't get up the stairs, no matter how good it is at other stuff, it's got a problem.'[57]

These challenges didn't exist back in the late 1990s when the carriers were conceived. Today, it is hard to find anyone either within the defence industry or government who would commission two ships exactly like HMS *Queen Elizabeth* and HMS *Prince of Wales* if they had their time again. There is a widespread acknowledgement that they are far bigger than necessary and that several smaller platforms would have been better, leaving more resources for smaller, more lethal destroyers and frigates.

Professor Gwythian Prins, a senior MoD adviser and member of the Chief of the Defence Staff's Strategic Advisory Panel, believes the entire programme was a 'serially mismanaged decision from the very beginning'.

'Why do we have these things? Because the government of the day wanted large pieces of metal to be built in Labour constituencies in Scotland. They didn't care what they were, as long as they were big.'[58]

A senior American naval source, now retired, is even more damning:

'In short, the carriers lack active defence capability; lack passive defence capability; and must operate relatively close to shore to generate deep strike capability, which in any case will be very limited. Never has a country spent more to achieve less in modern history!' he says.

> I understand the logic behind the concept, as a signal of the UK's role in world power, but no one accounted for the necessary escorts; the aircraft, including AWACS [Airborne Warning and Control System] and buddy tankers; or the required replenishment ships; or the number of personnel. It was like a child's wish list for Christmas, more often than not devoid of reasonableness.[59]

Given the scale of taxpayer investment, however, most of this is too painful for ministers and defence chiefs to admit. The majority remain genuinely proud of being in the 'carrier club', and still believe these types of platforms have both symbolic and practical value. The focus now is on making the best of it. The MoD's vision for the way they should operate is called 'carrier strike'. The thinking is that if the carriers are to be cost-effective for most of their working lives, they need to be operated as multi-purpose platforms, able to project the fighting power of all three services in support of UK interests around the world.[60] This project is so ambitious that it will become a focal point for much of the armed forces. In operations and conflict, military planners will have to take into account the way in which the carriers; their fighter jets and helicopters; their associated group of submarines, frigates and destroyers; and the collective ISTAR (intelligence, surveillance, target acquisition and reconnaissance) capabilities of all these platforms will work together to create maximum effect.[61]

PROPOSED COMPONENTS OF UK CARRIER GROUP

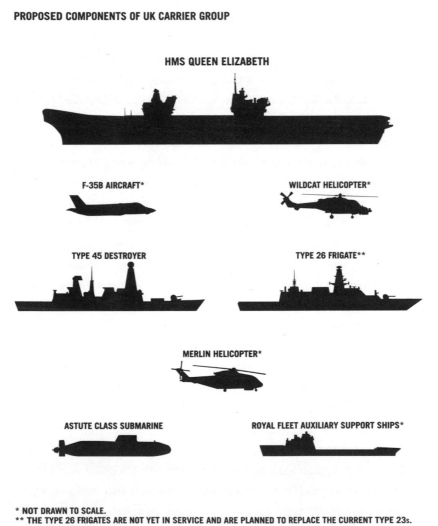

HMS QUEEN ELIZABETH

F-35B AIRCRAFT*

WILDCAT HELICOPTER*

TYPE 45 DESTROYER

TYPE 26 FRIGATE**

MERLIN HELICOPTER*

ASTUTE CLASS SUBMARINE

ROYAL FLEET AUXILIARY SUPPORT SHIPS*

* NOT DRAWN TO SCALE.
** THE TYPE 26 FRIGATES ARE NOT YET IN SERVICE AND ARE PLANNED TO REPLACE THE CURRENT TYPE 23s.

ESCORTING HMS *QUEEN ELIZABETH*/HMS *PRINCE OF WALES* WILL REQUIRE MUCH OF THE NAVAL FLEET.

For the navy, it will require a new way of thinking. The carrier group will represent almost a third (by tonnage) of the naval fleet, and soak up a fifth of naval personnel.[62] Instead of deploying single ships on operations, as they are used to doing, the navy will have to work as a group.

Given the potential vulnerability of the carriers themselves, some defence analysts believe the escort ships – as opposed to the carriers themselves – should become the focus of the so-called strike. Professor Peter Roberts, Director of Military Sciences at the Royal United Services Institute, says:

> The Royal Navy is thinking about the carriers being the centre of a carrier strike group and the most important piece. They [assume] the carrier is what needs to get within striking distance of the enemy, in order to have an impact. I think we're at a stage where we need to re-think that, and instead, think about the individual ships that you push forward being the front end that's facing the enemy, supported by aircraft from the carrier. The carrier itself then isn't the critical part. It isn't the focus for the military effort.[63]

Figuring all this out will take time, but there are encouraging signs that the project is now coming together. After much public derision about carriers without any planes (video footage of naval officers larking around with a remote-controlled toy helicopter on an empty deck didn't help), the RAF has finally taken possession of the first set of F-35B fighter jets.[64] By 2020, the MoD hopes all the various moving parts will fall into place, with the ships; the jets (known as the Lightning II programme); and a helicopter-borne radar system called *Crowsnest*[65] working in perfect harmony, finally transforming 'carrier strike' from concept to a real-life capability.[66]

However, many question marks remain. Officially, the project is 'on time and on budget', but the National Audit Office has warned that there are not enough people to fill specialist jobs and important parts of the plan are still unfunded.[67] The MoD has yet to specify what the carrier group will comprise in terms of ships and aircraft.

There remains a serious concern over whether there will be enough destroyers and frigates to keep the carriers safe, especially in view of disastrous technical failures involving the navy's Type 45 fleet.[68] All six ships are now undergoing a major refit to what the National Audit Office diplomatically calls a 'taut' timetable.[69] The MoD admits only a limited number will be ready to support the *Queen Elizabeth*'s first deployment. There are further question marks over *Crowsnest*, a radar and air command and control system which is designed to be fitted to existing Merlin helicopters. Though it is a modest part of the overall carrier strike budget (£0.3 billion relative to £12 billion on the carriers and fighter jets),[70] it is critical to providing the group with the information it needs to be effective. The fear is that there are simply not enough helicopters for the job.

All this has led Sir Michael Fallon to a controversial conclusion: our new symbols of national pride should be shared with other countries. Given the costs of the carrier, and the fact that other ships must guard it, it may be better as an 'allied carrier', he believes.

Former First Sea Lord Admiral Sir George Zambellas thinks that both ships will eventually be adapted for unmanned jets. He is still confident they will prove excellent value for money. 'The carriers are many things, from strategic assets to flexible sovereign territories, to mobile airfields,' he says.

> I don't expect the F-35s to be the only highly capable aircraft flying off them. Even with price rises invoked by governmental delays to the programme, and allowing for technical differences, the UK carriers are about a quarter to a third of the cost of an American carrier and, when in a few years it becomes routine to launch waves of unmanned aircraft, we'll think they've been a fantastic price. And fantastic value.[71]

Professor Peter Roberts warns the worst outcome would be to condemn either of the two ships to languishing in port.

> We are talking about these things as totemic symbols of British power. If you are alongside, you are losing capability; wasting your money. The

current way the carriers are planned is that they will go alongside, to do cocktail parties and influence. That's not the best way a carrier does influence. You bring the politician; you bring the leader out. And when you bring them out, you bring them to a deck that is flying off jets; loaded with bombs, and then recovering them. *That* is a very potent symbol of what you can do.

'A carrier alongside just looks like a big ship,' he says.[72] That is unlikely to happen on Williamson's watch: he too is adamant that the carriers must be pressed into service.

Soon, voters will have a better idea of whether all the woe was worth it.

HALF MAST

ATHENIANS

I n 483 BC, the Athenians discovered a rich vein of silver near the sea port of Laurium. Politicians offered the local population a choice between spending the proceeds on a fleet of 200 triremes (ships) or sharing the spoils, like a tax rebate.[1] One might have expected people to choose cash over national strategic assets, but that wasn't what happened. A popular general called Themistocles persuaded voters to choose ships, just in time to defeat Persia, the superpower of the day.[2] The revitalised fleet became the basis of the Athenian seaborne empire.

Today, head-on battles between rival navies are unlikely: the world's most powerful maritime powers also have nuclear weapons, which will probably prevent such an escalation. However, the threat of local and regional naval conflict is rising – and for a long while, British governments have had nobody like Themistocles.

Sea power provides the ability to control access to food, energy, water and raw materials, and to trade manufactured and other goods, without which no country can support economic growth and prosperity. Nations do not need to own these resources; but they do need to be able to buy materials at a reasonable price; use or add value to the material; and transport it, as well as their own goods, to other markets. Thus, sea-trade routes are vital strategic interests. Countries that depend on access to markets by sea need to be able to protect maritime highways in case the routes are restricted or blocked, and nobody else is willing to help.

In his book on the importance of maritime power in the twenty-first century, Rear Admiral Chris Parry explains why the British armed forces should be investing in more ships and submarines.

He describes the sea as a 'watery wide web' – a vast, largely ungoverned space which belongs to everybody and nobody and connects us to the rest of the world. Today, anyone could set sail from Dover, Portsmouth or the Outer Hebrides to any of the 150 or so countries with a coast, without needing anyone's approval or licence.[3] The open architecture of the sea underpins global trade and is vital to preserving our way of life. On a day-to-day basis, voters have no reason to think about it – it is simply taken for granted. If it were taken away, however, the economic impact would soon be felt.

If it were just about trade, the Merchant Navy (commercial ships) could do a lot to look after itself. However, freedom of navigation is hugely important to the armed forces, making it possible to dispatch warships anywhere. Vessels can set sail without upsetting anyone or committing to doing anything; drop anchor somewhere strategic; and stay as long as they like. No offence is taken if they simply withdraw. As Parry points out, this is much less aggressive or revealing about intentions than sending fighter jets or army formations.[4]

Sensing that the historic 'gentleman's agreement' on freedom of navigation might not be sustainable, in the 1980s, the United Nations put it in writing, defining the extent to which anyone can claim ownership of parts of the sea. Under the United Nations Convention on the Law of the Sea (UNCLOS), countries have 'territorial' rights extending twelve nautical miles (22 km) from the coast, or to a median line where the territorial seas of two countries are less than twenty-four nautical miles apart. Within twelve nautical miles, foreign ships are allowed innocent passage, but unless they have permission, they cannot conduct military operations in these waters.[5] If they're within twenty-four nautical miles (44 km) of shore, they are subject to the law of the state.[6]

Out to 200 nautical miles (370 km) from a coast, or, again, to a median line where two countries are less than 400 nautical miles apart, states have an 'Exclusive Economic Zone' (EEZ) defined by UNCLOS.[7] Within its EEZ, a state has exclusive rights to the exploitation and use of rights to the resources of seabed and the water column, as well as proprietorial rights relating to continental shelves, islands and rocks. However, states may not limit freedom of navigation for foreign ships, nor the full range of operations by warships. Outside these zones, almost everything else is categorised as the 'high seas', upon which anyone can sail, as long as they don't stop others from going about their lawful business.[8]

WHO OWNS THE SEA?

| INLAND WATERS | TERRITORIAL SEA | EXCLUSIVE ECONOMIC ZONE | HIGH SEAS |

THE FIVE MAIN ZONES ESTABLISHED BY THE UN CONVENTION ON THE LAW OF THE SEA (UNCLOS). SOME REGIMES ARE IGNORING THESE RULES AND TRYING TO PREVENT FREEDOM OF NAVIGATION.

These rules are now being tested as never before. In a scramble for sovereign control over extensive stretches of water as extensions of exclusive state power; and in competition for underwater resources, whether fish; oil and gas deposits; seabed minerals; or places to construct wind, wave and tidal power facilities, all states are starting to encroach on what has traditionally been shared space. As governments become greedier, hungrier, more ambitious and less fearful of repercussions, they will be increasingly tempted to push their luck and attempt to colonise and (in Chris Parry's words) 'territorialise water'. A range of (largely spurious) excuses is likely to be used to deny foreign vessels freedom of passage, from environmental protection to historical claims.

CHINA'S GREAT SEA GRAB IN THE SOUTH CHINA SEAS

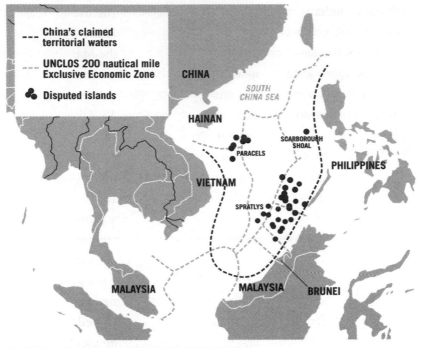

THE CHINESE REGIME IS ATTEMPTING TO APPROPRIATE STRETCHES
OF THESE WATERS, BREACHING INTERNATIONAL RULES.

Tensions between those who can control parts of the sea and those who
want to defend the existing arrangements are already intensifying. As
we have seen, the behaviour of the Chinese authorities is a case in point
and shows how things might come to blows. The regime has produced a
series of maps showing a tongue-shaped line enclosing most of the East
China and South China Seas. A variously so-called nine-, ten- or elev-
en-dash line, claimed as China's territorial seas (with the associated full
sovereign rights) and extending 1,500 nautical miles from China's coast,
rides roughshod over the exclusive economic zones of Japan, Taiwan,
Malaysia, the Philippines and Vietnam.[9] As part of their great sea grab,
the regime is busily reclaiming land on top of rocks and outcrops (in
the Spratly and the Paracel Groups) and presenting them as 'islands' in
a bid to confer on them territorial seas and EEZ rights.[10] The operation
is being underpinned by permanent expressions of hard power, such

as the construction of military installations, weapons stores and even full-length military runways on these artificial structures.[11] A string of armed enforcement agencies, such as China Marine Surveillance; China Fisheries Law Enforcement Command; and the Maritime Safety Administration, keep a threatening and coercive watch on comings and goings by foreign vessels and see off perceived interlopers, most of whom are operating in their country's legitimate EEZ.[12] This cavalier approach to freedom of navigation is a source of alarm in neighbouring countries and mounting concern to the US, which staunchly maintains its freedom to patrol these seas by conducting freedom of navigation transits by warships in defiance of China's pretensions.

Russia is up to the same sort of tricks. In a highly provocative stunt in 2007, the Kremlin attempted to stake a claim to billions of pounds worth of oil and gas by planting a one-metre-high Russian flag on an underwater ridge two and a half miles beneath the sea surface at the North Pole. The Kremlin claims this feature is connected to Russia's continental shelf. The regime's behaviour was condemned by the other four Arctic Council members (the US, Canada, Denmark and Norway) and by the Canadians specifically as 'fifteenth-century colonialism', as they insist that that part of the sea belongs to them.[13]

In April 2014, Putin passed an ominous new law allowing Russian energy companies to establish armed response forces to deal with anyone they don't like. The new legislation is ostensibly designed to protect infrastructure like platforms and pipelines from terrorists. It doesn't take a genius to work out how else these unaccountable militias could be used. The *Rossiyskaya Gazeta*, a Russian state newspaper, predicted it would trigger a huge expansion in private security companies with sophisticated weapons and quasi legal powers of enforcement.[14]

For all these reasons, sea power seems more important than ever. Yet the Royal Navy is short of sailors – especially in key disciplines like engineering and other technical trades – and ships.[15] According to the latest figures, the service, which should stand at 30,450 regulars, is almost 4 per cent below strength.[16] It has been staggering along without enough people since 2011. The knock-on effects are stark: every week, defence ministers receive a gloomy report detailing ships confined to port because of insufficient personnel. This bleak picture makes moves to cut some of the Royal Navy's most capable human resources – the Royal Marines – even stranger.

AMPHIBIANS

By and large, backbench MPs are too preoccupied by day-to-day problems to worry about defence strategy, which suits governments very well. It means potentially controversial measures can often be slipped through without too much fuss. Now and again, however, something touches a nerve, which is what happened in 2017 when reports emerged that the Ministry of Defence was secretly considering cutting the Marines.

The Royal Navy's amphibious troops are widely regarded as one of the world's elite commando forces, ready and able to deploy anywhere by land, sea or air. For centuries they have proven a formidable all-weather, all-terrain fighting force. Their role in the Falklands is the stuff of legends. As one of the most prestigious components of the armed forces, they seem an unlikely target for cuts, which is why there was widespread surprise and dismay. Before ministers had time to stutter that it was only an idea, they were being walloped from all sides. Something had caught the public imagination: tens of thousands of voters signed petitions; the Defence Select Committee launched an urgent inquiry; and Defence Secretary Sir Michael Fallon, on whose watch the idea was mooted, came under mounting pressure.

Fallon was conflicted. In the run-up to the 2015 general election, the Tories had promised that defence spending would not fall below NATO's recommended minimum level of 2 per cent of GDP if they won.[17] Following their surprise victory, Cameron had ordered a new defence review, designed to mark a line in the sand after the savage cuts of the coalition years. He wanted to show how a proper Tory government approached defence, representing a return to the good old days when Conservatives spent more than other parties on national security. Haunted by the misery and mayhem of the 2010 review, this time defence chiefs were determined to be very clear about what they wanted. Chief of the Defence Staff General Sir Nick Houghton was an accomplished 'Whitehall Warrior', and produced a crystal-clear shopping list for all three services. It included nine US-made P-8 Poseidon planes; funding to ensure both aircraft carriers could be fully used; two squadrons of twenty-four F-35Bs for carrier operations; twenty new US-made Protector drones; accelerating the purchase of fifty upgrade Apache helicopter gunships; and hundreds of new troop carriers for the army.[18] In what looked like a stunning victory for the armed forces, Cameron agreed to it all. The trouble was that the Treasury was not willing to pick up the entire bill for the new hardware, leaving the MoD to fund many of the projects via the usual loosely defined and characteristically overly optimistic 'efficiency savings'. The amount of extra money the department had to find was far greater than the £24.4 billion required to buy the hardware itself, because of the cost of new bases, infrastructure, hangars and training.[19]

By autumn 2016, Fallon had belatedly realised that the ambitions of the 2015 review were hopelessly out of kilter with the money available. As we have seen, his appeals to No. 10 and the Treasury for an emergency bailout to tide the department over for at least two years were rebuffed. Confronting the grim reality of delivering Brexit with a small parliamentary majority, Cameron's successor Theresa May had other things on her mind.

Fallon now had no choice but to cut some services to fund others. In summer 2017, the National Security Council formalised the process. Describing it as another Strategic Defence and Security Review so soon after the last one would have been too embarrassing, so it was given a different name (the 'National Security Capability Review') and billed as a 'refresh' of the 2015 review. Brexit – which had not been adequately factored into the calculations by a Cabinet expecting to Remain – provided a convenient excuse. (As we have seen, contributing to this exercise was Gavin Williamson's first big challenge on his sudden appointment.)

The cuts under consideration were drastic: up to 14,000 members of the armed forces, the majority (11,000) from the army, would be axed.[20]

But it was the suggestion that as many as 2,000 Royal Marines – almost a third of the total force of 6,580 – could be axed, and the UK's two amphibious assault ships, HMS *Bulwark* and HMS *Albion*, could be retired, that attracted most public attention.[21] It would all but demolish amphibious capability.

Not everyone thought it was completely mad. Fallon had been influenced by some defence experts who argue that the UK no longer needs to be able to mount D-Day style landings. A senior defence industry figure who discussed it informally with the Secretary of State made an impassioned case that the ability to storm beaches is redundant in the modern battlespace. He argued that high-precision tactical missiles now make a nonsense of beach landings.

'An amphibious ship approaching a beach is slow-moving – it's a very easy target to pick off. Even if you get your Royal Marines to the beach, they'll be ceremoniously mown down,' he told Fallon, adding that if a beach wasn't contested, Marines might as well arrive on a commercial aircraft and 'land at the local airport'.

The Defence Secretary could see his point. He was also weary of the howls of protest from all three services whenever their own capabilities were under threat. He felt that it was up to the navy, not politicians, to decide how many Marines were required.

However, other countries were busy *investing* in amphibious capabilities. Since the beginning of human conflict, man has reached opponents by sea. Most countries have vast coastlines, offering scope for deception to avoid opposed landings. Amid a mounting backlash, critics questioned the wisdom of jettisoning the UK's ability to project force across the world by the most logical and sustainable means available. Some also pointed out that amphibious shipping is essential for logistical support and landing conventional equipment: a helicopter cannot carry a tank. The potential knock-on effect on the Special Boat Service was another serious concern. The navy's elite Special Forces unit is primarily drawn from the Marines. There were fears that reducing the talent pool for recruitment could result in lower standards.[22]

A public petition attracted almost 30,000 signatures, some 25,000 more than other petitions on military matters to date.[23] When the defence committee's report came, the conclusions were damning. Published in February 2018, it described the proposed cuts as a 'short-sighted, militarily illiterate manoeuvre totally at odds with strategic reality'.

'Given the disproportionate contribution the Royal Marines make to Defence ... the country's security would be significantly undermined ... Wider global trends and the overall direction of UK foreign policy all point to the absolute necessity of retaining a meaningful amphibious capability that can project power far from its home base ... virtually every other international defence power is investing in them,' it thundered.[24]

The report stopped short of attacking Fallon personally. In a highly pointed section, however, MPs on the committee made clear they were deeply unimpressed by his line that it was up to defence chiefs to decide such matters.[25] As we shall see, the reality is that the size of the UK armed forces is primarily determined by funds allocated by politicians, not assessments of the threat by defence and intelligence experts.

The issue was unresolved when Williamson took over from Fallon at the end of 2017. The new Defence Secretary was instinctively uncomfortable about pressing ahead. Cuts to the Marines were not ruled out, but if they happened, they would be on a smaller scale. The two amphibious ships would be saved.

THE PERISHER

Submarines are some of our most powerful defence assets. They are commanded by men with a reputation as the best in the world at their jobs. They pass through the armed forces' ultimate trial by fire to get there: an infamous command course known as 'the Perisher'. The name is a reference to the proportion of candidates that fail and can never return to submarine service.

Since submarine command training was formalised in 1917 and the first set of students graduated from the 'Periscope School' aboard HMS *Thames* at Portsmouth, some 1,200 prospective commanding officers have completed the training. Allies including the United States,

Canada, Australia, Denmark, Germany, Greece, Norway, Poland, Sweden, France, the Netherlands, Portugal and Israel have all sent students on the course, in the hope that their own submarine commanders will meet the standards the UK demands.

Under the stewardship of coaches known as 'Teachers', over the past 100 years, Perisher has endured by evolving to take account of developments in equipment, technology, weaponry and tactics as well as the introduction of new classes of submarines with increased speed, mobility, endurance and stealth. For eighty years it was conducted in diesel electric submarines. Today, it takes place on nuclear-powered boats based on the Clyde and in exercise areas around Scapa Flow in the Orkneys and around the coast of Scotland.

Submarines play a vital role in UK defence and security. In addition to keeping the nuclear deterrent on permanent patrol, the service is responsible for launching Cruise missile attacks; tracking what potential adversaries, especially the Russians, are up to underwater; launching boats off enemy shores to soak up intelligence; and covertly deploying the Special Boat Service.[26]

For Perisher candidates, sea training starts with a gruelling series of tests designed to assess critical thinking and physical and mental resilience. They must demonstrate ability in torpedo firing, dodging ships and surveillance, often while sleep-deprived. A different skillset is required to earn the respect and goodwill of the crew, who keep a secret and uncannily accurate book on who they think will pass. The course lasts for months, but old hands can often spot failures within the first twenty-four hours. Rear Admiral Roger Lane-Nott, now retired, who passed the Perisher in 1974, says:

> Usually the ship's company can tell you on day one who has got it and who hasn't. We had a nice Norwegian on my course who couldn't get his head around the safety aspects – getting too close to ships – and knowing when to go deep. We could tell right away. It was sad because he was a lovely chap and a good submariner but [he] wasn't capable of grasping one of the crucial aspects of submarine safety. In all, I lost three of six out of my cohort.[27]

Admiral Sir John Woodward, quoted in a colourful newspaper article about the Perisher, describes the scale of the challenge for young recruits trying to familiarise themselves with the seascape. The former Commander of the UK's naval taskforce in the Falklands War says:

> Imagine sticking your head out of a manhole in Piccadilly Circus, taking one quick, swivelling look round, ducking back down into the sewer and then trying to remember everything that you had seen. The idea is to generate sufficiently accurate recall and timing to avoid a double-decker bus running over your head next time you pop up through the manhole.[28]

The point of all this, says Lane-Nott, is:

> getting the brain fully engaged in what you are doing. Planning all the time. Where do I look at next? What is my nearest danger? And being ready to change course at any moment. You've got to constantly change, and you need the ability to train your mind to be able to do that.

Towards the end of the course, candidates come ashore for their final challenge, a two-week underwater ordeal designed to bring together all their new skills. They plan to drop off Special Forces; lay mines; undertake periscope photography; and various other exercises. Candidates take it in turn to act as duty captain in conditions of a simulated war. By this stage they are extremely tired and must show a continued ability to think straight. To push them to the limit of mental endurance, the Teacher and regular crew may use some bizarre tactics.

'I once had the chef burst in and [start] chasing the steward through the control room with a knife to distract me,' Lane-Nott recalls.

Those who triumph emerge elated, secure in the knowledge that they have joined a very elite club. Lane-Nott still has a vivid recollection of the moment he learned he had survived Perisher.

'Toby Frere – my Teacher – called me in and said: "Congratulations,

Captain: HMS *Walrus*," which was the submarine to which I was being assigned. It was the best thing I have heard in my entire life,' he says. 'Afterwards we'd scheduled a film night with our comrades to celebrate, but we were so exhausted we all fell asleep straight away in the chairs and the old 60mm roll ended up falling out of the projector, so I can't even remember what the film was.'[29]

That the Ministry of Defence has consistently resisted the temptation to find ways to reduce the £2 million-a-head cost of the course indicates just how important submarines remain to UK defence.

'It prepared me for when I did 110 days at sea during the Falklands War,' says Lane-Nott.

> There we never got more than two hours' solid sleep a night. I learned to become a great cat-napper, and to this day I can shut my eyes for twenty minutes and get four hours' worth of stamina. You develop the intuition to know if things are 'off'. When I was a Second Lieutenant I could never understand how the captain would come into the control room just as something was about to go wrong, such as the hydraulics about to burst. But you develop a sixth sense for it – whether it is a change in the ventilation note or a slight tilt in the angle of the submarine.[30]

The beauty of submarines is stealth. A Prime Minister can claim he or she has submarines sitting off the coast of a nation with Cruise missiles ready to strike and naval mines ready to be laid, and the adversary has no immediate way of knowing whether it's true.*

The boats do not need to be accompanied by a destroyer or carrier to make such a threat. Submarines are also excellent at spying and can be positioned in areas that are inaccessible to surface ships. In a surveillance role, they can observe activities under water, on the surface, in the air and over the electromagnetic spectrum all at the same time. There are no cheap substitutes for this capability.

---

* For the time being, at any rate. One concern about submarine power is the development of new underwater technology to detect enemy submarines.

BLACKOUT

Deep beneath the sea that is the 'watery worldwide web' lie hundreds of fibre-optic cables that really do keep the internet running. When the Russian state decided to annexe Crimea, one of the Kremlin's first moves was to cut the communication line connecting the region to the rest of the world.[31]

Nothing particularly complicated was required. Thanks to maps available to anyone, they knew exactly where the cable lay, and as it was only a couple of centimetres thick, it wasn't hard to sever. At the same time, Russian Special Forces (*Spetsnaz*) were dispatched to seize the main internet exchange point in the city of Simferopol. In a few easy steps, they were able to gain total dominance over the flow of information to and from Crimea.

The criss-cross network of underwater cables that carries 97 per cent of the world's communications is clearly delineated in navigational charts to prevent accidental damage by shipping, but as the Crimean experience shows, the map can be used by terrorists or hostile states to devastating effect. Close to shore, the lines are armoured with nothing more than two layers of galvanised wire, a copper sheath, and a layer of insulation, and buried just under the sea bed, making them very vulnerable.[32] Defence chiefs are increasingly concerned that they could be targeted.

In December 2017, the then Chief of the Defence Staff Air Chief Marshal Sir Stuart Peach warned of 'immediate' and potentially 'catastrophic' consequences in the event of such an act.[33] Around the same time, former GCHQ Director Robert Hannigan said it would be possible to 'make life pretty difficult' for the UK 'without going for full conflict' using this technique.[34]

As Keir Giles, an expert in Russian information warfare at Chatham House, puts it, the fact that people wouldn't be able to log on to Facebook would just be a 'tiny, tiny aspect of all the disruption that would be caused'.[35]

In a report for the think tank Policy Exchange on this emerging threat, Tory MP Rishi Sunak called for new laws to protect such cables,

warning that existing legislation is 'far more suited to the comparative-
ly peripheral role the infrastructure played in the '70s and '80s than to
the indispensable status they now hold in the internet age'.[36]

The operation of Russian submarines along cable routes suggests
the Kremlin is serious about developing its ability to weaponise these
fragile communication systems. The use of its Yantar-class 'intelligence
ship' – which carries two submarines designed for underwater engineering missions and believed to be capable of destroying cables or
tapping them for information – is further evidence that disrupting
infrastructure is now part of Russian military strategy.[37]

NATO has another pressing submarine worry: the spike in Russian
underwater activity in the High North. If this continues unchecked,
it could jeopardise the Alliance's freedom to operate at sea. In a crisis
situation, the build-up of Russian military assets in this most inhospitable of regions could limit NATO's ability to move reinforcements
between North America and Europe, but also in the immediate back-
yard of four NATO countries: the United States, Canada, Denmark
and Norway.[38]

These disturbing manoeuvres by the Russian military present a
growing challenge not only for the navy, but also the RAF.

THE RAF

FLYPAST

A NOTE ON AIR POWER

There was an unusually cheerful item on the agenda of the Royal Air Force board in 2017: how to celebrate the centenary of the service. The Ministry of Defence had designated 2018 as 'The Year of the RAF' and was eager to mark the milestone with suitable pomp and ceremony. The RAF board set to work devising a fabulous programme of commemorative events.

The 100th anniversary of the world's first independent air force fell on Easter Day 2018, and was marked with a service at St Clement Danes on the Strand.

Three weeks later, 600 distinguished RAF men and women gathered at the Guildhall in the City of London for a sparkling black-tie charity dinner. Among the VIPs mingling with the Chief of the Defence Staff and Chief of the Air Staff were two former Battle of Britain pilots; retired Squadron Leader Benny Goodman, of Bomber Command, who flew Lancasters with the 'Dambusters' squadron against the Nazi battleship *Tirpitz*; and a pilot who took part in Operation Black Buck to bomb Port Stanley runway in the Falklands War in 1982, which involved eleven in-flight refuellings and an 8,000-mile round trip from Ascension Island. The arrival of the squadron leader who led the UK Tornado missile strike against Syrian chemical-weapon facilities just a week earlier brought the assembly of distinguished pilots right up to date.

The atmosphere in the splendour of the Great Hall of the Guildhall, which had been lit to show off the RAF Colour Standard, was as special as the organisers had hoped, combining ceremony with history, pageantry, pride and camaraderie. It was not only a night of nostalgia, but also of cautious optimism. With the formation of the new Lightning Fleet of F-35B stealth jets well under way, and delivery of nine long-awaited P-8 maritime patrol planes just around the corner, there was reason to feel that the bleak years of austerity associated with the 2010 Strategic Defence Review were coming to an end.

In summer 2018, there would be further events designed to project power and positivity. The Royal International Air Tattoo (RIAT) at RAF Fairford in Gloucestershire, widely considered to be the world's greatest air show, would be more spectacular than ever. The royal family would also be involved in the celebrations, with the Queen, the Duke and Duchess of Cambridge and other royals due to watch a stunning flypast over Pall Mall from a balcony at Buckingham Palace.

There was one question troubling organisers, however: would there be enough aircraft for the display? Back in 2008, the RAF had managed to rustle up ninety aircraft for a flypast for Her Majesty to mark the RAF's 90th anniversary. Even that had been an effort. This time, they needed 100 – and with the RAF at its smallest since the First World War, it was going to be a challenge. In the event, they managed it, with 103 planes and helicopters involved in the display.[1] As Air Chief Marshal Sir Stephen Hillier told colleagues proudly, the RAF always tries to exceed its targets.

But, as airmen sometimes say wryly: 'Don't confuse air shows with airpower.'

SKY RISE

THE RAF

HELLFIRE AND BRIMSTONE

The RAF is less than half of the size it was twenty-five years ago – and it is at war.[1]

Given the fuss in spring 2018 when Theresa May decided to join a US-led operation against the Syrian regime over its use of chemical weapons, it might seem that air strikes on Syria were a radical departure from the norm. In fact, the RAF has been firing missiles at targets in that troubled country and neighbouring Iraq practically every day since the end of 2015. The government simply does not go out of its way to remind people it is happening.

In December 2015, following a highly charged debate, MPs voted by an overwhelming majority for the UK to join a global coalition against so-called Islamic State.[2] The parliamentary process was painful for both government and opposition – the government because, eighteen months earlier, the then Prime Minister David Cameron had spectacularly failed to persuade MPs to back strikes against President Bashir al-Assad's regime;[3] and the Labour Party because it was split. Corbyn, who was only a few months into his job as Leader of the Opposition, had been forced to give his MPs a free vote, and had suffered the humiliation of watching eleven members of his shadow Cabinet support the government while he shuffled through the No lobby.[4]

Little wonder, then, that it suited both sides to complete the formality of securing parliamentary assent for the strikes, and move swiftly on. Soon after, Westminster was engulfed in the EU referendum campaign, and what the armed forces were up to in Syria and Iraq became Ministry of Defence small print.

For the RAF, however, the repercussions of that vote were enormous. It has been engaged in combat missions over Syria and Iraq ever since. Initially, they were told it was a temporary campaign. The last thing the government wanted was to alarm voters by suggesting the UK was about to get involved in yet another open-ended military operation overseas. The artifice that it would all be over soon had various logistical implications for RAF chiefs, who had no way of knowing whether it was worth establishing a dedicated base in the region. Had they known they would still be engaged in the operation several years down the line, they might have chosen to set up shop somewhere convenient like Jordan. Instead, it was decided to run the campaign, codenamed Operation Shader, out of RAF Akrotiri in Cyprus. Figures released through Freedom of Information requests suggest that nearly 6,000 missions have been conducted since October 2014.[5] The continuing operation involves eight Tornados; six Typhoons; numerous drones;[6] and some 1,000 RAF personnel.[7] According to a senior RAF source, so many Hellfire and Brimstone missiles have been expended in the process that the MoD is 'almost out of ordnance'.[8] The intensity at which the RAF is working far exceeds anything it did in Afghanistan.[9]

This is a contribution to a noble cause of which the UK can be proud. Yet nobody is talking about it. It is not because the MoD is being unreasonably secretive. Every month, basic facts and figures relating to the aerial campaign are published on a government website and circulated to the press. Such media interest as there is tends to centre on civilian casualties (officially none or almost none)[10] or the cost of the campaign to date (heading towards the £2 billion mark when last reported, but figures are incomplete).[11] Nor is the lack of political noise about the UK's role in the operation because it is any source of shame to ministers. Quite the reverse: attacking a foreign regime is highly controversial, but when the targets are terrorists, as in this case, public opinion is more favourable. The conspiracy of silence is probably first and foremost because nobody knows how long this particular mission is going to take, and what happens when it stops.

As one minister put it:

> Military action is an extension of politics: we don't agree with ISIS ideology; we can't do the politics; so we are killing them. But the extension of war to replace politics means that when the war stops, the politics has to begin. And that raises all sorts of awkward questions. Look at Syria and it's crazy – there's no space for the politics. What the hell is our long-term strategy for this area? We're strong against Daesh, but have no idea how to fill the vacuum that's been created. Those who've analysed it don't want to open up that Pandora's box.[12]

It would also be unhelpful and uncomfortable to acknowledge what the same minister referred to as the 'daftness' of taking on an enemy that is not contained by national borders.

'You take on an enemy; you have to hit it wherever it is. You can't have a line in the sand that we respect and nobody else respects,' says the source (who believes our armed forces should be doing even more, not less, to neutralise ISIS).

Finally, there is the UK's domestic problem with religious radicals. There is nothing to be gained – and a great deal to be risked – by provoking the handful of extremists in this country that object to UK military action against brothers-in-arms abroad. As one Tory MP put it: 'We do not want Operation Shader to become a recruiting sergeant.'

Thus it suits everybody – Downing Street, the MoD and MPs – to let the RAF quietly get on with it.

Their contribution is modest relative to the US effort. The American-led operation, codenamed Operation Inherent Resolve, has cost US$13 billion to date.[13] For the shrinking Air Force, however, Operation Shader is massive. If it is to continue at this tempo, RAF sources say there will need to be a re-think – because if anything else crops up, they may run out of pilots and planes.

THE MIGHTY HUNTER

As a self-confessed petrolhead, Defence Secretary Philip Hammond understood roads and cars. Having been Transport Secretary for a year or so, he also understood trains. Planes, however, were a mystery to him – particularly when it came to how many were available for ministerial travel. In May 2013, the then Defence Secretary took it into his head that he ought to visit Mali in West Africa, where British troops were helping to train local forces against Islamic extremists.[14] They had been deployed on the basis that it was not in the UK's interests for the region to become an ungoverned space, but MPs were becoming increasingly twitchy about potential 'mission creep'. Hammond was keen to hammer home the message that it was just a short-term thing and British forces were not there to fight.[15] He asked the RAF to sort him out with a plane for his trip, and was dismayed to be politely informed that they were too stretched. Still heavily committed to Operation Herrick, the war in Afghanistan, the RAF had just one aircraft available for anything discretionary on those dates, and unfortunately the Defence Secretary's travels were not top priority. He would have to make alternative arrangements.[16]

Back in the mid-1980s, such a request would not have been a problem. In those days, the RAF had some 93,400 personnel and more than enough planes to transport Defence Secretaries wherever they wanted. Since then, the service has been in steady decline in numerical terms, falling to 56,900 personnel in 1997; then to 48,700 towards the end of the Blair years in 2006; and further still under the coalition, with the 2010 Strategic Defence and Security Review setting out plans to cut personnel numbers to around 33,000 by 2015.[17]

There is no more powerful symbol of the RAF's ordeal as a result of austerity measures than the brutal destruction of a number of its long-awaited Nimrod maritime patrol planes. In one of the most embarrassing defence procurement debacles in modern history, the aircraft were unceremoniously smashed to pieces on a bleak Cheshire airfield in January 2011, after ministers decided that demolishing them would be less painful than attempting to make them fly. Before bulldozers set to work cutting off the wings, manufacturers BAE Systems erected screens around the demolition site, a bit like the way vets shield the public from the upsetting spectacle of injured racehorses being euthanised.[18] The half-hearted attempt to spare voters the spectacle did nothing to ameliorate the trauma for the RAF, which has neither forgotten nor forgiven the episode.

'It was the fact that they chose to *destroy* it,' bemoans a retired air chief.

> If you break an aeroplane up, that is not how you normally do it. You dismantle it; sell pieces off bit by bit. What they would do in America is stick it in the desert in Arizona; and one day they might choose to get it out again. But they literally broke the planes up. Was Nimrod a finished task? No. Had we put a lot of investment in? Yes. But there was no rush to do it the way they did.[19]

Maritime Patrol Aircraft are a key part of naval air capability; most of our neighbours have them. The planes had been used for anti-submarine warfare operations, protecting Royal Navy vessels; 'screening' the nuclear deterrent to ensure no hostile nation is in pursuit; and monitoring the UK's Exclusive Economic Zone for counter-narcotics, people-trafficking and smuggling. They had also been used for search-and-rescue operations.[20]

In March 2010 – a few months before the tumult of the general election that ousted Labour and marked the beginning of the austerity era – the government decided to retire the existing Nimrod MR2 a year earlier than planned. The aircraft was over thirty years old, and there was serious concern over its safety record after a crash in Afghanistan in 2006.[21] All fourteen of those on board were killed in the biggest single loss of life in the conflict.[22] At the inquest into their deaths, the coroner ruled that the aircraft were 'never airworthy'[23] – a damning indictment if ever there was one.

The RAF did not feel the need to shed too many tears at the demise of Nimrod MR2 because a new model was on its way. At RAF Kinloss, where Nimrod was based, Station Commander Group Captain Robbie Noel said he would miss the old aircraft, but was looking forward to the arrival of the replacement 'in a few months'.

'The new version of "The Mighty Hunter" is a huge leap forward, and I am particularly excited to be introducing it to Kinloss in the very near future,' he declared, in a cheerful MoD press release.[24] It never came. As we have seen, the replacement programme, known as Nimrod MRA4, was cancelled by the new coalition administration as part of the economies linked to the 2010 Strategic Defence Review.[25] The move sent shockwaves through the RAF. Though the project had been plagued by difficulties for years, it had never occurred to senior officers that it would be abandoned altogether. The UK now had no maritime air patrol capability, save for that which could be undertaken by helicopter.[26]

The decision was one of the most controversial and painful taken by the coalition in the 2010 Strategic Defence and Security Review, which hit the RAF harder than either of the other two services.

A senior air chief took the highly unusual step of speaking out publicly about the scale of the cuts, saying they 'worried the hell' out of him. Air Marshal Greg Bagwell, who was head of the RAF's fighter and bomber force at the time, suggested that squadron numbers would be left only 'slightly above Belgium'.[27]

His intervention infuriated the Ministry of Defence but was not that wide of the mark: the RAF currently has seven frontline fighter squadrons, only slightly more than Belgium, which no longer even has a stand-alone air force.[28] Instead, it has an 'air component', which has five fast-jet squadrons. In squadron terms, the RAF of 2020 will be only slightly larger, though it will have significantly more aircraft, with an estimated minimum of 127.[29]

In an open letter to the *Telegraph*, six former defence chiefs from all three services decried the scrapping of Nimrod as 'perverse', warning that it risked leaving 'a massive gap' in UK security. They argued that the aircraft was vital for the provision of long-range maritime and over-land reconnaissance, including over the UK, as well as anti-submarine

surveillance, air-sea rescue co-ordination and, 'perhaps most importantly', the protection of Trident submarines.[30] The move also had
implications for manufacturing jobs in the UK, prompting the trade
union UNITE to protest – not unreasonably – that when a government
orders the MoD to break up £4 billion worth of world-class defence
equipment, 'The lunatics have taken over the asylum.'[31]

In reality, the writing had been on the wall for years. An initial £2
billion contract for twenty-one aircraft, drawn up with BAE Systems in
1996, had been steadily whittled down to just nine planes.[32] By the time
Labour left office in 2010, the programme was almost £800 million
over budget, and the unit cost for each aircraft had tripled.[33] They were
still nowhere near ready to enter service. Indeed, the single aircraft that
had been delivered to the RAF was so riddled with faults it could not
pass its flight tests. In the words of the then Defence Secretary Liam
Fox, it was 'simply unsafe to fly'.[34]

Fox knew there were risks to abandoning the project. The RAF
would be furious, and it would be a political and diplomatic embarrassment. NATO would take a dim view. However, he had come to the
reluctant conclusion that ploughing on would be even worse. Nimrod
MRA4 had begun to remind him of the world's first jet airliner in the
1950s, which had been the subject of great hopes but was ultimately
doomed. The British-made de Havilland Comet looked beautiful and
could cross the Atlantic in style, but turned out to be fatally flawed.
In 1953 and 1954, three Comets broke up soon after take-off, killing
all on board, two over the Mediterranean on the ascent from Rome's
Ciampino airport, and a third caught in a thunder squall on the Cal-
cutta-to-Delhi leg of a flight from Singapore to London. Comet flights
had to be suspended, and production of the British jet was halted.[35]

Shortly after Fox's arrival at the MoD, BAE Systems begged him
for more money to fix a problem with Nimrod's fuselage. He refused,
deciding that the RAF would just have to beg and borrow to get by
without maritime patrol aircraft for the foreseeable future, until such a
time as the Ministry of Defence had more cash.[36]

The final figures relating to the project were staggering. The last wholly British-designed military aircraft had ended in complete failure, having been deemed unfit to fly. The nineteen-year saga had cost roughly the same as an entire *Queen Elizabeth* aircraft carrier and failed to produce anything airworthy. At its peak, the project was sucking up £444 million a year.[37] In a final insult to taxpayers, the MoD spent half a million pounds on the scrappage operation, receiving only £1 million for spare parts.[38] Not a single officer, civil servant or minister was ever blamed.

The operational impact was considerable. Just when Russia was beginning to ramp up incursions into UK waters and airspace, the military was stripped of one of its most powerful surveillance platforms. Indeed, according to a well-placed source, on the very day Nimrod was withdrawn from service, the RAF was busy shadowing a Russian submarine. In the years that followed, defence chiefs were forced to appeal to NATO allies to help carry out such tasks. Parliamentary questions reveal that American, French, German and Canadian Maritime Patrol Aircraft all stepped in.[39]

Twice a year the gap in capability was rudely exposed in NATO's 'Joint Warrior' exercise, which takes place in Scottish waters out of HMNB Clyde.[40] Russian submariners delight in trying to disrupt the games. Allies always send Maritime Patrol Aircraft to take part in the exercise. For some weeks after the event, these planes tend to hang around RAF Lossiemouth to continue the hunt. Humiliatingly, in recent years, the UK has been unable to contribute its own aircraft to the maritime patrol element of the exercise.[41]

In all, during the coalition years, the service lost almost a sixth of its total staff and 295 aircraft. For the first time since 1914, it was left with fewer than 200 fighter planes.[42]

Recently retired, Bagwell stands by his warnings all those years ago, pointing out that there is no fast way of restoring the RAF to its former shape and size if it is needed.

By all means go down the curve, but when you are doing that, think long and hard about your ability to either halt or come back up again. The ability to recover is limited. The problem is that capability atrophies quickly and unless you can bring the very same people back, you can't just say to a nine-teen-year-old, 'Alright, you're a maritime patrol specialist.' It takes fifteen years to become super good. I think our ability to come back up the other side, which we are now trying to do with a few minor increases, is going to be a long-term struggle. You can't just flick it back on.

Gavin Williamson shares these views, echoing Bagwell's concerns about the length of time it takes a depleted armed forces to recover. 'It's like a nursery. If you don't have any seedlings, you can't grow a new crop. Even if you have something which is not, at the moment, the size you'd want it, you need the potential to grow it,' he says.[43]

Eight years on from the Nimrod debacle, things are looking up for the RAF. As we have seen, the 2015 Strategic Defence and Security Review confirmed the MoD order for nine P-8 maritime patrol aircraft, marking the beginning of the end of the long maritime patrol capability gap.[44] Moreover, the service has just reformed its legendary Dambusters squadron to operate and fly F-35 Lightning II planes – billed as the world's most advanced fighter jets.[45] The centenarian is about to be rejuvenated.

AUGUSTINE'S LAW

Ambassadors usually steer well clear of domestic politics in their host countries, so defence reporters summoned to the US Embassy in London for a briefing about the Pentagon's largest ever weapons programme were surprised when the debate turned to one of the most sensitive subjects in British politics: the NHS.

Perhaps it was the unusually warm weather; perhaps it was the stress of President Trump's decision to tear up the Iran nuclear agreement twenty-four hours earlier; or perhaps he simply felt he was among friends. Whatever the reason, on a bright London morning in May 2018, when Ambassador Robert Wood Johnson was supposed to be doing the hard sell for American-made F-35 fighter jets, he veered off message and began questioning the amount of money the British government spends on the health service. He expressed the view that the UK should be ready to increase defence spending at the expense of the NHS to safeguard security and remain a strong ally. Healthcare would always be an issue, he acknowledged, 'But how important is it to defend yourself?' It was time for the UK to have a long hard think about its priorities, he advised, adding pointedly that the US did not want to 'pay for everything'.

'You're going to have to make trade-offs, and go through the emotional and practical philosophical arguments in terms of what you want to do, what you want to be, how important is defence, how you want to be perceived, by the US, but also by Russia and others,' he said.[46]

For a senior diplomat, this was a highly unusual intervention. Under the circumstances, however, the Ambassador's frustration was understandable. After all, more than twenty years after agreeing to become a prime customer for American-made F-35 Lightning II fighter jets, the UK still hasn't decided how many planes it wants. An initial pledge to purchase 138 of the jets came without any timeframe.[47] So far, the UK has only ordered forty-eight and there are continued rumblings that the final number may be far fewer than was originally suggested.[48] Moreover, the MoD is not sure which of the three available models of the aircraft it wants for the remainder of the order – if it is fulfilled.[49] All this when we promised to be first in line for the new aircraft. No wonder the Pentagon, which is under mounting political pressure over the programme, is both irritated and nervous.

To date, the US has poured US$100 billion of American taxpayers' money into the scheme with defence giant Lockheed Martin.[50] As a presidential candidate, Trump said it was 'out of control' and promised to beat the price down if he won.[51] He later took credit for a significant reduction in the cost of each plane – though his critics say it would have happened anyway, as more rolled off the production line.[52]

Yet as far as the RAF is concerned, the money being poured into the F-35 fighter jet programme on both sides of the Atlantic is a fantastic investment. From 2019, the Tornado fighter jets that have been at the heart of UK air power for the past three decades, flying bombing missions over Iraq, the Balkans, Afghanistan and Syria, are expected to be retired.[53] In the long term, they will be replaced by this so-called fifth-generation wonder jet.

To its cheerleaders, the F-35 is a modern marvel, designed to address the formidable new challenges and opportunities associated with air power. As Air Chief Marshal Sir Stephen Hillier and his US counterparts have publicly acknowledged on many occasions, the West can no longer rely on supremacy in the air.[54] Russia, China and other potential adversaries now have ways of preventing fighter jets entering their airspace. The F-35 is designed to dodge those systems, outflanking the enemy just as it catches us up.

According to Lockheed Martin, the jet will be 'four times more effective' in air-to-air combat than current aircraft and 'three times more effective' at detecting and foiling enemy air defences.[55] It is supposed to be more stealthy, have better range and require less logistics support than anything currently on the market. The Pentagon has gone so far as to describe it as 'the most affordable, lethal, supportable, and survivable aircraft ever to be used'.[56]

Though it will spearhead the UK's new 'carrier strike' capability, another selling point is that it is suitable for different branches of the military. To that end, there are three variants: the F-35A, designed to take off from conventional runways; the F-35B, a jump-jet model designed for aircraft carriers; and the F-35C, an alternative aircraft carrier model which takes off and lands using catapults and arrestors.[57] If Lockheed is to be believed, it will be all things to all people. Who wouldn't want a piece of this action?

The British government certainly did. When the programme was first announced back in the mid-1990s, ministers leapt at the chance to get involved, signing an agreement to become the US's premier partner. To show they were serious, they put down a US$200 million deposit towards eventual manufacturing costs.[58] The hope was that the project would not only provide the armed forces with the world's most advanced fighter jet; it would also prove a money-spinner for the British defence industry. The agreement gave the UK a significant stake in the entire process, with British defence companies providing around 15 per cent by value of each F-35 built.[59]

Anyone hopeful that the US would prove more efficient at delivering massive defence procurement projects than the UK was to be disappointed, however. It took more than twenty years for the first F-35s to arrive in the UK – and when the big moment finally came, the arrival was delayed by poor weather.[60]

Indeed, the project has suffered all the delays, cost overruns and technical problems characteristic of big military hardware projects in this country, leading one particularly sceptical former US airman and academic to label it 'one of the greatest boondoggles in recent military purchasing history'.[61]

For military planners, perhaps the most critical question is whether the jet is as stealthy as both the manufacturers and the Pentagon claim. After all, its capacity to fly without detection by hostile forces is supposed to be its primary selling point. Lockheed Martin and the Pentagon claim its ability to evade radar means it gets 'first look, first shot, first kill'. However, analysts say that the technology with which it is equipped 'greatly reduces, but does not eliminate' the signal that radar receivers see bouncing back off a jet. As one critic put it, 'The plane looks smaller on radar – perhaps like a bird rather than a plane – but it is not invisible.'[62] The same critic argues that it has been designed to circumvent the most commonly used radar frequency range in aerial combat, the so-called X band, and is less effective against alternative radar frequencies. In any case, he argues, radar is not the only way to locate and target aircraft these days: they can also be detected via infrared emissions created by the engines and friction-generated heat.[63]

Ironically, there are also worries that the jet's computer systems are too sophisticated to communicate effectively with other platforms, including the HMS *Queen Elizabeth* carrier and her escorts. The MoD has been accused of failing to buy 'critical support technology' for the planes, including a Battlefield Airborne Communications Node (BACN) 'that allows secure signals from the F-35 to be read by older aircraft'. According to an investigation by *The Times* newspaper, this means F-35 pilots trying to share data with older aircraft will have to use a less secure channel, potentially giving away their position.[64] In the same investigation, *The Times* raised the alarming spectre of US$100 million worth of metal and software and several million pounds worth of fighter pilot (they are extremely expensive to train) being accidentally shot down as they return to the carrier. The fear is that computer systems on HMS *Queen Elizabeth* and her escorts will not be capable of communicating with the F-35 when it is flying in stealth mode, as it would be on a bombing mission. According to *The Times*, this could render it 'indistinguishable on radar from an enemy missile' – leading to friendly-fire disaster.[65]

The newspaper investigation, which prompted an inquiry by the Commons Defence Select Committee,[66] highlighted a catalogue of other software and hardware problems, including a test flight in which the night-vision component on the pilot's £309,000 helmet failed, forcing him to land in almost total darkness.[67] In its damning report, published in July 2017, *The Times* condemned the aircraft as 'way over budget, unreliable, full of software glitches and potentially unsafe'.[68]

The MoD was unable to brush this off as media mischief-making. Meanwhile, in its annual assessment of the programme in 2018, the Pentagon itself identified more than 300 unresolved 'high-priority deficiencies' with the aircraft, including potential vulnerability to cyber-attack.[69] At the time of writing, the F-35B does not even have a decent set of wheels. The Pentagon admits the manufacturers have 'struggled to find a tyre that is strong enough for conventional high-speed landings, soft enough to cushion vertical landings, and still light enough for the existing aircraft structure'.[70] The tyre they are currently using has to be replaced after ten landings.[71]

As for the cost of the aircraft, nobody quite knows – or if they do, they would rather not say. Much to the irritation of MPs on the Defence Select Committee, the Ministry of Defence has repeatedly refused to provide a 'per aircraft' figure. Nor will ministers give an estimate for the entire programme.[72] This is probably because there are so many variables that it is almost impossible to calculate.

What is known is that the F-35 has become the most expensive weapons programme in history[73] – and the fluctuation in exchange rates has made it considerably pricier than the MoD anticipated. By the time the jet is phased out in 2070, it is expected to have cost around US$1.5 trillion.[74] Luckily for the MoD, nobody seems to have done an equivalent calculation for the cost to UK taxpayers. The most that can be said at this stage is that when spares, maintenance and training are taken into account, there will probably not be much change from £191 million for each aircraft.[75]

None of this has dampened RAF enthusiasm. Some 200 RAF and navy personnel spent much of 2017 and 2018 training alongside the United States Marine Corps at Beaufort Air Station, South Carolina,[76] mostly in simulators, counting the days until the aircraft arrived in the UK. Though they gripe that it is not a thing of beauty ('It's ugly as sin, which is always bad for an aeroplane, and you should also get its undercarriage up as fast as possible because it looks rubbish on its spindly little legs,' was how one very senior RAF man put it), pilots love flying it. One of the first British pilots to take to the skies in the F-35 said the experience was 'almost indescribable … After over seven years of training … to finally get into the real aircraft and take it airborne was one of the proudest and most exciting experiences of my life so far.'[77]

The aircraft will be based at RAF Marham in Norfolk, where £500 million is being spent on custom-made hangars and maintenance depots. The new facilities will include three landing pads for practising vertical take-offs and landings.[78] Ministers are keen to stress the wider benefits of the F-35 programme, which is said to have generated 1,800 jobs at BAE Systems.[79] Lockheed Martin claims that UK companies have already received '$12.9 billion in F-35 related orders' and that the programme will support 'more than 500 companies and 20,000 jobs in the UK throughout the thirty-year production phase'.[80] The downside, for the RAF at least, is that they will have to share their long-awaited new toys with the navy.

Back in 1984, Norman Augustine, a former US Under Secretary of the Army, seemed to see all this coming. He wrote a series of tongue-in-cheek aphorisms which became known as 'Augustine's laws'.[81] Law No. 16 predicted that, by 2054, 'the entire defense budget will purchase just one aircraft. This aircraft will have to be shared by the air force and navy 3½ days each per week except for leap year, when it will be made available to the Marines for the extra day.'

The observation proved spookily prescient. On a project of this scale and complexity, however, challenges and setbacks are hardly surprising. If all goes to plan, the acquisition of this remarkable aircraft will position the RAF alongside the US Air Force at the forefront of global air power.

How long that superiority lasts is another question.

GRIM REAPERS

Armed with nothing more offensive than two small trees, a little group of demonstrators once broke into RAF Waddington in Lincolnshire and set to work creating a 'peace garden'.

Though their activities ended with a night in a police cell, theirs was a very British protest, led by two priests (one Catholic, one Anglican); a Quaker pensioner; a teacher; and a grandmother.[82] Their plan was to plant a fig tree and a vine near the control centre for UK military drone operations.[83]

Apparently, the trees were a reference to the words of the prophet Micah: 'They shall all sit under their own vines and under their own fig trees, and no one shall make them afraid.'[84] Later, the police removed most of the garden, though they let an RAF officer rehome the vine.[85]

Some weeks earlier, in April 2013, a more familiar figure was to be found at the same site – though being a politician he was careful to stay on the right side of the barbed-wire fence. Then just a lowly backbencher, Jeremy Corbyn led a separate protest at the site organised by Stop the War campaigners. There, the future Labour Party leader took to a soapbox to call for drones to be scrapped.

'We're here today to say that we don't agree with these drones. We don't agree with this obscenity that's going on before our very eyes here. That's why just as much as we want to get rid of landmines, small arms, nuclear weapons, we want to get rid of drones as well, he declared. He went on to describe the use of unmanned aerial vehicles to kill people as 'the ultimate in sanitised warfare', saying the devices allowed the armed forces to 'immunise themselves' against the reality of what they were doing 'knowing full well that a family with barely enough to eat are going to be killed by a multi-million-pound weapon at the press of a button by someone in an air-conditioned office in the Midwest of the USA or right here in Lincolnshire.'[86]

As Corbyn headed home, he jabbed out a tweet:

'Well done to everyone who made it to Lincoln to protest at Drone deployment from RAF Waddington. Afghan war now waged from Britain by video link.' It attracted just seven 'likes'.[87]

That was five years ago. Not long after those protests, the British combat role in Afghanistan ended, but instead of marking the end of lethal drone strikes, as peace activists had hoped, the activity simply moved to new targets in the Middle East.

Today, so-called unmanned aerial vehicles (UAVs) are used by the army, navy and RAF. For the armed forces, any novelty factor has long gone: they are simply considered part of the 'core equipment programme'. The vast majority of the machines are used for surveillance. They range from tiny contraptions about the size and weight of a biscuit, designed to enable soldiers to peek round corners and over walls; to devices the size of small conventional aircraft. As we shall see, defence companies and academics think that in the near future, so-called swarms of small UAVs could be used to lethal effect[88] – for example, to imitate a deadly bird strike to bring down enemy aircraft.

For the time being, however, the armed forces only have one drone designed to kill: an unmanned aerial vehicle made by General Atomics called Reaper.[89] Over the past four years, it has been a vital weapon in Operation Shader, delivering lethal strikes against meticulously re-searched terror targets.[90]

Corbyn and other left-wing activists continue to caricature this capability, painting a distressing picture of innocent civilians casually annihilated by remote control. The Ministry of Defence insists the reality is not at all like that. The aircraft may be controlled by pilots thousands of miles away in the safety of the English countryside, but every operation is approached with the same gravity as would apply if the pilot were in the sky.[91] Each strike involves exhaustive intelligence-gathering, legal deliberation and days – sometimes weeks – of reconnaissance to ensure nobody innocent is hit.

Once in a blue moon, something does go wrong, as happened in Syria on 26 March 2018, when a Reaper armed with a Hellfire missile fired at three suspected Islamic State fighters, and accidentally killed someone else. After days of monitoring what the military call the 'pattern of life' in the area, RAF personnel had concluded it was safe to launch the mission – only for an unfortunate motorcyclist to burst onto the scene at the last minute. Amid continuing political pressure from Labour over potential collateral damage linked to drone use, the MoD decided it was best to come clean about this accident, which was disclosed to Parliament.[92]

It was the first time the MoD had admitted responsibility for a civilian death since Operation Shader began. They insist it was a one-off, though sources familiar with the way drone strikes work suspect there have been other cases. There is no suggestion that the MoD is deliberately covering these up; rather that (in the words of an RAF source who should know) 'you can't always see bodies in the rubble.' Drone strikes may be precise, but they make a giant hole in the ground and throw up a lot of dust.

According to a well-placed MoD source, there were a number of errors involving Reapers in Afghanistan, details of which were rarely made public.[93]

He cited an incident involving an intelligence failure about a truck.

The source says: 'We did not understand what was in the vehicle the man [target] was riding in. It was loaded to the gunnels with explosives. So when we hit it, it had a much bigger impact than expected. That did injure people. But that is very rare. It was a mistake.'

The same source, who had the highest level of security clearance, recollected what he called a 'very unpleasant business' (again in

Afghanistan) in which a drone strike failed, necessitating a second (and ultimately successful) attempt to kill the target as he fled.

'He was running around over the landscape. But, of course, he couldn't see the drone, which was miles away; couldn't hear it, he had no understanding of where the fire had come from. They got him in the end,' he claims.[94]

Such incidents are vanishingly rare, however. In most cases, only the target is eliminated, and he or she knows nothing until a few seconds before being hit, when the descending missile breaks the sound barrier. Seconds later, they are what the American military call 'vaporized'.

None of this appeases Corbyn or those who object to this type of operation on some kind of principle. Such is the intransigence of the Labour leader's opposition to drones that he struggles to contemplate their use against even the biggest of terror targets. In the run-up to May's snap general election in 2017, he repeatedly refused to say whether, if elected Prime Minister, he would be willing to authorise a drone strike against an ISIS leader.[95] The Ministry of Defence continues to work on the assumption that he will not make it to No. 10, and is planning to double the RAF's unmanned air fleet. By 2021, all ten Reapers will have been replaced by twenty so-called Protectors. According to the MoD, the new models can go further; stay in the air longer; and carry more powerful weapons. As an added bonus, they are even 'resilient against ice, fire and lightning'.[96]

All this touches on an existential question for the RAF: how long before unmanned aerial vehicles replace humans in cockpits? For now, drones make up just 5 per cent of the RAF's assets.[97] Air Chief Marshal Sir Stephen Hillier believes that could rise to one third within the next fifteen to twenty years.[98] Pilots will not be out of work for a long time yet. Meanwhile the service has other technology related challenges in a rapidly evolving defence domain: space.

ORBIT

SPACE, SATELLITES AND WAR IN THE FREEZER

PROJECT ICE

With a paltry £1.2 billion annual budget, the Foreign and Commonwealth Office tends to prefer selling real estate to buying it.[1] In spring 2016, however, a unique opportunity arose to establish a British outpost in what may become one of the most strategic positions in the world.

The Svalbard Archipelago already had a special association for David Cameron as the scene of one of his most successful initiatives as Leader of the Opposition.

Dramatic pictures of the young MP 'hugging huskies' on an expedition to the region to witness the effects of climate change burnished his environmental credentials and became a symbol of his campaign to modernise the Conservative Party.[2]

Now the UK had the chance to acquire a small piece of the island, from which it would be possible to do all sorts of exciting things.

'An area of land the size of Guernsey is privately owned and is to be sold. The owner is offering the UK first refusal. The strategic significance of UK land ownership inside the Arctic Circle cannot be overstated,' enthused the then Foreign Office minister Tobias Ellwood in a letter to Chancellor George Osborne.[3]

Half way between continental Norway and the North Pole, the Svalbard Archipelago is a place of mesmerising natural beauty; a frozen wilderness of midnight sun and polar nights. For more than two months between mid-November and the end of January it is in total darkness, the barren landscape illuminated only by the moon and the

Northern Lights.[4] Come May, the fjord ice begins to melt, and boats can once again make it through the waterways.

With a population of just over 2,500 dispersed in a smattering of towns reachable only by plane, boat or snowmobile, it seems an unlikely focus for an international power struggle.[5] Yet there are ominous signs that this remote region is assuming extraordinary geopolitical significance and could be the backdrop to the next major conflict involving the UK's armed forces.

When, almost a century ago, fourteen nations signed a treaty to define the status of Svalbard, the area did not seem much of a prospect. Having long been written off as 'no-man's land',[6] it attracted international attention at the end of the First World War only because political leaders were trying to minimise the prospect of future territorial disputes.

The so-called Spitsbergen Treaty of 1920 handed sovereignty of the archipelago to Norway, but with some very unusual conditions. Citizens of all fourteen initial signatories, and a further thirty-two nations that subsequently signed, were given the right to live and work there.[7]

The new agreement did not prompt a stampede – in those days, the region was simply too remote for prospectors. Now it is opening up. As the icecaps recede, there are potentially lucrative opportunities for energy exploration, commercial shipping and tourism. According to a US geological survey, as much as a fifth of the world's undiscovered oil and gas reserves may lie in this area, raising the spectre of heated disputes over sovereignty and future freedom of navigation.[8]

Against this backdrop, the opportunity to acquire one of the few parts of the archipelago that is not governed by the treaty looked like an exciting potential investment for the UK.

It was on the market for £250 million, or £12 million a year.

In his letter to the Chancellor, Ellwood highlighted a catalogue of potential benefits, including the opportunity to establish a new radar station and a strategic base or small port on the transpolar sea route, which he said was 'expected to become a critical East–West sea route within the next thirty years'.

'Assets include deep water anchorage (i.e. could accommodate our new aircraft carriers) and basic infrastructure,' he explained. 'A US geopolitical survey estimates that the Arctic holds about 13 per cent of the world's undiscovered oil reserves and 30 per cent of gas reserves, some of which would be accessible from this land. Ownership also comes with significant fishing rights,' he explained.[9]

Attached to Ellwood's letter was a detailed briefing note put together by the estate agents, headlined 'Project ICE'. They thought the place might make a good tax haven. However, the primary focus of their pitch was more sophisticated.

The key benefit of land ownership in Svalbard, they felt, would be the chance to create and control a private satellite ground station for earth observation.

For defence, this would be 'impossible to put a value on', they believed.[10] This was an opportunity to acquire real estate not only on land, but also in space, a domain which is becoming increasingly important to defence.

STEEL RAIN

Some 90 per cent of the UK's military capability is now dependent in some way on space.[11]

The 'space race' began with the so-called Sputnik Shock more than sixty years ago. In October 1957, the US was amazed when the Soviet Union managed to launch a satellite into orbit for the first time in history. Four years later, they sent the first man into space. The Americans launched an urgent catch-up operation, throwing money at scientists to accelerate their own space programme. Within months, they were able to launch their own satellite, Explorer 1.

It was not until the first Gulf War that space became integral to military conflict, however.

In January 1991, a US-led coalition of nearly a million troops amassed on the dusty border between Saudi Arabia and Iraq. The Berlin Wall had just fallen, the Soviet Union was in its death throes and the United States was eager to consolidate what President George H. W. Bush called the 'new world order', based on US leadership of an international community.[12]

The annexation of Kuwait by Saddam Hussein threatened all this. Brazenly flouting international law, the dictator had seized Kuwait's lucrative oilfields and dared the rest of the world to stop him.[13] If they could not defend small states from the aggression of larger neighbours, the rules-based international order was nothing but empty rhetoric. Bush announced that this reckless disregard for sovereignty would be met with a response of overwhelming force.[14] It would not be easy. Coalition forces would have to mount a ground invasion in the desert. The barren, windswept terrain offered few landmarks for troops to orient themselves, and the pace at which they would need to advance gave artillery support teams little time to survey the unfamiliar landscape to ensure complete cover of advancing troops.

The US Department of Defense decided to rely on what was then a novel capability: the emerging Global Positioning System. The idea was to use it to guide troop movements and position artillery. At this stage it was only accurate to within around twenty metres. It did not even provide 24-hour coverage. The bulky receivers cost thousands of dollars apiece. It was a major gamble: it had never been tested before in a battle of such high stakes.

The experiment paid off, providing an overwhelming advantage. Aided by GPS, the precision bombing campaign was so effective and relentless that Iraqi troops called it 'the steel rain'.[15] Coalition troops pushed Saddam Hussein's forces out of Kuwait and into the heartlands of Iraq in under a week. They inflicted around 30,000 casualties on Ba'ath'ist troops while receiving only 300 in turn, a significant proportion of which were from friendly fire.[16] The US Army now says that during the Gulf War, 'a new era for the military began, as space technology first played an integral role in military conflict'.

From an early stage, it had been clear that the 'space race' might eventually turn nasty. In 1967, the US, Soviet Union and UK signed a 'Treaty on Principles Governing the Activities of States in the Exploration and Use of Outer Space, including the Moon and Other Celestial Bodies'. At the time of writing it has 107 signatories, and forms the basis of international space law. It is designed to prevent the 'weaponisation' of this domain.[17]

Experts make a distinction between 'militarisation' and 'weaponisation' in this realm. The former is the use of space for military purposes such as positioning and targeting and is considered acceptable. The latter is the placing or use of offensive weapons in space, and is not. The law has not been updated since the original Treaty was signed, creating considerable scope for malign opportunism.

Since the fall of the Soviet Union, the West has taken space dominance for granted, so the issue has not been pressing. Now senior military figures are more concerned about the future of space than at any time since the depths of the Cold War. They know that certain regimes will have few qualms about starting a war in the stars.

In an indication of how important this area is becoming to the armed forces, in spring 2018, the Ministry of Defence held its first ever Defence Space Conference. Speaking at the event, Air Chief Marshal Sir Stephen Hillier admitted that the military's heavy dependence on GPS 'creates vulnerabilities'.

'We are at acute risk from those who might now seek to deny, degrade and disrupt our capabilities,' he said, adding that the armed forces, led by the RAF, will 'have to work increasingly hard to secure and ensure the space capabilities on which we are utterly reliant'.[18]

Around the same time, Donald Trump began talking openly about the possibility of putting soldiers into space. At a speech to Marines at Air Station Miramar in San Diego, the President raised the idea of a dedicated 'space force' to fight future interstellar battles. 'From the beginning, many of our astronauts have been soldiers, sailors, coastguardsmen and marines,' he said. In an unusually frank admission, he acknowledged that the US has already been left 'way behind' – a reference to China, which has invested heavily in this domain.[19]

ICARUS

On 23 July 2017, the Chinese government issued an urgent warning to all airlines to avoid a narrow flight path over the Mongolian steppes. At first, operators were confused. There were no planned military exercises in the area, and there had been no warning of severe weather in that region. All became clear when it emerged that the Chinese had been testing a powerful new weapon designed to destroy satellites. American intelligence agents watched with alarm as the Dong Neng-3 'direct ascent missile' thundered through the sky from the Jiuquan Satellite Launch centre in China's north-west near the Mongolian border. Local Chinese social media users gawped and posted photos and videos of the test – images which were hastily removed by the Chinese authorities.

In some ways, the test was a false alarm. The missile malfunctioned before it reached orbit, showering debris over the plains. But the implications of such a weapon are profound: it could potentially knock out US or European satellites. This would leave drones unable to fly beyond the line of sight, fleet commanders unable to communicate with their ships, and ground troops without maps or location information.

The Chinese see the ability to deny the US command and control interfaces provided by satellite technologies as crucial to a future war. The regime knows the US has significantly superior conventional forces – for the time being at least – but has identified the Pentagon's heavy reliance on space-based systems for communications as a potential vulnerability.[20]

Nobody knows how a space war would unfold. However, the nightmare scenario looks increasingly plausible. For civilians, the first sign might be the malfunctioning of everyday facilities like ATM machines. Then, traffic lights and satnav systems would begin cutting in and out, bringing cars and lorries to a standstill. The real panic would probably come when the finely tuned technology that keeps financial markets running stopped working. Mobile phone coverage would fade. Then the internet would crash.

Most of the real war would be invisible on earth. Cyberattacks would strafe back and forth across networks to overload the ability of NATO military satellites to communicate with receivers on the ground. Directed energy laser or microwave beams would streak out from a swarm of tiny satellites based in low-earth orbit, firing their pinpoint beams at delicate optical sensors on our communications satellites.

Finally, a volley of Chinese Dong Neng 3 or Russian Nudol missiles would snake upwards from their launch pads in the steppes. This time, they would hit their targets, causing them to explode into thousands of pieces of space debris. Unconstrained by gravity, these burning chunks of metal would start orbiting the earth at hypersonic speed, creating a hail of projectiles that would destroy any satellites in their path.

The potential for an adversary to flood orbit paths with outer-space debris is known as the 'Kessler syndrome'.*[21] It could be enough to take the UK's space-based communications systems offline indefinitely.

By this time, the Western world would have been plunged into a metaphorical dark age in a matter of hours. The armed forces would have their command and control abilities crippled. The civilian world would be in pandemonium and economic meltdown as cloud-based computing systems and financial records were wiped. Perhaps then, a real invasion would begin.[22]

This is still science fiction – but for how long? According to the 2018 US Intelligence Community's Worldwide Threat Assessment, offensive space weapons could have 'initial operational capability in the next few years'.

Military chiefs know they have to accelerate efforts to confront this emerging threat.

GALILEO

Until recently, Western allies have co-operated well in the space domain. During the Gulf War, the US gave dozens of coalition forces access to sensitive security information provided by GPS. This continued through the wars in ex-Yugoslavia in the 1990s, and the Middle East in the twenty-first century. The UK has invested heavily in co-operation in developing space capability not just with the US but with other allies. Brexit has threatened to change all this.

In spring 2018, as negotiations between London and Brussels ground on, an unexpected row broke out over a space project. For years, the UK had been ploughing money into an EU project called Galileo, the construction of a new EU global positioning system.[23] It is designed to

---

*   The Kessler Syndrome was a theory proposed by NASA scientist, Donald J. Kessler. The theory is that if two objects collide in space, it will generate more debris, which will create more collisions. This could increase the risks for satellites.

give European countries a sovereign alternative to the current US Air Force run GPS, in case the White House ever takes a drastic decision to cut off the EU.[24] Though the chance of this happening seems vanishingly remote, theoretically it is possible: the US did it to India during the Kargil War with Pakistan in 1999. Brussels empire-builders liked the idea that they would not be beholden to Washington over such a crucial asset.[25] Perhaps more importantly, Galileo would create jobs.[26]

Successive Labour and Conservative governments embraced the project, lavishing around a billion pounds of taxpayers' money on the early stages. Ministers even provided land on several British overseas territories – the Falklands, Ascension Island and Diego Garcia – for the installation of satellite dishes and boosters to enhance the system.[27]

Less than a year before the UK was due to leave the EU, Brussels negotiators suddenly threatened to lock the government out of the scheme.

Downing Street was furious. Since the EU referendum, ministers had assiduously avoided using defence as a bargaining chip with the EU. The Cabinet was unanimous that even hinting at the possibility of withdrawing military co-operation with European allies would be a mistake, setting the wrong tone for negotiations and damaging the UK's reputation. Now Brussels was playing that card.

A seething Gavin Williamson lashed out at the European Commission, accusing them of 'play[ing] politics with defence and security'. He hinted that Brussels officials were not in tune with what individual member states wanted, saying his own discussions with defence ministers across Europe indicated that they fully supported Britain remaining part of the project, in the interests of common security.[28]

To some, the whole scheme is a waste of time and money anyway.

Professor Julian Lindley-French, who was a Senior Fellow at the Paris-based Institute for Security Studies when the project was conceived back in the early 1990s, sees it as little more than a 'glorified, taxpayer-funded boondoggle for French, German, and to a lesser extent British and Italian defence industries'.

He goes so far as to argue that Galileo has weakened European defences, by diverting funds from other capabilities:

One argument advanced by the proponents of Galileo was that such a space-based architecture would enable Europeans to deploy advanced military forces independently from the Americans. What advanced military forces? By spending €10 billion (it is in fact far more) on a duplicate system to GPS, Europeans helped ensure they lacked the very advanced deployable military capabilities that would use the system.[29]

For Downing Street, it was a point of principle. Having offered unconditional co-operation on European security matters, No. 10 was shocked and indignant to be treated this way. The Chancellor – no supporter of Brexit – made it clear that if the EU didn't back down, the UK would simply go it alone. A new satellite system was, he said, vital for the UK's national security.[30]

This was exactly what Tobias Ellwood had in mind when he was pushing the Svalbard opportunity. At that time, he was the government minister with responsibility for space policy, and was acutely aware of the growing importance of space to UK defence and foreign policy.

Clauses in the Svalbard Treaty specifically grant permission to landowners to install wireless communication equipment on their own land.[31] This is not as odd as it sounds, because the archipelago's high latitude makes it a particularly good spot for satellite ground stations linked to so-called polar orbiting satellites. These have particular defence implications because they orbit the earth much faster than other satellites, while remaining close enough to the ground to provide high-quality imagery – ideal for spycraft or precision targeting for ballistic missiles. This means they can cover a huge amount of ground, but also are close enough to provide high quality images of the terrain below.[32]

Whoever bought that slice of Svalbard would, according to the property particulars, be able to 'build, operate and control a private facility, without the reliance on a third party' – a position the Ministry of Defence would presumably like to have been in when the EU started playing hard ball on Galileo.[33]

Ellwood's timing was unfortunate. Had the land purchase

opportunity come up a little later, the UK might by now be proud owners of an Arctic outpost. As we have seen, Gavin Williamson is keen to make the UK's presence felt around the world and likes the idea of establishing new bases – however modest – in strategic locations.

MILITARY INSTALLATIONS IN SVALBARD/ARCTIC CIRCLE ARCHIPELAGOS

DEFENCE EXPERTS BELIEVE COMPETITION FOR NATURAL RESOURCES IN THE HIGH NORTH/ARCTIC COULD LEAD TO WAR.

Sadly, by the time he became Defence Secretary, the Svalbard ship had sailed. Ellwood's letter to Osborne was dated 13 April 2016. That was just two months before the EU referendum. Though the then Chancellor acknowledged receipt of the proposal, his mind was elsewhere. A few weeks later, he would be out of office, and Project Ice melted in the hot seas of Brexit hysteria.

In his letter, Ellwood had warned of a potential rival bidder.

'China has expressed an interest and it is worth considering how they would exploit such an opportunity so close to Europe and the North Sea,' he wrote.[34]

Potential adversaries are unlikely to let such opportunities pass – and they are particularly interested in this part of the world.

WAR IN THE FREEZER

In the run-up to Theresa May's 2017 snap election, the Royal United Services Institute think tank staged a lively defence debate involving all the main political parties.

To the disappointment of organisers, the then Defence Secretary Sir Michael Fallon was too busy to turn up, spending that morning campaigning in an east London constituency instead. In his place, junior defence minister Harriett Baldwin gave a competent enough performance, featuring the usual dull party lines about the Conservative commitment to spending at least 2 per cent of GDP on defence and the risks to national security of a Corbyn premiership.

One question about the threat of conflict in the High North seemed to throw all five speakers, however. None displayed any particular knowledge of the subject.[35]

By contrast, Major General Mitch Mitchell, the man in charge of the Development, Concepts and Doctrine Centre, the MoD's think tank, has issued the starkest of warnings about the prospect of the armed forces being drawn into a war in the region.

In a keynote speech at the RAF's Air Power Conference in London a few weeks after the Royal United Services Institute debate, he identified the High North and Arctic as the place the service is most likely to find itself fighting in the next ten to fifteen years. He urged airmen and women to get ready, warning that space power would be critical to any fight.

'The tyranny of time and distance is very significant in this region. War at minus 76 degrees Fahrenheit is a very powerful obstacle to military operations, as is the fact that the area is four times the size of the US,' he declared, adding that 'good space support' is already essential for weather and climate change observations in the region, and 'as the region becomes more militarised, space surveillance will play a key role in providing indicators and warnings of intent. But only if you've got the sensors in the right place and at the right time.'[36]

The Norwegian government likes to talk about the High North being an area of 'low tension', arguing that what is needed is 'order and stability, not military solutions.'[37]

For its part, Russia claims it is only interested in 'peace and neighbourliness' in the Arctic and that NATO officials need not worry.[38]

This is whimsy. The reality is that Putin's regime has adopted an increasingly aggressive stance in the region. Russia now has a dedicated Arctic Command, with four specialised brigades, and many military installations in the region. While the US has just one functioning icebreaker, Russia has forty, with an additional eleven in development – showing just how much they are prepared to invest in the ability to navigate these icy waters.[39]

In recent years, Svalbard has become a particular focus of tension with Norway. NATO's decision to hold a Parliamentary Assembly on the archipelago, involving around 100 politicians, policy-makers and academics, in summer 2017 indicates the level of concern.[40]

Under the terms of the 1920 agreement, military installation and activity on the archipelago is forbidden: Article 9 of the treaty specifically outlaws the establishment of naval bases and fortifications and the use of Svalbard for 'war-like purposes'. According to a recent Norwegian government White Paper on Svalbard: 'Foreign military activity ... would entail a gross infringement of sovereignty.' Publicly, Russia insists it has no intention of stirring things up; privately, a leaked Russian Defence Ministry report identifies Svalbard as a key future hotspot.[41]

The UK's armed forces are already feeling the pressure. According to an impeccable Foreign Office source, Russian MIG fighter jets have been known to train weapons on Royal Naval ships in the region. To the alarm of the crew, in one incident, the jet 'locked the weapon on', as if the vessel were about to be targeted.[42]

Such provocations hint at the risks of complacency in this most inhospitable part of the world.

THE ARMY

SOLDIERING ON

THE ARMY

BONSAI ARMY

There's a lesson the Germans learned the hard way which some say applies to the state of the British Army today. It is about a tank called the T-34.

The T-34 wasn't perfect: it was cramped; there were visibility problems; and some of the workmanship was shoddy. However, it was tough, agile and reliable in all weathers, and crucially, it was easy to produce.[1] During the Second World War, the USSR churned out thousands of T-34s from a remote place in Siberia that became known as 'Tankograd'.[2] Soon they had more tanks than the rest of the world's armies combined. By 1941, they had four times as many as the Germans, and the vehicle played a decisive role in Soviet victories on the Eastern Front.

When word reached Hitler about the Russian wonder tank, he demanded something similar. So German arms manufacturers set to work designing an even better model. The problem was that their tank took far too long to make. Meanwhile, Russia kept the T-34 production line rolling. By the end of the war, the Soviets had made more than 55,000 T-34s. The Germans just couldn't keep up. Their new tanks may have been more sophisticated than the rival model, but there were simply too few to compete. The result was a series of devastating German defeats.[3]

Commanders sometimes tell this story to emphasise the importance of what they call 'mass'. The point is that quantity has a quality of its own. This is not a difficult concept to grasp. As a senior army officer puts it: 'If you're a small army and you go up against a big army, you're going to get a good kicking.'[4] However, two decades of cuts to the army suggest politicians either reject the premise; struggle to understand the argument; or just have other priorities. Today, few dispute that the British Army has lost the quality of quantity, and it is unclear how far the downward trend will go.

At the height of the Cold War, the British Army was 163,000 strong. At the time of writing, its official strength is around half that figure at 81,500 regulars, but many posts are unfilled, leaving a full-time force of less than 78,500.[5] There is a serious prospect of further decline.[6] As recently as December 2017, Chancellor Philip Hammond was said to be privately arguing that it could be reduced to just 50,000 – at which point the British Army, once feared and revered all over the world, would be half the size of the French Army and smaller than armies in Italy, Spain and even Germany.[7] Some already call it a 'bonsai army'.

To some in the service, this feels little short of an existential crisis. The 2010 Strategic Defence and Security Review was brutal, chopping 20,000 troops off an already diminished force.[8] Eight years on, the army is still adjusting to its new circumstances and remains deeply anxious about what may be to come.

Once upon a time, nobody thought twice about flying thousands of troops to BATUS, the British Army's training base in Canada, to exercise on the prairie. In the 1990s, they went six times a year. In 2017, they were lucky to go twice.[9] That year, resources were so stretched that a decision was taken to double the length of rotations for brigades switching between states of 'high readiness', training and rest. Each rotation would now drag on for two years, far longer than commanders believed was optimal for producing effective fighters.[10] Other blows included the cancellation of the live fire portion of an annual demonstration for officers from Staff College in Shrivenham designed to show future chiefs 'what land power looks like'.[11] The pyrotechnics were considered too expensive.

Gavin Williamson's appointment offered a glimmer of hope. His predecessors had reluctantly accepted that pressure on public finances meant the service had to shrink. With his punchy public interventions about making the UK's presence felt in the world, the new Secretary of State seemed different. So, when in his first few weeks in the job he visited the headquarters of the army's warfighting division near Salisbury, commanders seized the opportunity to give him a tutorial about the dangers of the army getting any smaller. They found him receptive.[12]

Williamson had come into the job determined to change the direction of the armed forces from retreat to forward charge. He was desperate to reverse what he saw as the 'hollowing out' of the service. But, like all his predecessors, he was constrained by the budget.

In an ideal world, money would not be the primary determinant of the shape and size of the army – or any other branch of the military. If the primary job of any government is to keep citizens safe, the starting point should be an assessment of what that requires and the allocation of resources accordingly. That is certainly how military people are instructed to approach their responsibilities, first defining the objective and then deciding what is needed to achieve that effect.

In the real world, politicians have to prioritise, which results in a rather arbitrary decision about defence spending, based on what is left after other departments with more voter-friendly remits – like health and education – have had their slice of the pie.

'The defence budget isn't really set according to the threat. What happens is that the government decides how much threat it can afford,' says one defence academic wearily.[13]

This is nothing new. Sometimes ministers are quite frank about it. Following the watershed Strategic Defence and Security Review in 2010, the Permanent Secretary simply informed the then Chief of the General Staff, General Sir Peter Wall, what size the Regular Army would be.[14] It was, as Sir Michael Fallon later admitted to MPs, 'designed to fit a financial envelope'.[15]

The military will always want more cash; it is up to politicians to decide what level of insurance cover is required. The trouble is that an approach that is not primarily based on a dispassionate and continually updated assessment of the threat has resulted in an army that is in danger of becoming so small that it can no longer do what it may be required to do.

BRITISH ARMY DEPLOYMENTS OVERSEAS

Afghanistan – Providing NATO/ISAF assistance to keep the Taliban out of power.
Baltic – Britain is involved in the Enhanced Forward Presence in the Baltic. 800 British troops are stationed in Estonia.
Brunei – There is an infantry battalion of Gurkhas and an Army Air Corps stationed in Brunei.
Belize – British Army Training and Support Unit Belize (BATSUB).
Canada – British Army Training Unit Suffield (BATUS).
Cyprus – British troops are part of the UN's Peacekeeping Force that has been in Cyprus since 1974.
Falkland Islands – British Armed Forces are present to deter military aggression.
Germany – British troops present until 2019.
Gibraltar – British Armed Forces are present due to the strategic location of the Straits of Gibraltar.
Iraq – Part of the global coalition to defeat ISIS.
Kenya – British Army Training Unit Kenya (BATUK) is a training support unit.
Nigeria – Britain is providing training to the Nigeria Armed Forces in order to combat Boko Haram.
Somalia – British troops are supporting four organisations in Somalia: the UN, the AU Mission in Somalia, the EU and direct support for the Somali National Army.
South Sudan – Nearly 400 British troops are part of the UN Mission in South Sudan.
Ukraine – Providing Ukrainian Armed Forces with training following the illegal annexation of Crimea.

THE ARMY HAS A RANGE OF REGULAR COMMITMENTS ALL OVER THE WORLD.

Part of the problem is that the majority of MPs in Parliament today simply cannot imagine the circumstances in which the army might be deployed on any scale. They have a visceral reaction to anything they classify as putting 'boots on the ground'. This attitude has become so entrenched since Iraq and Afghanistan that army reductions prompt only limited political protest.

As Prime Minister, David Cameron used to wince at the prospect of criticism over defence cuts from what he privately labelled the '35th Regiment of Briefers and Broadcasters', but it did not deter him from pressing ahead.[16]

Some now question whether the army is large enough to constitute a credible fighting force. MPs on the Commons Defence Select Committee have repeatedly urged the Ministry of Defence to define 'critical mass' to ensure it does not fall below such a threshold.[17] Ministers are reluctant to put a figure on it. They prefer to talk about what the army can *do* than engage in uncomfortable debates about numbers. Privately, they are under no illusion about the parlous state of affairs. In early 2018, a damning internal assessment of the army's warfighting ability concluded that it is not in a position to fight a conventional war, either by itself or as part of a coalition.[18] The review concluded that the army has boxed itself in by focusing on quality rather than quantity.

In 2017, several exercises – one organised by the Chief of the General Staff in January; another by the United States in the summer, and a third organised by the Vice Chief of the Defence Staff in the second half of September – resulted in British forces being swiftly defeated by a notional 'near peer' enemy.[19]

In recent years, nobody in government has talked about the possibility of increasing troop numbers. The height of political ambition seems to be to hold on to what is left. The government is relying on part-time soldiers to reinforce the dwindling number of regulars.

The new emphasis on Reserve forces dates back to the early years of the coalition, when ministers outlined plans to recruit thousands of extra part-timers. The old 'Territorial Army' would be re-branded the 'Army Reserve' and would increase in size by around 50 per cent.

The aim was to create a 30,000-strong force that could be called upon in a crisis.[20] It was a perfect fit with Cameron's 'Big Society' ethos, which aimed to encourage volunteering.[21] New recruits were to be tempted with the prospect of adventure, fitness training and a financial 'bounty' if they stayed the course. The new approach to manning the army sounded reasonable – but nobody could be sure how many people would sign up.

Take a company with a long track record of handling tricky government projects, offer the management hundreds of millions of pounds to find part-time soldiers, and sit back and relax, knowing they will deliver the goods. That was the Ministry of Defence's plan in 2012 when it hired outsourcing giant Capita to manage a mass recruitment drive for the new Reserves scheme.[22] Ministers assumed a 2018 deadline was ample time.[23] What could possibly go wrong?

Almost everything, as it turned out. Starting with a dismal saga over a new computer system,[24] the project, around which the entire Regular Army was being re-designed for the post-Afghanistan era, slowly descended into what one former civil servant summed up as 'endless horror'.

'At one point, the Taliban were recruiting more than the British Army,' he recalls gloomily.[25]

The Reserves were the centrepiece of a wider package of army reforms prompted by the 2010 Strategic Defence and Security Review. The changes facing the service were traumatic: forced redundancies; regiments disbanded; and a deeply uncertain future.

Downing Street had managed the optics carefully, instructing General Sir Peter Wall, who was overseeing the redundancy programme, to ensure the axe did not fall too heavily in the most sensitive parts of the country, which at the time meant Scotland. With a resurgent Scottish Nationalist Party, No. 10 was nervous about anything that might stoke resentment over the treatment of the armed forces north of the border.

The delicate handling of what could have been a political disaster paid off: to Cameron's relief, nobody resigned in protest over what were radical changes to the way the army would be structured.

Wall, then Chief of the General Staff, says that both he and his senior team briefly considered quitting, but concluded that it would only make matters worse. So they did what senior military figures disillusioned by their political masters generally do: kept their grumbles private and got on with it. Recognising that the army had to change, they decided to take pride in creating something new.[26]

'Ultimately there was an opportunity here to redesign an army within a new budget, which would be very effective and very credible although not as big as we would like,' Wall recalls.

> That was quite a creative opportunity. It wasn't just about cuts – it was about a complete redesign. Admittedly, it was going to be smaller, because we were pulling out of Germany; we were coming back from Afghanistan; we've got the emerging prospect of hybrid warfare … and we also had the Big Society stuff with the Reserves. We thought there is a real opportunity here for us and we had to lead it.[27]

The challenge of re-organising the newly scaled-back army for life after Afghanistan fell to General Sir Nick Carter, then Director-General Land Warfare. His brief was to devise new formations capable of reacting to a range of threats and to oversee the full integration of the Reserves with the Regular Army.[28] Following a historic decision to withdraw British troops from Germany, almost all army personnel would now be based in the UK.[29]

The plan Carter came up with was considered 'the most radical army shake-up since the end of National Service'.[30] Part one involved developing a 'reaction force' based on a division of three armoured infantry brigades. These would be heavy forces, equipped with a mixture of Challenger tanks and armoured infantry in Warrior fighting vehicles. They would be used for hard fighting against both conventional and 'hybrid' enemies, including in urban areas, and more difficult peacekeeping missions. Part two involved creating an 'adaptive force' of partnered regular and reserve infantry and light cavalry regiments to be used primarily in the UK in civil emergencies and to provide training to other countries.[31]

Luckily for Carter, responsibility for figuring out how to make the

Reserves initiative a success fell to someone else: General Sir Nick Houghton, then Vice-Chief of the Defence Staff. Houghton had been none too pleased to discover he had been lumped with this task at exactly the same time as the rest of the nation heard about it, which was when it was publicly announced by Cameron.[32] However, he threw himself into the job, optimistic he could come up with a scheme that worked.

'I absolutely bought into the fact that it was strategically mad for a country not to have a strong reserve component. I hated the idea that you should put all your money into a small professional elite and have no capacity to expand; no conduit into society; and no access to a larger pool of talent,' he recalls.[33]

The existing Territorial Army was 'haemorrhaging away' in any case, he says, so a new approach made sense. Houghton's report the following year became the basis for government policy. The idea was to work with employers to find part-timers who could replace regulars, primarily in logistical and support roles. Ministers were prepared to spend up to £1.3 billion creating a partnership with the private sector to sign up recruits.[34] Following a typical pattern for large Whitehall procurement projects, however, things quickly started to go wrong, and soon vast sums of money were being thrown at new systems that didn't function as they should.

By early 2014, Capita had received £50 million of taxpayers' cash;[35] millions more had been lavished on a fancy advertising campaign; and Reserve manpower had increased by the grand total of twenty people, from 19,290 to 19,310.[36]

As one commentator observed wryly: 'At that rate, they will reach full capacity in around five centuries' time.'[37]

This was not just Capita's fault. In a depressingly familiar Whitehall scenario, the MoD bungled a key computer contract, making Capita's job extremely difficult.[38] For several years, everything conspired against the scheme: the war in Afghanistan, which had proven an effective recruiting sergeant for the armed forces, was winding down; unemployment was low; and the combination of the austerity programme and the long-running inquiry into Iraq left the armed forces looking battered. Meanwhile, potential recruits prepared to give the whole thing the benefit of the doubt found themselves mired in an application process that took, on average, 300 days.[39]

As Capita foundered, senior civil servants with a keen sense of self-preservation ran a mile.

'There were several attempts to give this poisoned chalice to me, which I resolutely refused to accept,' recalls one of the MoD's most effective mandarins at the time.

'I was asked "Did I want to do this?" and I said, "Not in a million years, thank you very much. My death wish is not that strong."'[40]

It's no surprise that the career-minded avoided the Reserve recruitment debacle. One familiar with the workings of the scheme recalls:

Saying it was third rate was charitable. The people just had no idea what they were doing. They hadn't done any proper research. The IT systems they were running were completely incapable of taking people on to the books. It was catastrophic. But the army had negotiated a shitty contract that gave them no recourse.

'They couldn't push Capita out or punish them for not doing things effectively. It left them up shit creek without the proverbial,' he said.[41]

Hammond had pledged that the 30,000-strong force would be up and running by 2018.[42] It was clear it would take far longer. Mounting desperation to bump up the figures resulted in various modifications to eligibility criteria, including a reduction in the number of training days to which recruits were required to commit, from an initial minimum of twenty-seven to just nineteen. Nor was it essential for applicants to be very fit. In a seminar at the Institute for Government in 2017, one former Reservist claimed that 'at least a third' of Reservists he observed applying for tours of duty in Afghanistan failed basic fitness tests. 'And they were the keen ones, volunteering for active service,' he claimed. Turning on the MoD's Permanent Secretary Stephen Lovegrove, who was giving a speech at the event, he accused ministers of grossly overestimating the value of Reservists to the armed forces.

'We hear these extraordinarily optimistic estimates of what the military is going to be able to achieve with Reservists in future. In Afghanistan, a very high proportion of them were [kept] at base,' he said.[43]

By April 2018, the project had finally turned a corner. According to official figures, the trained strength of the Reserves was just shy of 27,000, putting the Holy Grail 30,000 target in sight.[44]

All may not have been quite as it seemed, however. Academics monitoring the debacle say the number was artificially inflated by relaxing the definition of 'trained strength' to include soldiers that had only passed the first half of their training.

Dr Patrick Bury, who served as an infantry captain in Afghanistan, subsequently authored *Callsign Hades* and is now a lecturer in Defence and Strategic studies at the University of Bath, says, 'Around 3,100 of the current total is just the army changing the metrics. They've only really managed to add 900–1,000 a year. It will take them another five years to hit their original total.'[45]

Reflecting on how things have worked out, Houghton says now that he knew the government's original timeframe was unrealistic. His report had not recommended such a tight deadline. However, he believes the principles behind the programme remain solid, and is impressed by the progress that has been made.

'We were talking about a cultural change that would take ten years. In fact, they've almost got there now,' he says.[46]

For his part, General Sir Peter Wall feels he was 'over optimistic' about the redesign of the army. He says David Cameron privately promised defence chiefs that when the economy picked up, he would reinvest in defence, a commitment Wall feels the then Prime Minister 'at least sought to honour'. He is disillusioned about the direction of travel since Cameron's departure.

'The current government is not prepared to invest properly for a post-Brexit world … This is a political choice that is already losing us credibility with our allies and emboldening our opponents,' he says.[47]

As the long operation in Afghanistan slipped into history, however, and the new Cold War with Russia grew chillier, the army in 2018 faced another challenge: remembering how to fight a conventional battle. For years, the enemy had been peasants with IEDs in remote villages and mountains. The next adversary looked likely to be a much more formidable prospect.

ATROPIA

Fort Bragg in North Carolina is the largest military installation in the world.* Spanning 251 square miles, it is home to more than 50,000 active-duty US military personnel – and (inconveniently for the US Army) a lot of birds.[48]

The sheer scale dwarfs anything familiar to the British Army, but some of the land-management issues are similar. Both Fort Bragg and Salisbury Plain, the largest military training area in the UK, are evidence that bullets and rare creatures aren't a good mix. Every year, parts of the MoD's Wiltshire estate are off-limits to troops to protect butterflies and buzzards. Fort Bragg is the only known habitat for the endangered St Francis Satyr butterfly, and complicated arrangements have to be made to avoid upsetting hundreds of rare woodpeckers. (Back in 1990, a government decision to declare the red-cockaded woodpecker an endangered species caused chaos: training had to be stopped; ranges were closed; and troops were moved to other zones. Eventually a deal was thrashed out between conservationists and the military involving cordoning off habitats. White stripes had to be painted on certain trees and various protective zones were established. Since then, everyone has been happily co-existing.)[49]

In April 2017, around 160 British soldiers descended on this place of unusual flora and fauna for a joint exercise codenamed Warfighter, involving around 6,000 US servicemen and women. The British lot set up camp on the estate, and for the best part of two weeks they all congregated in hangers and tents to simulate a ten-day military operation.[50]

---

* By population.

Set in a fictional country called Atropia and notionally involving a US Corps and two divisions – one British – as well as a logistics head-quarters, the exercise involved re-establishing the territorial integrity of a 'third party country'. It was multi-dimensional, with a strong air component; a role for Special Forces; and cyber and information op-erations. The adversary was a thinly disguised Iran. For ten days, all of those involved were required to fight an enemy that outmanoeuvred them, outgunned them and outmatched them. They were expected to conduct the mock operation twenty-four hours a day, seven days a week, without a break. The exercise proved highly constructive – and sobering. On more than one occasion, British troops were wiped out in one day.[51]

Before joining the exercise, the British had been given a detailed dossier explaining the background to the conflict or 'road to war'. They were warned that the fictional enemy would be impressive. While UK military exercises tend to be based on a generic adversary with medium capability, US commanders like to ramp up the pressure by basing exercises on adversaries with world-class capabilities.

Pitted against such a formidable opposing force, the British were in for a shock. The first blow was the realisation that Ministry of Defence rules and regulations governing the use of weapons were inadequate for such a fight. The so-called targeting policy was based on years of counter-insurgency operations in Afghanistan and was not suited to the sort of 'peer-on-peer' confrontation that Warfighter simulated, and for which the army is currently preparing.[52]

'It was not only inappropriate, but also impossible to follow. It re-quired a burden of proof and a degree of certainty; a degree of preci-sion, which is impossible in that kind of fight. In a real-life battle under that targeting policy, by the time we'd ticked all the boxes, we'd all be dead,' according to an army source.[53]

The UK's targeting policy applies to the entire armed forces, gov-erning the use of all weapons, from aerial strikes and Cruise missiles launched from ships to rifles and artillery fire. Joint Service Publica-tion 903, a classified document, sets the parameters, and the rules are familiar to everyone. According to army insiders, the consequences of applying the wrong rules can be severe: 'by the time we've ticked all the boxes, we're all going to be dead.'[54]

The British Army takes huge pride in its approach to the moral and ethical dimensions of modern warfare. Soldiers of all ranks continually emphasise their commitment to high standards. In Afghanistan, where Allied forces had the luxury of time to monitor the pattern of life around enemy compounds for long periods before any strike, this meant adopting an ultra-cautious approach to targeting.

According to one officer:

> In Afghanistan that was all really easy, because we had masses of ISTAR [intelligence, surveillance, target acquisition, and reconnaissance] and the Taliban didn't contest the air. So we could find a target and position a *Predator* [drone] over it for days at a time, and just sit and watch video frames to get a really good understanding of what was going on. We would know when the locals were active; when they would go and work in the fields and when they were at home. If we were trying to strike a target that was somewhere near civilian infrastructure, or civilian population, we could match our weapons to the target, selecting exactly the right system to do the damage needed and keep innocent people safe. You could mitigate the effects of the warhead in a number of ways.[55]

However, in high-tempo operations with a peer or near-peer enemy, lengthy deliberations could be fatal. According to an insider:

> One of the questions you have to ask yourself [under current policy] is, 'Are you satisfied that you understand the pattern of life on the target.' And the answer almost invariably in warfighting is 'No'. You just don't have that opportunity with a first-tier enemy. If you're dithering around, saying, 'Should we, shouldn't we?', they'll engage you, pack up, and move somewhere else.'[56]

Though Warfighter was an elaborate computer game, those involved say it felt remarkably similar to a real-life operation. In theatre, they are used to orchestrating campaigns from bases tens or even hundreds of kilometres from the frontline. So what happened was a good indication of how a real battle would evolve. It prompted an immediate re-think about targeting policy.

The exercise also raised questions over how well the British and American armies would work together in a genuine campaign. In the US, security leaks fuelled by the Edward Snowden scandal have encouraged the development of military computer systems so impenetrable they would cripple a joint operation. This became obvious during Warfighter. 'We'd all ratcheted up information security to the point that it was almost impossible to interact with allies,' according to a British Army source.

> Almost everything a modern army does relies on a computer-based system of some description or other. If none of those computers have been built to be inter-operable – in fact, worse than that, they've been built to be secure, which means they're inherently difficult to get to talk to each other – it's very difficult.[57]

The US Army was equally concerned by the experience. After Warfighter 2017, they launched an urgent programme to make computer systems more 'British friendly'. By the time Warfighter 2018 came around, the two sides were working together much better. But there were other challenges ahead.[58]

AMNESIA

Warfighter was evidence of a problem the army already suspected it had: after years in Afghanistan, it had forgotten how to do conventional warfare. Such is the scale of concern about the loss of core skills that, in 2017, Lieutenant General Patrick Sanders, Commander of the Field Army, launched a 'Back to Basics' programme.[59]

Officers cringe at the name ('It was a working title, which somehow took root'), but agree that it's needed. They had rushed into 'combined arms warfare' – an advanced approach to battle which involves hitting the enemy in multiple ways at the same time – before they were sure they were good at executing each type of attack.

According to an army source familiar with the issue:

I think we thought, post-Afghanistan, that we could just turn it back on overnight, and it would all be there. We failed to recognise how much rust there was. When we tried to go back to combined arms warfare, yes, we could do it – it was slow and it was clunky – but we recognised that the basic skills; the tradecraft; the business of being a good infantry soldier; a good tank soldier, were not there. So what we're doing at the moment is taking a step back from this for two or three years to focus on core skills.[60]

'By way of analogy, when you're learning to drive, there are just some things you shouldn't start off doing,' the source explains.

If you're only on your third lesson, navigating the Bull Ring in Birmingham might be a bit much for you. I think there was a view that what we've done is race back to the complex stuff without paying proper attention to the basics. This is about core skills and battlecraft.

Part of the problem is the rapid turnover of army personnel. Many new recruits only stay between four and six years, meaning there is little institutional memory in lower ranks.

One bonus is that 'Back to Basics' training is cheaper than more sophisticated exercises, but it will take time to rebuild skills that were not required in Afghanistan. Meanwhile, if war threatens to break out sooner rather than later, the army is developing a secret weapon.

IMAGINE

A NOTE ON A NEW BRIGADE

Moldova, 2025: *After mass demonstrations calling for unification with neighbouring Romania, the Moldovan government launches a crackdown. Hundreds of 'ring leaders' and 'agitators' are rounded up by local police.*

The Romanian government, which has been anxiously monitoring developments, fears its impoverished neighbour will descend into anarchy. It begins mobilising troops on Moldova's southern border.

In Moscow, this decision is greeted with confected outrage. An ageing President Vladimir Putin – whose thinly disguised militias stirred up the trouble – declares he will head off what he labels 'NATO-sponsored regime change'. His first move is to announce an air and sea 'quarantine' around Romania to prevent NATO member states delivering weapons to what he calls the 'illegitimate regime' in Bucharest. It is the Cuban missile crisis in reverse, with the Russians daring NATO to challenge their dominance of the Black Sea.

Putin warns that Russian warships and land-based Cruise missiles will target any NATO ships delivering arms to Romania. He dispatches a battery of S-400 surface-to-air missiles to Moldova, which he makes clear will be used to shoot down any NATO transport aircraft flying reinforcements into Bucharest airport. Putin means business: thousands of Russian paratroopers start landing in the Moldovan capital of Chişinău; while Russian marines can be seen loading armoured vehicles and stores onto amphibious landing ships at Sebastopol naval base in Crimea. It looks as if the Russians may attempt to seize Romania's Black Sea coast and open up a direct route to land-locked Moldova.

In London, the government is in full crisis mode. The 800-strong British regiment on exercise in Romania appears to be cut off from air and sea re-supply, just as thousands of Russian paratroopers seem poised to invade. Other NATO member states are vacillating, reluctant to provoke Moscow.

A newly elected Labour government led by a Blair-like Prime Minister is determined to prove it has shed the last vestiges of Corbynism, and will not bow in the face of Russian bullying.

Defence chiefs are cautious. The RAF fears there could be huge loss of life if it attempts to fly transporters into the region and is targeted by Russian missiles. The Admiralty is equally pessimistic that it can force a passage through to the Black Sea without a major Royal Navy warship being hit and sunk by the latest generation of Russian hypersonic anti-ship missiles.

There is another option, however: the Chief of the Defence Staff tells the National Security Council he can get reinforcements to Romania without provoking a war with Moscow.

Within minutes, orders are issued to the 1st Strike Brigade on Salisbury Plain to prepare to move to Estonia. The CDS tells ministers it can reach Estonia in three days of hard driving. Back in 2017, when he established the new brigade, he taught his soldiers and officers to operate like German panzer divisions during the blitzkrieg campaigns of the Second World War. The Strike Brigade will move fast to keep the Russians guessing, until it is too late for them to react.

Later in the day, columns of Ajax Scout vehicles and Boxer troop carriers can be seen heading along the M4 towards London and then down the M20 to the Channel Tunnel entrance near Folkestone. Behind the 250 armoured vehicles are more than a hundred supply trucks carrying ammunition. A traditional armoured brigade would have fuel tankers or ration trucks. Not Strike: its 3,000 soldiers travel light. Nor does it manoeuvre in huge columns, like brigades of the past. Instead, it is split into smaller convoys of no more than twenty vehicles to confuse Russian surveillance and make targeting more difficult. Convoy commanders control the manoeuvre using encrypted text updates sent to drivers via mobile phone.

Once each convoy of twenty or so Ajax and Boxers is through the tunnel, it is sent on its way around Europe's motorway network. Time is of the essence. Each convoy commander has a platinum Visa credit card to buy fuel and food; a pass to get onto toll roads in Germany and Austria; and European Union-issued customs exemption certificates allowing them to sweep past French, Belgium, German, Austrian and Hungarian border posts. They use Google Maps on tablet computers to follow a pre-programmed route. They will not see comrades from their regiments until they arrive in Romania.

It is now a race against time. When they need fuel and food, they simply pull into motorway service stations for a brief pit stop. Columns of Ajax and Boxers can be seen lining up behind HGV trucks and VW camper vans at diesel pumps to fill up and go. As the fuel is being pumped, soldiers descend on McDonald's and Pizza Hut outlets at service stations and order takeaway food. To keep the advance moving, tired drivers swap places with relief drivers who have been sleeping in the back of the Ajax and Scout vehicles. Within half an hour of re-fuelling, the convoys are on their way again, heading east.

Across Germany, Austria and Hungary, twenty or so British convoys are speeding down different motorway routes, making it difficult for the Kremlin's spy network to work out where they are going or how many British troops are on the move. Following Putin's playbook, the British start spreading fake news to further confuse Moscow. Social media posts suggest the troops are heading for exercises in Poland or Germany.

The Ajax and Boxer vehicles are not too heavy to drive long distances at speed. They can clock up 60 or 70 kmph as they cruise along mo- torways. Two days into their epic journey, the convoys are approaching Romania's northern border. At this point, they switch to minor roads. As they make their way through the dense forests of Transylvania, the Strike convoys are almost invisible to Russian surveillance drones and satellites.

Each British convoy now moves to a network of pre planned defensive positions just to the west of the Moldovan border, near the Black Sea coast. Anti-tank missiles are positioned to cover roads from the east; mini drones are sent up to watch over the border; and infantry teams begin digging trenches for machine guns and mortars.

In Bucharest, the British Strike Brigade commander is ushered into a press conference with the Romanian Minister of Defence. The British Brigadier makes an up-beat speech re-affirming Britain's commitment to defend Romania. As the briefing continues, each Romanian journalist receives a text message with a link to a streaming video site. It shows a British Corporal standing on top of an Ajax vehicle of the Household Cavalry, with an oversized Union Jack fluttering from its radio antenna.

The Ajax is parked next to the bridge over the Prut River, which forms part of the border between Romania and Moldova. It is just possible to make out the sleepy border town of Giurgiulești on the Moldovan side of the river. In other words, British troops have arrived on Moldova's border.

Romanian civilians come out into the fields by the border crossing to greet the British troops. They cheer every time the corporal speaks during the press conference.

'We are here, we're a bit tired but we are ready for a fight', he says.

Russia Today broadcasts the press conference live. The Kremlin's favourite television network is quick to denounce the 'reckless adventurism' of the British move. But there is no sign of President Putin. He appears to be in retreat. A few days later, at the urging of Moscow, Moldovan leaders agreed to meet with the Bucharest government to de-escalate the crisis. There will not be an invasion this week.

SALLYING FORTH

THE ARMY AT WAR

PRE-EMPTIVE STRIKE

In the event of a military crisis, politicians want choices. They like to keep their options open for as long as possible, so anything that can be deployed fast is a bonus.

Looking at what kind of war it might be called upon to fight in future, the British Army realised it had a problem: it would not be able to offer ministers brigades that could both move fast and survive.

The business of getting forces to a war zone is Eddie Stobart stuff: raw speed, distance and time. The most efficient way to transport troops is by air. The most efficient way to transport armour is by ship, with rail a third option. What you can't really do is fly tanks. It may be physically possible – the Americans do it – but it is phenomenally inefficient, because you can only fit one tank on a plane.

To date, the British Army has been able to offer ministers 'heavy' and 'light' troop options, but nothing in the middle, which is why the army is developing a third way.

'Light' brigades – soldiers with rifles and boots – can get to theatre quickly, but if the enemy has artillery, the soldiers will probably all die. 'Heavy' brigades with 60-tonne tanks are better protected, but they take weeks to get anywhere. As the character of war changes, the army has come up with something in between: two new 'medium-weight' brigades called 'Strike'.[1]

'It's about having a third option,' says a source familiar with the scheme.

It addresses two problems: it gets at the protection problem – because it will be well kitted out – and the mobility problem, because it can get places fast. It also addresses the strategic options problem. We will be able to tell ministers we can put this stuff on a plane, and it will be there in two days' time – and that is an advantage.[2]

The world's largest arms fair seems an unlikely place for the British Army to advertise an experiment, but that is where they chose to plug 'Strike' in autumn 2017. As smooth-talking salesmen plied their wares to ministers and mercenaries, a handsome young British brigadier was busy selling a concept.

'I have no idea where this journey is going to go,' admitted Brigadier Zac Stenning. 'And a critical point up front: the bottom line is that as an army officer I have absolutely no money.'

All the same, the commander of the army's Strike Brigade was fired up. 'There is a real sense of responsibility, opportunity and excitement across my team. I want to inspire you all to join us on this endeavour,' he enthused in a presentation to industry figures and defence journalists. 'It could help us to threaten our opponents on multiple fronts; place our opponents on the horns of a dilemma, and allow us to seize the initiative.'[3]

That Stenning is excited is little surprise. While his comrades spend their days managing routine training, he gets to develop a whole new approach to battle that could transform the army's fighting potential.

Not everyone buys into it, however. Should they find themselves pitted against Russian armoured units, the new brigades will be exposed, because they have no tanks or heavy artillery. They will be heavily dependent on air support, leaving them vulnerable to Russian forces equipped with modern surface-to-air missiles. There are also questions over how a 'live off the land' approach will work in hostile territory. It may be realistic in Europe, where the population is friendly and there are plenty of petrol stations and supermarkets, but in parts of North Africa or the Middle East, they would probably need 'heavy metal' logistics, including fuel tankers and food stockpiles simply to sustain themselves, never mind fight. All this has led some army crit-ics to dub the new Strike brigades 'mobile speed bumps' – organised and equipped to move fast as a sign of political intent, but lacking the hardware to win a stand-up fight with a heavily armed and armoured opponent.[4]

If Strike commanders can overcome these challenges, the hope is that hundreds of highly trained troops will be deployed to conflict zones so fast that they are either able to stave off a full-blown fight or make it easier for the rest of the army when it eventually arrives.

This is important, because accessing contested territory is getting harder for armed forces. Traditionally, armies have dealt with the heavy/light problem by buying the heavy contingent time. This is done by getting the light contingent to the conflict zone fast. This is only possible if they arrive by air. The trouble is that potential adversaries have learned the hard way that allowing Western armies into a conflict zone means probable defeat. As a result, they are investing heavily in so-called anti-access area denial weapons systems designed to keep Allied aircraft out (as we have seen in relation to emerging challenges for our aircraft carriers).[5]

The hope is that Strike will get around this problem by being light enough for troops to reach a conflict zone fast (by ship or road) and robust enough to survive and shape the environment for 'heavier' forces bringing up the rear. The idea is that Strike troops are on the first ship that lands; require only minimal preparation, logistical assistance and support; and that they can get up country quickly.[6]

'The point is that you've got a portion of a force that can get into theatre fast, and do all sorts of things there that will be helpful later,' explains a source associated with the brigade.

So, for example, if there was a particular city you wanted to seize, that you might otherwise only reach in sixty days, and then spend six weeks taking, Strike could seize it for you now. We call it pre-emption.

Another example would be if there is a particular defile [route between mountains] that the enemy would have to come through, Strike could seize that defile. If you can seize that defile early, you've got an advantage. It's about coming off the ship, not pausing to do anything, and driving, several hundred or several thousand kilometres, and being ready to fight at the other end.[7]

Central to the whole concept is elasticity. This stems from the simple observation that armies that conglomerate risk being found and destroyed. While the traditional distance between two armoured vehicles would be a few hundred metres, Strike brigades will disperse for protection.[8] The plan is to use technology to overcome the downsides of being further apart, which can make so-called command and control and logistics more difficult. If necessary, Strike brigades will also be able to pull together before dispersing again.[9]

For the army, this is radical, and will present significant challenges. A commander explains:

Armoured warfare at the moment is the business of formations: if I were commanding an armoured infantry battlegroup, I would have quite a lot of tanks and other vehicles, but I would not expect them to operate independently. We stay within arm's reach of each other. And right now, the average vehicle commander in a tank or a lorry is quite comfortable with that.

Being more dispersed means that a vehicle commander, who might be a 22-year-old lance corporal, suddenly has to make a lot more decisions. Right now, you have one guy [at the head of a convoy] who map-reads and steers. Everyone else follows. With Strike, the 22-year-old would navigate for himself; make tactical decisions about where to cross a river; whether to go left or right; all by himself. He's got to think much more about his own ammunition supply; his own logistics. It places much more of a cognitive and responsibility burden on everyone, instead of just a few people within the organisation.[10]

Strike is designed to address another problem relating to the army's artillery systems. At the moment, they fire big shells weighing 96 lb, which can travel about 35 km. By definition, this means the army can only shoot targets at a distance of 35 km or less, so the positioning of artillery systems is very important: the enemy will be looking for them. If they are located too near the frontline, they will be vulnerable; if they are too far back, they won't hit anything. Strike is designed to give the army a chance to move artillery systems and sensors to the position in which they will be most effective. The hope is that Stenning's brigades will be able to force their way into a contested area and protect themselves, some 700 km or 800 km away from the rest of the army.[11]

The so-called Strike Experimental Group is not only road-testing new structures and tactics, but also new kit, specifically a family of armoured vehicles made by General Dynamics called Ajax.[12] Within the army, these vehicles are a source of both excitement and uncertainty.

'Some of our kit at the moment, if you drive it in a straight line for 60 km, the chances are, it's going to fail, because it's old. In terms of reliability, in terms of average distance before it goes wrong; in terms of fuel economy; and all the digital systems you can hang off it, Ajax is an order of magnitude different to what we've got now,' according to a well-placed source.[13]

The Ministry of Defence is spending £3.5 billion on 600 of the 'mini tanks', to be delivered by 2024. They have been billed as the first ever fully digitalised armoured fighting vehicles and are expected to become the 'eyes and ears' of the British Army on the battlefields of the future. As with all new bits of kit, however, there are already concerns over performance, as well as fears that they will come to replace the army's tougher main battle tank.[14]

Strike will also use a new armoured personnel carrier, or 'Mechanised Infantry Vehicle' (MIV), but it will be some years before it is delivered.[15]

Some fear the Strike concept is overly dependent on Ajax, currently its only real hardware asset, and will need further investment if the army is to realise its full potential.

'Strike is intended to be a formation-level capability. It's not just a couple of new vehicles,' says a source. He believes that, in order to work, the new brigade will need much more gear, including armoured bulldozers and vehicles to lay bridges, neither of which can be too heavy, or they will slow the whole thing down.

> We probably need a new kind of engineer vehicle, specifically to support Strike Brigade. We probably need a new kind of artillery system, tracked or wheeled. We probably need a new suite of ground control stations for UAVs. So all those bits – the slightly less obvious, less glamorous bits of the capability – are planned for, but money hasn't been put against them.[16]

It is ambitious, but if Stenning and those who follow him pull it off, it could be transformational.

TEPIDOIL

Like all emergency workers, firefighters sometimes spend dull shifts hanging around waiting for someone to dial 999. If, after a long period of low call-outs, someone decided to use half of them to direct traffic instead, there would be a problem if a major blaze broke out. It would take a while to get them all back together again, and you couldn't be sure they would still be a fully functioning team.

That is challenge facing the army today as it tries to put together a warfighting division when a significant proportion of highly trained troops are deployed on routine overseas operations.

To be taken seriously as an ally, almost everyone agrees that the UK needs to be able to field a division. It would be helpful for politicians if a division were a fixed size or scale, but it all depends on the task. Lots of armies have divisions, but no two quite mean the same thing. The term comes from Napoleon, who made his army manageable by dividing it first into corps, and then sub-dividing them into 'divisions'. Today the word is used loosely to describe a fighting force of anything from 10,000 to 20,000 personnel.

In general, a division consists of at least two brigades, under two-star level command (major general), with what the army calls 'close support enablers' (artillery, engineers, helicopters and so on).

Within the army and among defence analysts, there is a general consensus that this is the minimum basic requirement if we want to hold onto our status as a nation with genuine warfighting capability and maintain the respect of the Americans as a serious military partner.

'It is the standard by which you are judged,' General Sir Nick Carter has said. In a speech to Chatham House think tank in 2015, he went on to say that the UK has to be able to stump up 'credible hard power' for Allied operations, which in his view – and in the eyes of American defence chiefs – means contributing a division.[17]

What the US wants is for the UK to be in a position to provide a fully functioning division that can be plugged into a US Corps (the main objective of joint exercises like Warfighter).

'There's no doubt about it – if you're trying to have a conversation about fighting alongside the Americans, their frame of reference is a division,' says one senior serving officer.[18]

Before Afghanistan and Iraq, nobody would have regarded the concept of being able to field a division as in any way revolutionary. It was a division that the UK sent to the First Gulf War when, in 1990, Iraq invaded Kuwait; and a division that was deployed in the operation to topple Saddam Hussein in the Iraq War of 2003.

Afghanistan was different. From 2007 onwards, in Carter's words, the army 'bent itself significantly out of shape' to deal with the unique challenges presented by the Taliban.[19] Instead of deploying a division to Helmand Province, which would not have been a suitable formation for a counter-insurgency operation, the British Army sent smaller units known as brigade taskforces, controlled by brigade headquarters. Staff at these brigade headquarters, which became far larger than the traditional model, were forced to adopt many of the roles of a divisional headquarters, such as dealing with NATO officials and keeping politicians in London happy. Traditional divisional capabilities were not needed and became eroded.[20]

'In the long years in Afghanistan, we forgot – and I use that term deliberately – we forgot how to do divisional-level warfighting,' admits a commander.[21]

On paper, the British Army today has two divisions: 3rd Division, based at Bulford Camp in Wiltshire, with around 15,000 personnel in barracks;[22] and 1st Division, which is headquartered in York.

Confusingly, however, 1st Division isn't deployable in its own right, focusing instead on what the army calls 'defence engagement', meaning non-combat operations.[23] Meanwhile, the ability of 3rd Division to deploy – and survive – is in some doubt.

According to a source familiar with the army's divisional capability:

If you said tomorrow, 'We need a division to go and do something,' it could be done. Would it be a slightly funny-looking division? Yes, it would. Would it be logistically sustainable in the short to mid-term? Yes, but only at a stretch. Would there be big holes in our capabilities? Yes, and some pretty significant ones.[24]

As with everything else about the army, this is largely about numbers – or rather lack of them. The ongoing struggle to recruit soldiers has left brigades undermanned.[25] Meanwhile, hundreds of battle-ready troops are currently on NATO and other Allied missions in the Baltics; eastern Ukraine; Iraq and elsewhere.[26]

For the army, the ability to do something unexpected at short notice – as opposed to carry out routine engagements – means keeping units and formations 'idle' but at a high state of training, which is very inefficient when money is tight. When there's pressure to save cash, 'spending' readiness on tasks like the Enhanced Forward Presence in Estonia makes sense,[27] but it comes at a cost, depleting the numbers available to form a division.

If push came to shove, overseas troops could all be called back to base. However, the thin dispersal makes it more difficult to be sure how effectively they would all come together in the time of need.

Amid mounting concern over a possible confrontation with Russia, the army is under significant political pressure to sort this out. The 2015 Strategic Defence and Security Review – written when diplomatic relations with Russia were significantly warmer than they are at the time of writing – made clear that they must rebuild the ability to field a full division of three brigades.[28]

Good progress is being made, but nobody denies it is challenging. This is about weapons, too: the army is acutely aware that if it were to march a division off to war, it might be lost in an afternoon, because of what one source described as an 'enormous hole' in air defences.[29]

In Afghanistan, there was no need to shoot down enemy aircraft, because the Taliban didn't fly. It was much the same in Iraq. Potential adversaries know the British and other Western armies have not invested in such capabilities. As we have seen, they are now ploughing resources into air power, posing a serious threat to a divisional ground force operation.[30]

'We are not in a good place there,' according to the same source.[31] 'The fact is that we lack a credible ability, in terms of the number of weapons systems we have, and their range and effectiveness, to shoot down enemy aircraft because we didn't need it in Afghanistan and Iraq.'

This is not easy for the army to resolve, not least because (aside from two air defence regiments) it does not control air capability. Using aircraft involves working with the RAF, which has other priorities. Tensions between the two services are nothing new: they have existed ever since the creation of an independent air force. There is no evidence relations are getting worse. Nonetheless, the availability of air cover for the army will become an increasingly pressing issue if it appears they might be required to deploy a division.

The RAF (and indeed any air force) would say that it's inefficient to 'park' aircraft over land forces. They take the view that the best way to protect troops is to gain and maintain overall control of the air. This invariably means going 'deep' and striking at source – hitting airfields, infrastructure, logistics and command and control centres – and positioning aircraft 'up threat' so that they can make interceptions a long time before they're even visible to those on the ground.[32] The army always acknowledges the logic of this argument, but remains uncomfortably aware of its dependence on another service. Commanders grumble that they don't get the support they need, because the air force is obsessed with 'dog fighting' at the expense of dropping bombs and doing other things the army would like. Both perspectives have some validity, and few officers of any cloth are outright chauvinists for their service. Most see it as a healthy creative tension that has to be managed, rather than a problem that needs to be solved.[33]

Meanwhile, in common with many other European armies, the British Army simply does not have enough land-based air defence systems (missiles on trucks) for a conflict with an enemy like Russia. These weapons are expensive and until recently have just not been a priority.[34]

How easy would it be to get what they need in a crisis? Not very. To explain the complexity of procuring complicated systems against the clock, the army talks about something called TEPIDOIL – an acronym for training, equipment, personnel, information, doctrine and concepts, organisation, infrastructure and logistics.[35] When it comes to air defences, says a source, 'you could just say, we don't have enough, so click, buzz, whir, let's go and buy some tomorrow, and then you'd have some shiny new equipment.'

But what about the T – training, and the P – personnel, and the I – infrastructure? Who is going to use it; how are they going to be trained; and where is the new stuff going to be stored? In order for something to be a genuine capability, rather than just a piece of equipment, you need all those things to line up behind it. Could we buy stuff off the shelf? Yes. Would our allies give us stuff? Yes. Would that be the complete answer? No.[36]

The UK's ability to field a division is still very much a work in progress.

LITTLE GREEK MEN

The mythological Greek King Agamemnon surveyed his battle-weary troops on a beach by the Aegean Sea on the shores of modern-day Turkey, and tried to figure out his next move.

For a decade they had been engaged in a fruitless siege of the great fortress of Troy. Until then, the war had followed strict codes of honour and decency, but his conventional forces had proven no match for the city's high walls and determined defenders. The king needed a new approach.

In despair, he turned to a bright young commander named Odysseus. The cunning Odysseus, known for his forward thinking, had a brilliant plan: a form of 'hybrid warfare' that would involve using the enemy's rules against them. Greek Special Forces would hide inside a great wooden horse and it would be given to Troy as a tribute to their successful defence.

This would be a deniable operation – the Greeks would first declare the war over, accompanied by a carefully targeted 'fake news' campaign. As the great Trojan warrior Aeneas recalled: 'They pretend it is an offering for their safe return; this is the rumour that goes abroad.'[37]

As the enormous wooden horse trundled into Troy, a local priest named Laocoon sniffed treachery. He pointed out that Greece was not known for its adherence to the rules-based international order.

'What monstrous madness is this... some trickery lurks inside!' he warned.[38] The Trojans ignored him and, in a tale that remains familiar over 3,000 years later, Greek troops hidden in the horse burst out,[39] threw open the city gates to the full Greek Army, which had been hiding around the bend of the bay, and Troy fell within hours. This most ancient of wars was won by the first great psyops campaign.

Psychological operations have a history that goes back as far as war itself. It encompasses everything from leaflets dropped on fleeing British troops at Dunkirk, telling them they were surrounded and urging surrender;[40] to the bullhorns on both sides of the Korean de-militarised zone (DMZ) between north and south, blaring out propaganda;[41] to the Kremlin's carefully co-ordinated social media campaign telling eastern Ukrainians that Russian speakers would face a 'genocide' from Nazi forces controlled by Kiev.[42] Conscious of the increasing challenges and opportunities presented by the information age, the British Army is stepping up its own psyops capability, with a growing team that is specifically dedicated to the art.

Launched in a blaze of publicity in January 2015, 77 Brigade is devoted to what ministers call 'Special Influence Measures'.[43] It is a response to the changing character of war: a new era in which ISIS can recruit British jihadists on social media and Putin's propaganda machine seizes every opportunity.

It is also born of bitter lessons of the Afghanistan campaign, which showed that the use of military power alone is not enough to deliver lasting victory. Officially, 77 is a 'tri service' brigade, staffed by a mix of regulars and reserves from the army, navy and RAF. In reality, it is heavily dominated by the army, a source of concern among those who believe that what the brigade is trying to achieve is so important that it should be a wholeheartedly joint effort.[44]

The origins of the new brigade date back to the First Gulf War, when the Americans urged the British Army to step up psyops capabilities in Iraq and beyond. According to a source familiar with the dialogue between the US and the UK at the time, US defence chiefs were taken aback when – in his words – the UK's response to their appeal was to 'send one bloke and his dog' to Iraq. 'And the dog did actually go with him.'[45]

'The Americans were disgusted. They said, "You can't get away with this," so the government of the time said they would build up a psyops group.'

That single desk officer and his pet were the beginnings of what became 15 Psyops Group. Formed in the early 1990s, it acquired over 150 staff and played an active role in the campaign to win hearts and minds in Afghanistan, running a network of radio stations using local Afghans as DJs, broadcasting music, poetry, debates and even a Helmandi soap opera. It also produced posters and leaflets and ran information campaigns designed to reduce the number of civilians, particularly children, being killed or maimed as a result of stepping on or handling unexploded bombs.

Within the MoD, 15 Psyops was widely considered a success story.[46]

The decision to expand its remit and transform it into what became 77 Brigade was problematic from the outset.[47] Introducing the new brigade in January 2015, the army had invoked the memory of the legendary 'Chindits' in the Burma campaign of 1942–45, suggesting 77 would share their 'spirit of innovation'.[48] In the Burmese jungle, these Allied

Special Forces (formally known as 'Long Range Penetration' groups) had carried out a series of daring operations deep behind enemy lines, to target Japanese communications. To emphasise the supposed parallel, 77 Brigade was even given the old Chindit insignia, a mythical Burmese creature which is half lion, half flying griffin.

Veteran Chindits, who had not been told anything about the plan, were somewhat bemused, struggling to see what the celebrated historical force and the new brigade had in common.[49]

Whatever the logic, in its first two years, 77 Brigade foundered. According to a source who has been involved with the unit since its inception, it was stymied by a paucity of resources and an absence of support from the MoD.

'It was not just that the MoD didn't get it – officials there were actively hostile to the brigade. They treated it as if it were some kind of virus,' he says.

From the start, money was an issue. According to the source, Brigadier Alastair Aitken, its first commander, did an 'amazing job' attracting staff from companies such as Google and eBay, but it was 'all down to his skills as a salesman', as opposed to the benefits package he could offer potential recruits from the private sector.

In the early days, the brigade did not help itself by failing to turn up for an important joint exercise.[50] The fictional scenario was an operation to assist an African country following an illegal invasion. Around 2,000 troops were involved in the exercise in Cornwall in December 2015.

When MoD officials assessed the 'information component', 77 Brigade received what one official derisively described as 'nul points'.

'This was not surprising, because they didn't show. We tried to ring them, and they didn't answer the phone,' says the official, wincing at the memory.

The following year, the exercise was repeated, with 77 Brigade given a bigger role. They spent nine months preparing.

'This time they did show up, and they still got "nul points",' says the same source.[51]

Speaking about 77's teething problems, the source says:

From the very conception, it was a disaster, from linking it to the Chindits without talking to them first; to the abolition of a psyops training programme, which was one of our better programmes and was not replaced; to a recruitment policy that seemed to involve going around Charlotte Street [in London's advertising district] and finding luvvies we didn't know how to use; to the fact that all the basics of psyops and information operations were either not understood or not implemented. They claimed to have a military deception cell, but nobody understood what military deception is. They didn't have the basics in place.[52]

In a move that was particularly controversial within the MoD, a decision was taken to incorporate media operations with psyops – functions some experts saw as fundamentally incompatible.

A fiasco surrounding the dispatching of an undercover psyops team to Ukraine – only for it to have to be urgently recalled after the MoD accidentally issued a press release announcing its arrival – underlined the conflict. 'The Russians must have been laughing their heads off at us,' the source recalls gloomily.[53]

The new brigade also suffered from a shortage of linguists and the type of intelligence required for the work it was supposed to be doing.

A serving officer who joined the brigade in 2016 says his initial excitement quickly turned to disappointment. Speaking in 2017, he described it as 'massively understaffed and underfunded'.

If you hear the word brigade, you think thousands, but we only have 100–150 people. It was sold by the initial brigade commander as being able to do everything – all singing, all dancing – and quite frankly it could not do any of them, because it did not have the infrastructure, it did not have the IT and it did not have the permission to do some of the stuff he was looking at doing. Under the original leadership, I've never seen an organisation in which morale was so low.[54]

He claimed that the brigade's efforts were constantly hamstrung by the reluctance of bosses to take risks – a complaint echoed by other 77 Brigade sources.

There is certain stuff that is not getting signed off on a daily basis because of the risk associated with it backfiring. We're talking really simple stuff, the likes of which a civilian company would not think twice about banging out there, and facing the consequences later on. It's a reputational thing, for UK Plc if it backfires, and secondly, the legal side.

For example, in Estonia, the Americans attached to the Enhanced Forward Presence have a 'playbook' which sets out what to do if 'this happens' or 'that happens'. They know their responses to each situation and it's signed off, so they can be first with the news. Normally it's the person who gets in first who gets the upper hand. We don't have that.[55]

According to the source, the US 'playbook' features instructions on how to respond to various potential PR crises, such as a rape allegation against an American soldier.

'If an American is accused of raping an ethnic Russian in whatever town they're stationed in, they will know what stuff to put out there, in the information space, with the target audience being ethnic Russians in Estonia. We don't have anything like that.'[56]

He claimed senior officers were too afraid to give junior ranks any discretion over how to respond to challenging situations.[57]

There is also frustration within the brigade that Regulars are only able to stay for two years before being rotated to new posts, a career system those who are passionate about information operations do not believe reflects the mounting importance of such capabilities.

'If people can only stay for two years, what sort of message does that send out? This should be a brigade in which people can develop real expertise and make their careers, not just do a temporary stint,' says the source.

At the time of writing, 77 Brigade is said to be in better shape.[58] The Ministry of Defence is reluctant to advertise details of its achievements, but morale is much higher and there is optimism about the contribution it can make. Just as well: as potential adversaries become more ruthless and effective in the information space, a small brigade with limited resources and leaders too timid to take risks cannot hope to compete.

CONCRETE JUNGLES

A NOTE ON URBAN WARFARE

GROZNY

When strong armies fight weak armies in dense urban terrain, everything can go wrong very quickly, as the Russians discovered in Chechnya. The fighting was so intense that in the 1994 siege of the breakaway Chechen Republic capital of Grozny, according to one veteran, 'the air was so thick with bullets you could have walked from one end of the street to the other on a pathway of lead'.[1]

At the height of the conflict, 4,000 shells an hour were pounding into the grey, featureless concrete blocks of the rebel capital. The *Times* correspondent Anthony Lloyd wrote that 'it left anything in my experience so far behind as to make it almost insignificant. You can grade conflicts according to intensity if you desire: low, medium and high. Chechnya blew the bell off the end of the gauge.'[2]

For the heir to the mighty Red Army, it should have been a pushover. The Russians had expected to be able to move their infantry and tanks through the streets with little resistance. After all, they outnumbered the defenders nearly ten to one. But despite the heaviest bombing campaign in Europe since the firebombing of Dresden in the Second World War, and a huge advantage in men and materiel, they would be chased out with their tail between their legs.

The Chechens – tough, proud people from the North Caucasus – had tried to secede from the Russian Federation shortly after the fall of the Soviet Union. The Kremlin refused to countenance it and invaded. The Russian defence minister had boasted he could take Grozny with a single airborne brigade. The battle demonstrates how even the most powerful state can be drubbed on the urban battlefield by a much weaker force.[3]

Urban warfare presents a very different military challenge to the counter-insurgency operations of Afghanistan. During the siege of Grozny, Chechen fighters exploited features such as high-rise buildings, sewers and the subway system to harass advancing troops and hide from artillery and aerial bombardments. They knew the terrain intimately and had support from a sympathetic local population. Russian heavy armour was of virtually no use in the narrow streets, where it was vulnerable to mines, rocket-propelled grenades and other explosives.[4] Federal troops lost 225 armoured vehicles, including sixty-two tanks, to the wily defenders.[5]

Eventually, after throwing the kitchen sink at Grozny and suffering extremely heavy casualties, the Russians managed to capture the city, but the Chechens continued a guerrilla insurgency. After wearing the Russians down, they were able to infiltrate and recapture the city with around 1,500 men. Russia was forced into a humiliating withdrawal.[6]

The British Army has lessons to learn from this urban debacle, and fast. At the time of the First World War, around 10 per cent of the world's population lived in cities. Now the figure is about half, and is expected to rise to 70 per cent by 2045. There are likely to be around 280 megacities with more than 20 million inhabitants. Slums around these urban sprawls often feature large pools of disaffected or unemployed youths, rendering them fertile recruiting ground for terrorism, organised crime or extremism. As the MoD acknowledges, heavy concentrations of impoverished city dwellers are 'likely to become frustrated – and with increasing access to information, there is likely to be a growing awareness of inequality. If not dealt with effectively, this could lead to violent protest and possibly full-blown urban insurgencies.' Many senior military planners believe the urban environment could be the defining battlespace of the twenty-first century.[7]

Of course, armies have engaged in urban conflict since the beginning of time. However, in the past, battles tended to take place around cities and for control of them, rather than actually within them. Defenders would hide behind walls or natural fortifications and hope to wait out the enemy in siege, rather than expect to fight concerted campaigns in the streets. That is now changing, as the conflict in Syria, with its huge offensives against cities such as Aleppo and Homs, has shown. American defence chiefs are concerned about the extent to which US forces are ready for this shift. General Mark Milley, the Chief of Staff of the US Army, has warned that 'the [US] Army has been designed, manned, trained and equipped for the last 241 years to operate primarily in rural areas ... in the future, I can say with very high degrees of confidence, the army is probably going to be fighting in urban areas.'

'We need to man, organise, train and equip the force for operations in urban areas, highly dense urban areas, and that's a different construct. We're not organised like that right now,' he has said. [8]

If this is the case for American forces, it is even more so for less well-resourced allies.

EXPLODING DUSTBINS

In the middle of Salisbury plain is a sparse block of buildings said to be modelled on a rural German village. It is used by the British Army for urban warfare training.

Nothing about this mock village ever changes: it is small and static, with the same obstacles and hiding places for the 'enemy' from one year to the next. Soldiers quickly learn where everything is. The village can hold around 600 'players' for a military exercise, but there are no facilities for live fire training. Soldiers can only pretend to shoot.

By contrast, the French Army has an urban training estate for 1,200 players. They are able to fill the town with a replica population and adversaries and the set is equipped for live fire drills. An even more sophisticated American facility can hold up to 4,500 personnel at a time. [9]

Speaking about the facility on Salisbury Plain, one officer who remembers it from his youth was scornful.

'I bet the dustbins still explode, I bet the dummies still talk to you as you go through the range, and I'm betting I'm still seeing a video tape playback that I saw as a second lieutenant aged nineteen,' he told a conference on urban warfare.

There was a palpable sense of frustration at the event, staged by the Royal United Services Institute think tank in April 2018. The feeling among the mainly military attendees was that the army needs to step up the pace to adapt to this new environment. At one point, the officer asked delegates to rate, on a scale of one to ten, the army's proficiency at urban warfare. The average response was between four and five.

'When I asked this question to a collection of brigadiers, the average answer was a three. One engineer even gave us a zero,' he told the audience bluntly.

The challenges presented by urban warfare go to the heart of the debate over the importance of mass in the army. Fighting in cities soaks up soldiers, putting very small armies at a critical disadvantage (though, as we have seen with Grozny, mass alone does not guarantee victory).

According to a senior army officer who led troops in Iraq and Afghanistan:

> I used to command an armoured infantry battle group, and I owned about 250 infantry soldiers in that battlegroup – soldiers who actually got out and fought. Now that was in a battlegroup of over 1,000 people, so the ratios aren't great for a start. When you look at an urban area, 250 soldiers probably give you the ability to clear one floor of a multi-storey office block, depending how heavily it's defended.

The officer stressed the sheer numbers required to seize buildings in urban environments.

> If you're fighting against an enemy that will try to counter attack, and will infiltrate every room that you clear, firstly somebody has got to make entry to that room; sometimes you have to blow your way in; you've got to clear through that room. You might take casualties doing that. So that ties you down to dealing with casualties, or prisoners. Then before you move on you've got to leave someone in that room. So as you're progressing up a street, you're spending the force, so very quickly you run out of soldiers.

'Every corner you go around requires someone to be a link man,' he says.[10]

The stark contrast between headline numbers of troops deployed on an operation and the proportion of those troops trained and available for combat at any one time is highlighted in a detailed account of Operation Telic, the codename for the British military campaign in Iraq from 2003 to 2011. Describing the occupation of Basra, author Tim Ripley tells how troops were 'spread hopelessly thin'.

'Out of the 9,500-strong British force, it was lucky if on a daily basis 1,600 troops could be operational. If they were allowed to sleep, this would push the numbers of deployable manpower down to around 1,200 in an area the size of England,' he writes.[11]

Defence chiefs remain haunted by how events unfolded there. There were simply not enough troops to contain Iraqi insurgents who inflicted a regular drip, drip of casualties on a daily basis from low-tech roadside bombs and sniper attacks. In the end, this broke the will of the British government to remain in Iraq and they ordered the British Army to retreat back to Basra airport in a bid to cut their losses, leaving the city in the hands of militants. The US Army had more stomach to take the fight to the insurgents and ultimately launched a successful bid to clear Basra in 2007.

IMPROBABLE

The ongoing campaign against Islamic State is a reminder of the urgency of developing the armed forces' urban warfare capabilities.

In June 2017, an exhausted but elated Iraqi Army forced its way into the wreckage of the al-Nuri Grand Mosque in central Mosul. The minaret had survived, but much of the once-splendid structure had been reduced to rubble.

Three years earlier, Islamic State cleric Abu Bakr al-Baghdadi stood outside this mosque and declared the beginning of a new global caliphate. By 2016, the expansion of ISIS had been reversed, and the Iraqi Army, assisted by Kurdish Peshmerga and heavily supported by a US-led international coalition, mounted an operation to retake the city.[12] Operation Eagle Strike was far more challenging than the bare numbers suggested. On paper, coalition forces far outmanned and outgunned the insurgents. In reality, vastly superior numbers were not enough to overcome the challenges presented by the urban setting. ISIS fanatics, assured by their mullahs they would go to paradise for their martyrdom, were determined to make the coalition pay. They started with an army of no more than 5,000 light infantry, but dug in. With extensive fortifications, they were able to hold off an international coalition of approximately 100,000 for close to a year.[13] A US Army study group report on the battle noted with concern that:

> Despite years of air operations against ISIS in Mosul, it still took a nine-month land campaign, enabled by capabilities from the other domains, to retake the city. Operation Eagle Strike also reinforced that operations in dense urban terrain are exceedingly difficult … Mosul provided a seemingly unlimited number of opportunities for ISIS to create a near unassailable defense-in-depth. Thoroughfares into the city, manipulated by heavy equipment, offered obstacles for tracked vehicle movement and provided a lull in momentum that allowed ISIS to concentrate its fire.

The report also highlighted the ease with which insurgents can exploit modern technology to level the playing field. Cheap drones ordered for a few hundred pounds from Amazon or IEDs thrown together with scrap metal and household chemicals can multiply an opponents' natural advantages. The report admits that this has 'significantly reduced the technological edge of the U.S. Army'.[14]

This is just a glimpse of what may be to come. A war in a true megacity, such as to repel a North Korean invasion of Seoul, or to take the streets of Moscow or Beijing, would involve fighting on a scale never before seen. Static training facilities like the one on Salisbury Plain cannot hope to replicate the likely conditions. Instead, the Ministry of Defence has been working with a technology company called Improbable Worlds Ltd on programmes to simulate the complexities of urban warfare in virtual reality. The idea is being pushed by General

Sir Richard Barrons, who sees huge training potential in military computer games. Crucially, new technology can simulate a multi-dimensional battle.

As Barrons says:

> You can replicate London or Damascus, or any part of the world, in extraordinary detail. 50,000 people can be in this universe at once. You can do 50–70 completely disparate activities in this virtual world – all your military training in one universe. You represent what goes in the sky, on land, under the land, at sea, under the sea, in space. You not only use it for training individuals to do their thing but the entire joint force.[15]

NATO will have to learn fast. After all, Russia, currently considered the Alliance's most likely peer-to-peer adversary, now has significant experience of battle in urban terrain. In 1999, the Russian Army returned to Grozny in 1999 to finish the job. This time they acted with ruthless efficiency. Instead of charging into the city, they besieged it with a force of 50,000 troops, executing a slow 'clear and hold' strategy that involved eliminating rebels block by block before moving on. They arrived with a large reserve force, allowing them to rotate men in and out of combat to recover from the intense psychological stress of this type of fight. To avoid losing the battle of wills, they ruthlessly enforced press censorship, banning Russian media from interviewing rebel commanders. The offensive was bolstered by an aerial barrage, the objective of which was 'demoralising the will of the populations to resist and the complete ruination of the internal infrastructure of Chechnya ... Targets included dams, weirs, water distributions systems, fuel dumps, oil installations, the telephone system, and the electricity supply system.'[16]

An estimated 200,000 civilians were killed[17] and both sides have been accused of war crimes.[18]

Since then, Russian ground forces have been able to keep their skills sharp with urban operations in the industrial cities and towns of eastern Ukraine. Few in military circles believe the UK armed forces can match this expertise.

JOINT FORCES

BALACLAVAS

SPECIAL FORCES

DOORKICKERS

In the dying days of his premiership, Gordon Brown struggled to control his volcanic temper. Aides would cower as he stabbed pens at upholstery, hurled staplers and once even shoved a printer off a desk when things didn't go his way.[1]

By contrast, David Cameron was exceptionally cool under pressure. Very occasionally a negative headline would get to him, however – as was the case over claims that the SAS and other Special Forces could be affected by plans for more defence cuts.[2]

It was January 2013, and the Prime Minister was on his way to North Africa on a charter jet accompanied by a dozen or so political journalists when the story appeared in the *Daily Telegraph*. At the back of the plane, reporters were waiting for him to emerge from the VIP section for the friendly off-record briefing that is a standard feature of such trips. Safely out of earshot of the assembled press, Cameron asked his Director of Communications Craig Oliver whether the author of the offending newspaper article was on board.

'Yes,' replied the spin doctor. 'But don't engage with him over the story.'

Oliver was worried about Cameron's mood. Earlier that day, the pair had discussed the *Telegraph* report, and the Prime Minister had not hidden his anger. He knew that any suggestion his government was running down Special Forces was politically toxic. The elite secret warriors are the pride of the British military, their real and imaginary heroics chronicled in countless books and movies. A daring SAS assault on the Iranian Embassy in 1980 which involved abseiling through the roof to end the infamous siege cemented their reputation as the most impressive troops of their kind in the world.[3] Almost four decades have passed since those heroics, and nothing has diminished their prestige. No Prime Minister wants to be seen putting that at risk.

All the same, Oliver felt the best response was to say nothing. As they made their way to the back of the plane, he once again urged his boss not to get into a row over the story. It was advice the Prime Minister couldn't bring himself to take.

Turning to the reporter directly, he made a sarcastic remark he would come to regret.

'Nice scoop today! What you forgot to mention is I'm also cutting the Red Arrows and Trooping the Colour,' he said.

Oliver flinched. 'For the avoidance of doubt, the Prime Minister was being ironic,' he told journalists. There was no plan to cut the Red Arrows.[4]

For the next few days, rumours persisted that one or other of the journalists was contemplating reporting that Cameron really did intend to cut the legendary Royal Air Force Aerobatic Team. Sure enough, at the end of the trip, as the Prime Minister's plane made its final descent into Heathrow, Oliver's BlackBerry lit up with messages about an article in the *Mirror*, claiming the Red Arrows 'faced the axe'.[5]

The aircraft was about to touch down, but Oliver could not wait. Furious, he unbuckled his seat belt and (ignoring appeals from stewardesses to sit down) marched to the back of the aircraft to confront the sheepish *Mirror* reporter.

Back in Downing Street, Oliver telephoned the editor, who was dismissive, grunting that he would deal with it later. The following day, there was no sign of a correction in the *Mirror*. Instead, the paper launched a 'Campaign to Save the Red Arrows'. With extraordinary brass neck, after whipping up a lot of entirely unnecessary public indignation over a proposal that did not exist, two and a half weeks later the tabloid claimed 'victory', announcing that the Red Arrows would be saved.[6] It was a bitter lesson about what can happen when premiers make flippant remarks.

Though the Red Arrows story was entirely spurious, there was a grain of truth in the original report about the possible impact on Special Forces of wider defence cuts. The small print had rightly explained that any reduction to the overall size of the army and Marines would automatically reduce the talent pool from which Special Force recruiters draw. As one defence academic puts it: 'These are not forces with special weapons but forces with special people and "special people" in an organisation are only ever a tiny percentage of the total. Less manpower inevitably means a capacity for fewer Special Forces, not more.'[7]

Indeed, the elite regiments were already – and continue to be – undermanned, not because there are insufficient applicants, but because of a resolute refusal on the part of defence chiefs to compromise on standards. Selectors would rather have slightly fewer men, all of exceptional calibre, than accept anyone without exactly the right qualities.

'I've never known any single Special Forces regiment to be fully staffed. Typically, in a good year, you'd be looking at 80–90 per cent,' according to a former SAS officer.[8]

For Prime Ministers, the beauty of Special Forces lies as much in the way they can be used as what they achieve militarily. Crucially, there is no need to tell MPs what they are up to. A premier can use Special Forces to contribute to one-off missions or ongoing Allied campaigns in war zones like Syria and Iraq, all the while proclaiming that the UK has no 'boots on the ground'. In recent years, Special Forces troops have had a continual presence in both of those countries supporting Operation Shader against so-called Islamic State terrorists.[9] If asked, Parliament would be highly unlikely to authorise the deployment of regular troops to the region, but they have no say over the deployment of the Special Air Service, Special Boat Service and other Special Forces teams.

If a particularly interesting or dramatic Special Forces operation is successful, there is an opportunity for positive political publicity via a carefully managed leak. If it doesn't work out, with luck, nobody will know. Everything from the way Special Forces train; the weapons they use; the type of operations they undertake; and their rules of engagement (as well as individual identities) is covered by the Official Secrets Act. The operational imperative to keep such information out of the public domain is obvious, but the mystique also serves a political purpose. It is deliberately cultivated by the Special Forces community for their own agenda, enhancing their professional status both within the armed forces and more widely. This remains so high that unlike any other branch of the armed forces, Special Forces have few complaints about resources. In a mark of the esteem in which they are held, to a considerable extent, they are able to short-circuit the onerous standard Ministry of Defence procurement process and buy what they need to facilitate operations, from small arms to weapons sights and light radios. On overseas operations, they may even be authorised to purchase armoured vehicles. Generally, defence chiefs ensure that they get what they need.[10]

As an illustration of the pragmatic attitude to spending on Special Forces, private jets are sometimes used to transport their ammunition when no RAF aircraft are available. A former Special Forces officer told of the eye-watering cost of this arrangement, which is linked to selection exercises in the jungles of Brunei.

'Flying one hundred plus people out to the jungle for six weeks, with helicopters, doctors, all the rest of it, is a very expensive business. On every selection, there is an issue over whether the RAF will be able to fly out the ammunition. Sometimes they just don't have the capacity, and Special Forces have to charter a civilian jet for an astronomical amount of money,' he says.[11]

The source, who has detailed knowledge of how the transport arrangements are made, estimated that the bill for such flights was in the region of half a million pounds each time, because of the nature of the cargo.

'It's not just a case of getting your average charter, on which you could put a couple of crates of bullets and grenades,' he says.

> You need a lot of ammunition, which means a special aircraft, in case there is a fire, and very expensive insurance. You tell them what you want to take

out there – huge amounts of grenades and heavy-calibre ammunition – and that is going to cost you serious money. The insurance, the additional customs controls and procedures – it all adds up. Plus you have to give the pilots danger money.[12]

There is no culture of casual extravagance, however. The source stressed that the hiring of private jets was always a last resort and efforts are always made to secure the most competitive possible quote.

To those in parts of the armed forces grappling with over-stretched budgets, this special treatment is an occasional source of envy and resentment. Such is the sensitivity of Special Forces operations, however, that there would be no mercy for politicians or military leaders who penny-pinched at their expense. After all, these men are supposed to epitomise everything the British military does best.

Tabloid tales tend to focus on the Special Air Service (SAS), but the famous regiment with the winged dagger badge is now very much a minority within the Special Forces community. The 22nd SAS Regiment (22 SAS), as the Regular Army unit of the SAS is officially known, only comprises about 350 men out of nearly 4,000 personnel assigned to what is formally called UK Joint Special Forces Group, or just 'the Group' to its members.[13]

The 'doorkickers' of the popular imagination are the tip of a very long spear of hundreds of enablers that facilitate precise strike missions behind enemy lines. For every 'blade', there are about ten back-up personnel. The wider group includes some 600 paratroopers, Royal Marines and RAF Regiment 'Gunners' who provide the heavy firepower and manpower needed to capture and hold airfields and other enclaves in hostile territory.[14] These operatives are part of the so-called Special Forces Support Group. Covert intelligence-gathering – at home and abroad – is the job of the Special Reconnaissance Regiment; while the RAF and Army Air Corps have dedicated air transport and helicopter squadrons to move Special Forces squadrons around the world in conditions of great secrecy. Specialist units of the Royal Signals, Intelligence Corps and Royal Army Medical Corps are also attached to the Group.

Newspaper reports about Special Forces' exploits have common features: no quotes from named sources; stock photographs of heavily armed men dressed in black; and a routine 'we do not comment on Special Forces' response from the Ministry of Defence. Within the higher reaches of the Ministry of Defence, the British Army and Special Forces themselves, these stories are regarded with amusement and seen to have their uses. They distract from real operations; burnish the reputation of the British armed forces; and help recruitment, both to Special Forces and the army in general. As a result, the Ministry of Defence press office never complains about inaccuracies or demands retraction. The reports are simply left out there for people to make up their own minds. This approach enables the Special Forces community quietly to continue going about its work without anyone being much wiser – unless something goes very wrong.

GOATHERD

Just how high the stakes can be on clandestine missions was exposed in an extraordinary episode involving Special Forces and a 'goatherd'.

It was March 2011 and Libya was in turmoil following a revolution against dictator Muammar Gaddafi. The British government was trying to figure out how to react.

Anxious to ensure the UK would have influence under the new regime, MI6 hatched a plan to dispatch a small delegation of intelligence agents to the east of the country to talk to rebel leaders.

This was always going to be risky and a degree of protection for the travelling party made sense. However, the revolutionaries were generally grateful for the UK's vocal support of the uprising, and there was no reason to expect a very hostile reception. The spies could have made their way to the meeting overland without attracting undue attention. Instead, it was decided that they should arrive by helicopter, accompanied by a highly sensitive unit of the Special Forces known as E Squadron, made up of Special Air Service and Special Boat Service operatives who work closely with MI6.[15] As per usual protocol, detailed plans for the operation were submitted to government lawyers for approval and signed off by the Ministry of Defence and the Foreign Office. With everything in place, sometime between 2 a.m. and 3 a.m. on Saturday 5 March, a black Chinook helicopter roared into the desert around 30 km east of Benghazi, disgorging eight men bristling with weapons onto a dusty field. They landed by an agricultural facility which was being watched over by a man variously described as a 'farmer', 'security guard' or 'goatherd'.[16]

Unsurprisingly, the sudden appearance of the aircraft and its suspicious-looking passengers alarmed the gentleman concerned, who feared an attack by Gaddafi's mercenaries. It did not help that when the team was confronted, they lied about whether they were armed. Mari Ghaith, the guard on duty at the farm, told how warning shots were fired by locals, and the British men were swiftly surrounded.

'We asked them to step aside. When we searched their bags we found guns and bombs. We asked, "How did you come here?" They said in a private aircraft. We asked, "Why did you come?" They said, "To reconstruct Benghazi."'[17]

Locals were unconvinced, and moved to arrest them. Fearing that resisting would only make matters worse, the Special Forces unit and intelligence agents allowed villagers to seize their belongings, which included highly sensitive communications equipment. They were then handcuffed and taken to a detention facility in the nearest town. Television footage later showed Libyan villagers rifling through the men's bags. Among the items displayed for the benefit of the cameras was a pair of Calvin Klein briefs with a secret pocket.[18]

The episode was a diplomatic disaster. Not only did two of the UK's most prestigious institutions   UK Special Forces and MI6 – look ridiculous; the debacle also shone a very unwelcome spotlight on the true scale of British involvement in the uprising in Libya.

Cameron was at the Welsh Conservative Party conference in Cardiff when he was informed. He did not take it well.

'DC was fucking furious. Absolutely furious,' according to a Special Forces insider, who describes the mission as a 'monumental cock-up'.[19]

The hours that followed brought more humiliation for the UK

government. A telephone conversation between the then British Ambassador to Libya, Richard Northern, and a rebel leader, in which the former claimed the incident was all a big misunderstanding, resulted in the men being released, but any relief for the Foreign Office was short-lived, as a recording of the excruciating telephone conversation was gleefully leaked to Libyan state TV.[20]

Worse, it transpired that among the belongings that had been confiscated during the initial confrontation with locals were five laptops, six GPS trackers, two 'Bgans' (broadband systems) as well as eight satellite phones and various shortwave radios from the Special Forces unit – a significant security breach.[21]

Members of E Squadron returned to their base at Hereford in shame.

According to a former Special Forces officer who witnessed the fallout:

When those guys came back, it was like the Red Sea parting as everyone tried to avoid them. Among the things that were captured was an encrypted laptop which is a portal into our system. Not a great look. If we had lost access to our portal – which we hadn't, fortunately – it would have not only put our own intelligence at risk, but also that of our allies, and lots of other things as well. It looked so amateurish.[22]

It has now emerged that what happened was much more serious than was reported at the time. The men involved in the mission not only lost sensitive communications equipment, but also the means to access some of the devices – a potentially catastrophic blunder. According to an impeccable source, they 'broke a cardinal rule' and wrote down passwords for their encrypted radio systems, taking the details with them on the trip. These access codes were seized by the Libyans along with their other belongings and may have been offered for sale to rogue states. The source, from the intelligence community, describes it as 'a huge failure of standard operating procedures'.

'You never, ever write passwords down, and for those passwords to fall into the hands of anyone else is a disaster,' the source says.

One concern was what the Americans would make of it. Special Forces are a very important element of the defence relationship between Britain and the US, and many missions are conducted jointly, not least because the US has more military assets around the world, particularly intelligence, surveillance and reconnaissance platforms, including drones and airborne warning and control systems.

'They have far more operationally deployable drones which they keep forward mounted in various places around the world, like Djibouti and so on. So if we have an operation in the Horn of Africa, for example, nine times out of ten we would be speaking to US counterparts asking what intelligence, surveillance and reconnaissance assets they have in the area that we might be able to use,' says a Special Forces source.[23]

UK Special Forces also lean heavily on their US counterparts for transport, particularly aircraft, and practical back-up in the event that a mission does not go to plan.

'We do have our own medics, including trained SAS guys who are also trained medics, and combat search-and-rescue units, but quite often we can't put together this type of capability as well as the Americans, especially if it's an ad hoc mission,' according to the same source.[24]

He said that the vast majority of Special Forces operations were conducted in co-ordination with American Special Forces.

'The first thing we do is check where the Americans are because if we take a contrary position, we know we won't necessarily have the capabilities to follow through. So we are incredibly judicious about that. There aren't many instances where we have to do something absolutely unilaterally.'[25]

Fortunately, the Libyan fiasco did not inflict any lasting reputational damage: American defence chiefs continue to hold UK Special Forces in the highest regard.

'They're exceptional; truly rank with the very best in the world,' according to former Director of the CIA General David Petraeus.[26]

They do not have all of the bells and whistles that only the US has. Only the US has the armada of special operations aircraft. Virtually all our special operation aircraft can be refuelled during flight; and they have enormous night flying capability. The UK has some of this, but it is a much smaller number than the US. And then when it comes to the intelligence surveillance and reconnaissance platforms; the variety of intelligence collection tools and so forth; again, the US is in a class of its own. But having said all that, the UK Special Forces are truly exceptional. As a doorkicker, someone from 22 SAS is the equal of someone from the best of anywhere.[27]

WHO DARES WINS

The Channel 4 TV series *Who Dares Wins?* has thrown a spotlight on the gruelling selection process for Special Forces. The physical challenges in the show are realistic, but what the programme cannot hope to replicate is the forensic psychological assessment of real life candidates as they undergo six months of intensive training and exercises designed to identify those best suited to the extraordinary demands and pressures of life in the Special Forces.

Every year, around 200 hopefuls are put through their paces in a variety of settings, from the rugged hills of Wales to the jungles of the Kingdom of Brunei. At the end of the process, only a handful remain.

Selection courses begin at the home base of 22nd SAS Regiment outside Hereford on the Welsh border. The first phase, known as 'the hills', involves a series of route marches over the Brecon Beacon mountains. The format of these hikes is well established and involves navigating against the clock through various checkpoints while carrying very heavy backpacks. Distances and loads are progressively increased and times between checkpoints reduced. Recruits who fail to meet deadlines are sent back to their base – or 'returned to unit' as it is known – ending their aspiration to become a Special Forces soldier. The hill tests culminate in an event known as 'The Long Drag', a march across Pen Y Fan, one of the highest mountains in the Brecon Beacons. Those who don't make the cut at this stage, either through injury or substandard fitness, are given an opportunity to try again in future. Attitudes to failure on subsequent phases are very different. Recruits can now be 'returned to unit' without a second chance.[28]

Phase two of selection is known as 'the jungle' and involves six weeks in the Kingdom of Brunei. This is considered significantly tougher than the first phase, involving intensive military training in very small groups in extremely challenging conditions. Candidates live out of their rucksacks for the duration. Many voluntarily withdraw part way through; others are disqualified by instructors who are as interested in the personality of each individual as their physical condition.

By the end of the 'jungle' stage, three quarters of entrants will have failed. For the remaining three months of the course, those who are left learn advanced Special Forces tactics, undergoing training in counter-terrorism, surveillance and reconnaissance, parachuting and resistance to interrogation. It is at this stage that they are introduced to some of the unique weapons used by Special Forces.

As the selection process reaches its finale, candidates are put under increasing pressure, deprived of sleep and given minimal time to recover between training events. Psychological evaluations come into play to spot those who might crack in a real-life situation. It all culminates in a mock escape and evasion exercise across the mountains. With minimal food, clothing and equipment, recruits are expected to hide from 'hunters' using helicopters, tracker dogs and night-vision sensors to run recruits to ground. Once captured, they are subject to the sort of treatment real prisoners of war might expect to receive in war zones: deprived of sleep, strip-searched, repeatedly soaked in water, starved of food and questioned by hectoring and verbally abusive interrogators from the Intelligence Corps. In real life, this would probably breach the Geneva Convention.[29]

'They just try to see how far we can be pushed and try to trip us up with trick questions about our service or private lives,' according to one veteran.

If you can't think on your feet or keep your story straight during the tactical questioning then you fail and are out. It's really a question of seeing how resilient you are in shit conditions. They know it's not about seeing how you would react to being threatened with execution or having your family meet with a fate worse than death, because that can't really be simulated.[30]

The last men standing still have to face a final cut by a panel comprising serving SAS or SBS officers and senior non-commissioned officers. This experience can be brutal, leaving some of those rejected at the last hurdle feeling as if they have failed simply because their 'face didn't fit'.[31]

The refusal on the part of those in charge of selection to cut candidates any slack has occasionally had tragic consequences. In July 2013, three Special Forces Reservists died of heat exhaustion during a selection training exercise in the Brecon Beacons in Wales. Carrying military rucksacks, they were on a 16-mile timed individual navigation and endurance test over the mountains on one of the hottest days of the year.[32]

An official investigation revealed that organisers did not know enough about heat exhaustion to recognise the risks. Insiders say it is not unusual for candidates vying for selection to collapse during exercises, sometimes as a result of deliberately carrying less water and rations than advised so that their Bergen rucksacks are lighter.

For the select few who make it through selection, the rewards are incredible.

'No amount of money can buy what it does to a man's ego,' says a former SAS officer.

A billion pounds can't buy it. It is that feeling of being the elite of the elite. Only around one in ten candidates make it through selection, but remember that most of the people at the start line are already elite: Commandos, Paras and so on. To come through that makes you walk ten inches taller. When you leave, you can live and trade on it for the rest of your life. There are guys who were only Special Forces for five minutes, and dine out on it for ever. To an extent, all service people feel special. Take that to the power of 100, and that's how it feels to be in Special Forces.

If there is any concern about Special Forces – and few are raised – it is that these highly trained warriors should continue to be allowed to do what they do best, and not asked to perform tasks for which they are over-qualified.

The respected General Sir Richard Barrons, who under David Cameron narrowly missed promotion to Chief of the Defence Staff, warns that Special Forces are increasingly being drawn into training foreign troops for operations in which the UK and its allies have an interest but which they do not wish to conduct directly. He believes this type of work should be conducted by regular soldiers.

'There is a danger of our Special Forces being drawn into things that are well below their capability,' he says.

> Since we got bored with having other people's wars for them, we now want them to do the fighting and the dying, and we'd like to provide risk-free help from the back. Special Forces have always done this, and they do it superbly. However, the sort of special forces that you need for this particular work are not that special. It's just that they operate with greater licence. What the UK has is superb Tier 1 Special Forces. They're as good as Seal Team 6 and Delta [American equivalents to the SAS and SBS]. Man for man. They should really do high-end, high-risk things at the strategic level. What they shouldn't do is teach the Peshmerga [Kurdish fighters in northern Iraq, who have been fighting Islamic State militants] to shoot straight. The rest of the army can do that. Our Special Forces are a fabulous thing, but they exist in very small numbers, and we will not generate any more. So don't waste them on small tasks.[33]

PLATO

On an otherwise ordinary afternoon in central London, a car crossing Westminster Bridge mounted the pavement and began mowing down pedestrians. Within minutes, five people were dead and dozens more had been injured. The driver, a British-born jihadi called Khalid Masood, then crashed his vehicle into the security barrier outside the Houses of Parliament and ran into the courtyard. In the shadow of Big Ben, he fatally stabbed an unarmed police officer before being shot dead.

Amid the chaos and confusion of what was to be the first of four terror attacks in the UK in quick succession, it was not immediately clear how many assailants were on the loose and whether further attacks might be imminent.

At Special Forces headquarters in Hereford, a call went out to the counter-terror squadron on permanent standby to respond to such incidents. Members of the unit are expected to be airborne within twenty minutes of a call-out. No time is wasted discussing tactics on the ground: the team simply grab what they need and race to a waiting helicopter. It is only en route that they discover whether they are being 'employed' or 'deployed'.[34]

This may sound like a nicety, but it goes to the heart of the very strict rules surrounding Special Forces conduct. In the UK, police always have primacy over the armed forces. If a Chief Constable wishes to release command to the military, there is a strict protocol known as 'Plato'.

For Special Forces, Plato has important associations. It means they can use their weapons. Until and unless Plato is called, they may have the best kit and training in the world, but they can't use it.[35]

On the occasion of the Westminster Bridge tragedy, the SAS helicopter roared over the Thames and came to land at the scene. The men leapt out of the aircraft, ready to go.

Armed with the best available weapons; the best available communications systems; and with years of training for a moment just like this, the men felt they could not have been better prepared. On this very rare occasion, when they were about to 'go live' in the UK, there was nothing they were lacking. When they landed at Westminster Bridge, pedestrians started clapping.[36]

In the event, Plato was not called. Armed police already had the situation under control. They had done a brilliant job: the lone attacker was dead. Special Forces flew back to Hereford, having played only a cameo role.

The deployment – rather than employment – of Special Forces in this case is just one example of how their role is regulated. Even on the most dangerous missions, they do not have a simple 'licence to kill'. Operations are generally signed off by the Secretary of State for

Defence and the Prime Minister and involve many lawyers. In emergencies such as hostage situations, the Cabinet emergency committee, COBRA, is involved. Together with Special Forces officers based at the Ministry of Defence, the Director of Special Forces presents ministers with a plan and everything must be approved by the Attorney General. Rules of engagement are clearly specified. As always, these rules vary significantly according to circumstances. On an overseas hostage rescue mission, troops might be authorised to fire if they believe they, or civilians, are under threat. On an undercover mission in central London, the threshold for firing a weapon would naturally be higher.[37]

Among regular troops, there are frequent complaints over legal constraints on operations. Surprisingly, the law appears to be less of a source of frustration for Special Forces, though they are far from immune from investigation over complaints.

A Special Forces source says:

People have this understanding of Special Forces that we do what we like, but it is all signed off at the highest level. Accountability is even more important to Special Forces than it is to ordinary troops. It matters because Special Forces work on the most dangerous, strategically sensitive operations, in which the stakes are very high. You can't afford to have them operating beyond the law or oversight.

Of course, that always needs to be balanced between duty and care to those individuals who are working in very dangerous environments where they are having to take autonomous decisions because they can't fall back on anyone's instructions. I think we do a very good job of moderating that. We can't afford to cut loose.[38]

Without such controls, the risk is that troops would have too much discretion during operations in remote places when their 'chain of command' is hundreds or thousands of miles away.

There have been suggestions that this is exactly what happened in Afghanistan, where Special Forces were involved in a long-running campaign to capture and if necessary kill Taliban leaders. The operation was so intensive that one former officer described the level of killing as 'industrial'.[39] There have been disturbing claims that during this period, one particular Special Forces unit 'went rogue', killing a number of suspects 'in cold blood' rather than taking them captive, as rules of engagement require.[40]

Unnamed Special Forces operatives have been accused by one Afghan Commando Force 333 commando of planting guns and drugs on corpses to cover their tracks. At the time of writing, an official investigation into the allegations appeared to be ongoing, though details are classified and the precise situation remained unclear.*

According to a Special Forces source, lurid reports of this nature are based on a misunderstanding of the instant judgements required on life-or-death night raids. 'You have to put yourself in their position,' he says.

> It's pitch dark. Your adrenalin is pumping. Everybody is on a hair trigger. You see a movement. You have a split second to make a decision whether to fire. You're relying on the best possible intelligence. If the intelligence you have been given is not right, and you've shot someone who should not have been targeted, it's a bit crap, but you live to see another day. But if you hesitate in those situations, you are probably dead.[41]

He revealed that the troops accused of 'going rogue' had 'conducted themselves with absolute honour in Libya', where they apparently played a key role in helping the Libyan rebel army take control of Tripoli – resulting in the toppling of Gaddafi.[42]

'They got rid of Gaddafi. It pays to remember the whole picture about those troops,' he says.[43]

Attorney Generals rarely block proposed Special Forces operations, but sometimes they impose so many restrictions that a decision is

---

*   The allegations are part of a much wider inquiry called Operation Northmoor. In February 2017, it was announced that 90 per cent of cases would be dropped. The remaining cases are not expected to conclude until 2021. It is unclear whether these remaining cases include the Special Forces claims.

taken not to go ahead. Missions that do not go to plan – leading to civilian fatalities, for example – trigger a 'post-incident review'.

> There is a clear record of all the orders given; a very specific audit trail. What happens is that the Ministry of Defence will send out a lawyer, who will examine all the paperwork. It is not a witch hunt – they don't cut straight to the individual. That is the last bit: sitting down with the individual or individuals who may have pulled the trigger.

'It is a forensic analysis, matching what the orders were, what the controls were, and what actually happened,' according to a Special Forces source familiar with the process.[44]

In his experience, '9.9 times out of ten nothing further comes of it', 'because of the professionalism of the guys'.[45]

Given how very few individuals have the superlative qualities required to join the UK's Special Forces, that is little surprise.

ORCHESTRAS

JOINT FORCES

In a crisis, different branches of the armed forces need to stop acting like separate musical bands and come together like an orchestra. In 2014, their ability to do this was put to the test in an extraordinary humanitarian mission in west Africa. Ultimately, it was a success and British troops helped save many lives, but there were moments of farce and high drama which exposed the weaknesses of what defence chiefs call 'joint force' operations. When time was of the essence, military figures found themselves doing battle with ministers and officials overwhelmed by the complexity of it all and anxious about how the operation would evolve. Having committed to the rescue operation, they were loath to authorise the deployment of naval ships to assist, fretting about what British voters would think.

It was November 2014, and the Ebola virus was sweeping through the West African nations of Guinea, Liberia and Sierra Leone and threatening to spread further across the region. The World Health Organization labelled it 'the most severe acute health emergency seen in modern times' and appealed to the international community to act.[1] A global pandemic could have caused more devastation than any number of conventional bombs, bullets or ISIS-inspired jihadis. Tackling the virus required an unprecedented multinational operation of considerable sophistication and put the UK's newly developed 'joint forces' concept to the test.

The British involvement began on the sidelines of a meeting of the United Nations General Assembly, when representatives of the nations of the G7 sat down to lunch. The then Prime Minister David Cameron and Foreign Secretary Philip Hammond had returned home, so junior Foreign Office minister Tobias Ellwood was the UK man. US Secretary of State John Kerry was holding court.

'What are we going to do about Ebola? There are a lot of us here, we should be able to work something out?' Kerry asked.

After some discussion, Ellwood took out a map.

'Why don't we do it geographically? It would be easier if we [the British] took Sierra Leone, for example, as we have a relationship with that country. Others can take countries they have a relationship with, and so on,' he suggested.

The delegates nodded in assent.

'Sounds like a good idea. Let's do that,' Kerry agreed.[2]

The UK armed forces contribution to the multinational effort would be codenamed Operation Gritrock. It would be nice to imagine that once the decision had been made to get involved, Her Majesty's Government swung into action, with the Foreign Office, the Ministry of Defence, the Department of Health and the Department for International Development all working together seamlessly. Two ships, RFA *Argus* and the amphibious flagship HMS *Ocean*, were particularly suited for this sort of operation: *Argus* was fitted with world-class medical facilities and both vessels were designed to transport and land heavy equipment including helicopters.

Here was a moment when these unique and expensive platforms – which are constantly under threat in defence cuts – could come into their own.

However, according to Lieutenant General Sir David Capewell, who co-ordinated the armed forces' response to Ebola in his role as Chief of Joint Operations at Joint Forces Command (2011–15), it took 'three weeks of lobbying' for permission from Whitehall to send either vessel.

'There was huge prevarication in Whitehall and the Cabinet Office to release RFA *Argus*,' he says.

Either RFA *Argus* or HMS *Ocean* was the perfect platform to provide offshore medical relief for our own people, and the boats and helicopters needed by the team 'up country', at the sharp end of the operation. But Whitehall was worried about mission creep and optics while the bodies piled up...

Capewell emphasises that everyone in government 'wanted to do the right thing'.[3]

> It's not that people were being difficult. I think this was a collective anxiety about what we were walking into. Nobody knew about Ebola. We didn't understand it. Naturally there was an anxiety about investing in something when we really didn't know what the outcome would be. When you are faced with uncertainty and complexity, navigating your way through is really difficult.

'People get paralysed,' he says.[4]

Eventually, RFA *Argus* was dispatched and British Army engineers arrived in Sierra Leone to build facilities where people who might be infected could be isolated and treated.[5] The army tarmacked surfaces; built medical centres; and supported a force of more than 750 personnel from across government to curb the spread of the disease.[6]

While Operation Gritrock was not officially under military control, with the Department for International Development taking the lead on the ground, the thread that held together all the different agencies – the Department of Health, DFID, the United Nations and the Ministry of Defence – was the Ministry of Defence's 'Permanent Joint Headquarters' in Northwood, which heads up so-called combined operations. Capewell – a Royal Marine officer who earned a reputation among American defence chiefs as the most impressive UK operational commander of a generation – had to manage not only the real risk of British troops being infected by Ebola; but also the paranoia of panicky Westerners who were not in any danger. At one point, cabin crew on a Russian private jet funded by British taxpayers refused to leave the plane for fear of catching the virus.

According to Capewell:

At vast expense, the Department for International Development hired a Russian jet to take the President of Sierra Leone to London. It broke down for two weeks in Freetown. We had hysterical Russian stewardesses who looked like expensive hookers who would not get off the jet unless we gave them Marigolds and a gas mask! Not a very convincing approach to barrier protection! I don't think they showered for two weeks.[7]

Amid all the hysteria, his own return journey to the UK was complicated by Spanish authorities who thought the wings of his military aircraft might be contagious. He recalls:

I was heading back to the UK after seeing the Sierra Leone President. We wanted to refuel in Spain, but Spanish air control would not allow us into Spanish airspace because they thought we had Ebola on the wings. It turned into a farce. This was how scared everybody was. They wouldn't allow us into airspace and quarantined my jet in Tenerife![8]

Troops and medics on the frontline of the operation were working in very dangerous conditions to defeat the disease, an 'enemy' they had never encountered before.

Critical to the success of Operation Gritrock was understanding the local culture. Only when it became apparent that grieving relatives of victims were inadvertently spreading infection because of certain traditions did efforts to bring it under control begin to bear fruit.

Capewell says:

The thing that changed the course of events was the late discovery that burial practices – body washing – were a key vector and multiplier for the disease. As soon as we stopped this in the villages, all the science, the hospital-building and border control efforts began to have a measurable effect – thankfully.[9]

By November 2015, Sierra Leone was declared free of Ebola.[10] The global disaster health agencies had feared was averted. There was a single isolated case of a UK nurse being infected, but she recovered.[11]

The belated discovery that cultural practices were exacerbating the crisis was a reminder of lessons learned in Afghanistan. Without significant investment, tribal and socio-religious dynamics can take a very long time to grasp.

'Cultural understanding was key, and we lacked that to start with,' admits Capewell. 'This is where much more effort is required. It took us ten years to get a meagre handle on this in Afghanistan, with huge investments in anthropology. These were hard lessons to learn, even harder to resource, and very easy to forget.'[12]

Many in defence circles believe that in crises such as this, a heavy price is paid for the neutering of the Foreign and Commonwealth Office. Its budget has been decimated in recent years, now standing at just £1.3 billion a year – around a tenth of the Department for International Development's budget.[13] When the armed forces are deployed on overseas operations, they now have less local intelligence.

Sir Nick Harvey, a Liberal Democrat defence minister during the coalition years, is still appalled by the hammering of the Foreign and Commonwealth Office budget under that administration.

> Can I tell you what I think was one of the most scandalous pieces of vandalism of the coalition's austerity programme? It was cutting the Foreign Office budget and saving peanuts. They closed embassies here, there and everywhere, laid off diplomats and staff, and the savings probably amounted to about a quarter of the Ministry of Defence's coffee budget.

'And the loss of diplomatic and intelligence reach from that has probably undermined our security as much as any reduction in aircraft,' he says.[14]

He claims the decision had a heavy impact on the UK's military campaign in Libya:

> When we went into Libya suddenly and unexpectedly, we had no up-to-date intelligence of what was going on in that country at all. There is a graphic example: we were using a mix of Second World War maps and

Google Maps because we had so under-invested. Quite rightly the government put more and more money into intelligence services, MI5, MI6 and so on, but if you haven't got embassies and outposts in all these places, with the spooks hidden in the back, you haven't got the intelligence.[15]

Becoming a military 'orchestra' is a significant cultural challenge for the different branches of the armed forces, requiring the casting aside of generations of rivalry. When major procurement decisions are being made, this competition is understandable: if the Ministry of Defence opts to spend billions on new planes or ships, generals will naturally worry about what that means for the army. However, army, navy and RAF tribalism is so ingrained that it is sometimes very petty, as a spat over a failure by RAF chiefs to namecheck the navy in a speech about the F-35 fighter jets shows.

Air Chief Marshal Sir Stephen Hillier made the omission at an event in spring 2018 to mark the 100th anniversary of the RAF at the Smithsonian National Air and Space Museum in Washington DC, during which he spoke about the reformation of the Dambusters squadron to fly the new Lightning II warplanes off the aircraft carriers.

'He did a very good speech. But there was no mention of the navy and no mention of the aircraft carrier or going to sea,' according to a sailor.

'He mentioned more about working closely with the Americans than his own services in the UK. It was a very blatant omission and it was very noticeable. It was an attempt to undermine the unity between the services. I was quite shocked. A number of people were.'[16]

By contrast, navy sources say they are 'punctilious' about acknowledging the RAF whenever the aircraft carriers and the F-35 jets are mentioned in public.

This corrosive low-level bickering indicates the scale of the challenge facing those charged with promoting 'jointery' in the armed forces. There is nothing particularly new about the concept, but efforts to save money have pushed it up the agenda. The 2010 Strategic Defence and Security Review identified it as a way to reduce duplication across the forces and make more efficient use of so-called enabling capabilities (like intelligence, surveillance, acquisition and information systems), which are like the operational 'glue' between the army, navy and RAF. Bringing together capabilities that all three services need was also a way to improve cyber defence. A decision was taken to put a four-star officer in charge of a new operation to ensure the UK armed forces could take full advantage of developments in the joint realm.

For General Sir Richard Barrons, Commander of Joint Forces Command between 2013 and 2016, 'jointery' represented a very different way of thinking for the armed forces, focusing on effects – what the armed forces wanted to achieve – rather than the 'platforms' like tanks, planes or ships. He hoped it would usher in a cultural change, discouraging the army, navy and RAF from endless squabbling over pieces of an ever-shrinking pie.[17] However, he found it was often just used as an excuse for more cuts. During his time at head of Joint Forces Command, he says he was called upon to make 'Herculean efficiencies' in an economy drive that left defence 'locked in a serial process of reduction'.

> For a long while you can call this efficiency, and yes, there's been fat to cut over the years, where things were done badly or duplicated, or were profligate. The whole march of 'jointery' is part of that. But there does come a point where what you're doing is pretending it's efficient, when you've got vehicles you've got no spares for; or you've got no fuel; or you cancel exercises in Canada because you can't afford the ammunition.

'It happens all the time,' he says.[18]

Capewell sees 'jointery' as vital to the success of the armed forces in future operations. He believes the Ebola experience offers valuable lessons about the type of conflict the military may face: highly complex, multi-layered, and full of the unexpected.

'It is a weather vane of what the future might be. We are going to have to get used to this if we are going to deal with the hybrid threats of tomorrow,' he says.[19]

He warns that efforts to fight back will not be effective unless the armed forces and other government departments and agencies spend more time rehearsing together.

> The Whitehall apparatus has to practise this to the point of failure, so we know how good or not we are. That's why the Ebola lessons are an important insight into how we will have to organise for the hybrid challenges of the future. History repeatedly tells us that it takes a catastrophe to put things right. The requisite habits to co-operate, see the synergy, spot the anomaly and opportunity in a 'whole force' or 'cross government' approach is much harder to grasp and embed if we only become joint when it suits us.[20]

Joint exercises are expensive, so they are often cancelled.

'The result is that we do not really train for how we want to – or would – fight. This is tantamount to the England squad turning up for the World Cup Final the night before,' he says.

'It's hard to maintain the instinct and nous for joint operations if you don't practise persistently – shadow boxing is no good in a street fight.'[21]

READY OR NOT

IF WAR COMES TOMORROW

SWEDEN'S WARNING

During the Cold War, the British armed forces held a dress rehearsal for World War Three. 'Exercise Crusader 80' saw roads leading to the Channel and North Sea ports clogged with convoys of army trucks as more than 20,000 Territorial and 10,000 Regular soldiers headed to Germany.[1]

Such an exercise today might create some alarm. In the 1980s, however, every single soldier, sailor and airman – as well as hundreds of thousands of Reservists – had a role to play in plans to mobilise the nation for total war against the Soviet Union. Across the country, warehouses, dockyards, airfields, vehicle stores and ammunition depots were rammed with everything needed to get the British armed forces onto the battlefield. In every military base in the UK and around the world, commanding officers and their senior staff had keys to a safe containing their unit's secret instructions for what was called 'transition to war'. Fleets of tanks, ships and aircraft were ready to go. Every year, units rehearsed their parts. Little thought was given to how to keep the war going for more than a few weeks: World War Three was expected to be very short.

The Ministry of Defence never really got round to cancelling or recalling the secret battle orders. They were left locked in safes across Britain, gathering dust. An officer recalls finding one of these plans during a routine inspection in the mid-1990s.

'It was a massive typed document, several inches thick. Every eventuality was covered, down to how we were supposed to bury hundreds of dead soldiers who had been contaminated by radioactive fallout,' he recalls. 'You felt like you were reading our nation's suicide note to itself.'[2]

Had the plans been called upon after the Cold War, they would not have been much use: mobilisation on the scale envisaged in the 1980s would simply no longer be possible. Today, there is mounting concern within military circles over the UK's readiness for war. If the next conflict is not at a time or place of our choosing, the ability of the armed forces to mount a credible, timely response could hardly be more important.

As we have seen, the collapse of the Berlin Wall in 1989 changed assumptions of the previous forty-four years. With no enemy at the gate, there seemed little point in keeping the armed forces on a near-permanent war footing. The government adopted a peacetime psyche. A new system was introduced under which many ships, tanks and aircraft were simply not ready for action.

The new regime became known as a 'readiness cycle' or 'graduated readiness'. Every major army, navy and air force headquarters set up schedules in which units were rotated through stretches of 'high readiness' when they were supposed to be manned, equipped, trained and prepared to deploy overseas on operations at a few days' notice. The system continues to this day.

During these 'on-call' periods, each service is expected to have a certain number of personnel fully trained and fitted out with the right uniforms, tropical disease jabs, guns, ammunition and in-date passports. All their major kit – tanks, helicopters, fighter jets or field guns – is supposed to be fully serviced with enough spare parts to keep them going on foreign battlefields. They remain in barracks, on alert.

The system has significant implications for how the military operates and is funded. Personnel held at high readiness cannot go on training or promotion courses and cannot holiday abroad. Preparing them requires what is known as 'collective training', in which everyone in the unit practises their combat role together. In army regiments, after soldiers have completed basic training, they must learn to use more complex weapons such as artillery, mortars and machine guns. They are also taught to drive tracked vehicles, operate radios and then bring all these skills together to fight as a unit. With between 6,000 and 10,000 new recruits arriving in army regiments every year – more than a quarter of the frontline army's strength – there is a constant churn of people requiring this training.[3]

The cost of a collective exercise like this, for a single army regiment, can run to more than £8 million.[4] Because it is all so expensive, over the past thirty years, governments have progressively reduced the percentage of armed forces that are combat-ready. Politically, it makes sense: the 'headline' number of tanks, planes and ships still looks good, masking the reality that barracks are full of tanks being cannibalised for spares; fighter jets are stuck in hangars; and ships are tied up in docks.

Some European governments are beginning to acknowledge that if war comes tomorrow, ordinary people as well as soldiers, sailors and airmen and women will need to play their part, or at least know how to react. The continuing peacetime mentality, and a reluctance on the part of the government to cause unnecessary alarm, means there has been little public debate about this in the UK. Other countries have been bolder. In May 2018, leaflets began dropping through letterboxes of every household in Sweden, offering advice on preparing for various potential disasters, including armed conflict. The government suggested keeping tins of food, tea lights and wet wipes, and being ready for power cuts. If that happens, the leaflet suggested, families should 'gather together in one room, hang blankets over the windows, cover the floor with rugs and build a den under a table to keep warm.'[5]

SWISS ARMY KNIVES

If war comes tomorrow, the Swiss will be even better prepared. They may not have not taken part in a foreign war since Switzerland's neutrality was established by the Treaty of Paris in 1815, but that does not mean they eschew arms. On the contrary, the Swiss Army has more than 150,000 soldiers at its disposal. Most train periodically over a ten-year period of military service but live at home and have other full-time jobs. The aim is that they are ready to be deployed if the country faces an existential threat.[6] Around 20,000 young soldiers a year attend basic training for eighteen weeks, and uniforms and weapons are then kept at home, ready for rapid mobilisation. A high proportion of Swiss civilians therefore own guns. Military service is mandatory for men, but women can volunteer, and conscientious objectors can do community service instead.[7]

In 2016, the Swiss Senate and House voted to reduce the size of the Swiss Army to 100,000.[8] Parliament prioritised the ability to deploy 35,000 troops within ten days. It is an aspiration the British Army can only dream of.

Until the war in Afghanistan, the British Army was organised into two main combat divisions, each with three combat-deployable armoured or mechanised brigades of around 8,000 troops.[9] By 2009, the campaign against the Taliban was soaking up so many troops that both divisions had to be trawled to keep 10,000 troops in the campaign. The war in Helmand Province was so different from armoured combat with tanks that it required a complete re-think. When General Sir David Richards took over as head of the army in 2009, he launched Operation Entirety, cancelling almost all training that did not relate to the war effort.[10]

After 2010, 'readiness' hit a new low in units not earmarked to fight in the Afghan war. Operation Entirety remained in force until the end of 2014, and for a five-year period the army's armoured forces were only funded to keep a single armoured battlegroup with just thirty-six Challenger tanks and twenty-eight Warrior troop carriers ready for battle at five days' notice.[11]

The way kit was acquired for Afghanistan had long-term repercussions for readiness after the campaign. The number of casualties to Taliban-improvised bombs, snipers and ambushes had forced the British Army to rush new equipment like helmets, body armour, sniper rifles, machine guns and rocket launchers into service. Under a fast-track procurement system called 'urgent operational requirements', an array of other materiel like electronic jammers, mine detectors, battlefield internet communications, medical kits and bomb-proof vehicles was hurried into service. Only enough was bought for troops in Afghanistan, however, leaving the rest of the British Army to make do. When the campaign ended in 2014, the best kit was re-distributed to high-readiness units, which took turns to use it during their periods on alert duty. Meanwhile, a new vehicle management system, also designed to save money, involved the bulk of the army's Challengers, Warriors, AS-90 self-propelled howitzers and other armoured vehicles being removed from British Army bases and dumped in warehouses near ports in Germany and southern England. These vehicles were supposed to be modified with the latest counter-mine systems, radios and armour plates. The idea was that they should be stored in climate-controlled warehouses, ready to be collected by army units heading for overseas missions in time of crisis, or for major exercises. The flaw in the plan was exposed in November 2014, when a squadron of the King's Royal Hussars flew to Poland to pick up a fleet of Challengers for a military exercise called Uhlan Eagle in Poland and found several of the vehicles did not work. Troops ended up having to call back to their base in Wiltshire and arrange for replacements.[12]

The 'readiness cycle' effectively creates a two-tier army, a small part of which is fit to go to war, while the rest muddles along with sub-standard equipment. If only a very small fraction of troops can be mustered at short notice, headline figures for the overall size of the army become considerably less meaningful.

ARGY BARGY

When an Argentinian submarine vanished in the southern Atlantic in November 2017, the RAF joined the search-and-rescue mission.

Laying to rest the decades of enmity following the Falklands War, ministers sent a Voyager aircraft carrying equipment and submarine specialists on a sixteen-hour emergency flight from RAF Brize Norton in Oxfordshire to the southern Argentinian city of Comodoro Rivadavia.[13]

Sadly, the mission failed – the submarine was never recovered – but it is a tribute to the RAF that it mustered the resources, because it has very little spare 'readiness'. As we have seen, the demands of Operation Shader mean it is already very stretched, and its ability to respond to emergencies is continually tested.

As with army regiments, RAF squadrons (their basic fighting units)* work on readiness cycles, typically culminating in a bombing exercise with live weapons in the USA. Readiness is complicated by aircraft maintenance requirements, which take a significant proportion of jets out of circulation at any one time. At regular intervals, every aircraft needs to be completely dismantled and overhauled, putting it out of service for several months. In February 2017, twenty-one of the RAF's sixty-seven Tornado GR4 bombers and forty-three of its 135 Typhoon fighters were in bits. These overhauls are paid for through five- or ten-year-long contracts with BAE Systems, which are extremely costly. A recent maintenance contract for Typhoons, for example, covering the aircraft till 2026, will cost taxpayers £2.1 billion.[14]

In a further challenge, the RAF must keep some Typhoon fighter jets on continuous alert to respond to threats to the UK homeland. After the 9/11 terrorist hijackings in the US, this previously mundane activity took on far more importance. It is now the RAF's prime operational tasking.

Known as Quick Reaction Alert duty, it requires keeping a pair of RAF fighters poised for take-off at one base in Lincolnshire and another in the north of Scotland. In the traditions of the Battle of Britain, pilots and ground crew live and sleep next to their jets so that they can be airborne in less than ten minutes. It is a 24/7, 365-day-a-year mission that gobbles resources. On both bases, a second pair of Typhoon pilots is ready to step in if the first pair is scrambled, so at any one time, there are four pilots on Quick Reaction Alert duty, plus four more on standby. In a typical week there are fifty-six Quick Reaction Alert pilot slots to be filled by some ninety pilots. A further six Typhoon pilots also have to take turns to be on duty in the Falklands. In effect, this

---

* Most flying squadrons are commanded by a wing commander who oversees around 200 personnel and between twelve and sixteen aircraft.

means that three out of five RAF Typhoon squadrons are locked into Quick Reaction Alert duty at any one time. When holidays, illness and training commitments are thrown into the mix, it means the RAF Typhoon Force struggles to free up anything more than a squadron's worth of aircraft and pilots to deploy overseas.

As with the army, the 2010 defence review hit RAF readiness hard. Plans to expand the Typhoon force beyond five squadrons were put on hold. The Harrier jump jet force was disbanded. The seven-squadron Tornado bomber force was supposed to be reduced to just two units when the Afghan war ended in 2014.

It was a cut too far, effectively ending the RAF's ability to conduct a major mission involving strike operations for more than a few months.

According to one RAF officer: 'Everyone knew what it meant when the government announced it. The Typhoon had yet to be cleared to carry the same air-to-ground weapons as the Tornado so the government was taking a "strike capability holiday".'[15]

The risks were exposed in summer 2014 when Islamic State launched its operation to capture Mosul and Kurdistan in Iraq. RAF Tornados were scrambled to fly to Cyprus to launch air strikes, marking the beginning of Operation Shader. It soon became clear that the mission was not going to be over quickly, and the government was forced to find the money to keep the third Tornado squadron in service for another four years.

'It was a close thing. If Islamic State had delayed their offensive by a couple of months the Tornado guys would have been paid off and the RAF would not have been in the game,' said a senior RAF officer involved in running the air war in Middle East.[16]

OPERATION COUGAR

When Prime Minister Theresa May ordered punitive air strikes on President Bashir al-Assad's regime in Syria in spring 2018, it was widely reported that Astute submarines were sent to the Mediterranean in support.[17] In reality, none went. It has emerged that for all the media excitement, there was never a plan to deploy them in the first place.

According to Whitehall sources, after news of the chemical attack broke, it took No. 10 several days to communicate to the MoD how the Prime Minister wanted to respond (which says something about political readiness for a military crisis). During this period, Downing Street spin doctors are said to have become increasingly twitchy about potential criticism over the time it was taking to formulate a plan, so they 'filled the void' by briefing that she was deploying submarines. According to a source who was involved:

> After the attack, I was in Downing Street trying to find out what the PM was thinking so I could report back to the MoD. Nobody could tell me what was going on. It felt as if it was not even on their radar. There was a complete absence of information coming out of the government. Eventually, someone in No. 10 told people she was sending a submarine, which I think was just their way of trying to show she was doing something. It was never an option that was actively pursued.[18]

In any case, no submarines were available within the required time-frame. 'There was pressure to strike and we had no assets on location,' says an MoD source simply.[19]

This was probably down to maintenance issues, the key problem for the navy when it comes to readiness. Hulls need cleaning to stop them rusting, engines need overhauling, and nuclear reactors need to be flushed. When you don't have very many ships, taking one or two out of circulation leaves quite a gap. In 2015, of thirteen Type 23 frigates, three were in harbour being overhauled, and another three were just out of dock and being prepared to go back into service. Four of the six nuclear-attack submarine fleet were out of action that year.[20] Fast-forward to 2017, and the situation with the Type 45s was equally embarrassing. Thanks to long-running engine problems, they were out of action for 80 per cent of the year.[21]

The Royal Navy's diminished fleet makes it extremely vulnerable to accidents and unforeseen technical problems. When HMS *Ambush* collided with a ship off Gibraltar in July 2016, the submarine overhaul schedule was thrown into turmoil. A few months later, it emerged that the navy did not have a single seaworthy submarine.[22]

Personnel problems also play a part. As we have seen, some 5,000 sailors were cut as a result of the 2010 Strategic Defence and Security Review – and then the service found it couldn't fill certain positions.[23] The recruitment problem left the fleet several hundred sailors short, resulting in remaining crews having to spend longer at sea. The pressures prompted more sailors to quit.[24]

By 2015, there was a full-blown manning crisis just as the navy was trying to ramp up recruitment for the new aircraft carriers. A drastic decision was taken to tie up a Type 23 frigate and Type 45 destroyer in Portsmouth indefinitely, to free up crews for other ships.[25] In the 2015 Strategic Defence and Security Review, ministers also announced that the helicopter carrier HMS *Ocean* would be retired early so her crew could be released to man HMS *Queen Elizabeth*.[26]

Before 2010, Britain's amphibious strike force, the Royal Marine Commando Brigade, was kept at a state of high readiness. It had one battalion-sized infantry unit, or 'Commando', with some 700 Royal Marines fully trained to conduct both helicopter and sea-borne landings at seventy-two hours' notice. Another 'Commando' – and the bulk of the brigade's specialist engineering, logistic, artillery, medical, communications and other support regiments – was ready to go at fourteen days' notice.

All this changed with the Strategic Defence and Security Review. Now the Marines were only expected to have a single Commando or landing force on fourteen days' notice and a solitary company of 120 Marines on seventy-two hours' notice. One of the navy's four landing ships was sold off, leaving only two ready to go at any given time. Meanwhile, one of its two dock ships was placed in what was termed 'extended readiness' – a euphemism which meant it would not be ready for service for many years.[27]

The biggest cuts hit the navy's 'flat top' carriers, with further serious implications for the Royal Marines. HMS *Ark Royal* and her Harrier jump jets were taken out of service immediately after the defence review in early 2011.[28] HMS *Illustrious* limped on until 2014, but once she was retired, only HMS *Ocean* – which had also been condemned – remained as the flagship of any amphibious task group.[29]

As a result, the navy and Marines could only form a full amphibious task group – combining landing ships, helicopters and marines – on a part-time basis. For several months of each year since 2011, there have simply not been enough of the right ships in a fit state to carry out amphibious operations. For a few years, navy chiefs tried to keep things going with *Operation Cougar*, an annual three-month-long amphibious task group deployment to the Mediterranean or Middle East. By the middle of the decade, however, it was becoming clear that even this was beyond the resources available. The 2016 Middle East deployment comprised only an expanded 200-strong landing force, a handful of RAF and army helicopters on HMS *Ocean* and just one landing ship.[30] There was no longer any pretending that the navy was ready for war.

TODAY?

The 2015 Strategic Defence and Security Review was supposed to improve readiness. In theory, the army would now have a full division capable of taking part in high-intensity warfare; the RAF would be allowed to take dozens of Typhoon jets out of storage and form two new squadrons to replace the soon-to-be-retired Tornado bombers; and the navy would be given the cash to use its second aircraft carrier, HMS *Prince of Wales*, to support amphibious operations. All this would be in place by 2025. Cameron and the then Defence Secretary Michael Fallon trumpeted the £178 billion spending on equipment over the coming decade as a symbol of the increased ambition of Britain's armed forces.[31]

Though the army now had more money for armoured training exercises, ambitions to put all four of the high-readiness brigade's four armoured battlegroups through a live firing training exercise in 2017 had to be scaled back to save money. At the same time, concerns remained about the readiness of vehicles to go to war.

According to one senior officer, in a report on the army's conflict readiness, anecdotal evidence suggested that 'a percentage of platforms [vehicles] that are held in storage are unfit, or have been cannibalised, and could not be made deployable within lengthy warning times.'[32]

Despite the funding boost, the army remained short of tank transporters to move more than a few dozen tanks over long distances at a time. Officers reported that hundreds of mine-proof vehicles brought back from Afghanistan were parked up because of a lack of spare parts. Several infantry regiments had none at all.

Meanwhile, the recruitment and retention crisis continued. In 2016, the army announced that four infantry battalions would have their manpower halved so they could be converted into training and advisory teams to work with Third World armies, further reducing the number of infantry regiments available for combat operations.[33] The shortage of basic kit for the bulk of the army was exposed when, in the aftermath of the May 2017 Manchester terror attack, 1,000 troops were drafted in to help the police. There was not enough new Virtus body armour to go around, and they had to make do with protective kit that was rated obsolete a decade earlier.[34]

Following a review of combat readiness in 2017, the conclusion of the army's own think tank was stark. A damning report from the Centre for Historical Analysis and Conflict Research questioned whether it could fight a major war.

With the army reduced to 79,000 regular personnel (at best) the report said: '...if one merely sees preparedness through net manpower and kinetic force capacity, the answer might be a simple "no": the British Army is at its smallest and has faced years of budget cuts.' It claimed repeated rounds of defence cuts over the past twenty years had 'resulted in the hollowing out or deletion of the army's deployed capabilities'.[35]

As for the RAF, 'the 2015 defence review appeared to set lots of up arrows for the RAF terms of getting new aircraft and capabilities, but it did not. It was only a slowing down of the down arrows from the 2010 Strategic Defence and Security Review', according to a senior officer who was involved in writing the document.

It hides the fact that our numbers are at an historic low. You can't just turn the tap back on to train people to fly the new aircraft we are supposed to be getting ... In the Cold War, we had plenty of spare people – there is now no capacity in the system to find the people we need.

Nor did the 2015 Strategic Defence and Security Review solve the problem of readiness at sea. 'The navy are in big trouble – they can't guarantee anything that is dependent on people – they just don't have enough of them,' was the assessment of a senior Ministry of Defence official.[36]

As for amphibious capability, the review did not address the long-term shortage of shipping to fill the gap and allow 24/7/365 readiness for 3 Commando Brigade for amphibious operations. While the HMS *Prince of Wales* carrier offers great potential to carry a fleet of RAF Chinook heavy-lift helicopters, it does not have a dock to take landing craft to carry vehicles and heavy kit ashore.

British soldiers, sailors and airmen have a can-do spirit by their very nature. Time after time they rise to the occasion – whether running security during the 2012 Olympics, scrambling jets to stop the Islamic State advance in 2014 or rescuing migrants from the Mediterranean in 2015. But something has changed. The armed forces are just not equipped, funded or trained to carry out sudden mass mobilisations as they were during the Cold War. If peace can be relied on for the foreseeable future, that is fine. If not, it is a deeply worrying state of affairs.

PART FOUR

THE HOME FRONT

THE MIGHTY O

The morning after the night before dawned bright for the Conservatives. It was 4 May 2018, and they had been spared the battering they had expected to receive in local elections across England. To the party's surprise, bitter divisions over Brexit and a furore over the treatment of so-called Windrush-generation immigrants that cost the Home Secretary her job just before polling day did not translate into hundreds of lost seats. After failing to win a string of target constituencies, Labour leader Jeremy Corbyn cut a chastened figure.[1] The Tory Party leadership breathed a collective sigh of relief.

One result cast a dark shadow over the picture, however: the loss of Plymouth Council to Labour.[2] Captain Johnny Mercer, formerly of 29 Commando Regiment Royal Artillery, was sure he knew why. As the local MP, he had thrown himself into door-to-door canvassing in the run-up to the election. In addition to the usual gripes about potholes, bus services and bin collections, one subject kept coming up: defence.

Plymouth is a naval city. To the west is HMNB Devonport, one of the Royal Navy's three operating bases in the UK. It is home to the UK's two amphibious assault ships, HMS *Bulwark* and HMS *Albion* – for the time being at least. Both vessels are threatened with the axe. If they go, almost 2,000 jobs could be hit.*[3] Until recently, Devonport was also home to the UK's largest operational warship, HMS *Ocean*,

---

* A study commissioned by the council showed that, when the supply chain is taken into account, the economic impact on the region from the amphibious assault ships is £61 million in GVA (Gross Value Added) and a total of 1,776 jobs.

303

affectionately known to the fleet as 'the Mighty O'. In a ceremony led by the Queen, in March 2018 she was decommissioned and sold to Brazil.[4]

The Royal Marines are also based in the area, although the Ministry of Defence has announced plans to sell off the base. As we have seen, the Marines themselves are under threat. In a further blow, less than a month before polling day, workers at defence giant Babcock's Devonport dockyard, which services Royal Navy ships and submarines, began receiving letters warning of redundancies. The company is shedding 500 jobs in the area.[5]

The morning after the night before, Mercer delivered his verdict: 'It's pretty clear to me the biggest factor in this city is defence. It always has been.' Local party activists had been 'hammered' over the government's handling of defence as they went door to door trying to drum up votes, he said.[6]

Some politicians like to shrug that there are 'no votes in defence'.

Plymouth knows better.

THE WAR BUSINESS

THE DEFENCE INDUSTRY

On the outskirts of London, beyond the reach of the Tube, is an enormous exhibition centre that has been used for everything from *X Factor* auditions to the Miss World Competition. It has been the setting for a *Doctor Who* convention; the scene of a *Star Wars* extravaganza; an exam hall for students from King's College London; and a venue for numerous international conventions, including G20 summits.

But it is an event with a rather mundane name that attracts the most controversy: the bi-annual Defence and Security Equipment International (DSEI) exhibition. This is the world's biggest arms fair.

Nothing about the appearance of the throngs of be-suited delegates who descend on the docklands for the event every other September indicates their unusual trade. They might just as well be heading for a day touring display stands about e-commerce or the insurance industry. Behind the heavily guarded doors of the exhibition centre, however, are millions of pounds worth of lethal weapons.

It takes three forms of identity and an expensive conference pass to make it through security. The stringent approach is understandable, not only to ensure none of the exhibits fall into the wrong hands, but also because the exhibition always triggers protests. In 2017, London Mayor Sadiq Khan threw his weight behind a long-running campaign to have it banned, expressing distaste at the use of the city as a 'marketplace' for the trade of weapons to questionable regimes. A year earlier, a court acquitted eight anti-arms-trade protestors who tried to shut down the fair, ruling that there was 'clear, credible, and largely unchallenged evidence of expert witnesses of wrongdoing' at DSEI – a reference to the suspected touting of munitions that could contravene international human rights conventions.[1]

Organisers insist they go to every length to ensure that none of the extraordinary array of military hardware on offer breaches any rules. Given the scale of the event, however, it would be no surprise if something slipped through the net.

Spread over 100 acres of air-conditioned halls, the display is eye-popping in size and variety. It attracts some curious characters.

'Ever since I was a little girl I knew I wanted to sell firearms,' says an elegant young Taiwanese woman, pouting over a wine glass. With her dark red lipstick, Chanel earrings and Louis Vuitton bag, she looks as if she has dressed for a fashion shoot. Gleefully exhibiting an assortment of pistols, shotguns, machine guns and the odd mortar for a major European arms company, she stands out in the mostly male throng. Apparently, her parents still set her a curfew at home, but they seem to have fewer qualms about her travelling half way across the world to sell automatic weapons.[2]

THE WORLD'S BIGGEST ARMS COMPANIES:
TOP ARMS-PRODUCING AND MILITARY SERVICES COMPANIES IN 2017*

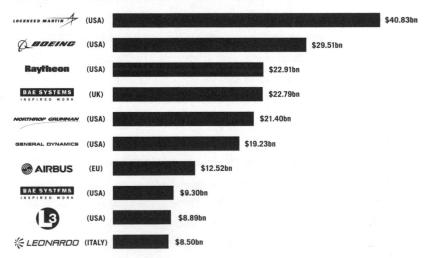

Company		Value
LOCKHEED MARTIN	(USA)	$40.83bn
BOEING	(USA)	$29.51bn
Raytheon	(USA)	$22.91bn
BAE SYSTEMS INSPIRED WORK	(UK)	$22.79bn
NORTHROP GRUMMAN	(USA)	$21.40bn
GENERAL DYNAMICS	(USA)	$19.23bn
AIRBUS	(EU)	$12.52bn
BAE SYSTEMS INSPIRED WORK	(USA)	$9.30bn
L3	(USA)	$8.89bn
LEONARDO	(ITALY)	$8.50bn

***EXCLUDING CHINA DUE TO A LACK OF DATA**

DEALING WITH THE DEFENCE INDUSTRY IS A CHALLENGE FOR EVERY UK GOVERNMENT.

Around thirty countries, including the USA, UK, Germany, France, Italy, Australia and Canada, have individual exhibition stands. Pakistan, Turkey and Saudi Arabia are all represented. Conspicuous by their absence are the Russians, because of EU sanctions.[3]

BAE Systems is by far the UK's largest arms company, with a market share of just over 55 per cent and many lucrative government contracts.[4] Its stand takes up almost an eighth of the conference centre. Staff are pushing a new sharpshooter bullet, which a salesman notes with a wink is 'referred to by soldiers... although not us' as the 'Widowmaker'. It is a 7.62mm round, which has twice the range of standard ammunition and is supposedly being used by SAS troops in Syria and northern Iraq against Islamic State militants. Richard, a tall, lanky man in an impeccably tailored suit and blue tie, demonstrates the hardened steel tip and upgraded propellant which mean it can be used to take on anti-armoured vehicles.[5]

On a podium, someone else from the company is demonstrating how a series of drones can be synchronised – a glimpse into the potential future of warfare. A robotic voiceover invites spectators to imagine how it would be if 'autonomous machines could give you an operational edge in contested environments'.

'What if all long-range weapons could give you surgical precision?' the disembodied voice asks.

'The future is here!' gushes a salesman.

'And it is terrifying,' mutters an observer under his breath.

At a drinks reception later in the evening, a salesman reminisces about his former job campaigning on environmental issues.

'Believe it or not, there used to be an ethical component to my work!' he quips.[6] Everyone laughs.

At the stand of a company called Ripple Effect Systems, a young South African woman can be found showing off a 40mm belt-fed automatic grenade launcher. 'Wouldn't want to get on the wrong side of this!' one prospective buyer exclaims.

'Oh well, we also sell a less lethal variant,' she tells him cheerfully, as if she were a barista offering extra sugar with his coffee. 'For crowd control.'

'How do you get a less lethal one of these? Does it only blow your legs off or something?' he replies.[7]

Depending on who is selling, the sales patter varies from the euphemistic to the blunt. Meopta night sights promise 'victory over the darkness'; but the Barrett REC7 DI assault rifle offers to 'shoot holes in every excuse'. An American sales rep shows off a fancy bullet, holding it next to the highest-tech armoured helmet.

'It'll go in the side, through the head and out the other side. Problem solved!' he enthuses.

Meanwhile, heavy explosive ammunitions are euphemistically referred to as '40mm solutions', as if they were designed to fix a software bug. At its stand, a firm which specialises in field-testing arms and vehicles displays several dozen double shots of expensive vodka poured from specially designed crystal skulls.[8]

Small arms – a category that includes mortars and miniguns – are just a fraction of the offering at the DSEI exhibition. All manner of vehicles, from speedboats to frigates, from trailers to tanks, are on sale.[9]

Tucked away in a corner, so far from the main action that few delegates pass by, is a particularly striking display. It is manned by real-life amputees with alarmingly convincing fake wounds. They are selling first-aid kits for the battlefield. Among the sanitised exhibition stands with their free ballpoint pens and bright displays, the actors are an arresting sight.[10]

The exhibition is a window on an extraordinarily secretive world that generates billions of pounds for the UK economy. Though it supports hundreds of thousands of jobs, it has a lousy image. This doesn't just stem from what the products do; it is linked to the controversies that have lodged in the public mind, particularly the so-called Al-Yamamah scandal. The notorious deal involved the sale of £43 billion worth of Typhoon and Tornado fighter jets made by BAE Systems to Saudi Arabia.[11] There were hefty kickbacks to members of the Saudi royal family responsible for signing off on the contract and claims of a slush fund for entertaining Saudi clients abroad, some of which was spent on prostitutes.[12] The Ministry of Defence is said to have been fully aware of some of the tawdrier aspects of the deal, but looked the other way.[13] BAE was forced to pay a fine in the hundreds of millions of pounds.[14] Though Al-Yamamah was decades ago, the stench around the industry has never quite gone away.

MONEY SPINNER

For every government, dealing with the defence industry is a heavy burden, forcing ministers to reconcile what are often deeply conflicting agendas.

On the one hand, they have a duty to equip the armed forces with the most effective and technologically advanced kit available, to protect and safeguard the lives of British citizens and minimise battlefield casualties. Intense political pressure to sustain the UK's manufacturing industry; the self-interest of MPs whose seats depend on supporting jobs in local shipyards and defence companies; and the impetus to avoid jeopardising national security by becoming overly dependent on foreign suppliers creates a bias towards British defence companies. On the other hand, they have a duty to extract best value for taxpayers, meaning they must consider buying cheaper tanks, planes, ships and munitions overseas. As if this were not complicated enough, there are then tricky moral and ethical dilemmas about exports, specifically sales to countries with dubious human rights records.

All this is high-risk territory for politicians of all parties. Get the delicate relationship with the defence industry right, and there is no credit from voters, who simply expect ministers to make the necessary judgements. Get it wrong, and it is resignation material.

In recent years there has been remarkably little variation in the approach of Labour, coalition and Conservative governments, whatever their idealistic stances in opposition. That is because beyond the political rhetoric is a cold, hard reality: the arms business is pivotal to the economy. As of 2016, it directly employed around 142,000 people and had a turnover of £23 billion.[15] The UK share of the global defence export market is around 9 per cent,[16] making this country the second largest arms exporter behind the United States.[17] These economic considerations have a huge bearing on decisions about where to buy equipment for the armed forces.

**TOP TEN GLOBAL DEFENCE EXPORTERS
(ESTIMATES BASED ON ORDERS/CONTRACTS SIGNED 2007–2016, IN $BN)**

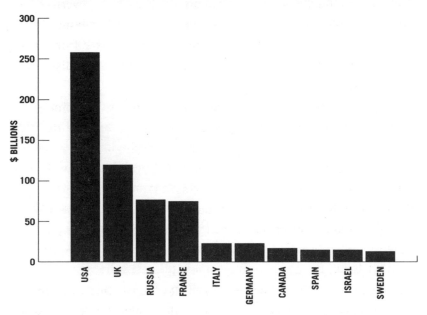

ARMS EXPORTS ARE A KEY COMPONENT OF THE UK ECONOMY BUT CAN BE VERY POLITICALLY SENSITIVE.

By law, certain defence-related products have to be made in the UK, including key components of the nuclear deterrent; electronic warfare materials; and cryptography services crucial to the intelligence services. The so-called Sovereign Requirement list can be a source of frustration and anxiety for both industry and ministers – especially in the context of Scottish independence.[18] A few months before the referendum in 2014, Philip Hammond, then Defence Secretary, visited a factory in Glasgow owned by French defence company Thales. For nearly a century, the company and its precursors have made the periscopes for every submarine in the Royal Navy in a Glasgow plant. Hammond told workers that in the event of independence, production would have to be halted, because the components would be deemed to emanate from a 'foreign' supplier.[19]

In theory, goods that are not on the Sovereign Requirement list can be bought anywhere. In practice, British defence manufacturers are always favoured, even if the same quality product is available cheaper elsewhere.

Sometimes, this approach is official policy, as with the government's 'national shipbuilding strategy'. In other cases, it is less transparent. The Ministry of Defence is constantly under pressure from MPs to award contracts to companies in their constituencies, distorting decision-making.

'The number of times we're asked to give a contract to somebody, because it would create jobs, *significantly* undermined the defence budget', according to one former MoD special adviser.[20]

The most notorious example is the contract to build the new aircraft carriers in 1999. As we have seen, this was driven by Gordon Brown's determination to prop up jobs in Scottish shipyards. The then Chancellor agreed to an 'unbreakable' deal with BAE Systems that guaranteed work for 10,000 people for the next fifteen years. In return, all they had to do was find efficiency savings for shipbuilding.[21]

A former adviser to General the Lord (Richard) Dannatt, who was Chief of the General Staff at the time, recalls a senior admiral urging Dannatt to back the carriers on that basis.

He said to me, 'I hope your boss is going to vote for the carriers.' I said, 'Why is that?' He said, 'Because if he doesn't, and we don't build them, we're going to have to build something else, or else pay for 10,000 people to sit around doing nothing, because the agreement is that there will be 10,000 people in the shipyard business! So, what are we going to build, if we don't build the carriers?'[22]

Brown's 'terms of business agreement' effectively meant the government would have to pay BAE Systems whether they were working or not. It dogged Defence Secretaries for over a decade. When he became Defence Secretary, Michael Fallon was determined to overturn it, but it did not prove easy. It took until autumn 2016 for the Ministry of

Defence to wrest its way out. During negotiations over construction of the Type 26 Frigate, Fallon laid his cards on the table, telling BAE's chairman Roger Carr that he would only go through with the order if they had a 'gain share; pain share' agreement. Under the new terms of business, if the job overran, BAE would cough up 50 per cent of additional costs; if it ended up costing less than the estimate, BAE would get to keep 50 per cent of the savings. The condition was that Brown's terms of business agreement would never apply to any contract ever again. Carr grudgingly agreed. Fallon tells friends that breaking the BAE monopoly was one of his greatest achievements, wryly acknowledging that it is unlikely to be one for which he will be remembered.[23]

Defenders of Brown's contract say that it was crucial to ensuring shipbuilding jobs stayed in the UK and prevented cash-strapped administrations from turning to cheaper shipyards, such as in South Korea. The industry certainly needed the support: shipbuilding has suffered a precipitous fall since the halcyon days of the nineteenth century. At the Defence and Security Equipment International exhibition in 2017, Lord Prior, the Parliamentary Under Secretary of State for Business, Energy and Industrial Strategy, lamented that 'In the UK in the 1890s we produced 80 per cent of world shipping tonnage. Then, thanks to a fragmented industry, lack of investment, poor management, we couldn't stop shipbuilding going east. In 2015, Japan produced 19 per cent of world tonnage, Korea 23 per cent, China 37 per cent.' The UK had just 0.004 per cent.[24]

As UK defence manufacturing shrinks, ministers regularly find themselves with the unpleasant task of handling announcements about job cuts. This can lead to ugly tussles over which politician should face the music. Shortly before he resigned as Defence Secretary in autumn 2017, Sir Michael Fallon was involved in a bitter row with Business Secretary Greg Clark over whose department should respond to a BAE decision to cut 2,000 staff in the UK.

A Ministry of Defence insider claims Clark 'hid in his office' to avoid dealing with the controversy, leading to a shouting match between the two Secretaries of State.

Greg refused to go out and deal with BAE job cuts, and pushed it onto the Ministry of Defence. It led to a stand-up row outside Cabinet, during which the immortal words 'Do your job, Greg!' were uttered. There was a more sweary version within the Ministry of Defence. We knew he was hiding from the media. His people were claiming he was incredibly busy; but we knew he was just in his office. He didn't want to handle the presentational stuff on the job losses, or put out ministerial statements. Yet his department had a team dedicated to economic shocks! We told him it was his fucking job![25]

DILEMMAS

With his gentle manner, enthusiasm for ballroom dancing and intellectual kudos for predicting the global financial crash, as an opposition politician, Vince Cable could do no wrong.

In government, however, the MP affectionately known as 'Saint Vince' was immediately forced to confront the challenges of combining high moral principles with high office.

As a backbench Liberal Democrat, Cable had had strong views about the defence exports, once even appearing as a court witness for the pressure group Campaign Against Arms Trade (CAAT).[26]

Then, in 2010, he was appointed Business Secretary in the new coalition government. Suddenly he found himself in charge of export licences for the UK defence industry, and it all became more complicated.

Just two years before joining the Cabinet, the then MP for Twickenham had supported an attempt by the CAAT to release official documents relating to the Al-Yamamah deal.[27] The hearing had been deeply uncomfortable for BAE Systems. Now he found himself responsible for the government's relationship with the aerospace company, and in a position to judge what they should and should not be allowed to sell to regimes like Saudi Arabia.

Cable was not the only one in the Department for Business, Innovation and Skills who was conflicted. The minister in charge of exports, Lord (Stephen) Green of Hurstpierpoint, was equally uncomfortable with this aspect of his job. Having made a fortune in the City, Green had agreed to give up his position as group chairman of HSBC and accept a Tory peerage, along with an appointment as Minister of State for Trade and Investment at the Department for Business, Innovation and Skills and the Foreign and Commonwealth Office.[28]

What complicated matters was that he was also an ordained minister of the Church of England and prided himself on an ethical approach to financial matters.[29] He and Cable were not the obvious candidates to manage arms sales.

Cable recalls:

> The two of us had quite serious misgivings about having to oversee the export licensing. I actually had a conversation with him at the start – we talked about how to handle it and concluded that it was on balance best for us to be involved than to refuse to do it. We thought we better get our hands dirty.[30]

Under what the government insists is a rigorous arms export licensing policy, companies cannot sell arms abroad if the economic or political reasons for doing so are outweighed by 'concern that the goods might be used for internal repression or international aggression'.[31] In practice, a bar or limit is only applied if there is considered to be a 'clear risk' that materials could be used in ways that breach international human rights agreements. Routine applications are dealt with by the business department, with contentious cases referred to the Foreign and Commonwealth Office; the Ministry of Defence and Downing Street if necessary. The system is scrutinised by an MP-led committee on Arms Export Controls, but it has limited power: ministers always make the final decision.

During the coalition years, Cable and Green rolled up their sleeves and got stuck in, doing their best to reconcile their ethical instincts with the imperative to do their best for the economy. As time passed, Cable was surprised to discover that the way the issue was handled in Whitehall was more nuanced than he had imagined. He had expected others to be too quick to sign off deals. In fact, some licence applications that he personally considered to be low risk or harmless were blocked by colleagues, while others he believed should have been stopped were given the go-ahead.

'I used to do factory visits every week and would get very deserving cases of companies with wonderful high-tech stuff; they would be tearing their hair out because they couldn't export it. These businesses would be crippled,' he says.[32]

He recalls a case in which a British company was exporting a toothpaste ingredient to Syria and was suddenly ordered to stop in case it could be used for something sinister.

> There was a row. We were sending some stuff over with fluoride in it, either for toothpaste or cleaning windows. Someone pointed out that it could be used as a component for chemical weapons. That was technically true, if you went to a very, very great deal of trouble, but really, it was just toothpaste.

'I lost that battle,' he recalls.[33]

In another case, an Aberdeen-based company called SubSea 7, which installs underwater infrastructure and safety equipment, wanted to export diving safety kit to Russia. Cable was impressed by the firm and supported its application but was overruled by Cabinet colleagues.

'The Ministry of Defence and No. 10 objected, on the grounds that it breached sanctions,' Cable says. 'I took SubSea7's side, but I lost that battle too. There were also things companies wanted to sell the Argentines that were pretty innocuous but were blocked.'[34]

On the flip side, he was unable to persuade Cabinet colleagues to stop British defence companies exporting arms to Israel.

> There were things I thought we should be questioning and weren't. I spent a lot of one summer in anguished conversation with Philip Hammond [then Foreign Secretary] about exports to Israel. I remember I was on holiday in France and was on the phone to Philip all the time. The result was a score draw. He was representing the view of the Foreign Office and of David Cameron, that we were reliable suppliers to the Israeli Defence Force, and that the kit would not be used to create any kind of human rights problem.

But when you are talking about components for aircraft that might be used for bombing [Palestine], I think that's different. The Israeli argument took place while conflict was actually raging in the Gaza strip.

'By the time we reached agreement on what to sell and not sell the fighting had stopped,' he says.[35]

British arms exports to Saudi have always been the most controversial deals. Entering London via the M40 in early March 2018, drivers would have passed a series of billboards showing a young bearded man with a benign expression. It was Prince Mohammed Bin Salman, the Crown Prince of Saudi Arabia, who – the poster explained – was 'bringing change' to his country.[36] One newspaper ran a half-page advertisement for the foreign royal, showing a woman in a hijab behind the wheel of a car. According to the puff, the Prince had been busy 'empowering' Saudi Arabian women.[37]

This was his first visit to the United Kingdom, and the government rolled out the red carpet. Under pressure, Downing Street promised to challenge him over human rights abuses and the role of Saudi Arabia in the war in Yemen,[38] but for diplomacy's sake, any such conversations were probably kept to a minimum. The Prince was entertained personally by the Prime Minister; enjoyed lunch with the Queen; and was a guest of honour at a banquet with Prince William and the Duchess of Cambridge.[39]

The warmth of this welcome infuriated those who have long campaigned against arms exports to his kingdom. Some 500 protestors descended on Downing Street on the day of his arrival, holding signs that read 'Hands off Yemen'.[40] Labour MPs condemned the visit, dispatching shadow International Development Secretary Kate Osamor to speak at the protests.[41]

Cable himself had planned to attend the demonstration, but it was made clear he would not be welcome because of his old role signing off arms deals to the regime. He regrets that he ever did so, and feels the Ministry of Defence misled him about the possibility of the weapons being used for human rights violations.[42]

Reflecting on how difficult it can be for ministers to make the right judgements about arms exports, Cable points out that until the illegal invasion of Ukraine, Russia was one of the UK defence industry's biggest markets.[43] Now weapons sold to the Russian regime by British companies before sanctions were imposed could be used against us, or our allies.

JUST ENOUGH, JUST IN TIME

At the start of the Falklands War in 1982, HMS *Sheffield* was hit by an Exocet missile, killing twenty sailors and injuring twenty-six more. The crew had been sleeping on highly flammable foam mattresses which gave off clouds of toxic smoke when they caught fire.[44] The Ministry of Defence was horrified. Within a day, any ship involved in the conflict was re-fitted with horsehair mattresses, which burned less easily and gave off none of the dangerous fumes.[45]

It soon transpired that the Ministry of Defence had known of the risk all along. They had simply not anticipated a war, so they didn't bother sorting it out. David Webb, a former Ministry of Defence civil servant, recalls:

> During my time in naval training in the '70s, people always knew that the mattresses in ships gave off noxious fumes if the ship was hit. We knew that for at least a decade before the Falklands, but what we hadn't had until then was ships being hit by missiles, so no one bothered to do anything. Then, within a day, any ship yet to go down was getting new modern mattresses. So, this problem that we couldn't solve in twenty years we were able to do in twenty-four hours![46]

The mattress episode took place decades ago, but it represents the best and worst of Ministry of Defence procurement today. In a crisis, the department rises to the occasion. As we have seen, during the wars in Iraq and Afghanistan, the Urgent Operational Requirement system was used to get kit to troops quickly, and generally worked well. It was paid for by a Treasury contingency fund.[47] When time is not precious, however, procurement can take decades (as we have seen in relation to the aircraft carriers).

An industry figure who has experienced the problem from all sides, having risen to the higher echelons of the army and held procurement-related positions in the MoD before taking up a senior role in a defence company, observes that when time is not of the essence, *performance* becomes paramount, at the expense of everything else.

'In the days of Urgent Operational Requirements, there was no way we could delay getting whatever it was into service, so we were prepared to compromise on performance and cost,' he says.

> But when we are buying something for our core programme, the critical thing is performance. What goes then? Cost and time! So there are enormous cost overruns on programmes, and enormous time overruns on programmes, because the only thing that's nailed to the ground, which is absolutely demanded, is performance.
>
> The Urgent Operational Requirements did their job and did it well. It might have been a bit more expensive to go down that route, but by God we got stuff quickly. Today we've gone from one extreme to the other, and there is no urgency at all. We need some middle way.[48]

There are many reasons defence manufacturers get better deals with the government than they should, but there are some recurring themes. Until 2008, there was a continuing tension between various streams of money coming into the Ministry of Defence from the Treasury. One stream of money, known as Capital Development Expenditure Limit (CDEL), was generally for procurement; the other, Resource Departmental Expenditure Limit, known as RDEL, was for running costs.[49] As Chancellor, Brown instituted a 'golden rule' that the government would never borrow money for running costs; only for capital expenditure. While this sounds sensible, it had perverse consequences,[50] meaning the Ministry of Defence could afford to buy big-ticket items – like aircraft carriers and submarines – because the Treasury would allow it to borrow money; but could not afford upkeep and running costs, like pay and pensions. As a result, the department was constantly short-staffed. The rule was abandoned after the 2008 financial crash, but the continued 'ringfencing' of certain streams of money still skews decision-making in the department.

Another issue is a spending system called annuality, which dictates that departments cannot carry money from one financial year to the next if they have any left over.[51] This 'use it or lose it' system discourages saving for a rainy day, resulting in ill-advised spending sprees as the cut-off point approaches.[52]

A former brigade commanding officer recalls:

> I was running Thorney Island, a base on the south coast, and got a phone call from a colleague saying, 'Hey, there's an underspend on the brigade this year. What do you want to spend it on? You've only got two weeks to spend it.' All we could do was tarmac the roads! You end up spending on silly things because you can't save the money.[53]

Another Ministry of Defence civil servant recalled his office splashing out on new computer monitors because they had nothing better to buy.[54]

Perhaps most importantly is the fear among defence chiefs that if they settle for basic models (whether it's planes, tanks, ships or anything else) on the basis that the kit can be upgraded over time, they will never get the upgrades. As a result, they demand 100 per cent of the potential capability up front, encouraging the purchase of a small number of extremely expensive 'exquisite' platforms which take so long to produce they are outdated by the time they are delivered, at the expense of kit that is just good enough and arrives just in time. (As we have seen, aiming high at the start does not stop service chiefs asking for more later.)

But many of those who have worked in both camps – the industry and the Ministry of Defence – say the government gets more right than it receives credit for. A senior defence industry figure who also worked in the upper echelons of the Ministry of Defence says things look very different inside the tent.

What those in the defence industry tend to do is sit around late at night, with a couple of glasses of red wine, bemoaning all the ridiculous things the Ministry of Defence does, complaining about how they've cocked everything up. What I found when I came into the Ministry of Defence was that about 80 per cent of the things that from the outside I'd have been very critical of had got a rational explanation behind them. Not one you'd necessarily have realised from the outside.[55]

SYMPATHY FOR THE DEVIL

It is not so much unfashionable as virtually unheard of to pity the UK defence industry, but there are many reasons to be concerned about its future, with all the associated implications for the economy.

It is not just that the industry has no idea what a future government will do with multi-billion-pound procurement programmes. The industry does not even know what an administration is going to do from one *month* to the next. A government might say it is going to buy this or that, but who knows if those plans will be shelved? Almost anything can happen, at any time, and though contracts are designed to protect the industry, that is more solace to chief executives and shareholders than it is to laid-off workers.

Another challenge is that overseas customers now demand lessons in how to make the kit they are buying, particularly software components. They may be prepared to import kit, but they want the right to produce their own version in future.

The problem that we have in [our company] and in other companies, is that the Middle East, and India, and the Far East, are more and more demanding that if they buy a product from us, that we must over time teach them how to make it themselves, because they want to build up the skills in their own country.

'So the transfer of technology is now normally a pre-condition of selling anything,' says an industry source.[56]

Some potential customers don't even bother paying. The Chinese in

particular are frequently suspected of stealing schematics or intellectual property through cyberattacks or espionage, and then reverse-engi-
neering it. Facing such pressures, it is little wonder that the slick-look-
ing arms dealers at the Defence and Security Equipment International
exhibition are eager for sales.

RAINBOW WARRIORS

PEOPLE AND POLITICAL CORRECTNESS

NOT THE BEST

In a dreary conference room at Army Headquarters in Andover, General Sir Nick Carter, then Chief of the General Staff, and the Executive Committee of the Army Board, sat down to discuss a pressing issue. Why, despite its illustrious pedigree, was the British Army in the midst of its worst manpower crisis for decades?

Was it the dilapidated accommodation that senior MPs publicly labelled 'disgraceful'?[1] The modest pay, which General Sir Nick Carter privately admitted to junior officers was 'crap' and had fallen every year in real terms since 2010?[2] Could they blame Capita, the company which had made such a mess of its lucrative contract to boost recruitment that many would-be soldiers just gave up in disgust?[3] What about the canning of overseas training exercises in Canada and Belize, a career highlight for many soldiers? Replacing these foreign adventures with Xbox-style simulations hardly made the job more attractive.

The bright sparks on the board scratched their heads, chewed the tips of their Biros and hit on another explanation: the army's image, which they concluded did not appeal to a generation of young people with diverse religious backgrounds, gender identities and sexualities – some more physically fit and emotionally robust than others. Old advertisements, like those from 1976, in which a soldier says, 'I wondered if I'd ever get through those first few weeks … I ached in places I didn't know I could ache', were deemed unfit for the modern world.[4] A recruitment video for the Marines warning that '99.99 per cent need not apply' certainly wouldn't do.[5] Now it was 2017, and they needed a fresh approach.

In fairness to Carter, there was evidence that the old methods had reached their sell-by date. The Marines struggled to recruit after their campaign, which appears to have made the service seem so elite that few dared apply.

As usual the army was strapped for cash, but everyone at the meeting could see this was important. Digging deep into their pockets, the board found just under £2 million to commission a campaign that would emphasise 'belonging and team building'.[6]

Inside the Ministry of Defence, everyone involved seemed happy with the finished product: a series of touchy-feely videos to pump out on social media. In one of the short films, a drippy male voice bemoaned how hard it can be for men to express their emotions. He assumed a testosterone-fuelled environment like the army could never accept someone effeminate. Guess what? On joining he found that it was 'OK to cry', and there was 'always someone to talk to'. Other ads stressed how a Muslim soldier, even on exercise, 'could always find a quiet moment to go into a corner and do my prayers', while those with wobbly bellies instead of six packs were assured they didn't have 'to be a Superman to join the army'. The footage appeared under saccharine taglines like 'find where you belong' and 'unique and united'.[7] As for why you would want to join the army, the ads were conspicuously silent.

Had the board left it at that, they would probably have got away with it. Traditionalists might have cringed at the methodology, but few would criticise attempts to encourage a broader section of society to consider the armed forces as a career. It was the simultaneous decision to scrap the traditional recruiting strapline 'Be the Best' – a slogan that had served the army well since 1993 – that would create a furore.[8]

In an internal document called *The Army Brand*, Carter declared that the phrase no longer 'resonated with key audiences' and dismissed it as 'dated, elitist and non-inclusive'.

'The retirement of Be the Best will commence immediately with all planned refreshes of Be the Best branded material cancelled in favour of brand-compliant products,' he declared.[9]

What happened next was a presentational disaster. With an inevitability that somehow bypassed the legions of communication experts on the Ministry of Defence payroll, all hell broke loose about abandoned aspirations and standards.

The first Defence Secretary Gavin Williamson heard about the plan was one Friday night, 22 December, when a reporter from the *Mail on Sunday* rang his department. The Defence Secretary listened in disbelief.

'What a load of bollocks,' was his private reaction.

He had been in post for just under two months but needed no time to work out what to do. He told the *Mail on Sunday* in no uncertain terms that the slogan would stay.[10]

Williamson's swift pronouncement did not prevent damaging questions about the culture in the armed forces today. Presumably, with a slight change of emphasis, the campaign slogans would not have caused such a fuss. Alternatives like 'I'm a Muslim, but that doesn't mean I can't be a patriot and fight for my country', or 'I started off out of shape, a bit of a wimp. The army helped turn me into a lean mean fighting machine ready to serve my country. It doesn't matter where you start; it's where you end up,' would have struck a better tone.

The Irish Defence Forces recently unveiled a campaign aimed at recruiting women that stresses the importance of physicality, exciting travel and the sense of accomplishment that comes with an army career.[11] It is conspicuously devoid of the patronising tone that accompanied the British Army's adverts.

It was the suggestion that a sense of belonging was more important than the ultimate mission – to engage and destroy the Queen's enemies – that was so misjudged. In a sign of the strength of feeling within the ranks about the adverts, the tattoo-baring, no-nonsense army Sergeant Major Glenn Haughton took to Twitter to suggest his men were being misrepresented.

'Not much crying going on and I couldn't care less what their sexual orientation is…As long as they, just like the rest of the Army are pre-pared to fight for their country, their Capbadge and @BritishArmy that's all that matters,'[12] he admonished.

The thinking behind the controversial recruitment campaign was well-intentioned, as was an edict to top brass to hoist the rain-bow-coloured LGBT flag on parade grounds to mark Gay Pride month.[13] The observance is common in many British institutions, in-cluding embassies and universities, and few people object. However, some in the armed forces – to whom flags are neither political nor dec-orative, but symbols of 'life or death' allegiance – were deeply uncom-fortable. Serving personnel have revealed that there was a backlash on a number of military bases.

A Royal Marine said:

> There was a big stink. In civilian life, nobody really pays attention to flags. However, flags are a big part of a soldier's identity. Traditionally, the only flags that fly on parade grounds are the regimental flag, the company flag, and the Union Jack, each representing a level of belonging.
>
> We had to go through a long process of hoisting down the regimental flag; hoisting up the gay pride flag; then saluting it. This was an issue, not because anyone has a problem with gay soldiers in the military, but because we felt we were being asked to make a political statement. To soldiers, flags are sacred. The feeling was that top brass were using them to virtue signal.[14]

The new adverts and efforts to demonstrate empathy and respect for the LGBT community were a logical response to a real problem across the armed forces. As we have seen, having spent years making people redundant, the army, navy and RAF all face a recruitment crisis. At the time of writing, the regular strength of the armed forces was 136,770 – 6 per cent below target strength.[15] In the year leading up to April 2018, 12,360 people joined the UK Regular armed forces, but in the same period, 15,170 left.[16] The Royal Navy and the RAF are running at around 10 per cent short of their annual recruitment target, while the army had a recruitment deficit of 31 per cent.[17]

This is partly a peacetime problem. Wars help recruitment, appealing to patriots, thrill-seekers and adventurers. The armed forces did not have a problem attracting personnel during the Iraq and Afghanistan wars. Moreover, unemployment is at a record low; society is ageing; more young people are going to university and there are more ethnic minority groups wary of joining the military. There are also problems with what defence chiefs call 'the offer', meaning pay and conditions.

One former adviser to a Labour Defence Secretary put it bluntly:

> It's a shit job, run by shit people where you are treated like shit … you are thrown into this environment where they have to share rooms, live in dormitories, treated like dregs, shouted at, screamed at, made to do horrible things, run for forty miles or whatever. It is not pleasant happy life and today's soft kids are not used to it.[18]

Studies show that the average private has suffered a wage decrease of £1,000 in real terms since 2010.[19] The challenge is not just attracting personnel but keeping them. Many young people see joining the armed forces as a short- to medium-term option, knowing their skills will be very marketable in the private sector. The way pay rises are 'frontloaded' early in careers – with rapid increases in the first few years quickly levelling off – makes leaving after a six-to-eight-year stint a logical option. As one former officer, who left the Household Cavalry to make the most of his Oxbridge degree and multilingual skills, put it: 'Good in, good out.'

> If you're doing well in the army, you'll be a high flyer outside. They're going to pay you, and promote you. Within a few years if you're good in an investment bank, you'll be earning a few hundred thousand. Whereas as a Lieutenant Colonel aged forty-five, commanding a group in Afghanistan, commanding 1,000 men, you'll still only be earning £70,000. Which is what friends who graduated from Oxford would have got in year one. That's the issue.[20]

Morale is a persistent problem. According to the Ministry of Defence's 'Continuous Attitude Survey', which records how servicemen and women feel about life in the armed forces, satisfaction rates have dropped from an already modest 61 per cent in 2009 to just 42 per cent in the most recent survey in 2017.[21]

A 2015 report by former defence minister Mark Francois MP, called 'Filling the Ranks', warned that 'the scale of the challenge of manning the armed forces cannot be underestimated.'[22] No wonder top brass are trying to cast the widest possible net. At the same time, they can make a virtue of arguing that the military should be more representative of the society it serves, with more women, LGBT people and ethnic minorities.

The question is whether, in this part-ideological, part-pragmatic quest to be inclusive, they might be compromising the UK's ability to win wars.

WAVING OR DROWNING?

Bayonet training, Sandhurst.

'Do you *know* how angry you need to be to push a knife into another human being?' enquires an officer cadet, recalling his training experience. 'They need to get you seeing red!'

Here's how they do it. Forty or so cadets are put through half a day of physical hell, crawling through dirt and ditches; hauling themselves along the ground in a press-up position and sprinting back and forth. All the while, they're instructed to chant: 'Kill! Kill! Kill!'

Then they are marshalled into lines in front of straw sandbags and ordered to charge, and stab at the heart of the sandbag with all their might.

'I remember being absolutely exhausted before we even began,' recalls the officer cadet. He will never forget the way the Falklands veteran who was in charge of the drill prepared cadets for the challenge.

> He shouted at us to 'CRAWL OVER THERE, GET OVER, GET IN THAT DITCH, GET OVER THERE!' so we were completely done in; and then he shouted, 'RIGHT. YOU ARE GOING TO FUCKING KILL! FUCKING KILL.' And we were like, 'YEAH!'
>
> I remember him roaring: '*What makes the grass grow?*' And we all

yelled, 'BLOOD, BLOOD, BLOOD!' And his eyes – I've never seen such crazy eyes in my life! He got right up close to us, grabbing us and shouting 'FUCKING KILL.' He was near enough frothing at the mouth.

Recalling the sergeant's uncompromising approach to other routines, the source said:

The guy would forget what he'd told you to write down in the morning. He'd yell: 'Did I fucking tell you to do that?' And you'd reply, all meekly, 'Yes, you did, Sergeant Major.' And he'd start shouting: 'I DIDN'T FUCKING TELL YOU THAT. GET OVER THERE AND TELL THAT TREE HELLO!' And you'd go over there and be like, 'Hello, tree!' and you'd run back, and he'd be like, 'I DIDN'T FUCKING TELL YOU TO COME BACK, YOU C*** – GET BACK OVER THERE.'[23]

Such is the training that transforms polite young men and women from civilians to soldiers.

As Officer Cadet Elizabeth Eldridge writes on an official British Army blog, 'You train hard to fight easy, but fighting does not come naturally to most; it is altogether "other"...' In her view, this sort of bloodthirsty ritual is exactly what is required to make the psychological leap.[24]

Far from being traumatised, many cadets cite exercises in which they are pushed to their physical and mental limits as highlights of their training. They relish the challenge, and believe few of those who join the armed forces expect – or want – to be treated like civilian workers.

'If you don't like the heat, get out of the fire. The army is NOT the place for you,' says one Sandhurst cadet bluntly.

In this attitude, surprisingly, young members of the forces appear to be increasingly at odds with their elders. Many young servicemen and women are quietly contemptuous of what they see as an obsession with political correctness on the part of politicians and the chain of command. One disgruntled soldier pointed to a blog by a civil servant on the Ministry of Defence's website which said straight colleagues should all take a training course on LGBT issues to 'explore your conscious and unconscious biases and make you think about how your behaviour and use of language can make others feel less included'. The author of the blog suggested colleagues become 'visible straight allies' by 'wearing an ally badge' and reminded people to avoid words such as husband and wife, recommending using the gender-neutral term 'partner' to 'avoid the awkwardness of someone having to correct you that their other half is actually the same sex'.[25] The soldier considered it unnecessary and ridiculous.

The blunt application of politically correct edicts, governing everything from the type of language used by drill instructors to how far recruits can be pushed, has given rise to a worrying narrative, both inside and outside the military, that the British armed forces are 'going soft'.

At all levels, but particularly in lower ranks, there are mounting concerns over the tension between wise and necessary reforms to ensure the military is an employer fit for the twenty-first century; and enabling the military chain of command to train recruits to survive in battle.

As one put it, 'There are no fucking safe spaces in Afghanistan … You think the Taliban would care about hurting our feelings?'[26]

The depth of frustration among ordinary serving personnel about these changes, and the extent to which they believe such preoccupations are literally weakening the British armed forces, has found voice on army message boards, where serving personnel express their disdain under a cloak of anonymity. As one contributor pointed out, if a commanding officer ordered his men to switch off their radios on the battlefield to allow a Muslim comrade to pray (as per a scene in one of the new recruitment ads), they would all be at risk: these radio communication systems deliver battlefield instructions and warn of incoming enemy fire.[27]

There is particular disquiet among ordinary servicemen and women for what they see as a fixation with LGBT rights and the amount of resources devoted to ensuring that nobody causes offence.

'When I'm asked how I want to be described, I feel like saying I'm transgender, so that I can get promoted. The whole thing has gone way too far. Perhaps I should say I identify as a goldfish? Tomorrow, I'll change it to a square. Or a triangle! It's become ridiculous,' according to one young serviceman.[28]

For the Ministry of Defence and defence chiefs, all this is a very difficult balance. The shocking death of four trainees at Deepcut Barracks in Surrey between 1995 and 2002, amid claims of systematic bullying, humiliation and harassment, rightly led to much soul-searching about the welfare of young recruits.[29] An independent review concluded that while the army did not cause the tragedy, it failed in its duty of care.[30] It had a lasting impact on the culture at military bases – for the better. However, a 'zero-tolerance' approach to bullying has had a significant impact on the nature and level of aggression considered acceptable during training exercises. In extreme cases, it has led to the prosecution of drill instructors accused of 'assaulting' troops.[31] Privately, young officers and soldiers frequently express concerns about how this might play out on the battlefield.[32]

It would be easier to dismiss suggestions that the armed forces are 'going soft' were it not for the extraordinary number of serving personnel who are officially classified as unfit to send to war. As at 1 January 2018, a total of 27,071 full-time trained members of the armed forces, including 17,054 members of the army, were medically downgraded, around half of whom (13,104) were classified as 'non-deployable' on operations. The number of army personnel classified as unfit for deployment stood at 7,082.[33]

A GP who works full time at one army base estimated that a quarter of men and women at her base fell into these categories and described 'many' as overweight. She claimed it was common for servicemen and women to be downgraded for far longer periods than necessary because of lengthy waits for medical investigations and treatment. She said:

> By the time they've gone through some physio; then it's decided they need to go to the rehab unit; then it's decided they need to see a specialist, and he or she says you need an operation; then they're on the normal NHS waiting

list, because there are no longer military hospitals, a year has gone by! And they're in danger of being discharged completely.[34]

This is partly a societal problem and is having a real impact on the size of the talent pool from which the military can draw. The army is having to turn away 'large numbers' of potential recruits because they are not 'medically or physically up to it'. In 2016, over 100,000 people applied to join, but only 7,441 were successful.[35]

Concerns about fitness standards are not confined to the British military. In 2017, an internal memo from Special Forces instructors at Fort Bragg in the United States claimed there are now almost 'no fitness barriers' to earning the coveted Green Beret.

> Students do not need to be able to pass a 2-mile run at an 80 per cent standard. They do not need to pass a 5-mile run in under 40 minutes. They do not need to be able to pass a 12-mile ruck march in under 3 hours. They are not required to find ANY points during their land nav training and assessment. They do not need to be able to perform 8 pull-ups. They do not need to be able to perform 57 push-ups, or 66 sit-ups. They no longer need to be able to climb a 15-foot rope with weight on. Students are no longer administered any form of physical or administrative punishment. After passing a 19-ish-day selection process, there are no physical barriers to earning the coveted Green Beret. These were standards for EVERY Green Beret in modern history prior to this month. To say that standards have not been eliminated would be laughable, were it not so tragic…[36]

Of course, it's possible to go too far the other way. Russian boot camp has long been notorious for its brutality. Terrified recruits call it '*dedovshchina*', or 'rule of the grandfathers'. Trainees are subjected to prolonged periods of physical and psychological abuse by their superiors, who are expected to instil 'discipline' in young recruits through a long series of indiscriminate beatings and starvation. An investigation by the website Vice described a series of stomach-churning practices, such as:

the Pheasant, where the *dukh* [recruit] has to crouch on the legs of an up-side-down bench while the *deds* [grandfathers; superiors] line up and whip his naked ass with a metal belt buckle. It varies according to unit, but the *dukh* can expect at least 100 blows. If at any point the *dukh* falls off the bench, the process starts from the beginning.[37]

In one infamous incident in 2005, a young private named Andrei Sych-yov was severely beaten while his superiors were on an alcohol-fuelled bender. Despite suffering grievous injuries, military doctors pro-nounced him healthy. Days later, his legs became gangrenous. Both had to be amputated.[38]

Such excesses have contributed to huge desertion rates within the Russian armed forces. Many soldiers suffer mental breakdowns, and suicides are not uncommon.

It is unclear how well a new generation of British troops could com-pete with enemy forces trained in this way.

'The Russians come out of training made of steel. If it came to a war, they'd walk all over us,' suspects one Sandhurst cadet.[39]

Some young British troops are so eager to be pushed to their physi-cal and psychological limits that they are taking matters into their own hands. In an unexpected encounter while on holiday in Indonesia, Nick Mutch, a contributor to this book, witnessed a group of young off-duty Sandhurst cadets voluntarily engaging in waterboarding – a form of torture notoriously used by the CIA on terror suspects – both on themselves and various hostel guests who volunteered to see what the procedure was like.

Mutch says:

I met 'Mike' and 'David'[40] in a dingy youth hostel on Gili Trawangan, an island just off the coast of Bali. David was in the Cavalry, Mike in Signals Intelligence. They'd just been through the gruelling training common to soldiers at Sandhurst, but expressed dismay at recent changes to what is tra-ditionally a more brutal side to military education. They told me that they did 'crazy shit' to each other just to test their limits. I asked them what it was like to be waterboarded. They told me that after about five seconds the water flows through your nose and into your lungs. You feel like you're drowning and your instinct is to take giant, panic breaths, but that just makes it worse. Apparently true panic sets in after ten seconds. Your limbs start flailing uncontrollably. You would be screaming in terror, but any noise is muffled.

According to Mutch, 'David' and 'Mike' played at waterboarding with fellow holiday makers every night of their stay. Volunteers would be held down on a hostel table; blindfolded; and have water poured over their faces. One volunteer lasted fifteen seconds – 'as long as the average Marine,' according to 'Mike'.

'After surviving this he jumped up, punched the air and exclaimed, "Too easy at this level!" For his efforts he received a round of backslaps and free drinks all evening,' Mutch recalls.

SPLITARSES

It was the day before New Year's Eve 2017 and a group of off-duty Marines was celebrating in time-honoured style. In a crowded bar in Bucharest, they were downing drinks and becoming increasingly loquacious – particularly about female colleagues.

Slamming his beer on the counter, one exclaimed: 'Our armed forces have been disintegrating from the inside. From *splitarses* in the military. The slags. Fucking splitarses cause all the problems.'

Referring to a scandal on board the nuclear submarine HMS *Vigilant* in October 2017, which resulted in nine service personnel being kicked out of the navy after testing positive for drugs and the captain being stripped of his duties after forming an 'inappropriate relationship' with a female crew member,[41] the Marine continued:

Look at the submarines. They've been going fine for over 100 years. Now one of the nuclear submarines got turned around because a load of fucking *splitarses* started fucking everyone to the point where one of them was walking around with a captain's hat wearing his uniform. They basically had to turn around a submarine because of *women*!

It wasn't the ability of female soldiers to fight with which he took issue ('It's just pulling a trigger. A child could probably do that, like the fucking African dictators get them to'), but allowing men and women to train and fight together.

'It's when you try and integrate them, that's the problem,' he declared.

The rest of the group did not demur. Speaking with a frankness they would never risk in a formal setting, the young officers poured scorn on the rationale for opening all roles to women, arguing that 'changing times' was insufficient justification.

All they say is 'It's the twenty-first century, innit?' Most people don't have a logical argument. The only argument they have is 'Ohhh, it's 2017!' As if we didn't win the last two world wars without women. In fact, we've won everything without them. So why do we really need them now?[42]

The Marines were drunk and letting off steam, so perhaps not too much should be read into this ugly exchange. However, their hostility towards female personnel points to a wider unease among some in the armed forces over the way the (rightful) desire to increase the representation of women is being handled by politicians and top brass. Few question the ability of women to serve in all roles, except perhaps Special Forces, where the exceptional physical requirements could be prohibitive. It is the indiscriminate integration of men and women in extremely challenging operational environments that is generating concern.

In July 2016, with the enthusiastic support of the then Defence Secretary Michael Fallon, David Cameron lifted the ban on women serving on the frontline in ground close combat roles (GCC).[43] Announcing the change, Fallon declared:

There are women flying fighter bombers at the moment over Iraq and I don't think it is right now to exclude women from considering any role that they want to apply for ... It has been done already in the frontline for police, for example, where women are serving in firearms units and smashing down doors.[44]

Defence chiefs were fully behind the reform. Carter, who had person-ally driven the policy, argued: 'By allowing women to serve in all roles, we will truly help to maximise the talent available to the army and make the armed forces a modern employer.'[45]

As General Sir Nick Houghton, who threw his weight behind the plans when he was Chief of the Defence Staff, points out, urban war-fare and counter-insurgency had made a nonsense of the concept of the 'frontline' in any case.[46]

In the ranks, however, there was a degree of scepticism about the sudden conversion of top brass to the equality cause. To some observ-ers, the sex scandal on HMS *Vigilant* – dubbed HMS *Sex and Cocaine* after nine sailors were kicked off for drug taking and four officers were removed over allegations of affairs[47] – hammered home the operation-al risks associated with a dogmatic insistence on equal opportunities. The degenerate behaviour was not just an embarrassment to the navy, but for the wider armed forces, undermining the effort that goes into projecting their professional image.

Sir Michael Fallon, on whose watch it happened, was appalled, summoning First Sea Lord Admiral Sir Philip Jones to his office for a furious dressing down. Some wonder why he was so surprised, point-ing out the likely effects of throwing a small number of young men and women together in extremely confined and pressurised conditions such as those on board a submarine.

'I don't think anyone would suggest that there aren't women who are better than men. The issue is the mix,' says one young Afghanistan veteran.[48]

Top brass argue, with justification, that occasional scandals and in-cidences of bad behaviour are a poor basis for changing policy. For now, just over 10 per cent of the armed forces are women, but the figure is increasing slightly every year.[49] The Afghan experience, in which women soldiers worked as bomb disposal experts, medics and radio operators, and lived and died alongside combat infantrymen, did much to promote a sense of equality on the battlefield. However, many soldiers question the time and effort being devoted to planning for a future generation of female combat soldiers that might never materialise. While commanders busy themselves re-organising training courses; planning new barracks; and educating instructors in how to deal with female recruits, women are not rushing to sign up for combat roles.

'So far it seems that only a handful of women want to be infantry soldiers – is this really the most important problem facing the army?' says an army officer involved in the project. 'Everyone will look really silly if we roll out the red carpet for the women and no one shows up.'[50]

As the military opens up, lawyers specialising in equality and human rights are doubtless smacking their lips. As we shall see, the UK armed forces are already a lucrative source of litigation work.

LAWFARE

WAR AND THE LAW

FUBAR

Volunteers who selflessly signed up to give blood to the NHS during the coalition years might have been surprised to discover that they could have been saving the Taliban.

Hospitals across the UK need more than 6,000 blood donations a day to keep supplies going, the vast majority of which is used to treat British patients. During the Afghanistan war, however, large volumes of blood were also sent to the field hospital in Helmand Province, where it was used to treat both our own soldiers and the men trying to kill them. This strange state of affairs encapsulates the contradictions of war fought with honour – and, increasingly, war fought with an eye on the law.

In his powerful eyewitness account of life in the field hospital in Helmand, the academic Dr Mark de Rond highlights the extraordinary lengths to which British doctors went to save wounded enemy fighters. The ethnographer, who spent six weeks embedded with the surgical team at Camp Bastion at the peak of the ISAF (International Security Assistance Force) operation, reveals that critically injured Afghan insurgents were given blood transfusions courtesy of the NHS, whatever the level of reserves. As the bodies of British soldiers blown to pieces by improvised explosive devices were sombrely repatriated in coffins draped in Union Jack flags, medical teams at Camp Bastion could be found patching up the hands of injured Afghan insurgents – enabling them to return to their deadly activities planting more roadside bombs. On one occasion, de Rond watched as a critically injured

Afghan dressed in 'black Taliban trousers' drained limited medical supplies at the field hospital – or, as one of the British doctors put it bluntly: 'Bloody well used up all of our platelets.'[1]

De Rond's account of day-to-day life in the field hospital, which was part-staffed by teams of British medics on release from the NHS and developed a reputation as the most successful trauma unit in the world, illustrates the anomalies and ambiguities thrown up by the responsibilities of the armed forces under the Geneva Convention, which governs the treatment of prisoners of war and those injured on the battlefield, and other international agreements.

It reveals the extent to which the admirable determination of the British armed forces to honour both the letter and spirit of those ob-ligations diverted resources from British and NATO troops. At times, this approach upset and exasperated doctors. Humanitarian efforts were not limited to treating Afghan insurgents. Locals suffering from a wide range of conditions, from sexual problems to burns caused by kerosene lamps, made their way to the field hospital for medical care courtesy of the British taxpayer. There they were shown compas-sion and respect, and almost always provided with the best available treatment. In one of many striking examples of the generosity of the British military towards sick Afghan civilians, de Rond describes how a drunken Afghan involved in a hit-and-run accident was airlifted to the field hospital, an expensive and dangerous act of charity (which received no thanks). De Rond says:

> The man was verbally abusive ... and fought off any attempt to help him or hold him down. He badly needed to go into theatre for emergency surgery, but ... given the level of intoxication, was wrapped in gauze before being ordered onto the ward to sleep it off. He'd hopefully be able to tell the dif-ference between a hangover and a head injury by the time he woke up the following morning.[2]

Afghans treated at the field hospital were routinely transferred to local clinics once their condition had stabilised. This system often created a dilemma for the British surgical team, who were reluctant to discharge vulnerable patients, particularly children, when the care at local medical facilities was so rudimentary they would probably die. De Rond says one of the lead surgeons was 'firm in the view that no resources be spent on Afghan casualties who have a better chance of winning the lottery than surviving their injuries. To keep them alive just because we can is, he said, heartless, seeing that they would be off-loaded onto a local hospital with fewer resources, inferior pain meds, and different standards of care. Better to let them go comfortably and be done with.'[3] He describes a number of cases in which mortally wounded Afghans were given very high doses of fentanyl until they slipped away.[4]

In other cases, mortally wounded Afghans with no hope of survival were kept alive for a period to make the paperwork easier. De Rond describes how 'US administrators' requested that the death of an Afghan who arrived at the hospital 'FUBAR' ('Fucked Up Beyond All Recognition'), having been spotted burying an IED which blew up in his own face, was 'postponed so as to give them time to complete the relevant paperwork.'[5]

'It seems things were easier administratively if he died a free man rather than the detainee he now was; and thus while his "release" was being processed through the usual channels, he lay in intensive care, killing time for the sake of managerial convenience,' he writes.[6]

For the most part, the surgeons de Rond observed accepted – even embraced – their humanitarian obligations, approaching each patient as a medical challenge rather than an individual who might be on the wrong side of the war. Nonetheless, they were acutely aware that the enemy did not share the same standards.

'I bet you a million these ragheads don't give our boys that sort of treatment,' de Rond quotes the lead surgeon as saying.

> We shoot a missile at them and they survive, and rather than finishing the job we fly in our most expensive asset and have our lads carry them two and a half miles on gurneys through the fucking heat with all their gear on

their backs just to get them to the helicopter and pump them full of blood even if we all know they're going to die.[7]

Ask members of the armed forces what they think of all this, and a few will roll their eyes and complain that it is topsy-turvy. War is war, they will say, arguing that when resources are limited, they should not be squandered on enemy fighters at the expense of British or Allied patients, particularly not on injured insurgents masquerading as civilians. The majority disagree. From the earliest days of their training, new recruits are taught to take pride in the way they treat the enemy. This is not a source of resentment. On the contrary, most members of the armed forces feel very strongly about embracing the highest standards of battlefield behaviour. Servicemen and women know that it is much easier to win hearts and minds in any given operation if their behaviour is beyond reproach.

The furore surrounding the plight of Sergeant Alexander Blackman, dubbed 'Marine A', who shot dead a mortally wounded Taliban fighter in September 2011 and was subsequently charged with murder, suggests that public opinion is more sympathetic to the mistakes made in extraordinary circumstances. Many ordinary voters were shocked that a highly experienced serviceman with an impeccable record should be so heavily punished for a temporary lapse of judgement in the heat of battle.[8]

Some fellow servicemen and women did feel the murder charge was too harsh.

As one former Household Cavalry Officer put it:

That's what he's in the war to do – kill people. He didn't rape a baby! In no other country would that have been brought to trial. You can't have civil rules on that kind of situation. Everything depends on reasonableness and what's reasonable in war is not reasonable in other circumstances.[9]

Within military circles, this is a rare expression of sympathy, however. The general view is that Sergeant Blackman's conduct sullied the hard-won reputation of the British armed forces. All pride themselves on their respect for the Geneva Convention and other international protocols surrounding the treatment of prisoners of war and those injured in conflict.[10]

All the same, his case was a powerful illustration of the legal risks faced by British servicemen and women in combat zones. Today, warfare is increasingly accompanied by lawfare, as individuals at all levels within the military seek to avoid being sued.

HAZIM

Perhaps the rot really set in with the death of a young man named Hazim, though there were others.

On the evening of 4 August 2003, the 23-year-old Iraqi tribesman was attending the funeral of a relative in a village called Al-Majidiyah near Basra. It was the early days of the Iraq War and Saddam Hussein was on the run. The British had become part of a 'caretaker administration' attempting to maintain order in what was still a very volatile situation until a new Iraqi government could be established. Basra was part of the British-controlled area.

According to Hazim's brother, shortly before midnight, the funeral ceremony became very noisy, as relatives engaged in an age-old custom of discharging guns to celebrate the life of the deceased. Hazim was making his way to the property where the funeral was taking place. As he turned down a street, he found himself face to face with British troops – and was shot dead.[11]

The British version of events was rather different. According to the sergeant who pulled the trigger, he and his comrades had been patrolling the area when they heard heavy gunfire from a number of different points. As they approached the centre of the village, they came across two Iraqis on the street. One of the pair, who was about five metres away from the patrol, was armed and pointing his gun at the British. In the dark, it was impossible to tell the position of the other man. Believing that his life and those of the other soldiers was at immediate risk, the sergeant opened fire on the two men without any verbal warning.

The following day, the sergeant produced a written statement describing what had happened. It was good enough for his command-er, Brigadier William Moore, who was satisfied that his actions fell within the so-called Rules of Engagement (ROEs) for British troops. As far as the brigadier was concerned, the matter was closed.[12]

That was not how Hazim's brother saw it, however. Furious at what he regarded as the summary execution of his sibling, he initiated legal proceedings against the United Kingdom on human rights grounds, re-sulting in a case known as *Al-Skeini* (the family surname) which went all the way to the European Court of Human Rights in Strasbourg. Judges there ruled that because the British Army was in 'effective control' over Basra at the time, Hazim was within the UK's jurisdiction, meaning he was protected by the European Convention on Human Rights, just as he would have been had he been attending a funeral in a village in England.[13]

The decision had profound implications for both the military and the government, opening the way for European and human rights laws to follow British troops onto the battlefield. At a stroke, the armed forces were now liable to be sued in any territory over which they could be held to exercise control.

Soon hundreds of Iraqis were lining up to seek compensation for alleged abuse and torture during the conflict. Such was the volume of claims that the Ministry of Defence set up a unit to investigate. The now-notorious Iraq Historic Allegations Team (IHAT) began with 149 claims.[14] Encouraged by unscrupulous British lawyers, the claims mul-tiplied, until IHAT was handling some 3,400 cases, most without any merit or foundation.[15]

This inquiry and Operation Northmoor (a similar inquiry into al-legations against veterans in Afghanistan) has cast a spotlight on the role of the courts in conflict. The armed forces should not be above the law, and they do not want to be above the law. As former Intelligence Corps Reservist Tom Tugendhat has acknowledged in a study called 'The Fog of Law':

> That discipline is what turns a group of individuals from a mob into one of the most respected fighting organisations in the world. It is based on

many things: ethos, values, tradition of excellence, and most importantly, self-regulated standards that demand professionalism despite the chaos of battle. Together, these are what make the Royal Navy, the British Army, and the Royal Air Force.[16]

The question is *which* laws should apply on the battlefield. A follow-up study to which Tugendhat also contributed, 'Clearing the Fog of Law', highlights how unsuitable international human rights legislation is for application on the battlefield. The authors point out that human rights laws stem from a fundamental principle that you should never use anything that could be described as 'excessive' or 'disproportionate' force; whereas the whole point of armed conflict is to use *overwhelming force* to beat an adversary into submission – in other words, the polar opposite to the 'no more than strictly necessary' principle that applies in a civil context.[17]

The combination of the *Al-Skeini* ruling; another decision in a case called *Smith* v *Ministry of Defence* (in which the UK Supreme Court established for the first time that relatives of servicemen and women killed in action can sue the government for negligence and for breach of the 'Right to Life' under Article 2 of the European Convention on Human Rights);[18] and a host of other test cases have entangled the British military in a mesh of human rights laws. This often benefits our adversaries.

Many in the armed forces feel the government has done very little to protect them from this corrosive new environment. They are particularly bewildered and resentful that the pursuit of veterans through the courts over decisions taken on the battlefield does not appear to be happening in other countries. While the Geneva Convention applies to all 196 signatories, interpretations of the responsibilities and restrictions on armed forces arising from the European Court of Human Rights vary widely from one EU member state to another, with British troops far more exposed to the threat of legal action than their European and American counterparts. British troops can't help wondering why they are especially liable to be sued and pursued.

All this has troubled successive Defence Secretaries, who have come under intense political pressure to protect the armed forces from the creeping judicialisation of warfare. Former Army Captain Johnny Mercer, now a Tory MP, has led a long-running campaign to bring an end to the misery of veterans caught up in the process. (One individual has been subjected to no fewer than four inquiries over the death of an Iraqi in 2003.) Mercer has said he feels 'ashamed' of what he sees as the government's lily-livered approach to the issue.[19]

Defence Secretary Gavin Williamson is now determined to act. At the time of writing, his attempts to persuade the government to introduce some kind of statute of limitations on allegations of historical abuse, and other legislation to protect troops in the heat of battle, were being frustrated by the apparent reluctance of the Prime Minister and Attorney General to risk falling foul of the courts by introducing measures that could be challenged.

Williamson's position remains that it is better to start with something imperfect and refine it as required than to decide it is all too difficult to bother.

'The problem is a culture of trying to find a risk-free option,' he says.

> There is no such option. There is nothing watertight. We need to do something; we don't have to get it totally perfect. If there is a challenge, then we will adapt it. Doing nothing is not an option I'm happy with. Someone needs to take the legal and political risk, and I am happy for that to be me.[20]

Tugendhat and his co-author Laura Croft are in no doubt where the buck stops. They argue in their study, 'The Fog of Law', that the problem stems from

> Parliament's incremental removal of the protections once granted to those who risked all for their country. Without a legislative re-wall to hold back the cases and with no other body stepping in to decide, the judiciary has been left in the unenviable position of having to hear cases and to decide what is, and what is not, right in battle.[21]

PART FOUR: THE HOME FRONT

To date, political attention over the role of the law in warfare has focused on the impact on veterans. In future conflicts, however, many will be watching anxiously to see how it affects military success.

DEATH BY JUDICIAL DIKTAT

The day-to-day experience of soldiers and airmen in Afghanistan offers a sobering insight into how a 'tick box' culture in the armed forces designed to minimise legal risk can affect military operations.

In his powerful account of his combat tours of Afghanistan, Captain Johnny Mercer, now a Conservative MP, tells how he and his men were caught up in a deadly firefight as a result of red tape. The prologue to his book, *We Were Warriors*, describes how he was prevented from destroying a compound – from which the Taliban would 'pour murderous machine gun fire' on a British patrol base – because his chain of command was worried about the impact of blowing it up on the surrounding landscape.

> I should have destroyed the compound months ago. Two 500lb bombs would do it, or a couple of guided rockets. Last time I attempted it we waited for six hours in a ditch, while battalion headquarters worked out the 'environmental impact' of me turning it into dust. What would happen to the watercourses? How would the trees recover afterwards?

'British soldiers' lives were tumbling down the priority lists out here,' he says.[22]

Mercer goes on to describe how, during his tours of Afghanistan, 'the most enormous pressure' was put on young field commanders and soldiers, whose actions were

> subject to an almost constant overwatch and second guessing – usually by someone who had yet to experience their first proper firefight … commanders became obsessed with analysing secondary and tertiary effects of almost every engagement. This had the effect of both paralysing ground troops and commanders and bringing friction to the relationship between

those of us on the ground and those commanding from Patrol Bases. In close contact with the enemy, this could prove fatal.[23]

This attitude was partly linked to the doctrine of 'courageous restraint' introduced by US Commander General Stanley McChrystal in an attempt to reduce civilian casualties.[24]

Mercer believes British commanders over-interpreted the approach. He writes:

The concept was good: 'should I, could I, must I engage the target?' with the emphasis on the last one. This however is a very easy process while sat in headquarters watching the action unfold on TV; it is a great deal harder to assess what 'must' be done if it is you that is involved in the mortal combat … British commanders, seemingly unable to think for themselves and now heavily deferent to the Americans … were falling over themselves to be the ones who instigated [McChrystal's] directive to the strictest degree.[25]

The MP's account of the constraints faced by British troops in theatre is far from unique. Another Afghanistan veteran, a former Household Cavalry officer, describes how British troops calling in air support after becoming caught in firefight hoped 'anyone' other than the RAF would respond because they were less able to engage with the enemy than allies operating under more relaxed rules of engagement. He says:

When I was in Helmand there was a kind of 'stack' of Allied jets above Afghanistan. If you looked up, there would always be this kind of donut in the sky. If there was a particular mission, you could call in advance with specific requirements; for example, if you were attacking a bunker, you might want a bunker-busting bomb. But in an emergency, there was this stack of planes, permanently burning jet fuel at extraordinary expense. It was a free-for-all up there – Americans, Dutch, French – but you would never want a Brit because of the rules of engagement. They were so narrow that unless someone actually started firing at the plane, pretty much they were not going to help you.[26]

For the British government, the politics surrounding civilian casualties in any conflict are particularly challenging. The widespread public perception that the Iraq War was illegitimate and unnecessary has contributed to a culture in which ministers are under constant political pressure over collateral damage in military campaigns, with anti-war campaigners and human rights groups demanding regular updates on accidents. In Afghanistan, restrictive rules of engagement designed to minimise the risk of civilian casualties were obsessively applied, sometimes at the expense of the wider war effort.

According to one former officer who experienced how this played out:

> I was sent up to an area where three of us got shot on the first day, myself included. We had to fight to contain it for a week, as they attacked us every day with a whole bunch of things, including mortars. They had an ammunition dump [storage unit] but we weren't allowed to call in a strike on the ammunition dump, because they [the chain of command] were worried about civilian casualties. They said people might be nearby and that we couldn't prove it was empty. I said, 'Yes, but I can prove it's full of ammunition. Everyone agrees on that!' I had to keep our guys sitting on a hilltop, being shot at every single day for a week, because we couldn't blow up the ammo supply. Just in case! Nobody had proven there were civilians there. It's just that I could not prove there weren't.[27]

Rules of engagement for troops in Afghanistan could change day to day, sometimes simply for political reasons. An Afghanistan veteran recalls how extra restrictions were suddenly imposed on British troops after American troops accidentally bombed a civilian convoy – only to be lifted when media attention had dissipated.

'We were out patrolling an area that hadn't changed at all, but we were now on more restrictive rules of engagement. A month later, when the press had forgotten about it, we went back to the old thing,' he says.[28]

In general, British troops were allowed to fire at anyone carrying a weapon if they were considered to pose a threat. They were not allowed to fire at individuals who were unarmed. A hostile that fired at British troops, then ran to a new position and fired again, was considered a legitimate target, because he was moving from position to position, in what was considered to be a 'continuing fight'. By contrast, a hostile that fired at British troops then ran away was considered to be 'withdrawing from battle'. Technically, that soldier no longer qualified as a threat, meaning he was no longer a legitimate target. For British troops, shooting an individual in those circumstances would carry the risk of disciplinary and potentially legal action.

The distinction may sound reasonable on paper, but little is black and white on the battlefield, where troops have a split second to judge whether someone is fleeing or re-positioning for a new attack. In practice, according to veterans of the Afghanistan conflict, these rules – and the fear of legal repercussions if they are broken – limit the scope of British troops to exercise their discretion in the unique circumstances of every firefight and can have serious unintended consequences.

'Someone may be running away, but how the fuck do I know if he's about to turn around and shoot me?' exclaims an officer who experienced the complications in Helmand Province.

> Why are we teaching eighteen-year-old soldiers that kind of nuance? It's meaningless; not at all helpful. We were in gun fights and I would have soldiers on the radio asking for permission to shoot because it's so confusing. What if he [the target] is moving away a little bit, or moving towards you but with the gun facing down? What if the guy is on the phone? That was one of our big problems. If the guy was on the phone calling in a mortar strike – if there was a hill, and we were on one side; and they were on the other; and he was on the phone calling in mortar strikes on us – we couldn't shoot him, unless we requested different rules of engagement.[29]

In such situations, according to the source, British troops would turn to Afghan soldiers supporting the Allied war effort and ask them to fire instead.

'This happened to me. I had a guy on the phone, in front of me, just looking at me, calling in fire, and I couldn't shoot him. Obviously in that situation you let loose your Afghan soldiers.'[30]

While troops in difficulty could request urgent changes to rules of engagement, the process would typically take too long to be of any help in an emergency.

'It was not as instantaneous as a gun fight – nothing is! And that's the issue. So whether I get new rules in thirty minutes or not, it's not quick enough,' says the officer.[31]

In Afghanistan, the enemy soon learned how to exploit all the restrictions on Western forces, for example by using children to carry ammunition to Taliban positions.

'They knew that we could not shoot anyone who didn't have a gun, and anyway, would we shoot a kid with ammo?' recalls an officer.[32]

Mercer recalls how a Taliban commander he was tracking on one of his combat tours of Afghanistan was meticulous about ensuring he was always surrounded by children. The army (rightly) went to huge lengths to avoid harming the youngsters, launching a high-risk operation to intercept the Taliban commander's vehicle – enabling troops to remove the children to safety before they seized him – rather than ordering an aerial strike, as would ordinarily have been the case.[33]

In Iraq and Syria, ISIS has also learned how to play the system. An RAF source familiar with measures taken to minimise the risk of civilian casualties in Operation Shader revealed that jihadis sometimes install mosques within buildings to deter air strikes. According to the source, the UK vetoes between 20 and 30 per cent of proposed attacks planned at the coalition's Combined Air and Space Operations Centre in Qatar.

'There is an RAF person who is the UK's red card holder, with an RAF lawyer sitting next to him. Any hint of collateral damage, they use the red card, and they use it quite a lot,' he says.[34]

He claims the US Air Force sometimes presses ahead with strikes the UK will not sanction.[35]

Many voters will wholeheartedly approve of such a cautious approach. The concern is how it would play out in a bigger, more desperate battle. If the law loomed too heavily over the campaign in Afghanistan, how much worse would it be in a war of national survival? Tugendhat believes that without urgent changes to the law to protect the armed forces, the courts 'risk paralysing the military' with coroners' inquests; health-and-safety legislation; and human rights cases. 'The paperwork alone would simply overwhelm the Ministry of Defence, even if the eventual findings of the inquiries ascribed no blame,' he and his co-author have said.[36]

He goes so far as to warn of the prospect of 'defeat by judicial diktat'.[37]

For the time being, ministers have the luxury of peacetime conditions to redress the balance.

PART FIVE

TOMORROW

SIXTH SENSE

A NOTE ON RISK

Perhaps Squadron Leader Samuel Bailey had a premonition about how his life would end.

On 25 April 2012, the young pilot told a doctor that his fear of flying had reached 'crisis point'. He had become so anxious being in fighter jets at certain altitudes that he believed he was no longer fit to fly. The doctor signed him off for three weeks and arranged for him to see mental health professionals, after which he returned to duty, flying only in conditions in which he felt more comfortable.[1] Ten weeks later he would be dead, after his RAF fast jet collided with another fast jet in mid-air, killing three out of four of the airmen on board.

Fog was rolling in over the Moray Firth when Tornado ZD743 and Tornado ZD812 smashed headlong into each other off the north east coast of Scotland. However, an official investigation ruled that neither the weather nor Squadron Leader Bailey's fear of flying were to blame. There were seventeen other factors, the most controversial of which was the absence of a common safety device known as a Collision Warning System on the fast jets.[2]

In overcrowded skies, the possibility of mid-air collision is very real. RAF chiefs and ministers consider it the 'top air safety risk'.[3]

Collision Warning Systems are basic pieces of technology that alert pilots to such danger. If two planes are on a possible collision course, alarms go off in the cockpit, allowing them to take evasive action. All civilian airliners are fitted with such systems. The sorry saga surrounding their absence in the RAF's Tornado fleet says a lot about the mindset at the highest levels within the Ministry of Defence and the armed forces. It also offers an insight into attitudes to risk, an increasing source of concern within the military and among defence academics.

The way responsibility for safety works at senior levels of the Ministry of Defence is that 'duty holders' carry the risk of things going wrong. They need to ensure that those risks are 'as low as reasonably practicable' – or 'ALARP' in Whitehall speak. When it comes to the possibility of mid-air collisions between airliners and fast jets; or two fast jets; making the risk ALARP means installing Collision Warning Systems on aircraft. Ministers have long accepted this in principle.

The decision to fit Tornados with the safety systems was initially announced in the 1998 Strategic Defence Review, but it was classified as discretionary at the time, meaning it could be delayed.[4]

Crucially, under Ministry of Defence rules and regulations, setting money aside to do something qualifies as 'ALARP' even if nobody follows through with the project. It was enough that the installation was *planned*.

Now everybody involved had covered their backs, there was little incentive to get on with the job, especially when money was always tight. Consequently, during the Labour years, the fitting of Collision Warning Systems to Tornados was repeatedly deferred.[5]

Then, in 2010, the Ministry of Defence went a step further. All those years had passed without a catastrophe, so some bright spark thought the department might as well 'delete' the plan.[6]

Against all advice from the Chief of the Air Staff and the Director-General of the Military Aviation Authority, who warned that this would mean the risk could no longer be ruled ALARP, on 4 April 2011, the then Secretary of State Liam Fox cancelled the programme.[7]

At that point, the risk holder process kicked in. The person responsible for all fighter jets (the Area Officer Commanding 1 Group) became very nervous that he could be legally liable if the worst happened. He wrote to the Chief of the Air Staff, making it clear that he was only prepared to 'hold the risk' if the Secretary of State gave him cover. He asked Fox to 'endorse it as the departmental position'.[8]

When he didn't receive a reply, the hot-potato-passing started. The

Director-General of the Military Aviation Authority wrote to the Secretary of State declaring that the failure to fit Collision Warning Systems contravened air safety regulations, and warning that flying operations might have to stop. He was backed by the Chief of the Air Staff himself, who declared in no uncertain terms that the 'cessation of the Tornado CWS [Collision Warning System] programme now means that the risk of a MAC [mid-air collision] can no longer be considered ALARP.'[9]

With RAF chiefs now running a mile from 'holding the risk', it moved to the top of the food chain. On 11 June 2011, the risk transferred to its final holder, the Secretary of State himself. Returning to work after the weekend, Fox was 'invited to note' that both the Chief of the Air Staff and the Director-General of the Military Aviation Authority regarded the decision not to install Collision Warning Systems to be a breach of ALARP. He was reminded that the buck stopped with him. The 2nd Permanent Undersecretary made sure that Fox was in no doubt about the value of the safety systems, noting in a letter that they probably halved the risk of a mid-air crash. For the avoidance of doubt, the Secretary of State was further reminded, in typical Whitehall speak, that the Collision Warning System programme was 'no longer in being'.[10]

At this point Fox suddenly had a change of heart. Faced with the alarming prospect of being held personally responsible for a calamitous crash between a fighter jet and a civilian airliner, he immediately decided to reinstate the Collision Warning System programme 'to make the risk of a collision involving Tornado ALARP'. He had held the risk for only a few days.[11]

All this came too late for Squadron Leader Samuel Bailey and the other airmen involved in the mid-air crash over the Moray Firth. When the nose of the right underwing fuel tank of one jet smashed into the right engine air intake cowling of the other, the jets broke up in a ball of fire.[12]

In the end, work only began to install Collision Warning Systems on Tornados in 2015, a full sixteen years after the measure was agreed.[13] By this point, the Tornado was not far off retirement in any case.

Meanwhile, Collision Warning Systems have yet to be installed on Typhoon aircraft, which will eventually replace the Tornado fleet.[14]

The Moray Firth crash has been the only such disaster in the past twenty years. However, there have been numerous 'near misses'. In all, there have been seventy 'airprox' incidents with the Typhoon since it came into service in 2006.[15] In 2010, air operations were suspended around Warton due to a near miss involving a Typhoon and an airliner.[16] It happened again in 2014, when a Typhoon flying out of RAF Leuchars in Scottish airspace had a near miss with a commercial airliner flying from Aberdeen.[17]

Risk is at the heart of the fundamental rationale for the military. The armed forces exist to take up the burden of protecting society on behalf of the general population, thus saving civilians from having to defend themselves. Having signed up to the job, they train and deploy to put themselves in highly risky situations that others do not face. A healthy attitude to risk is therefore a vital component of capability. This episode reveals something very unhealthy about the Ministry of Defence's attitude to risk. As soon as an individual becomes personally accountable, they treat their accountability like a live grenade, to be thrown as quickly as possible.

Politicians and mandarins in the Ministry of Defence spend a great deal of time ensuring that no one person will individually assume risks, because the results of a wrong decision are potentially career-ending. In this case, it was only when the potential for a mid-air crash landed squarely on the shoulders of the politician that he appreciated the magnitude of the risk military people were being asked to assume. For the 'uniforms', the reluctance to take chances is linked to the brutal promotion system, which simply does not allow for mistakes. A single error over a 25-year period, or one appraisal graded less than excellent, ends any hope of reaching the highest rank.

In the case of lawfare, soldiers in contact with the enemy are avoiding action that could reduce British casualties because there is a risk they may be held personally accountable if they make a targeting mistake. In the MoD, individuals may avoid doing what is required to promote the safety of troops precisely because there *isn't* a risk they will be held personally accountable. These two positions may seem contradictory, but both are about attitudes to responsibility and liability.

One former senior officer contrasted this culture with the culture in the US military. 'There, the important thing is that you succeed. If you fail, you fall down on your feet and get back up. Here, the only important thing is that you don't fuck up.'[18]

These attitudes are distorting decision-making, whether on the battlefield or in the comfortable surroundings of an air-conditioned Whitehall department – and our armed forces are weakened by it. Only very strong political leadership can introduce the culture change required to liberate military people and civil servants to make better judgements.

ROBOTS

THE TECHNOLOGY CHALLENGE

WHEELBARROW

In a way, modern warfare began when Peter Miller got tired of trimming his lawn. In the early 1970s, tinkering in his garage, the retired Colonel had attached a remote control to his mower, allowing him to direct it from the comfort of his chair. By pure coincidence, an army colleague happened to drop by to discuss the Troubles in Northern Ireland, where the IRA was bringing terror to the streets of Belfast and Derry. Bombs hidden in car boots were blowing up British troops and maiming innocent civilians. Eight soldiers had been killed in less than a year. The army was desperate to find a solution.

Suddenly, Miller realised his invention could have potentially life-saving applications.

'This seemed a possible solution to the problem, so I went to a local garden centre with the intention of buying a gutted lawnmower. The sales manager suggested that the chassis of an electrically powered wheelbarrow might be suitable. I thought it was ideal and bought one on the spot,' he said later. With a little more work, he was able to build a robot that could disarm, defuse or, as a last resort, detonate the IRA's explosives. Between 1972, when the 'wheelbarrow' was first introduced, and the end of the Troubles in the late '90s, nearly 400 bombs were neutralised. Each success potentially saved the life of the bomb disposal expert, who would otherwise have had to destroy it manually, as well as those who would have been in harm's way had it detonated as the terrorists had planned.[1]

Miller was never rewarded or compensated for his work. The

Committee of Awards to Inventors claimed that he was already 'paid to invent' as an officer of a Ministry of Defence research establishment and it took decades for his work to be properly recognised.[2] However, one day he may be known as the progenitor of one of the most important military advances in history: the application of robots and unmanned systems to warfare. This is changing the character of war, and the race is on to exploit the opportunities the new technology offers. There are dangers, however: some of the armed forces' most expensive equipment could be rendered obsolete.

On a BBC website, anyone can take a quiz to see if their job is likely to survive the technological changes of the twenty-first century. Some people, like social workers and therapists, are safer than others. Roles that involve empathy, moral and ethical judgement and people management are more resistant to automation.

Clerks, accountants and even doctors are more vulnerable: robots could soon do their work.[3] According to a study by the accountants Deloitte, nearly 35 per cent of all jobs are at 'substantial risk' of automation over the next twenty years. Already, robots and artificial intelligence are performing medical surgery, driving cars and cleaning houses.[4]

Automation has the potential to revolutionise warfare. As Richard Box, an IT director at Ernst and Young, put it: 'Robots are a pretty attractive proposition. They can work 24/7, they don't get tired, they don't make mistakes late at night, and most them can be used for less than the minimum wage.'[5]

Robots could also bolster a shrinking army. In Singapore, a sharp fall in population threatens to reduce the armed forces, which rely on conscription, by almost one third by the year 2030. Defence chiefs hope technology can make up the numbers.

David Koh, Singapore's Cyber Security Chief, makes no secret of his government's plan to substitute machines for young men and women in uniform.

'The challenge that Singapore faces is that we have not enough babies. Despite the best efforts of our politicians in throwing lots of incentives at our young couples, they just refuse, for whatever reason, to procreate,' he says.

> Because we are a conscript armed forces, the challenge is quite evident for us. The people who will serve in our armed forces are in school today, and we see the numbers declining at a very steady rate. We hope, and we are working towards, technology making the difference, otherwise the armed forces capability of the Republic of Singapore will change dramatically ... It's not driven by innovation or desire, but really by necessity.[6]

The British Army is thinking the same way. Major General Chris Tickell, Director of Capability at Army HQ, believes robotics and autonomous systems could offset what is widely seen as the army's greatest weaknesses: its diminishing size.

'The army has got smaller in recent times. We definitely view robotics and autonomous systems as one way to mitigate that risk, particularly if we pair manned and unmanned systems – then we can start to buy back some of that lack of mass, as well as avoiding putting soldiers in harm's way when we don't need to,' he told an international security conference in 2017.[7]

Tickell acknowledged that robots have their shortcomings. 'They are very structured; they don't really like change in a big way; they certainly don't build relationships; they're not very empathetic or sympathetic, so for all of their good, they are not the perfect employee,' he said.[8]

Making the most of new technology will require a very different approach to procurement. As we have seen, it can take decades for the armed forces to acquire some bits of kit. In a world of daily software updates, the system will have to become more nimble.

'If we enslave ourselves to the current ten-year [procurement] process ... then we are not going to deliver the effect we need at the pace we need,' Tickell has said.

> We have got to deliver capability faster. If we're truly innovative, not everything we introduce will work. That is counter cultural. I understand

why it is, because we're dealing with public money, but if we don't get over that hump, we'll always end up reverting to a relatively safe procurement process, which arguably ends up with things that are not necessarily optimised at the time they're delivered.[9]

William Biggs, Campaign Leader on Autonomy for the company QinetiQ, has echoed concerns about the Ministry of Defence's procurement process in this context, describing it as 'hopelessly unsuited' to the acquisition of new technology.

'It's simply too linear, too slow, and too aligned to traditional capabilities,' he has said.[10]

The navy is already embracing the robotics challenge. In late 2016, off the west coast of Scotland, they took the lead in an ambitious joint exercise with NATO allies called 'Unmanned Warrior'. In the Scottish seas near the Hebrides and the Kyle of Lochalsh, they tried out over fifty different unmanned systems on a range of missions, including anti-submarine warfare and mine counter-measure exercises. Among the systems tested were various underwater drones; an autonomous BAE speedboat; a self-flying helicopter made by the defence giant Leonardo; and an unmanned aerial vehicle made by Boeing called Scan Eagle. The Ministry of Defence was pleased with how the exercise went, releasing a video on the Royal Navy's YouTube channel enthusing that 'all objectives' had been met.

'Deployment of systems was up to the challenge,' the department said, adding that the performance of joint forces in the exercise was 'beyond all expectations.'[11]

Other observers were more sceptical. Professor Peter Roberts, a naval expert at the Royal United Services Institute think tank, dismissed Unmanned Warrior as 'late to the game and not very ambitious.'[12]

AEGIS

The Super aEgis II doesn't need to eat; won't nod off on its shift; won't get distracted by its phone; and won't be tempted to clock off early. It is a fully automated gun turret armed with a 50-calibre machine gun that can lock on, aim and fire at a human target with perfect accuracy at a range of over 2 km. Thanks to infrared sensors, it is unaffected by harsh weather or the dark. Apparently, the South Korean government has acquired several of these weapons and positioned them overlooking the Demilitarized Zone.

For the time being, the turret is connected to a human observer armed with a joystick and trigger. Only he or she can give the order to shoot. However, the developers of aEgis candidly admit they are only a quick software fix away from giving the turret the ability to fire on its own. As one of the chief engineers for designer DoDaam told the BBC: 'Our original version had an auto-firing system. But all of our customers asked for safeguards to be implemented. Technologically it wasn't a problem for us. But they were concerned the gun might make a mistake.'[13]

Current rules of engagement for the armed forces in the UK, the US and all other NATO allies require humans to make the final decision to use lethal force. Sooner or later, however, others may well adopt a more relaxed approach to who, or what, is at the end of what defence analysts call 'the kill chain'. The emergence of autonomous systems that can decide for themselves whether to hold or open fire paves the way for a disturbing new front in robotic warfare.

The former Commander of Joint Forces Command, General Sir Richard Barrons, says:

> If you take the assault on Mosul;* what you've got is a load of Iraqis crossing the river, on a pontoon, and fighting their way through the grubby streets. So you have a human who is first to go round the corner; look over the wall, and so on. In future, you'd have a machine to do that. That machine can be either unmanned, controlled by a human somewhere else, or it can be autonomous, which means it's run by algorithms, which within certain parameters allow it to do things, and even kill.
>
> People here are very uncomfortable with that, but the North Koreans

---

* Allied operation against ISIS in Iraq, supported by Iraqi soldiers.

wouldn't be. I don't think any Western nation has an autonomous machine in production that kills on the basis of its algorithm, but Russia and China wouldn't even blink at it![14]

In April 2018, a group of 116 scientists wrote an open letter to the UN ahead of an arms convention demanding a blanket ban on the development of any 'lethal autonomous weapons'. They warned that such systems 'threaten to become the third revolution in warfare … they will permit armed conflict to be fought at a scale greater than ever, and at timescales faster than humans can comprehend … once this Pandora's box is opened, it will be hard to close.'[15]

Closing the box might even become a legal problem. The armed forces may find themselves damned if they do, and damned if they don't. It is easy to imagine bereaved relatives suing the manufacturers of a 'killer robot' over bullets accidentally sprayed in the wrong direction, yet a failure to employ such systems once they are on the market might also give rise to a legal challenge. Just as nobody serving in Belfast would have chosen to send a soldier to dispose of a bomb when the 'Wheelbarrow' could do the job, if infantry soldiers or pilots can be replaced with robots, keeping humans out of danger, society may demand that they are used instead. Some, including the Ministry of Defence itself, fear this could lead to a world in which war between states is more acceptable because the human cost is much lower.[16]

The logical path of all this leads towards robots fighting other robots. Apart from the technical complexity, protecting the lives of one's own troops in this way might mean that the only casualties are non-combatants. The ethics become extremely challenging: the 'will' of the government and the nation is one of the three essential components of military strategy. This is totally undermined if leaders are not prepared to spill the blood of their young men and women, and instead allow robots to become proxies (and possibly kill innocent bystanders).

Experts believe the way that technology is changing defence has particularly sobering implications for countries like the UK that have invested heavily in top-end equipment. At the 2017 Fortune Global

Forum, a prestigious annual economic conference held in Guangzhou that year, spectators were dazzled by a display involving a fleet of 1,180 drones flying in synchronicity.[17] The drones were just for show, but a swarm equipped with offensive weapons or packed with explosives could potentially disable some of the armed forces' most advanced platforms.

'Several thousand things that cannot be individually tracked and neutralised could render large platforms, whether the F-35 fighter jet or a naval vessel, into vulnerabilities rather than assets,' says a cyber-security academic.

> It's for the same reason we no longer put our infantry in phalanxes or in musket squares. If you put them all together in a neat geometric form, they are just a nice target for precision guided munitions. We've learned on the infantry and armour battlefield to decentralise the asset. Yet we are still producing huge valuable assets like aircraft carriers. The cost of losing twenty mini-drones is very small. If I am your enemy, why don't I send 20,000 mini-drones against your frigate or carrier?[18]

Al Brown, of the Ministry of Defence's Development, Concepts and Doctrine Centre, remembers US General David Perkins telling him that, in the Middle East, one of America's allies was forced to fire a £3 million Patriot missile to destroy a single kamikaze drone which cost £200 pounds on Amazon. A large swarm of those drones falling on the British base in Afghanistan, Camp Bastion, could have temporarily disabled most of the aircraft the UK was using in the campaign, a huge potential return on investment for insurgents.[19]

Defence chiefs in the UK are acutely aware of this danger. Vice-Chief of the Defence Staff General Sir Gordon Messenger has acknowledged the inherent risk of investing in a few very costly pieces of kit. 'We can't simply prioritise high-end platforms. If we did that, we'd end up with smaller and smaller numbers of more and more exquisite platforms,' he told delegates at the 2017 Defence and Security Equipment International exhibition.[20]

In certain conditions, very expensive high-specification platforms may be lethal to the enemy, but they are not much good at what Messenger called 'the prevent business, where one needs more platforms, more ubiquity; less survivability, and less lethality'.[21]

To date, defence chiefs have tried to design the armed forces for worst-case scenarios in a way they hope will optimise their chance of dealing with anything south of that level of threat. This approach looks unsustainable.

As Messenger put it: 'If your worst drives you down to a relatively small number of high-end platforms, that is a notion worth challenging.'[22]

To some defence experts, the F-35 fighter jet programme is indicative of the technology and automation problem facing Western militaries.

'In the UK and the US, we have a culture of idolising fighter pilots,' says a defence academic.

But everyone who knows physics and electronics knows that the minute you get the monkey out of the cockpit, the airplane can perform much better! Not only can it perform tactically better at higher G force than any human can endure, it can fly longer missions than any human can endure. The more I get the monkey out of the conflict, the more widely I can use the platform, because I'm not worrying about ISIS or whoever else may be seizing my downed pilot. Not only does it tactically improve performance, but operationally, having no pilot gives me much wider latitude. Yet, our 'next generation' fighter still has a human in the cockpit … I ask people, why are you preparing to fight last century's wars?[23]

In this new game, advantage will fall to whoever masters the new technology first. There is no universally applicable rulebook for conflict, and hostile regimes or individuals will not trouble themselves with ethics.

As Barrons put it: 'Much as we would like everyone to play by our rules of cricket, other people don't even understand what cricket is.'[24]

SHOWDOWN

POLITICAL PRIORITIES

KAMIKAZE

Gavin Williamson's first victory as Defence Secretary had been to buy himself time to consider the state of the armed forces before reaching any decisions that could make them weaker. Within days of his arrival at the Ministry of Defence, he had been asked to make sweeping recommendations about possible cuts to capabilities, a responsibility he felt was too important to rush. It did not take him long to see that what defence needed was more resources, not less. He decided the solution was to persuade Cabinet colleagues of the nature and scale of new threats to security, but he quickly became frustrated by the intractability of a Treasury desperate to keep control of the nation's spending and debt at a time when money was still tight.

Williamson had entered the Ministry of Defence with a rare advantage: a strong bond with a Prime Minister who did not have a close personal relationship with many Cabinet colleagues. At the time of his appointment, he was a figure some political observers believed could one day become leader of the Conservative Party. Others with his political prospects might have quietly accepted the hopelessness of persuading an administration in agonies over Brexit to devote serious thought and resources to defence matters, and simply waited to be moved to a new job. Instead, Williamson embarked on an increasingly high-stakes campaign to secure a better financial settlement for the armed forces, telling friends he would rather 'try and fail, than fail to try'.[1]

Throughout 2018, he made the state of the armed forces considerably more difficult for the party leadership to ignore, perhaps at a cost to his own career.

His bullish tactics alienated some colleagues. His supporters briefed against the Chancellor, and occasionally Downing Street, and he was constantly in the press in ways that were not always flattering. A live TV appearance from a Midlands safari park in May, during which he repeatedly failed to say whether he regretted declaring that Russia should 'go away and shut up', prompting presenter Richard Madeley to terminate the interview, was a particular low.[2] His relative lack of ministerial experience perhaps led him to be a little too zealous in pursuit of his goals, and critics began sniping that in his determination to win this battle over the defence budget, he had gone too far.

The trouble was that Brexit was all-consuming for Downing Street. There simply wasn't the bandwidth for much else. Moreover, the Prime Minister continued to view defence and security through the prism of the Home Office, where she had built her Cabinet career.

May's relations with military top brass during her first year in office had been business-like but not warm. She liked to play up the fact that her grandfather was an army sergeant major[3] but there were few major military decisions to be made during this period. The strategy for the war against Islamic State and confronting Russia in Eastern Europe had been largely set by her predecessor David Cameron. The low-profile Chief of the Defence Staff, Air Chief Marshal Sir Stuart Peach, and his successor General Sir Nick Carter, were largely left to get on with the job.

Privately, senior figures at the Ministry of Defence complained that the Prime Minister hardly every turned to the department for help or suggestions. 'It was as if we had been parked in a lay-by and forgotten,' according to one senior official. 'She only seemed interested in using the armed forces for props and backgrounds in photo-ops for non-military-related policies.' As a former Home Secretary, the Prime Minister was more comfortable with the security services and police. She knew most chief constables by name and had routinely worked with the heads of MI5, MI6 and the intelligence agency GCHQ (Government

Communications Headquarters). Those within the military who did interact with the Prime Minister found her courteous but aloof.

'When she was going to meet military chiefs we had to prepare briefs so she knew who she was talking to. It was obvious she was not comfortable with trusting strangers,' according to the same mandarin.[4]

One of May's most trusted officials was her National Security Adviser Sir Mark Sedwill, who had been the most senior civil servant with her at the Home Office from 2013 until early 2017, when he was moved to the Cabinet Office. The former Ambassador to Afghanistan shared her 'counter-terrorist and cyber warfare' take on the security threats facing the UK. The wave of terror attacks on the UK in spring 2017 reinforced this perspective. Invasion by hordes of Russian tanks or blockades by Moscow's silent submarines were not high on Sedwill's threat list.

The Prime Minister and her advisers had been relieved that, following the 2017 terror attacks in the UK, no sustained military mobilisation had been required to support the police (in contrast to the approach taken in France in 2015, when 10,000 troops flooded the streets of Paris after the massacre at the offices of the satirical magazine *Charlie Hebdo*). However, senior officers and intelligence chiefs warned that they might not be so lucky next time. They pushed for a dramatic increase in the number of armed officers and more funding for surveillance squads.[5] It would not be cheap.

This was the background to the sweeping review of all security-related spending across government announced in summer 2017. It was born of a need to find more money to ramp up police and intelligence counter-terror budgets, and the knowledge that the Ministry of Defence was in deep financial trouble. As we have seen, the ambitions of the 2015 Strategic Defence and Security Review had not been underpinned by enough money. Over the previous six months, the National Audit Office spending watchdog had warned that the department was nowhere near finding the 'efficiencies' required to fund the £24 billion cost of the new programmes announced.[6] The Cabinet Office's own Infrastructure and Projects Authority gave eight of the Ministry of Defence's thirty-three projects 'red' or 'red/amber' tags, warning that successful delivery was in doubt or in some cases unachievable. Another fourteen projects were listed as 'amber' by the government's internal auditors. They warned that urgent action was required or the position would worsen.[7]

The revisiting of British security spending – the exercise Williamson was keen to delay after his surprise appointment as Defence Secretary – was dubbed the National Security Capability Review. Sedwill was given a remit to examine the security services, police, counter-terrorism, cyber security and eavesdropping, Foreign Office diplomacy and defence spending and the cross-government Conflict, Security and Stability Fund. He was also asked to look at the potential impact of Brexit on defence and security.[8]

Crucially, the exercise was supposed to be cost-neutral, so any recommendations would have to be paid for by cutting existing activities. Neither Downing Street nor the Ministry of Defence under Sir Michael Fallon was keen to draw attention to the process. To that end, the review was announced on 'Trash-Out Thursday', the day before Parliament shuts down for the long summer recess, when Whitehall departments scramble to tie up loose ends and all but the most controversial announcements can be slipped out without much fuss. The plan was that Sedwill should report by Christmas, so that his recommendations could feed into the next Budget. The timing fuelled the impression that the exercise was primarily about money as opposed to big-picture strategy.[9]

When Whitehall returned that September, civil servants and military top brass in the Ministry of Defence accelerated work on their submissions. Sedwill repeatedly emphasised that the Ministry of Defence could not expect any more money. In a depressingly familiar routine, defence chiefs were sent off to come up with a menu of options for more cuts to make ends meet. The navy suggested making sailors redundant, and retiring two frigates, two amphibious assault ships, a helicopter training ship and seven minesweepers. They also offered to scrap a fleet of Wildcat helicopters which were only two years old.[10] As we have seen, there were also suggestions that the Marines could be cut, and the amphibious ships HMS *Albion* and HMS *Bulwark* could be scrapped.*

For its part, the army offered to disband one light infantry brigade and one armoured infantry brigade and scale back a project to upgrade its old Challenger tanks and Warrior troop carriers. They also suggested cutting Army Air Corps helicopter numbers.[11] The priority was saving Ajax, the armoured vehicle needed for the new Strike Brigade, and a contract for high-tech radios.[12]

For RAF chiefs, protecting P-8, the long-awaited maritime patrol aircraft, and the F-35B programme was key. They offered to ditch all their Hercules airlifters and E-3D Sentry AWACS radar early-warning jets. Other spy planes and drones would also be cut, along with part of the RAF regiment.[13]

To many in the armed forces, it felt like 2010 all over again. Just as ministers were talking up the Russian threat, the armed forces were being forced to contemplate yet more reductions to frontline capability. The whole package potentially involved the loss of 14,000 military personnel in the hope of saving £2 billion a year.[14]

Since leaving office, Fallon has told friends there would never have been reductions on this scale. At the time of writing, however, no decisions have been made, and the armed forces feel neither secure nor optimistic about what lies around the corner.

In late January 2018, Williamson managed to persuade the Prime Minister to separate the defence element from Sedwill's review. He was given an extra six months to look at what was going on with his department's budget. He secured a very important additional concession: the new mini defence review (dubbed the Modernising Defence Programme) would no longer be 'cost-neutral' – raising the possibility

---

* Fallon has told friends that defence chiefs never formally presented him with plans to cut the Marines or amphibious ships. He has told friends he would not have countenanced it. Apparently, he did not quash speculation about their future at the time on the basis that ruling out one particular saving would only raise question marks over others.

of more money for the armed forces.[15] And so began what some saw as his kamikaze mission.

BOILING POINT

It all came to a head in a heatwave. As London sweltered in one of the hottest summers on record, Williamson headed into Downing Street to appeal to the Prime Minister personally for more money. He was about to find out whether his rapport with May would be enough to transcend the Chancellor's objections.

In the room were the Prime Minister, Hammond, Sedwill and Chief of the Defence Staff General Sir Nick Carter. The meeting was not a success.

A few days earlier, on 16 June 2018, the Chancellor had stunned Tory MPs by signing off a £20 billion-a-year boost to the NHS budget, to come into effect from 2023.[16] The lavish additional funding, to mark the 70th anniversary of the health service, would mean tax rises[17] and even less resources for anything else.[18]

For Williamson, the timing of this decision could hardly have been worse. Washington was becoming increasingly anxious – and vocal – about the state of the armed forces in the UK. In an extraordinary intervention, US Defense Secretary Jim Mattis had warned that the UK's status as a global power was 'at risk of erosion' because of insufficient spending on the military. In a letter to Williamson, sent on 12 June 2018 and leaked on 2 July, he signalled that without budget increases, the UK might no longer be his country's 'partner of choice'.[19] The 2018 NATO summit was less than a month away, with the risk that President Trump could single out the UK for public condemnation over defence spending. Only a few weeks of the parliamentary term remained, and the Modernising Defence Programme needed to be wrapped up.

Williamson had asked Carter to kick off the meeting with a presentation on the scale and range of threats facing the UK. He had hoped that this would set the right tone for a serious discussion about resources for the armed forces. However, both May and Hammond are said to have appeared sceptical from the start. The Prime Minister reportedly looked confused by some of the military jargon used by the Chief of the Defence Staff and repeatedly stressed the importance of counter-terrorism and the 'wonderful' response of the police, MI5, MI6 and Foreign Office diplomats to the poisoning of the rogue Russian spy Sergei Skripal in Salisbury. She did not acknowledge the fact that military personnel trained and equipped to handle nerve agents had also been involved.

Following the presentation, Williamson and Carter were subjected to a forensic grilling by Sedwill, who looked unconvinced by their arguments. When the general stressed that extra money was needed to keep Britain as a 'Tier 1 military power', May appeared bemused. She admitted (not unreasonably) that she was not familiar with the term, and wanted to know what it meant. She failed to offer any reassurance that she would not preside over the relegation of the armed forces from the military premier league. Williamson and Carter left No. 10 empty-handed. Time had run out to agree a new settlement for the armed forces before the long summer recess. It would only be possible to publish some vague 'headline conclusions' of the Modernising Defence Programme and renew efforts in the autumn.

It was not long before details of the Downing Street meeting leaked. During a joint press conference with NATO Secretary General Jens Stoltenberg, May was challenged by journalists about what had happened. She claimed reports of the discussion with Williamson were 'not correct'.[20]

However, she once again refused to commit to maintaining the UK's 'Tier 1' military status, saying only that this country would remain a 'leading defence nation'.[21] It was not the reassurance MPs who care about defence needed.

The following weekend, sensational reports emerged that the Defence Secretary had secretly threatened to bring the Prime Minister down if she did not concede more cash.[22] Williamson seemed ready to go to war himself.

CONCLUSION

In spring 2018, a group of young British Army officers were treated to an unusual lecture at the Defence Academy in Shrivenham, Swindon. They listened intently as a commander described the kind of war they might have to fight in 2035. The imaginary scenario, loosely based on real events in Ukraine, was this: a surprise sporting victory triggers an outbreak of nationalistic pride in Georgia, unleashing a chain of events that leads to an illegal Russian occupation. The Kremlin starts by claiming Russians in Tbilisi feel threatened and launches a clandestine operation to 'support' its oppressed diaspora. The arrival of Russian forces is skilfully disguised, creating widespread confusion. The operation is accompanied by a sophisticated campaign of misinformation. Before anyone realises what has happened, the Russians have effectively invaded.

In the fictional example, British troops stormed to victory against the Russians after politicians took a 'massive leap of faith back in 2018' and transformed the UK's armed forces. Perhaps inspired by the 2011 movie *Moneyball*, in which Brad Pitt plays a small-town baseball team manager who takes his players to the top after finding new ways to win, MPs realised that if they didn't approach defence differently, the British armed forces would be 'destined to … irrelevance'. They decided to stop tinkering around the edges, refusing to let a modest defence budget stand in their way. Recognising that they were at a pivotal moment in history, when rapidly changing technology; new threats; and a shortage of resources were all coming together to create a huge challenge for the military, they ripped everything up, and started again with a blank sheet. They worked out where to 'bet big' and which capabilities to ditch; and found new ways to fight. The result? When war came in 2035, they were able to win an 'away match' they had no choice but to play.

Called 'Agile Warrior', the lecture[1] delighted students. Though they are the generals of tomorrow, many feel they spend too much time learning about yesterday's wars. Here was a remarkably frank assessment of the deep-seated problems facing the armed forces today – and a refreshing opportunity to debate how warcraft will have to change.

The presentation described how a terrifying new long-range rocket system called Zeus gave NATO forces the edge. Unmanned tanks; drones; robots; electronic jamming systems; and stashes of hidden weapons were also pivotal to the imaginary conflict in 2035. Much of the kit depicted in the presentation to young army officers was futuristic, but some of the winning tactics were used in the First World War. Students were reminded that the character of war may be changing, but the nature of war remains the same: in 2035, as in 2018, it will still be about killing people and breaking their stuff.

As we have seen, tomorrow's war could be fought in cities; under water; in space or cyberspace; using robotics and autonomous systems; unmanned aerial vehicles and hypersonic weapons. It could also require old-fashioned machine guns, bombs and tanks. There is now much more 'territory' to defend, and technology is changing so fast that weapons systems can become obsolete before they are even delivered. The UK's two new aircraft carriers, which have taken almost a quarter of a century to materialise, may appear to be magnificent symbols of hard power, but it is now evident they will have to be used in a very different way to that which was originally envisaged: deadly 'carrier killer' missile systems which did not exist when the ships were commissioned mean they will have to stay well out of range of conflict zones. The onus is on ministers and top brass to find ways to make the most of an investment that has dominated UK defence planning for the past decade. The Trident nuclear weapons system, too, is vulnerable to advancing technology, and to political leaders with a principled objection to its existence and deployment.

Regrettably, maintaining and renewing this ultimate deterrent is a price we must pay to remain at the international top table, but the time to consider whether there are smarter, cheaper ways to provide the same level of deterrence in coming decades is now. As we have seen, a government-commissioned review of alternatives, carried out during the coalition years, was unsatisfactory. It is a pity that the Ministry of Defence has not succeeded in a long-running quest to persuade the Treasury to foot the bill for renewal. It is insufficiently funded to carry this millstone, and the Chancellor should acquiesce.

Ministers like to talk about the extent of the UK's *soft* power, linked to the generosity of foreign aid. This is a legitimate source of national pride, but without visible and professional hard power to back it up, that too will be diminished. Our armed forces still need tanks, planes and ships. Working out where to invest and where to divest is as much about working out what will remain the same as what will change.

Some things are already coming full circle. In the intelligence world, the risk that electronic documents will be leaked is encouraging a shift back to storing some highly classified material on paper, which can be kept in safes. Meanwhile, the development of electromagnetic pulse systems capable of disabling communication between planes, ships and home bases means soldiers, sailors and airmen and women cannot afford to be totally reliant on satellite navigation systems. They may need to find their way with an old-fashioned map. In this new world of hyper-competition, it will not be the largest and strongest countries that survive and thrive, but those best able to adapt. States that do not accept the current world order; are willing to bend rules and fight dirty; and are ruthless about exploiting every opportunity will have a particular advantage.

We are now at a critical inflection point in defence. It is patently not safe to assume that the UK will have the luxury of choice over when and where the armed forces will next fight. It is all too easy for commentators to parody those who warn of danger by scoffing at the idea of President Putin's tanks rolling towards the UK. This is irresponsible and complacent. As we have seen, modern warfare takes many shapes, and our commitment to NATO allies without the comfort of distance from the Russian border might well require our armed forces to sally forth. Those politicians who blithely dismiss the notion of war with a peer or near-peer adversary are wilfully ignoring defence chiefs on both sides of the Atlantic and others better qualified than they are to assess the risk.

Our armed forces are nothing if not resilient, but they were hollowed out in the devastating cuts imposed by the Strategic Defence and Security Review in 2010, and have endured remorseless salami slicing ever since. Along the way, they have always skilfully adapted to their reduced circumstances, but there comes a point when what remains is not a smaller, neater version of the original – still able to fulfil the same functions – but an entirely different entity, with greatly diminished utility.

As we have seen, in the event of war tomorrow, the army would struggle to deploy and sustain a division – a state of affairs that would have seemed unimaginable during the campaign in Afghanistan only a decade ago. It is just about possible to make a persuasive case for a different type of army, leaner even than it is today, but highly trained and better equipped – but only if the lack of mass were very skilfully offset by other capabilities, and only as part of a radical re-think about the composition and structure of the entire armed forces. To date, politicians have not tried to make any such argument, axing troops simply on the basis of financial expedience.

Of the three services, the RAF appears the least troubled. Engaged in Operation Shader against ISIS targets in Iraq and Syria, an honourable campaign the government does not trumpet for fear of unnecessarily provoking opposition peaceniks, it is largely unaffected by public and political antipathy to the overseas deployment of 'boots on the ground'. However, neither fighter pilots nor fighter jets can be procured quickly, and the service is under no illusion about its capacity for additional tasking. As for the navy, as Theresa May learned when it was not possible to dispatch an attack submarine within range of Syria, because none was available, precious few ships remain, and they can only be in one place at a time.

All three services struggle to fill jobs, as good mid-ranking officers and non-commissioned officers decide they have a better future elsewhere. Armed forces personnel are the backbone of any military and the haemorrhaging of talent has grave implications for the quality of candidates for the highest office in years to come.

As if all this were not enough, our armed forces are now dogged by the fear of pursuit through the courts over decisions made in the heat of battle. Judicial encroachment is a very attractive conceit to liberal elites in wars of choice, where there may be the illusion of discretion and the advantage of time and military superiority to deliberate over targeting. It is very different for those under fire. The next war we fight is unlikely to allow for minute calculations about the remote possibility of collateral damage. The threat is likely to manifest at a pace and in ways that are unrecognisable, and there is no certainty that a rules-based approach will survive. That is not to say that our armed forces should not continue to operate with the highest of ethical standards, which they are rightly proud to espouse. However, they need to be liberated from the scourge of 'lawfare' to do what they do best.

In June 2018, the Prime Minister was widely criticised for questioning the meaning of 'Tier 1 status' in military terms. It was not unreasonable to ask: we should not expect ministers to be defence experts. Those trying to persuade politicians and voters of the true value of the armed forces do not help themselves by consistently assuming far more knowledge than exists among these groups of what can be a very technical subject. In the course of our research, we have been consistently impressed by the calibre of those at all levels of the armed forces, but especially the exceptional individuals who make it to the top. If they were given more licence to speak out and if they avoided endless jargon, there would be no more compelling advocates of their cause.

In fact, there is no universally accepted definition of a 'Tier 1' military power. But, as Gavin Williamson puts it, 'People know what it isn't.'[2]

Broadly speaking, the term refers to the possession of high-end globally deployable forces, trained and equipped to fight in the most intensive types of conflict. It means having credible air power, maritime power and land forces, and the expertise to bring them all together.

Along with the United States and France, the UK can just about claim this status. But for how much longer?

Since 2010, the debate over the state of the armed forces has been dominated by numbers: the size of the army now versus how it was in the old days; the diminishing number of ships and planes; the precise amount of GDP spent on defence. As we have seen, these things do matter. But recent administrations have not made time to consider the more profound question: what kind of country do we wish to be?

Military men and women are used to being given a mission. At lower levels, it might be to secure a bridge, to give safe passage to a unit or platoon whose mission is to move to a patrol base, from where they are tasked with helping to secure a piece of ground from an adversary. At higher levels, it might be to neutralise an international terror threat.

Within any given mission are parameters and constraints. All of those involved in a military operation should have a clear 'unifying purpose' and understand how they are contributing to the overall objective. The same should go for politicians.

Amid the chaos of day-to-day administration, insufficient thought is given to the mission, and the unifying purpose. For all his undoubted faults, Tony Blair understood this. His variety of benign military interventionism may have been discredited, but he could not be accused of lacking vision.

Today, wise decisions about the future of the armed forces would begin with a difficult but essential discussion at the highest level about what role the UK should play on the world stage. This is not a debate that should be rushed: it is far too important to relegate to 'any other business'. It requires Downing Street to take a step back from the maelstrom of Brexit negotiations and the pressures of day-to-day government and set aside some time to reflect on the big picture. Political leaders have a duty to do more than deliver policies: they must also provide strategic direction. A cross-party commission would probably struggle to reach any consensus, but the National Security Council, which was originally intended for grand debate of this nature, might be an appropriate forum.

The easiest option would be to limit our ambitions, accept a declining international status, and adopt a new 'UK first' approach in which we content ourselves with commenting from the sidelines in geopolitical crises.

It is a choice that would certainly appeal to some voters. However, repositioning the UK in such a way would have profound political, economic and diplomatic implications. If we are going to head down this route, it does not seem right to do so by default, as is currently the case.

The Ministry of Defence should play a more proactive part in the debate. No Whitehall department has more exciting stories to tell. Declining to advertise the contribution of the armed forces on the grounds that it is all too sensitive may be easier than working out what can safely be disclosed, and it makes the select few who are in the know feel more important, but it is self-defeating. There is so much good to say. The UK armed forces are not just keeping this country safe, but tackling wildlife poaching in Africa;[3] working to reduce sexual violence against women in conflict zones; and taking part in extraordinary rescue missions of which few voters are aware.[4] The MoD could take inspiration from the way voters value the National Health Service and aim to engender similar affection for the armed forces.

Defence planning and management is fiendishly difficult and becoming harder still. The time currently taken to procure major pieces of equipment and train people to use it makes agility in response to changing threats and innovation near impossible. In recent years, significant improvements have been made to the process, but it remains too inflexible. More thought needs to be given to adapting the system to accommodate the pace of technological advance.

Others are far better qualified than us to prescribe in more detail what needs to be done to equip the armed forces for tomorrow's world. Though it is not all about money, it is clear that a very substantial uplift in the defence budget will be required if we are to do anything more ambitious than maintain current diminished capabilities. The House of Commons Defence Select Committee, in a recent report, called for an increase in defence spending to 3 per cent of GDP in order to retain influence and credibility with our allies. Historically, this level of spending is the norm: the figure was 4 per cent at the end of the Cold War, and during the 2000s was consistently between 2.5 and 3 per cent.[5] It seems the right level of investment for deeply uncertain times.

It would also be sensible to review the scope of spending by the generously funded Department for International Development, which has around £13 billion a year – 0.7 per cent of UK GDP – at its disposal. Rules set by the Organisation for Economic Co-operation and Development, which decides what counts as official foreign aid, are clearly too restrictive, an issue brought into sharp relief in 2017 when the Ministry of Defence was forced to shoulder some of the cost of humanitarian relief efforts in the Caribbean following Hurricane Irma. Given that Whitehall departments struggle to spend all the overseas aid money they have been allocated,[6] this is clearly a nonsense, as a number of Cabinet ministers have acknowledged.[7]

The interviews we have carried out with military figures; academics; recently retired Ministry of Defence officials; and defence industry figures leave us in no doubt that these matters are pressing. The stakes could not be higher. If we do not take a conscious decision to invest in defence, not only will we lose global influence, we will also be vulnerable to adversaries who neither recognise nor respect the rules and values of Western democracies.

There is a grave danger that, in cases where the brazen flouting of the rules-based international order can only be remedied via military response, we will lose the practical ability to do good. Brexit and the protracted negotiations with our European Union partners have already given the impression that we are stepping back from the international stage. As we loosen ties with Brussels, if we do not have the assured ability to protect maritime trade routes in an era where freedom of navigation is increasingly challenged, we may also lose vital commercial opportunities.

This country has an enviable and well-earned reputation for stepping forward on the international stage when other nations hesitate. If we appear to be in retreat, those who have traditionally looked to the UK for leadership in times of crisis may gravitate elsewhere. Some colleagues may take issue with his style, but this is something that Gavin Williamson, Defence Secretary at the time of writing, understands well.

In recent years, American defence chiefs have repeatedly warned that we cannot take for granted our long-running status as their closest ally. To date, no minister has been in a position to offer the assurances Washington seeks about defence spending and investment. The French would dearly love to take our place. As the ambitious young President Emmanuel Macron steps up his country's military capabilities, we may soon learn that the US is not crying wolf.

For all this, there is much cause for optimism: we have yet to run up the white flag. Our armed forces are among the best in the world: professional, disciplined, reliable, committed and brave. As our own international research for this book has found, the UK is still widely seen as among the top five most powerful and influential countries in the world, after the USA, China, Russia and Germany (the latter owing more to Chancellor Angela Merkel's status within the European Union than her country's military capability). American voters still hold this country in particularly high regard, with two thirds citing the UK as 'one of the most influential world powers'.[8] It is striking that less than half of British people questioned in our survey felt the same way. They were also more likely than Australians, Israelis, Italians, Koreans and Americans to think the UK 'seems to overestimate its importance in world affairs'. This hints at a worrying loss of national self-confidence. The armed forces have a great role to play in restoring that aplomb, not via wars of choice, but by helping maintain our relevance in an era of rapidly shifting global power.

If the first duty of a government is to protect its citizens, there is a political peril here, too. Relative to health and education, defence has not been a significant issue on the doorstep in recent elections. That can change in the blink of an eye. Governments are judged on how secure voters feel at home and abroad; how they defend our shores, and how quickly they are able to support those affected by UK and international security incidents. While all is well, assessing their performance on these measures may not be a priority for voters, but adverse events would soon focus the public mind. It is ironic that the Conservative Party, with its proud history of understanding and valuing the armed forces, is gambling on not having to put that possibility to the test.

In recent decades, governments have had the luxury of deciding how much defence they can afford, and how they wish to use that capability. Tomorrow, the initiative may not be in our hands. Then our armed forces will have to deal with problems in the way they are presented – not in the way that is convenient.

The job of the armed forces is to be ready to fight war at its most feral: not the war they last fought, or the war they would like to fight, but the war they may have no choice *but* to fight.

It is time for political leaders to ensure they are ready to meet that grave challenge.

APPENDIX

GLOBAL DEFENCE SURVEY

2,*021 adults in Great Britain were interviewed online between 8 and 11 June 2018. 5,773 adults were interviewed online or by telephone in Australia, Estonia, France, Germany, Israel, Italy, South Korea, Poland, Russia and the United States between 30 May and 21 June 2018. Data has been weighted to be representative of all adults in each country surveyed. Full data tables are available at LordAshcroftPolls.com.*

PERCEPTIONS OF POWER AND INFLUENCE IN THE WORLD

How much power and influence do you think each of the following countries has in the world today – where zero means it has no power or influence at all, and ten means it has very significant power and influence?

Mean /10	ALL	Respondents in...										
		GBR	AUS	EST	FRA	GER	ISR	ITA	KOR	POL	RUS	USA
USA	7.94	8.21	7.61	8.57	7.17	7.28	9.02	8.40	8.42	7.73	7.65	7.30
CHI	7.12	7.43	7.17	7.80	6.35	6.54	7.25	7.42	7.36	6.58	7.81	6.62
RUS	7.06	7.13	6.59	7.88	6.22	6.59	8.00	7.54	6.42	7.02	8.06	6.16
GER	6.38	6.83	5.53	7.23	5.97	6.09	6.39	7.47	6.43	6.62	6.12	5.43
GBR	6.08	6.32	6.05	6.58	5.20	5.31	6.43	6.65	6.50	6.20	5.85	5.75
FRA	5.72	5.97	5.18	6.23	5.62	5.66	5.72	6.43	6.13	5.71	5.10	5.14
SAU	5.22	5.79	5.05	5.56	5.05	4.94	4.94	6.09	4.95	5.06	4.97	5.03
IRA	4.52	4.60	4.16	4.94	4.08	4.07	5.07	5.03	4.44	4.37	4.35	4.60
IND	4.43	5.15	4.50	4.70	4.08	3.87	4.34	4.62	4.81	3.94	4.33	4.44

- Of the nine countries we asked about, the UK was seen as the fifth most powerful and influential after the USA, China, Russia and Germany.

- The mean score given to the UK from other countries was 6.05, almost identical to that given by British respondents themselves.
- With the exception of France and Germany, all the countries surveyed thought the UK had more power and influence than France; only Australia, Israel, South Korea and the US thought the UK had more than Germany.
- People in Russia saw their own country as the most powerful and influential of those we asked about. They were the only nation surveyed to give the highest rating to a country other than the USA.

And would you say that the power and influence of each of those countries is currently increasing, decreasing, or staying about the same?

Inc/ Dec %	ALL	Respondents in…										
		GBR	AUS	EST	FRA	GER	ISR	ITA	KOR	POL	RUS	USA
CHI	64/4	55/4	70/4	75/2	57/5	61/4	53/5	67/7	71/6	55/4	85/1	56/4
RUS	44/11	38/13	42/9	52/11	41/6	41/8	55/7	46/6	17/27	40/16	74/9	39/12
USA	40/16	31/16	35/20	39/22	30/10	29/26	59/9	41/11	52/7	46/11	34/30	40/19
IND	24/12	25/11	26/11	34/10	27/11	22/15	19/8	23/14	25/17	13/16	34/8	20/13
GER	23/14	16/12	13/13	34/15	18/14	20/18	15/15	45/7	17/15	26/17	26/18	23/9
SAU	23/13	17/12	16/15	29/9	32/11	24/14	21/13	28/10	9/25	23/11	27/8	21/13
IRA	19/22	12/20	14/21	28/14	21/20	16/20	25/35	19/16	9/37	16/18	30/12	22/23
FRA	15/19	12/19	10/20	27/15	16/25	19/11	7/22	19/17	11/19	14/27	18/23	17/12
GBR	14/29	9/41	14/26	20/31	10/36	7/39	13/21	19/26	8/27	13/31	20/25	18/14

- Nearly two thirds of all respondents said they thought China's power and influence were increasing; just under half said the same of Russia – though nearly three quarters of Russians themselves thought this was true of their country.
- British people were more likely than those in any other country to say they thought the UK's power and influence were decreasing; they were by far the most likely of any nationality to say this of their own country. Americans were the least likely to think the UK's power was declining.
- Excluding British respondents, 14 per cent said they thought the UK's power and influence was currently increasing, 28 per cent

said it was decreasing, and 51 per cent said it was staying about the same.

PERCEPTIONS OF DIFFERENT COUNTRIES' ARMED FORCES

Now thinking in particular about military power, from what you know or have heard, how would you rate the armed forces of each of the following countries, where zero means they are extremely weak and ineffective and ten means they are extremely strong and effective?

Mean /10	ALL	Respondents in...										
		GBR	AUS	EST	FRA	GER	ISR	ITA	KOR	POL	RUS	USA
USA	8.01	8.05	7.54	9.01	7.08	7.43	8.90	8.19	8.22	7.85	7.87	-
RUS	7.34	7.54	6.94	8.39	6.69	7.02	8.26	7.81	6.88	7.35	-	6.50
CHI	6.88	7.08	7.01	7.80	6.00	6.50	6.76	7.06	6.97	6.52	7.60	6.34
GBR	5.98*	6.49	5.92	6.48	5.44	5.52	6.56	6.54	6.15	6.08	5.51	5.67
GER	5.89	5.92	5.54	6.47	5.20	-	6.17	6.55	6.08	6.04	5.54	5.37
FRA	5.71	5.79	5.25	6.26	-	5.72	5.99	6.37	5.93	5.61	4.95	5.21
IRA	5.17	5.10	4.74	5.68	4.82	4.97	5.72	5.81	4.95	5.18	5.01	4.96
SAU	4.90	5.16	4.48	5.47	4.70	4.97	4.56	5.62	4.78	4.91	4.60	4.71
IND	4.64	4.91	4.45	4.94	4.30	4.39	4.73	5.08	4.97	4.45	4.55	4.30

excludes score from GB respondents

- Overall, the UK's armed forces were seen as stronger and more effective than those of Germany and France, but behind the USA, Russia and China.
- 5 per cent of all respondents rated the UK's armed forces at 10/10 ('extremely strong and effective') – compared to 35 per cent for the US, 20 per cent for Russia, and 12 per cent for China. The proportion giving the UK armed forces 10/10 was just ahead of that for Germany (4 per cent), Iran and France (both 3 per cent).

A FORCE FOR GOOD OR ILL IN THE WORLD?

How much of a force for good or ill in the world do you consider each of the following countries to be, where -5 means it is very much a force for ill in the world, +5 means it is very much a force for good, and zero means it is neither?

Mean -5/+5	ALL	Respondents in...										
		GBR	AUS	EST	FRA	GER	ISR	ITA	KOR	POL	RUS	USA
GER	0.94	1.32	0.98	2.09	1.05	-	1.05	0.79	0.96	0.24	0.07	0.85
FRA	0.88	1.33	1.00	1.88	-	0.93	0.59	0.79	0.92	0.26	0.04	1.08
GBR	0.86*	1.80	1.40	1.62	1.02	0.58	1.26	1.07	0.91	0.66	-1.10	1.23
USA	0.34	0.67	0.79	0.85	0.24	-0.95	2.65	0.91	0.65	0.78	-3.08	-
IND	0.30	0.48	0.18	0.90	0.06	-0.02	0.55	0.12	-0.06	-0.42	1.30	0.28
CHI	0.06	-0.01	-0.37	1.85	-0.45	-0.52	0.22	0.31	-1.19	-0.45	1.81	-0.52
SAU	-0.66	-0.84	-1.04	0.51	-1.14	-1.14	-1.02	-0.44	-0.33	-0.74	-0.36	-0.67
RUS	-0.90	-1.55	-1.07	0.88	-1.02	-1.03	-1.31	0.33	-1.12	-1.93	-	-1.11
IRA	-1.46	-1.57	-1.64	-0.29	-1.67	-1.61	-3.25	-1.18	-1.15	-1.69	-0.06	-1.80

excludes score from GB respondents

- Overall, the UK was seen by non-British respondents as more of a force for good in the world than the USA, but received a slightly less positive score than Germany and France.
- The UK's highest score from overseas came from Estonia. Australians, Israelis and Americans also gave the UK more positive scores than average.
- Russians considered both the USA and the UK more of a force for ill in the world than Saudi Arabia or Iran.
- The highest score given by one country to another was from the Israelis to the USA (43 per cent of respondents in Israel gave the USA a maximum score of +5); the lowest was given by the Russians to the USA.

ALLY OR ADVERSARY?

How much of an ally or adversary to [RESPONDENT COUNTRY] do you consider each of the following countries to be, where -5 means it is very much an adversary, +5 means it is a very close ally, and zero is neither?

Mean -5/+5	ALL	Respondents in...										
		GBR	AUS	EST	FRA	GER	ISR	ITA	KOR	POL	RUS	USA
USA	1.36	1.99	2.28	2.60	1.07	0.23	4.19	1.43	2.12	1.21	-3.40	-
FRA	1.20	1.69	1.26	2.59	-	1.78	1.10	0.85	1.02	0.46	-0.01	1.30
GER	1.18	1.52	1.01	2.93	1.86	-	1.48	0.54	1.11	0.42	0.09	0.96
GBR	1.18	-	2.46	2.57	1.46	1.02	1.45	0.97	1.15	0.81	-1.62	1.65

IND	0.51	0.95	0.36	0.31	0.15	0.02	1.25	-0.02	0.32	-0.13	1.99	0.35
CHI	0.30	0.02	0.01	1.08	-0.29	0.20	1.14	0.14	-0.80	-0.44	2.76	-0.59
SAU	-0.31	0.14	-0.83	0.08	-0.52	-0.36	-1.21	-0.22	0.26	-0.43	0.02	-0.31
RUS	-0.74	-1.82	-0.97	-0.64	-0.57	-0.33	0.38	0.58	-0.62	-2.32	-	-1.21
IRA	-1.15	-1.60	-1.52	-0.18	-1.13	-0.93	-4.24	-0.72	-0.39	-0.95	0.91	-1.89

- People in Estonia and Australia were the most likely to see the UK as a close ally.
- Russians saw the UK more as an adversary than an ally. Excluding Russian respondents, the UK was the second most likely country to be seen by others as an ally.

INTERNATIONAL PERCEPTIONS OF THE UK

Here are some things that people have said about the United Kingdom. For each, please say how much you agree or disagree with the statement.

Agree/Disagree % The UK…	ALL*	Respondents in…										
		GBR	AUS	EST	FRA	GER	ISR	ITA	KOR	POL	RUS	USA
…represents decent values	62/15	63/13	74/9	61/20	73/7	60/14	48/15	63/9	60/16	62/19	40/36	75/7
…is more willing than most to deploy its military to defend its interests and help protect its allies	58/14	64/8	63/9	56/21	59/13	55/13	48/12	61/10	61/8	51/19	58/23	68/8
…is more globally influential than most other countries its size	58/17	60/14	64/11	61/25	52/21	47/22	42/16	62/10	63/8	65/18	51/34	69/8
…is still one of the most influential world powers	57/21	47/24	61/13	49/39	51/27	46/25	50/14	63/11	65/12	70/18	50/38	66/11
…seems to overestimate its importance in world affairs	52/17	52/19	44/21	59/23	53/18	53/13	51/8	46/16	46/12	60/17	66/20	45/21
…is more willing than most countries to deploy its military to support humanitarian goals	47/19	62/9	60/9	46/28	48/18	44/16	41/17	46/15	54/11	44/20	26/51	64/8

* excluding respondents in Great Britain

- People in Australia, France and the USA were more likely than British people themselves to agree that the UK 'represents decent values'. While 81 per cent of people in Britain aged sixty-five or above agreed with the statement, fewer than half of 18–24-year-olds agreed.
- International respondents were more likely than those in Britain to agree that the UK was 'still one of the most influential world powers'. British people were also more likely than Australians, Italians, Koreans and Americans to think the UK 'seems to overestimate its importance in world affairs'.
- Majorities in all the countries surveyed except Israel, and nearly seven in ten Americans, believed the UK was 'more willing than most to deploy its military to defend its interests and help protect its allies'.
- Majorities in all the countries surveyed except Germany and Israel agreed that the UK is 'more globally influential than most other countries its size'.

BRITISH PERCEPTIONS OF NATIONAL SECURITY THREATS

Thinking about the world today compared to thirty years ago, and the potential threats to the UK's national security from all sources, would you say the overall threat to the UK was higher today, lower today, or about the same as it was?

%	ALL	Men	Women	18-24	25-34	35-44	45-54	55-64	65+
Much higher today	41	40	42	26	26	36	45	53	52
Somewhat higher today	33	31	35	38	38	32	29	29	33
About the same	12	16	9	12	14	15	15	10	8
Somewhat lower	3	5	2	5	1	2	4	3	5
Much lower	1	1	1	2	1	1	1	1	0
Don't know	10	8	12	17	20	13	7	5	2

Three quarters of people in Britain thought the threat to national security was higher today than it was thirty years ago. 85 per cent of those aged over sixty-five thought the current threat was greater, compared to 64 per cent of those aged 18–24.

HOW MUCH OF A THREAT DO YOU THINK EACH OF THE FOLLOWING CURRENTLY POSES TO THE UK'S NATIONAL SECURITY?

Mean /100	ALL	Men	Women	18-24	25-34	35-44	45-54	55-64	65+
Terror attacks in the UK carried out by terrorist groups	51.81	48.47	55.01	53.29	42.93	51.31	53.68	57.03	53.30
'Cyberattacks' on computer systems in the UK carried out by terrorist groups	43.65	39.89	47.25	45.40	33.63	43.52	44.03	47.49	47.64
'Cyberattacks' on computer systems in the UK carried out by foreign states	43.26	42.37	44.12	40.22	34.51	43.09	41.80	48.30	49.33
The actions Donald Trump might take as US President	42.65	39.09	46.06	44.84	36.46	43.68	41.84	45.37	44.37
Russian expansionism and intervention in Eastern Europe	39.35	37.03	41.58	37.49	33.96	39.11	36.98	41.52	44.94
Growing instability and unpredictability in world affairs generally	38.29	35.30	41.15	38.79	33.06	39.93	36.19	41.56	40.32
Climate change	36.70	33.58	39.68	45.25	36.91	37.31	35.20	36.51	33.22
Refugees entering Europe from North Africa and the Middle East	35.63	34.64	36.58	30.82	26.64	34.99	34.37	42.29	41.87
Immigration and migration into the UK	35.62	34.15	37.02	31.42	27.69	36.37	34.25	42.20	39.89
The development of nuclear weapons in Iran	35.53	32.03	38.87	38.88	29.69	36.31	32.46	37.01	39.14
Nuclear weapons in North Korea	35.00	29.04	40.69	42.39	30.43	35.79	30.97	36.70	36.28
Attacks in the UK carried out by foreign states	32.72	28.19	37.07	39.03	29.01	35.58	30.34	35.27	30.63
Foreign interference in UK elections	28.63	27.28	29.92	31.38	28.05	29.07	25.97	28.01	29.89
A possible return of paramilitary activity in Northern Ireland	24.45	21.88	26.91	27.44	22.27	26.30	23.92	25.12	23.31

- Terror attacks in the UK and cyberattacks carried out by terrorist groups were regarded as the biggest threat by all groups.
- Cyberattacks by foreign states were seen as the third biggest threat overall. However, climate change was the third biggest danger for

18–24s, and the potential actions of President Trump were in third place for women and 25–34s.

- In most cases, older people assigned higher threat levels than younger people, especially for Russian expansionism and refugees entering Europe from North Africa and the Middle East. Notable exceptions were climate change and North Korean nuclear weapons, for which the highest scores came from the youngest participants.
- Women assigned a higher threat level than men to every scenario.

WILLINGNESS TO DEPLOY UK ARMED FORCES

Please say whether you would support or oppose the UK armed forces being involved in each of the following:

% support / oppose	ALL	Men	Women	18-24	25-34	35-44	45-54	55-64	65+
Helping police and security forces with anti-terror operations in the UK	83/7	84/9	82/6	65/20	73/10	76/8	87/7	91/3	95/2
Taking part in UN peacekeeping missions overseas	70/15	72/16	68/13	57/22	60/14	64/16	73/14	76/13	82/11
Humanitarian aid and overseas disaster relief	68/19	69/22	67/17	63/19	63/17	62/19	71/22	72/19	73/21
Using force to defend an ally that has been invaded by another country	63/18	70/16	57/19	51/25	57/17	58/17	68/17	70/14	70/18
Missions against terrorists abroad	62/22	66/22	57/22	53/27	56/18	59/20	67/21	65/23	65/24
Action to prevent foreign governments seriously abusing human rights in their country	53/27	54/30	53/24	54/25	54/20	59/19	59/24	53/31	44/37
Pre-emptive action against foreign states believed to pose a threat to the UK	50/30	50/34	49/27	42/32	47/26	47/28	49/32	55/32	55/32
Removing foreign dictators from power	38/39	36/46	39/33	40/34	44/24	43/31	42/38	32/50	28/54
Pre-emptive action against foreign states believed to pose a threat to a neighbouring state	33/44	35/48	32/40	37/35	39/33	37/35	36/43	30/53	26/56

- More than eight in ten, though only two thirds of 18–24s, supported the armed forces being deployed to help police and security services with anti-terror occupations in the UK. Only just over half of the youngest participants supported UK military involvement in UN peacekeeping missions overseas.
- Only just over six in ten, and only just over half of 18–24s, approved of using force to defend an ally that has been invaded by another country or missions against terrorists abroad. Exactly half, and a minority of those aged up to fifty-four, supported pre-emptive action against foreign states believed to pose a threat to the UK.
- Support for British military involvement in each scenario increased with age, with three exceptions: action to prevent foreign governments abusing human rights, removing foreign dictators from power, and pre-emptive action against foreign states believed to pose a threat to a neighbouring state.

ENDNOTES

SAXA VORD

1 https://www.theregister.co.uk/2018/02/05/raf_saxa_vord_radar_station_reopened/

INTRODUCTION

1 https://www.bbc.co.uk/news/world-middle-east-34011187
2 https://www.middleeastmonitor.com/20161022-yemens-al-hudaydah-a-childs-worst-nightmare/
3 http://researchbriefings.files.parliament.uk/documents/RP98-91/RP98-91.pdf
4 http://blogs.lse.ac.uk/politicsandpolicy/british-public-opinion-after-a-decade-of-war-attitudes-to-iraq-and-afghanistan/
5 https://www.theguardian.com/world/2016/feb/16/libya-gaddafi-arab-spring-civil-war-islamic-state
6 https://www.bbc.co.uk/news/uk-politics-23892783
7 https://www.independent.co.uk/voices/theresa-may-trump-syria-strikes-parliament-vote-britain-russia-chemical-weapons-latest-a8303146.html
8 https://www.embl.de/aboutus/science_society/discussion/discussion_2006/refl-22june06.pdf
9 National Security Strategy 2010, p. 30; https://www.gov.uk/government/news/national-security-strategy
10 http://www.dw.com/en/uk-army-chief-nick-carter-calls-for-cash-to-counter-russia-threats/a-42253039
11 https://www.reuters.com/article/us-usa-military-china-russia/u-s-military-puts-great-power-competition-at-heart-of-strategy-mattis-idUSKBN1F81TR
12 https://www.adsgroup.org.uk/wp content/uploads/sites/21/2017/09/DefenceOutlook2017-WebRes.pdf
13 IISS, *Military Balance* 2018, pp 502–8
14 http://www.janes.com/images/assets/097/71097/Evolving_expeditionary_capabilities.pdf
15 Interviews with US and Allied serving officials

BLOSSOM AND BLOOD

1 Interview with authors
2 Research trip to the Donbas
3 https://www.gov.uk/government/speeches/four-years-since-the-illegal-annexation-of-crimea-article-by-boris-johnson
4 https://www.theyworkforyou.com/wrans/?id=2016-10-31.51144.h&s=%22operation+orbital%22#g51144.r0
5 https://www.gov.uk/government/news/uk-extends-training-of-ukrainian-armed-forces
6 https://www.unian.info/politics/2394782-us-to-allocate-200-mln-for-ukraines-defense-in-2019.html
7 https://prometheus.ngo/wp-content/uploads/2017/04/Donbas_v_Ogni_ENG_web_1-4.pdf
8 Research trip to the Donbas
9 Interview with authors
10 https://www.unian.info/war/2009479-russia-deploys-over-60000-troops-along-ukraine-border-in-crimea-donbas-def-ministry.html
11 Interview with authors
12 Interview with authors
13 http://news.bbc.co.uk/1/hi/world/europe/7550354.stm
14 https://www.foreignaffairs.com/articles/ukraine/2016-04-18/why-putin-took-crimea
15 https://www.telegraph.co.uk/news/2017/07/18/separatists-ukraine-declare-creation-new-state-malorossiya/

16 https://www.telegraph.co.uk/news/worldnews/northamerica/usa/11023183/Russians-warned-not-to-use-humanitarian-crisis-as-pretext-to-invade-Ukraine.html
17 http://researchbriefings.parliament.uk/ResearchBriefing/Summary/SN07135#fullreport
18 https://www.reuters.com/article/us-ukraine-jevelin/ukraine-receives-us-javelin-systems-poroshenko-idUSKBN1I11ZY
19 http://www.bbc.co.uk/news/world-europe-31436513
20 Research trip to the Donbas
21 Private information
22 Research trip to the Donbas
23 'Average wage by region', April 2018, State Statistics Service of Ukraine. https://ukrstat.org/en/operativ/operativ2018/gdn/reg_zp_m/reg_zp_m_e.xlsx
24 Interview with authors
25 Research trip to Kiev
26 http://www.spiegel.de/international/world/viktor-yanukovych-interview-ukraine-has-become-a-wild-country-a-1135829.html
27 Interview with authors
28 Interview with authors

RED ALERT

1   https://www.telegraph.co.uk/news/2018/01/25/crippling-russian-attack-britains-infrastructure-could-kill/
2   Interview with authors
3   Interview with authors
4   Interview with authors
5   Interview with authors
6   https://www.reuters.com/article/us-usa-military-china-russia/u-s-military-puts-great-power-competition-at-heart-of-strategy-mattis-idUSKBN1F81TR
7   https://www.independent.co.uk/news/uk/home-news/cyberwarfare-russia-terrorism-british-army-general-nick-carter-us-france-nato-a8173136.html
8   Professor Mark Galeotti, Head of the Centre for European Security at the Institute of International Relations in Prague; interview with authors
9   http://news.bbc.co.uk/1/hi/4480745.stm
10 https://www.theguardian.com/commentisfree/2017/apr/04/putin-continuum-tsars-russia
11 Confidential source; interview with authors
12 Interview with authors
13 https://www.brookings.edu/opinions/pay-attention-america-russia-is-upgrading-its-military/
14 https://www.ecfr.eu/article/commentary_russias_heavy_metal_diplomacy_7208
15 https://www.nato.int/docu/review/2017/also-in-2017/zapad-2017-and-euro-atlantic-security-military-exercise-strategic-russia/EN/index.htm
16 http://eng.belta.by/society/view/details-of-belarusian-russian-army-exercise-zapad-2017-unveiled-99607-2017/
17 Confidential source; serving Ministry of Defence official
18 General Sir Nick Carter, Dynamic Security Threats and the British Army, RUSI, 22 January 2018, https://rusi.org/event/dynamic-security-threats-and-british-army
19 Interview with authors
20 https://publications.credit-suisse.com/tasks/render/file/?fileID=60931FDE-A2D2-F568-B041B58C5EA591A4; https://blogs.spectator.co.uk/2018/04/the-10-graphs-that-explain-vladimir-putins-russia/
21 I Sutyagin, *Russia's New Ground Forces: Capabilities, Limitations and Implications for International Security* (Routledge, 2017)
22 Interview with authors
23 Interview with authors
24 https://www.nato.int/cps/en/natohq/topics_136388.htm
25 https://www.gov.uk/government/news/uks-nato-southern-air-policing-mission-to-begin-in-may
26 Interview with authors

ENDNOTES

27 Private information
28 https://www.ft.com/content/dfbc0988-e0ee-11e7-a8a4-0a1e63a52f9c
29 http://henryjacksonsociety.org/2015/10/08/russians-are-spying-on-trident-subs-experts-say-nuclear-deterrent-is-under-threat-after-moscow-attempted-to-acquire-acoustic-signature-made-by-submarines/
30 Private seminar, 'Imagining War in 2030', Project for Study of the Twenty-First Century, September 2017
31 Interview with authors
32 Interview with authors
33 https://www.digitalhealth.net/2017/10/wannacry-impact-on-nhs-considerably-larger-than-previously-suggested/
34 Interview with authors

CHOPPY WATERS

1 https://www.theguardian.com/uk-news/2017/jul/27/britains-new-aircraft-carriers-to-test-beijing-in-south-china-sea
2 Private information
3 Private information
4 https://www.telegraph.co.uk/news/2018/04/12/hms-sutherland-arrives-japan-effort-curb-north-koreas-evasion/
5 Private information
6 https://www.telegraph.co.uk/news/2018/04/12/hms-sutherland-arrives-japan-effort-curb-north-koreas-evasion/
7 Interview with authors
8 Interview with authors
9 Private information
10 https://www.ft.com/content/3477fe5a-c809-11e6-8f29-9445cac8966f
11 Private information
12 2015 Strategic Defence and Security Review, para. 5.74
13 https://publications.parliament.uk/pa/jt201617/jtselect/jtnatsec/153/153.pdf, pp 13–15
14 Ibid., pp 15–16
15 https://www.ft.com/content/24bbea6e-ce87-11e2-ae25-00144feab7de
16 https://publications.parliament.uk/pa/jt201617/jtselect/jtnatsec/153/153.pdf
17 Keynote Speech, RUSI Land Warfare Conference, 27 June 2017, https://rusi.org/sites/default/files/20170627-rusi_lwc17-gen_milley.pdf, p. 3
18 Tim Marshall, *Prisoners of Geography* (Elliot and Thompson, 2015), p. 40
19 Ibid.
20 IISS, *Military Balance* 2018, p. 504
21 Ibid., pp 220–35, 249
22 https://www.iiss.org/blogs/military-balance/2018/05/china-naval-shipbuilding
23 Private information
24 http://nationalinterest.org/blog/the-buzz/how-russia-china-would-wage-war-against-america-kill-the-20658
25 https://www.wired.com/2009/07/china-looks-to-undermine-us-power-with-assassins-mace/
26 https://www.iiss.org/events/2018/02/milbal-london
27 IISS, *Military Balance*, pp 220, 249
28 https://pca-cpa.org/wp-content/uploads/sites/175/2016/07/PH-CN-20160712-Award.pdf; https://www.theguardian.com/world/2016/jul/12/philippines-wins-south-china-sea-case-against-china
29 Interview with authors
30 http://uk.businessinsider.com/china-internet-kim-jong-un-fatty-on-the-train-to-avoid-censors-2018-3?IR=T
31 https://www.express.co.uk/news/world/958444/North-Korea-nuclear-missile-nuke-bomb-Punggye-ri-test-site
32 http://www.bbc.co.uk/newsbeat/article/35605009/royal-marines-train-us-forces-in-arctic-over-fears-of-russian-aggression

33 Confidential source, interview with authors
34 https://www.thetimes.co.uk/article/troops-need-anthrax-jabs-as-north-korea-and-terrorism-threat-grows-wsqq6lnzn
35 https://edition.cnn.com/2017/05/29/asia/north-korea-missile-tests/index.html
36 https://edition.cnn.com/2017/09/18/politics/donald-trump-un-speech-iran-north-korea/index.html
37 https://www.mirror.co.uk/news/politics/london-closer-north-korean-missiles-11143643
38 https://www.gov.uk/government/groups/development-concepts-and-doctrine-centre#futures
39 Confidential source; interview with authors
40 'Future Operating Environment', pp 8–9, https://www.gov.uk/government/publications/future-operating-environment-2035
41 Confidential; serving personnel
42 https://assets.publishing.service.gov.uk/government/uploads/system/uploads/attachment_data/file/348164/20140821_DCDC_GST_5_Web_Secured.pdf, p. 3
43 Ibid., pp 4–7
44 Ibid., p. 17
45 Ibid., p. 18
46 Ibid., p. 21
47 Ibid., p. 28
48 Ibid., p. 52
49 Ibid., pp 33–6
50 Ibid., p. 67
51 Interview with authors
52 US Department of Defence, http://archive.defense.gov/news/newsarticle.aspx?id=45289
53 https://www.airforce-technology.com/projects/b2/
54 https://www.nytimes.com/1991/02/26/science/invention-that-shaped-the-gulf-war-the-laser-guided-bomb.html
55 https://www.theguardian.com/environment/2007/jun/27/climatechange.climatechange
56 http://news.bbc.co.uk/1/hi/sci/tech/7419752.stm
57 https://foreignpolicy.com/2015/03/02/why-the-war-in-afghanistan-was-lost-from-the-start-coin-taliban/
58 https://www.cnbc.com/2017/12/09/us-could-potentially-lose-next-war-to-russia-or-china-warns-rand.html
59 http://www.dailymail.co.uk/news/article-5317257/Minister-MOCKS-defence-secretary-Gavin-Williamson.html
60 https://www.ft.com/content/108ce242-0fef-11e8-8cb6-b9ccc4c4dbbb
61 https://www.standard.co.uk/news/politics/insane-absurd-and-ridiculous-journalist-julia-hartleybrewer-touched-on-knee-by-michael-fallon-a3674196.html
62 https://www.theguardian.com/world/2017/nov/02/theresa-may-angers-tory-mp-with-choice-to-replace-disgraced-fallon
63 https://www.telegraph.co.uk/news/2016/06/28/theresa-mays-campaign-accused-of-using-government-whips-to-stron/
64 https://www.telegraph.co.uk/news/2017/12/06/mod-bans-philip-hammond-using-raf-planes-row-unpaid-bill/

GUNFIRE

1   http://www.bbc.com/future/story/20160905-the-pilot-who-stole-a-secret-soviet-fighter-jet
2   Stephen Lovegrove talk to the Institute for Government, 26 June 2017, https://www.instituteforgovernment.org.uk/events/managing-ministry-defence-stephen-lovegrove
3   Interview with authors
4   https://assets.publishing.service.gov.uk/government/uploads/system/uploads/attachment_data/file/660158/QCPR_October_2017-Publication-Revised.pdf, p.4
5   Confidential source; interview with authors
6   Confidential source; interview with authors
7   Confidential source; interview with authors
8   Interview with authors
9   https://www.theguardian.com/politics/2009/mar/02/sir-michael-quinlan-obituary

10 Confidential source; interview with authors

GHOSTS
1   https://www.gov.uk/government/news/defence-budget-increases-for-the-first-time-in-six-years
2   http://www.bbc.co.uk/news/magazine-31750929
3   Interview with authors
4   https://www.gov.uk/government/news/new-national-security-council-established
5   'Securing Britain in an Age of Uncertainty: The Strategic Defence and Security Review', HM Government, October 2010, pp 5–6
6   http://www.bbc.co.uk/news/uk-politics-11569160
7   http://www.bbc.co.uk/news/uk-10812825
8   Private information
9   https://www.independent.co.uk/news/uk/politics/forces-left-unable-to-launch-lsquomajorrsquo-missions-overseas-2111341.html
10 Interview with authors
11 https://assets.publishing.service.gov.uk/government/uploads/system/uploads/attachment_data/file/224063/AFPS_Accounts_2010_11.pdf, p. 34
12 https://assets.publishing.service.gov.uk/government/uploads/system/uploads/attachment_data/file/34131/StrategicEnvironmentAssessment_1st_Stage_Scoping_Report.pdf
13 https://www.theguardian.com/uk/2012/nov/15/hms-astute-submarine-slow-leaky-rusty
14 https://publications.parliament.uk/pa/cm200506/cmselect/cmdfence/986/986we30.htm, para. 30
15 https://assets.publishing.service.gov.uk/government/uploads/system/uploads/attachment_data/file/62482/strategic-defence-security-review.pdf, para 2.A.5 and 2.D.13
16 2010 Strategic Defence and Security Review, para 2.D.13 and p. 22
17 https://www.theguardian.com/uk/2012/may/09/government-u-turn-fighter-jets
18 http://www.bbc.co.uk/news/uk-politics-11248603
19 https://www.army-technology.com/projects/scout-specialist-vehicle/
20 https://www.lockheedmartin.com/en-gb/products/armoured-vehicles.html
21 https://www.telegraph.co.uk/news/uknews/defence/8031385/Defence-cuts-Liam-Foxs-leaked-letter-in-full.html
22 https://www.gov.uk/government/news/defence-budget-cut-by-eight-per-cent
23 https://www.nao.org.uk/wp-content/uploads/2011/05/10121029.pdf, p. 22; https://www.nao.org.uk/wp-content/uploads/2012/02/10121791.pdf, p. 13; https://assets.publishing.service.gov.uk/government/uploads/system/uploads/attachment_data/file/62483/strategic-defence-security-review.pdf, p. 31
24 https://www.nao.org.uk/wp-content/uploads/2011/05/10121029.pdf, p.32
25 https://www.nao.org.uk/wp-content/uploads/2012/02/10121791.pdf, p.5 and p. 13
26 Private information
27 https://assets.publishing.service.gov.uk/government/uploads/system/uploads/attachment_data/file/62488/Factsheet6-Royal-Navy.pdf
28 https://assets.publishing.service.gov.uk/government/uploads/system/uploads/attachment_data/file/62490/Factsheet8-RoyalAirForce.pdf
29 https://publications.parliament.uk/pa/cm201012/cmselect/cmdfence/1373/137303 htm#a7
30 https://www.gov.uk/government/news/royal-navy-and-army-release-redundancy-scheme-details
31 2010 Strategic Defence and Security Review, para 2.D.12
32 https://assets.publishing.service.gov.uk/government/uploads/system/uploads/attachment_data/file/62489/Factsheet7-British-Army.pdf
33 2010 Strategic Defence and Security Review, para 2.D.9
34 2010 Strategic Defence and Security Review, para 2.D.5
35 2010 Strategic Defence and Security Review, para 2.D.5
36 https://hansard.parliament.uk/Commons/2010-10-19/debates/10101928000003/StrategicDefenceAndSecurityReview?highlight=not%20simply%20cost%20saving%20exercise#contribution-10101928000185
37 https://www.gov.uk/government/speeches/statement-on-strategic-defence-and-security-review; https://fullfact.org/economy/did-labour-leave-38-billion-black-hole-defence-spending/

38 https://assets.publishing.service.gov.uk/government/uploads/system/uploads/attachment_data/file/221550/autumn_statement_2012_complete.pdf, p. 58; https://assets.publishing.service.gov.uk/government/uploads/system/uploads/attachment_data/file/263942/35062_Autumn_Statement_2013.pdf, p.82

39 https://www.independent.co.uk/news/commando-swoop-on-serbs-1249970.html

40 Interview with authors

41 Interview with authors

42 1998 Strategic Defence and Security Review, p. 36

43 Interview with authors

44 https://www.independent.co.uk/news/election-97-labour-to-toe-tory-line-on-economy-1265050.html

45 Interview with authors

46 http://webarchive.nationalarchives.gov.uk/20121018172816/http://www.mod.uk/NR/rdonlyres/65F3D7AC-4340-4119-93A2-20825848E50E/0/sdr1998_complete.pdf

47 1998 Strategic Defence Review, p. 36

48 http://news.bbc.co.uk/1/hi/uk/71226.stm

49 1998 Strategic Defence Review, p. 32

50 https://www.ukpublicspending.co.uk/spending_chart_1997_2004UKb_17c1li111mcn_30t

51 Interview with authors

52 https://www.smh.com.au/articles/2003/03/28/1048653831705.html; https://www.telegraph.co.uk/news/newstopics/mps-expenses/6229121/MPs-expenses-armour-was-so-poor-that-troops-couldnt-wear-it.html

53 https://www.telegraph.co.uk/news/uknews/1352848/Six-out-of-10-RAF-bombs-missed-target-in-Kosovo.html and http://news.bbc.co.uk/1/hi/world/middle_east/1184086.stm

54 https://www.telegraph.co.uk/news/uknews/1458677/260m-SAS-helicopters-cant-fly-with-a-cloud-in-the-sky.html

55 https://www.theguardian.com/uk/2008/nov/01/snatch-land-rovers-army

56 https://www.bbc.co.uk/news/uk-35432341

57 Private information

58 https://www.bbc.co.uk/news/uk-22967853

59 Interview with authors

60 Interview with authors

61 HM Treasury, Spending review and autumn statement 2015, Cm 9162, November 2015, para 1.72

62 https://www.forces.net/news/fallons-legacy-never-going-set-world-fire

63 Private information

64 Interview with authors

65 https://www.globalfirepower.com/countries-listing.asp

66 https://www.iiss.org/publications/the-military-balance/the-military-balance-2018/mb2018-10-country-comparisons-copy

67 Ibid.

68 https://assets.publishing.service.gov.uk/government/uploads/system/uploads/attachment_data/file/707538/20180401-_SPS.pdf, p.4

69 https://www.gov.uk/government/uploads/system/uploads/attachment_data/file/706934/1_Apr_2018_-_SPS.xlsx, Table 8a

70 https://www.iiss.org/publications/the-military-balance/the-military-balance-2018/mb2018-10-country-comparisons-copy, pp 250, 192

71 Ibid., p. 107

72 Ibid., p. 102

73 Ibid., p. 340

74 https://www.independent.co.uk/news/world/politics/the-nine-countries-that-have-nuclear-weapons-a6798756.html

75 IISS, *Military Balance* 2018, p. 155

76 https://www.independent.co.uk/news/world/politics/switzerland-high-rates-gun-ownership-why-doesnt-no-mass-shootings-a8230606.html; https://www.vbs.admin.ch/fr/ddps/faits-chiffres/armee.html

77 IISS, *Military Balance* 2018, p. 183

78 Ibid., p. 286

79 Ibid., p. 161

80 Ibid., p. 164

81 Ibid., pp 102, 105

82 Ibid., p. 103

83 Ibid., pp 194, 198, 200

84 Ibid., pp 197, 199

85 Ibid., p. 251

86 https://www.telegraph.co.uk/business/boeing-uk/new-fleet-of-maritime-patrol-planes/

87 IISS, *Military Balance* 2018, p. 49

88 https://www.contracts.mod.uk/do-features-and-articles/delivering-carrier-strike/

89 https://www.flightglobal.com/news/articles/uk-re-forms-617-sqn-for-f-35b-era-447809/

90 https://www.royalnavy.mod.uk/our-organisation/the-fighting-arms/surface-fleet#frigates

91 https://www.defensenews.com/global/europe/2018/03/16/bae-systems-launches-the-type-31-frigate-for-export/

92 IISS, *Military Balance* 2018, p. 193

93 Ibid., p. 103

OPERATION TETHERED GOAT

1 https://www.forces.net/news/800-british-troops-deploy-estonia

2 Research trip by project contributors

3 Interview with authors

4 Interview with authors

5 Research trip by project contributors

6 http://www.bbc.co.uk/news/uk-wales-43218117

7 Research trip by project contributors

8 Research trip by project contributors

9 https://www.rand.org/content/dam/rand/pubs/research_reports/RR1200/RR1253/RAND_RR1253.pdf

SECURITY BLANKET

1 https://www.nato.int/cps/ic/natohq/official_texts_17120.htm

2 https://www.wsj.com/articles/nato-is-american-greatest-strategic-advantage-1471465396

3 Interview with authors

4 https://www.bbc.co.uk/news/world-us-canada-38635181

5 http://www.itv.com/news/2017-05-25/trump-berates-nato-countries-for-chronic-underpayments-for-defence/

6 http://www.bbc.co.uk/news/world-us-canada-39585029

7 https://www.nato.int/nato_static_fl2014/assets/pdf/pdf_2017_06/20170629_170629-pr2017-111-en.pdf

8 https://www.telegraph.co.uk/news/2017/01/10/france-aiming-take-nato-leadership-role-britain-brexit/

9 https://www.politico.eu/article/donald-trump-vladimir-putin-russia-nato-summit/

10 https://www.thetimes.co.uk/article/donald-trump-tells-nato-to-pay-double-5knd8stg0

11 https://www.nato.int/nato_static_fl2014/assets/pdf/pdf_2017_02/20170213_1702-factsheet-nnhq-en.pdf

12 http://video.foxbusiness.com/v/4722042954001/?playlist_id=937116503001#sp=show-clips

13 http://foreignpolicy.com/2017/05/15/nato-frantically-tries-to-trump-proof-presidents-first-visit-alliance-europe-brussels/

14 http://www.bbc.co.uk/news/av/world-us-canada-40050926/trump-pushes-past-montenegro-s-pm

15 http://www.bbc.co.uk/news/av/world-europe-40048008/nato-meeting-trump-and-macron-s-awkward-handshake-in-brussels

16 http://foreignpolicy.com/2017/05/25/trump-nato-meeting-brussels-defense-spending-transatlantic-alliance/

17 Interview with authors
18 https://www.bbc.co.uk/news/world-europe-38537689
19 Confidential source
20 Private information
21 Lt Gen Ben Hodges, speech to RUSI Land Warfare Conference, 28 June 2017
22 Ibid.
23 Ibid.
24 https://www.politico.eu/article/call-for-military-border-schengen-to-get-troops-moving-nato-eu-defense-ministers/
25 https://www.reuters.com/article/us-nato-germany/germany-chooses-ulm-for-new-proposed-nato-logistics-command-idUSKBN1GW1QM
26 https://www.bloomberg.com/news/articles/2018-02-13/u-s-germany-said-to-be-locations-for-new-nato-command-centers
27 Private information
28 Interview with authors
29 Interview with authors
30 Interview with authors
31 Interview with authors
32 Confidential source; serving government official
33 Confidential interview with senior UK military source
34 Interview with authors
35 Interview with authors
36 Interview with authors
37 Interview with authors
38 Interview with authors
39 https://www.independent.co.uk/news/uk/politics/eremy-corbyn-labour-defence-spokeswoman-nia-griffith-nato-doubts-deployment-estonia-russia-a7523361.html
40 https://www.theguardian.com/politics/2018/mar/15/corbyn-defies-critics-calls-for-calm-over-russia-nerve-agent-attack
41 https://www.telegraph.co.uk/news/worldnews/northamerica/usa/11030099/Diego-Garcia-The-facts-the-history-and-the-mystery.html
42 https://www.ft.com/content/abbc879a-ac1d-11e6-ba7d-76378e4fef24
43 https://www.cbsnews.com/news/diego-garcia-exiles-still-barred
44 http://www.nbcnews.com/id/6786984/ns/world_news-tsunami_a_year_later/t/tsunami-spares-us-base-diego-garcia/#.WuBSDq3MyYU
45 http://news.bbc.co.uk/1/hi/uk/2265159.stm
46 https://www.naval-technology.com/projects/diego-garcia/
47 Private information
48 Interview with authors
49 Interview with authors
50 Lt Gen. Ben Hodges, speech to RUSI Land Warfare Conference, 28 June 2017
51 Ibid.
52 https://www.telegraph.co.uk/news/2018/01/22/britain-may-reverse-decision-pull-germany-need-react-russian/
53 'Indispensable allies: US, NATO and UK Defence relations', House of Commons Defence Select Committee, 26 June 2018, p. 3
54 Ibid.
55 http://www.france24.com/en/20180208-france-hike-defence-military-spending-over-40-percent-nato
56 http://www.bbc.co.uk/news/uk-41903960
57 Ibid.
58 Private information
59 Private information
60 http://www.bbc.co.uk/news/uk-politics-23892783
61 Interview with authors

ENDNOTES

62 Confidential source; interview with authors
63 https://www.telegraph.co.uk/news/worldnews/europe/germany/11420627/German-army-used-broomsticks-instead-of-guns-during-training.html
64 http://csbaonline.org/uploads/documents/ALLIES_in_DECLINE_FINAL_b.pdf
65 http://www.bbc.co.uk/news/uk-25754870
66 Interview with authors
67 http://europa.eu/rapid/press-release_IP-16-4088_en.htm
68 https://eeas.europa.eu/headquarters/headquarters-homepage/34226/permanent-structured-cooperation-pesco-factsheet_en
69 https://news.err.ee/647993/pesco-established-by-25-eu-member-states
70 Ibid.
71 Interview with authors
72 http://researchbriefings.parliament.uk/ResearchBriefing/Summary/CBP-8149
73 https://www.thetimes.co.uk/article/uk-unconditionally-committed-to-protecting-europe-theresa-may-tell-troops-c3d2kjg5l
74 http://www.itv.com/news/meridian/2018-01-18/sandhurst-hosts-french-president-on-official-uk-visit/
75 https://assets.publishing.service.gov.uk/government/uploads/system/uploads/attachment_data/file/238153/8174.pdf
76 https://www.express.co.uk/news/politics/906687/macron-uk-visit-theresa-may-sandhurst-brexit-news-france-calais-border
77 https://edition.cnn.com/style/article/bayeux-tapestry-uk-france-agreement/index.html
78 https://www.standard.co.uk/news/world/theresa-may-treats-french-president-emmanuel-macron-to-pub-lunch-amid-postbrexit-talks-a3743701.html
79 Interview with authors

BUNKERS

1 Confidential source; serving official
2 http://www.bbc.com/future/story/20170821-how-prepared-are-we-for-the-impact-of-a-nuclear-war
3 https://www.standard.co.uk/news/the-doomsday-bunker-mods-secret-command-centre-including-a-pine-bed-for-the-principal-6937352.html
4 https://www.mirror.co.uk/news/uk-news/inside-prime-ministers-nuclear-bunker-8474816
5 Confidential source; serving official
6 https://www.wired.com/2011/01/inside-londons-secret-crisis-command-bunker
7 Ibid.
8 Ibid.
9 Research trip to Kiev by project contributors
10 Interview with authors
11 Interview with authors
12 Research trip to Kiev by project contributors
13 Research trip to Kiev by project contributors
14 http://content.time.com/time/magazine/article/0,9171,976207,00.html
15 http://www.aif.ru/archive/1632340
16 Interview with authors
17 http://uk.businessinsider.com/inside-burlington-bunker-britains-secret-underground-city-2017-1/#the-sluice-room-in-the-sites-hospital-21

THE BOMB

1 Interview with authors
2 https://www.telegraph.co.uk/news/2016/03/21/what-is-trident-britains-nuclear-deterrent-explained/
3 https://www.independent.co.uk/news/uk/politics/theresa-may-nuclear-weapons-first-strike-michael-fallon-general-election-jeremy-corbyn-trident-a7698621.html; https://www.telegraph.co.uk/news/worldnews/middleeast/iraq/1388364/UK-warns-Saddam-of-nuclear-retaliation.html
4 http://www.dailymail.co.uk/news/article-3310079/Military-chief-attacked-Corbyn-WON-T-disciplined-Ministers-stand-officer-said-Labour-leader-worried-him.html

5   http://www.thenational.scot/news/15436152.Trident_Two_freed_from_jail_then_head_straight_for_Faslane/
6   http://www.nukewatch.org.uk/?page_id=23
7   https://www.theguardian.com/uk-news/2016/sep/21/uk-nuclear-weapons-convoys-have-had-180-mishaps-in-16-years
8   Interview with authors
9   https://faslanepeacecamp.wordpress.com/2014/03/21/peace-campers-arrested-on-board-nuclear-sub/
10 https://faslanepeacecamp.wordpress.com/2015/05/27/faslane-security-breached-again/
11 https://ukdefencejournal.org.uk/us-navy-nuclear-submarine-departs-faslane/
12 Interview with authors
13 http://www.bbc.com/news/election-2015-scotland-32236184
14 *Yes, Prime Minister*, 'Grand Designs', BBC, 9 January 1986
15 http://www.bbc.co.uk/newsbeat/article/36824917/trident-what-are-the-letters-of-last-resort
16 https://www.theguardian.com/politics/2015/sep/30/corbyn-i-would-never-use-nuclear-weapons-if-i-was-pm
17 https://www.theguardian.com/uk-news/2016/oct/13/labour-continue-back-trident-shadow-defence-secretary-nia-griffith
18 https://www.telegraph.co.uk/news/uknews/1545508/Labour-rebels-vote-against-Blair-on-Trident.html
19 Interview with authors
20 http://www.basicint.org/sites/default/files/trident_commission_finalreport.pdf
21 Ibid., p. 32
22 https://assets.publishing.service.gov.uk/government/uploads/system/uploads/attachment_data/file/78977/coalition_programme_for_government.pdf
23 Interview with authors
24 Interview with authors
25 Communication with authors
26 https://hansard.parliament.uk/Commons/2016-07-18/division/27E40019-B844-4971-BE72-B5E192957044/UKSNuclearDeterrent?outputType=Party
27 http://survation.com/scots-want-second-independence-referendum/
28 https://hansard.parliament.uk/Commons/2016-07-18/debates/7B7A196B-B37C-4787-99DC-098882B3EFA2/UKSNuclearDeterrent
29 Ibid.
30 Interview with authors
31 http://www.bbc.com/news/uk-10812825
32 https://www.savetheroyalnavy.org/taking-down-the-arguments-against-trident/
33 https://wikileaks.org/trident-safety/
34 Ibid.
35 https://www.theguardian.com/uk-news/2015/may/18/trident-submarine-whistleblower-william-mcneilly-to-turn-himself-in
36 https://www.theguardian.com/uk-news/2017/jan/23/how-did-the-trident-test-fail-and-what-did-theresa-may-know
37 Interview with authors
38 https://www.theguardian.com/politics/video/2015/nov/09/general-houghton-would-be-worried-jeremy-corbyns-views-translated-power-trident-video
39 http://www.basicint.org/sites/default/files/HACKING_UK_TRIDENT.pdf
40 https://www.politico.eu/article/uk-trident-nuclear-program/
41 https://ukdefencejournal.org.uk/no-america-doesnt-control-britains-nuclear-weapons/
42 https://www.theguardian.com/uk-news/2017/dec/18/trident-may-be-removed-from-mod-budget-mps-told

TO THE RIGHT

1   https://www.defenseindustrydaily.com/race-for-the-door-drayson-resigns-from-uk-mod-04170/
2   http://www.bbc.co.uk/news/av/uk-politics-18063585/yawning-black-hole-filled-in-mod-budget-hammond

ENDNOTES

3   https://rusi.org/commentary/ministry-defence-facing-tough-financial-choices
4   Speech by Sir Bernard Gray at IISS, 2015
5   Ibid.
6   Ibid.
7   https://www.gov.uk/government/news/defence-budget-increases-for-the-first-time-in-six-years
8   https://www.gov.uk/government/publications/defence-reform-an-independent-report-into-the-structure-and-management-of-the-ministry-of-defence--2
9   https://assets.publishing.service.gov.uk/government/uploads/system/uploads/attachment_data/file/27408/defence_reform_report_struct_mgt_mod_27june2011.pdf, para. 3.8
10 Ibid., para. 7.6
11 Ibid., para. 4.4
12 http://data.parliament.uk/writtenevidence/committeeevidence.svc/evidencedocument/defence-committee/sunset-for-the-royal-marines-the-royal-marines-and-uk-amphibious-capability/oral/75152.html
13 Ibid.
14 Confidential source, interview with authors

CATS AND TRAPS

1   https://www.telegraph.co.uk/politics/2018/01/05/defence-secretary-gavin-williamson-wins-compromise-defence-spending/
2   https://www.independent.co.uk/voices/gavin-williamson-wants-to-be-prime-minister-theresa-may-cronus-tarantula-scheme-a8120191.html
3   Private information
4   https://www.thetimes.co.uk/article/go-away-and-shut-up-defence-secretary-tells-the-russians-k3ngjtds9
5   Private information
6   Private information
7   Confidential source, interview with authors
8   Confidential source, interview with authors
9   https://www.historic-uk.com/Blog/British-Navy-Size-Over-Time/
10 IISS, *Military Balance* 1981–1982, p. 28
11 IISS, *Military Balance* 2018, p. 23
12 Ibid.
13 https://www.royalnavy.mod.uk/news-and-latest-activity/news/2018/february/07/180207-ocean-arrives-into-portsmouth-for-last-time
14 https://www.ft.com/content/1125f706-d4f9-11e7-8c9a-d9c0a5c8d5c9
15 http://www.savetheroyalnavy.org/sustaining-royal-navy-manpower-the-greatest-challenge/
16 http://www.savetheroyalnavy.org/why-the-royal-navy-has-just-been-cut-by-another-2-ships/
17 https://publications.parliament.uk/pa/cm201617/cmselect/cmdfence/221/22109.htm#_idTextAnchor060
18 Chris Parry, *Super Highway* (Elliot & Thompson, 2014)
19 https://www.naval-technology.com/projects/nimitz/
20 https://publications.parliament.uk/pa/cm200203/cmhansrd/vo031023/debtext/31023-26.htm
21 https://www.naval-technology.com/projects/invincible/
22 https://publications.parliament.uk/pa/cm200203/cmhansrd/vo031023/debtext/31023-26.htm
23 https://www.independent.co.uk/news/uk/home-news/mod-signs-pound3bn-contracts-for-aircraft-carriers-859248.html
24 http://news.bbc.co.uk/hi/english/static/vote2001/results_constituencies/constituencies/210.stm
25 https://www.telegraph.co.uk/news/uknews/defence/8074625/Defence-review-decision-to-build-new-aircraft-carriers-made-in-Labours-1998-Strategic-Defence-Review.html
26 https://publications.parliament.uk/pa/cm200405/cmselect/cmdfence/45/4112403.htm
27 https://publications.parliament.uk/pa/cm200405/cmselect/cmdfence/45/4112404.htm
28 http://news.bbc.co.uk/1/hi/scotland/6914788.stm
29 https://www.f35.com/global/participation/united-kingdom
30 https://www.theguardian.com/politics/2010/nov/04/bae-cameron-aircraft-carrier-contract

31 https://www.telegraph.co.uk/news/uknews/defence/8072041/Navy-aircraft-carrier-will-be-sold-after-three-years-and-never-carry-jets.html

32 https://hansard.parliament.uk/Commons/2010-10-19/debates/10101928000003/StrategicDefence AndSecurityReview#contribution-10101928000193

33 Confidential source; interview with authors

34 https://hansard.parliament.uk/Commons/2012-05-10/debates/12051029000006/CarrierStrike Capability#contribution-12051029000116

35 http://www.bbc.co.uk/news/uk-politics-15300751

36 Interview with authors

37 http://www.bbc.co.uk/news/uk-politics-18008171

38 Ibid.

39 https://www.fleetairarmoa.org/content/sites/FAAOA/uploads/NewsDocuments/100/NAO-Carrier-Strike.PDF, p. 41

40 https://www.ft.com/content/40106756-4487-11e3-8926-00144feabdc0

41 http://www.bbc.co.uk/blogs/thereporters/robertpeston/2011/04/aircraft_carrier_costs_to_rise.html

42 https://www.theguardian.com/politics/2013/nov/04/aircraft-carrier-contract-costs; https://www.fleetairarmoa.org/content/sites/FAAOA/uploads/NewsDocuments/100/NAO-Carrier-Strike.PDF, para. 1.13

43 Confidential source

44 Confidential source

45 Confidential source

46 Confidential source

47 Confidential source

48 https://www.royalnavy.mod.uk/news-and-latest-activity/news/2016/january/13/160113-hms-prince-of-wales-iconic-structure-installed

49 https://rusi.org/sites/default/files/201309_op_leveraging_uk_carrier_capability.pdf, p.4

50 http://www.bbc.co.uk/news/world-asia-china-34125418

51 Ibid.

52 https://www.theguardian.com/world/live/2015/sep/03/china-military-parade-to-commemorate-second-world-war-victory-live

53 http://www.newsweek.com/2016/02/26/china-dongfeng-21d-missile-us-aircraft-carrier-427063.html

54 http://www.bbc.co.uk/news/world-europe-40442058

55 Parry, op. cit.

56 House of Commons Defence Committee Oral Evidence: Modernising Defence Programme, HC 818, 1 May 2018

57 Interview with authors

58 Interview with authors

59 Interview with authors

60 Christopher Parry, 'The UK's Future Carriers: What Are They Good For?', *RUSI Journal*, 11 December 2012

61 https://rusi.org/sites/default/files/201309_op_leveraging_uk_carrier_capability.pdf

62 https://www.nao.org.uk/wp-content/uploads/2017/03/Delivering-Carrier-Strike.pdf

63 Interview with authors

64 https://www.telegraph.co.uk/news/2016/06/29/long-awaited-70m-stealth-fighter-jet-arrives-in-britain-for-the/

65 https://www.gov.uk/government/news/crowsnest-helicopter-surveillance-deal-to-protect-carriers-sustains-200-high-skilled-uk-jobs

66 https://www.contracts.mod.uk/do-features-and-articles/delivering-carrier-strike/

67 https://www.nao.org.uk/wp-content/uploads/2017/03/Delivering-Carrier-Strike.pdf

68 http://www.savetheroyalnavy.org/type-45-destroyer-issues-continue-hms-diamond-breaks-down-on-gulf-deployment/

69 https://www.nao.org.uk/wp-content/uploads/2017/03/Delivering-Carrier-Strike.pdf, p. 16

70 https://www.gov.uk/government/news/crowsnest-helicopter-surveillance-deal-to-protect-carriers-sustains-200-high-skilled-uk-jobs

71 Interview with authors

ENDNOTES

72 Interview with authors

HALF MAST
1   https://classicalwisdom.com/themistocles-part-2/
2   http://ancient-greece.org/archaeology/lavrion.html
3   Parry, op. cit., p. 2
4   Ibid.
5   http://www.un.org/depts/los/convention_agreements/texts/unclos/unclos_e.pdf, Article 3
6   http://www.un.org/depts/los/convention_agreements/texts/unclos/unclos_e.pdf, Article 33
7   http://www.un.org/depts/los/convention_agreements/texts/unclos/unclos_e.pdf, Article 57
8   http://www.un.org/depts/los/convention_agreements/texts/unclos/unclos_e.pdf, Article 37, 38
9   https://www.economist.com/graphic-detail/2016/07/12/the-south-china-sea
10 http://nationalinterest.org/feature/china-america-clash-the-high-seas-the-eez-challenge-10513
11 https://geopoliticalfutures.com/chinese-military-installations-south-china-sea/
12 https://www.globalsecurity.org/intell/world/china/ccg.htm
13 https://www.theguardian.com/world/2007/aug/02/russia.arctic
14 Parry, op. cit.
15 http://www.savetheroyalnavy.org/tag/type-31-frigate/
16 https://www.nao.org.uk/wp-content/uploads/2018/04/Ensuring-sufficient-skilled-military-personnel.pdf, para. 1.4, 1.8
17 https://www.conservatives.com/manifesto2015, p. 77
18 https://assets.publishing.service.gov.uk/government/uploads/system/uploads/attachment_data/file/555607/2015_Strategic_Defence_and_Security_Review.pdf, p. 28
19 https://www.nao.org.uk/wp-content/uploads/2017/01/The-Equipment-Plan-2016-2026.pdf, p. 4
20 https://www.thetimes.co.uk/article/merger-threat-to-elite-forces-royal-marines-and-paratroopers-hjf9rm2wr
21 https://news.sky.com/story/royal-marines-at-risk-if-amphibious-ships-scrapped-11236133
22 https://www.theguardian.com/money/2002/jan/20/wageslaves.careers
23 https://petition.parliament.uk/petitions/202588
24 https://publications.parliament.uk/pa/cm201719/cmselect/cmdfence/622/62203.htm#_idTextAnchor004
25 https://publications.parliament.uk/pa/cm201719/cmselect/cmdfence/622/62205.htm, para.14
26 https://www.thetimes.co.uk/article/ultimate-test-of-leadership-under-stress-c3w6p2s3l
27 Interview with authors
28 https://www.thetimes.co.uk/article/ultimate-test-of-leadership-under-stress-c3w6p2s3l
29 Interview with authors
30 Interview with authors
31 https://www.theguardian.com/world/2017/dec/14/russia-could-cut-off-internet-to-nato-countries-british-military-chief-warns
32 Parry, op. cit.
33 http://www.bbc.co.uk/news/uk-42362500
34 https://www.thetimes.co.uk/article/economy-vulnerable-to-russian-attack-on-undersea-cable-links-rqqf0fxj8
35 http://www.bbc.co.uk/news/world-42365191
36 https://policyexchange.org.uk/wp-content/uploads/2017/11/Undersea-Cables.pdf, p. 17
37 Ibid., p. 30
38 http://www.dw.com/en/nato-chief-jens-stoltenberg-urges-calm-as-moscow-rattles-baltic-saber/a-43259850

FLYPAST
1   http://www.dailymail.co.uk/news/article-5938255/RAF-Centenary-Flypast-Watch-highlights-100-aircraft-took-skies-London.html

SKY RISE
1   http://researchbriefings.parliament.uk/ResearchBriefing/Summary/CBP-7930

2   http://www.bbc.co.uk/news/uk-politics-34989302
3   http://www.bbc.co.uk/news/uk-politics-23892783
4   http://www.bbc.co.uk/news/uk-politics-34989302
5   https://dronewars.net/foi/
6   http://www.warfare.today/2017/04/04/operation-shader-britains-war-in-iraq-and-syria/
7   https://www.forces.net/news/tri-service/raf-2016
8   Confidential source, interview with authors
9   http://www.warfare.today/2017/04/04/operation-shader-britains-war-in-iraq-and-syria/
10 https://assets.publishing.service.gov.uk/government/uploads/system/uploads/attachment_data/
    file/520366/PJHQ_FOI2016_03806___Number_of_enemy_combatants_killed_in_RAF_
    airstrikes_in_Iraq_from_2014_to_2016.pdf
11 https://dronewars.net/2018/02/26/cost-of-uk-air-and-drone-strikes-in-iraq-and-syria-reach-1-75-
    billion/
12 Confidential source, interview with authors
13 https://oig.usaid.gov/sites/default/files/other-reports/quarterly_oir_123117.pdf, p. 47
14 https://www.gov.uk/government/news/british-troops-support-mali-training-mission
15 https://www.telegraph.co.uk/news/uknews/defence/9834483/Hammond-UK-clear-about-Mali-
    mission-creep-risks.html
16 Private information
17 https://assets.publishing.service.gov.uk/government/uploads/system/uploads/attachment_data/
    file/62490/Factsheet8-RoyalAirForce.pdf
18 http://www.bbc.co.uk/news/uk-12297139
19 Confidential source, interview with authors
20 https://www.telegraph.co.uk/news/uknews/defence/8284935/Scrapping-the-RAFs-4bn-Nimrod-
    fleet-risks-UK-security.html
21 https://www.telegraph.co.uk/news/uknews/defence/7528840/Nimrod-officially-retires-after-three-
    decades.html
22 https://www.theguardian.com/uk/2009/oct/28/nimrod-crash-inquiry-blames-mod
23 https://www.telegraph.co.uk/news/2014178/Nimrod-inquest-Fleet-was-never-airworthy-says-
    coronor.html
24 https://www.forres-gazette.co.uk/Features/Kinloss-takes-its-leave-of-the-Mighty-Hunter-5777.htm
25 2010 Strategic Defence and Security Review, para. 2.A.II
26 http://www.bbc.co.uk/news/uk-england-12294766
27 https://www.telegraph.co.uk/news/uknews/defence/8212090/RAF-commander-our-air-force-will-
    be-little-better-than-Belgiums.html
28 https://ukdefencejournal.org.uk/12-squadron-named-new-typhoon-squadron/
29 https://www.telegraph.co.uk/news/uknews/defence/8212090/RAF-commander-our-air-force-will-
    be-little-better-than-Belgiums.html; http://www.bbc.co.uk/news/uk-33618484
30 https://www.telegraph.co.uk/news/uknews/defence/8284935/Scrapping-the-RAFs-4bn-Nimrod-
    fleet-risks-UK-security.html
31 https://www.theguardian.com/politics/2011/jan/27/nimrod-loss-massive-gap-former-defence-
    chiefs
32 https://www.airforce-technology.com/projects/nimrod-mra4/
33 https://www.nao.org.uk/wp-content/uploads/2011/11/10121520-I.pdf, para. 2.9
34 https://www.telegraph.co.uk/news/uknews/defence/8191690/3.6-billion-Nimrods-dismantled-for-
    scrap.html
35 http://www.bbc.com/future/story/20140414-crashes-that-changed-plane-design
36 Private information
37 https://www.theyworkforyou.com/wrans/?id=2015-02-27.225757.h&s=nimrod+section%3Awrans
    +speaker%3A11189#g225757.q0
38 https://www.theyworkforyou.com/wrans/?id=2014-06-09b.199145.h&s=nimrod+section%3Awrans
    +speaker%3A11189#g199145.q0
39 https://www.theyworkforyou.com/wrans/?id=2014-12-09.217871.h&s=lossiemouth+section%3Awr
    ans+speaker%3A11189#g217871.q0
40 http://www.bbc.co.uk/news/uk-scotland-highlands-islands-43836791

ENDNOTES

41 https://www.independent.co.uk/news/uk/home-news/uk-russia-submarines-patrol-planes-nimrod-poseidon-p8-nato-monitor-activity-navy-air-force-security-a8151931.html
42 https://www.telegraph.co.uk/news/uknews/defence/7931465/RAF-to-shrink-to-World-War-One-levels.html
43 Interview with authors
44 2015 Strategic Defence and Security Review, para. 4.49
45 https://www.telegraph.co.uk/news/2017/12/01/dambusters-squadron-reformed-fly-britains-new-stealth-fighter/
46 Confidential source; eyewitness account
47 2015 Strategic Defence and Security Review, para. 4.49
48 https://www.theregister.co.uk/2017/11/22/uk_f35_order_cuts_parliament/
49 https://www.theregister.co.uk/2017/12/05/uk_f35a_buy_still_on_cards/
50 https://www.flightglobal.com/news/articles/opinion-after-a-100bn-spend-it39s-time-for-f-35-to-413138/
51 https://twitter.com/realdonaldtrump/status/808301935728230404?lang=en
52 https://www.politico.com/story/2017/02/donald-trump-f-35-cost-234719
53 https://assets.publishing.service.gov.uk/government/uploads/system/uploads/attachment_data/file/492800/20150118-SDSR_Factsheets_1_to_17_ver_13.pdf, p.2
54 http://www.dailymail.co.uk/news/article-5564507/RAF-needs-money-airmen-deal-Russian-threat-says-chief.html
55 http://www.defense-aerospace.com/articles-view/release/3/66855/lockheed-touts-f_22%2C-jsf-at-s%27pore-show-%28feb-22%29.html
56 http://www.jsf.mil
57 https://www.telegraph.co.uk/finance/newsbysector/transport/farnborough-airshow/10977537/Everything-you-need-to-know-about-the-F-35-Britains-70m-new-stealth-fighter.html
58 https://medium.com/@DAUNow/the-joint-strike-fighter-when-construction-began-4aa3b8606fa3
59 https://www.f35.com/global/participation/united-kingdom-ip
60 https://www.thetimes.co.uk/article/bad-weather-delays-arrival-of-britain-s-new-warplanes-0j02qwwwc
61 https://theconversation.com/what-went-wrong-with-the-f-35-lockheed-martins-joint-strike-fighter-60905
62 Ibid.
63 Ibid.
64 https://www.thetimes.co.uk/article/jets-are-overbudget-unreliable-and-vulnerable-to-cyberattacks-v3gt8dcbb
65 Ibid.
66 https://publications.parliament.uk/pa/cm201719/cmselect/cmdfence/326/326.pdf
67 Ibid., p. 5
68 https://www.thetimes.co.uk/article/jets-are-overbudget-unreliable-and-vulnerable-to-cyberattacks-v3gt8dcbb
69 https://www.thetimes.co.uk/article/new-fighter-jets-have-more-than-300-faults-67bqlwjk9
70 Ibid.
71 Ibid.
72 https://publications.parliament.uk/pa/cm201719/cmselect/cmdfence/326/326.pdf
73 http://content.time.com/time/magazine/article/0,9171,2136312,00.html
74 https://www.flightglobal.com/news/articles/lockheed-f-35-service-life-extended-to-2070-423536/
75 https://www.theregister.co.uk/2017/11/22/uk_f35_order_cuts_parliament/
76 https://www.raf.mod.uk/news/uk-takes-delivery-of-final-f-35b-lightning-of-this-year/
77 https://www.forces.net/news/raf/fresh-out-training-and-f-35-fighter-jet
78 http://www.itv.com/news/anglia/2017-11-27/raf-base-continues-preparations-for-fighter-jet-arrival/
79 https://publications.parliament.uk/pa/cm201719/cmselect/cmdfence/326/326.pdf
80 Ibid.
81 Norman R. Augustine, *Augustine's Laws* (American Institute of Aeronautics & Astronautics, 1984)
82 https://www.theguardian.com/uk/2013/jun/04/six-arrested-drone-protest-raf-waddington
83 https://www.telegraph.co.uk/news/uknews/law-and-order/10360977/Clergymen-shut-down-base-that-operates-drones-in-Afghanistan.html

84 https://yorkshirecnd.org.uk/peace-activists-breach-security-at-uk-drones-base-to-plant-peace-garden/
85 https://www.theguardian.com/theguardian/2013/jun/07/drones-waddington-protest-greenham-common
86 https://www.telegraph.co.uk/news/2017/05/06/jeremy-corbyn-condemned-call-scrap-drone-warfare-dubbing-obscenity/
87 https://twitter.com/jeremycorbyn/status/328205367710470144
88 https://www.theatlantic.com/technology/archive/2018/03/drone-swarms-are-going-to-be-terrifying/555005/
89 http://researchbriefings.parliament.uk/ResearchBriefing/Summary/SN06493#fullreport, p. 11
90 http://www.warfare.today/2017/04/04/operation-shader-britains-war-in-iraq-and-syria/
91 https://www.telegraph.co.uk/news/uknews/terrorism-in-the-uk/10524075/Inside-drone-base-where-RAF-targeted-British-jihadists-in-Syria.html
92 https://hansard.parliament.uk/Commons/2018-05-02/debates/18050243000006/Counter-DaeshOperations#contribution-E367BCCC-DD50-44FA-A2D5-8B5CA970217F
93 There is one report: https://www.theguardian.com/uk/2011/jul/05/afghanistan-raf-drone-civilian-deaths
94 Confidential source; interview with authors
95 https://www.politicshome.com/news/uk/political-parties/labour-party/jeremy-corbyn/news/85312/watch-jeremy-corbyn-refuses-say-he
96 https://www.theengineer.co.uk/mod-to-invest-100m-in-drone-programme/
97 https://www.ft.com/content/c6755884-0034-11e8-9650-9c0ad2d7c5b5
98 Ibid.

ORBIT

1 https://www.gov.uk/government/publications/autumn-budget-2017-documents/autumn-budget-2017 Table 1.7
2 https://www.telegraph.co.uk/news/uknews/1516276/Cameron-turns-blue-to-prove-green-credentials.html
3 Original documents seen by authors
4 https://www.timeanddate.com/sun/norway/longyearbyen
5 https://www.ssb.no/en/befolkning/statistikker/befsvalbard/halvaar/2016-09-26
6 https://www.regjeringen.no/en/dokumenter/meld.-st.-32-20152016/id2499962/sec3
7 https://www.loc.gov/law/help/us-treaties/bevans/m-ust000002-0269.pdf Article 2 and Article 3
8 https://www.nytimes.com/2008/07/24/business/worldbusiness/24iht-arctic.4.14767779.html
9 Original document obtained by authors
10 Original documents seen by authors
11 https://modmedia.blog.gov.uk/2015/12/15/philip-dunne-defence-and-space/
12 http://www.presidency.ucsb.edu/ws/?pid=18820
13 http://news.bbc.co.uk/onthisday/hi/dates/stories/august/2/newsid_2526000/2526937.stm
14 http://news.bbc.co.uk/onthisday/hi/dates/stories/february/22/newsid_2518000/2518911.stm
15 https://www.scientificamerican.com/article/gps-and-the-world-s-first-space-war/
16 http://news.bbc.co.uk/1/hi/world/middle_east/2754103.stm
17 https://www.state.gov/t/isn/5181.htm, Article IV
18 https://www.thetimes.co.uk/article/britain-must-prepare-for-attacks-in-space-warns-raf-chief-xrbr3ggwr
19 https://www.cnbc.com/video/2018/03/13/trump-introduces-idea-of-space-force.html
20 http://freebeacon.com/national-security/china-carries-flight-test-anti-satellite-missile/
21 http://www.spacesafetymagazine.com/space-debris/kessler-syndrome/
22 http://nationalinterest.org/blog/the-buzz/get-ready-chinas-laser-weapons-arsenal-20138
23 https://www.telegraph.co.uk/business/2018/05/14/british-companies-may-banned-european-satellite-programme-brexit/
24 https://www.independent.co.uk/news/uk/politics/uk-galileo-satellite-system-eu-security-brexit-defence-a8343146.html
25 https://timesofindia.indiatimes.com/home/science/How-Kargil-spurred-India-to-design-own-GPS/articleshow/33254691.cms

26 http://www.mobilecomms-technology.com/projects/galileo/

27 http://www.bbc.co.uk/news/uk-politics-44232269

28 https://www.thetimes.co.uk/article/may-fights-to-stay-in-range-of-10bn-eu-satellite-deal-thstqd8bx

29 http://lindleyfrench.blogspot.co.uk/2018/05/schuman-galileo-and-return-of-great.html

30 https://www.telegraph.co.uk/politics/2018/05/25/uk-should-go-alone-build-satellite-system-brexit-chancellor/

31 https://www.loc.gov/law/help/us-treaties/bevans/m-ust000002-0269.pdf, Article 4

32 http://www.esa.int/Our_Activities/Space_Transportation/Types_of_orbits/(print)

33 Original document seen by authors

34 Original documents obtained by authors

35 https://rusi.org/event/pre-election-defence-debate

36 Major General Mitch Mitchell, Air Power Conference 2017

37 http://eu-arctic-forum.org/allgemein/what-future-for-the-high-north-debate-with-norwegian-foreign-minister-jonas-gahr-store-mep-michael-gahler-and-david-o'sullivan-chief-operating-officer-eeas-in-brussels/

38 http://www.mid.ru/ru/foreign_policy/news/-/asset_publisher/cKNonkJE02Bw/content/id/2732562?p_p_id=101_INSTANCE_cKNonkJE02Bw&_101_INSTANCE_cKNonkJE02Bw_languageId=en_GB

39 http://foreignpolicy.com/2017/01/25/heres-what-russias-military-build-up-in-the-arctic-looks-like-trump-oil-military-high-north-infographic-map/

40 http://www.highnorthnews.com/security-implications-in-focus-at-nato-pas-svalbard-meeting/

41 https://thebarentsobserver.com/en/security/2017/10/kommersant-russia-lists-norways-svalbard-policy-potential-risk-war

42 Confidential source

SOLDIERING ON

1 https://warisboring.com/the-t-34-was-a-war-winning-tank/

2 http://www.vaguelyinteresting.co.uk/tankograd-chelyabinsk-and-the-salvation-of-the-soviet-union/

3 https://warisboring.com/the-t-34-was-a-war-winning-tank/

4 Confidential source; serving personnel

5 https://www.bbc.co.uk/news/uk-39968776

6 http://researchbriefings.files.parliament.uk/documents/CBP-7930/CBP-7930.pdf

7 https://www.thesun.co.uk/news/5066989/chancellor-philip-hammond-armed-forces-cuts/

8 http://www.bbc.co.uk/news/uk-33638492

9 https://www.thetimes.co.uk/article/british-army-cuts-threaten-crucial-battlefield-training-37m2pbc3k

10 Confidential source; serving personnel

11 Confidential source; serving personnel

12 Private information

13 Interview with authors

14 Private information

15 https://publications.parliament.uk/pa/cm201415/cmselect/cmdfence/387/387.pdf, p. 4

16 Confidential source; interview with authors

17 https://publications.parliament.uk/pa/cm201415/cmselect/cmdfence/387/387.pdf, p. 5

18 Confidential source; MoD official

19 Confidential source

20 https://www.telegraph.co.uk/news/uknews/defence/11230930/Will-the-Army-be-able-to-rely-on-the-reserves.html

21 http://www.bbc.co.uk/news/uk-10680062

22 https://www.nao.org.uk/wp-content/uploads/2014/06/Army-2020.pdf, para. 2.11

23 Ibid., para. 2.27

24 Ibid., p. 10

25 Confidential source; interview with authors

26 Interview with authors

27 Interview with authors

28 https://www.telegraph.co.uk/news/uknews/defence/9076527/Territorial-Army-not-fit-for-new-role-warn-Generals.html
29 2010 Strategic Defence and Security Review, para 2.D.12
30 https://www.theguardian.com/commentisfree/2012/jul/05/army-2020-fighting-future
31 Ibid.
32 Author interview with Houghton
33 Author interview with Houghton
34 https://www.telegraph.co.uk/news/uknews/defence/10572453/Philip-Hammond-admits-millions-wasted-on-army-IT-failure.html
35 Ibid.
36 https://www.telegraph.co.uk/news/uknews/defence/11229680/Shocking-recruitment-figures-show-Army-Reserve-barely-growing.html
37 https://www.telegraph.co.uk/news/uknews/defence/11230930/Will-the-Army-be-able-to-rely-on-the-reserves.html
38 https://www.thetimes.co.uk/article/army-wastes-millions-on-botched-it-system-fb609p5hp5q
39 http://www.bbc.co.uk/news/uk-43111121
40 Interview with authors
41 Interview with authors
42 https://assets.publishing.service.gov.uk/government/uploads/system/uploads/attachment_data/file/28392/reserve2020_leaflet.pdf
43 https://www.instituteforgovernment.org.uk/events/managing-ministry-defence-stephen-lovegrove
44 https://assets.publishing.service.gov.uk/government/uploads/system/uploads/attachment_data/file/707538/20180401-_SPS.pdf, p. 9
45 Interview with authors
46 Interview with authors
47 Interview with authors
48 https://www.army-technology.com/features/feature-largest-military-bases-world-united-states/
49 https://www.nytimes.com/2010/02/22/science/earth/22endangered.html
50 Private information
51 Private information
52 Private information
53 Confidential source; interview with authors
54 Confidential source; interview with authors
55 Interview with authors
56 Interview with authors
57 Interview with authors
58 Private information
59 Private information
60 Interview with authors

SALLYING FORTH

1   https://rusi.org/publication/newsbrief/explaining-british-army's-strike-concept
2   Private information
3   Lecture at DSEI, 14 September 2017
4   https://www.thinkdefence.co.uk/light-strike-brigade/
5   https://www.economist.com/special-report/2018/01/25/using-clever-technology-to-keep-enemies-at-bay
6   https://www.thinkdefence.co.uk/light-strike-brigade/
7   Private information
8   https://rusi.org/publication/newsbrief/explaining-british-army's-strike-concept
9   Ibid.
10 Interview with authors
11 https://rusi.org/publication/newsbrief/explaining-british-army's-strike-concept, p. 4
12 https://www.generaldynamics.uk.com/solutions/vehicles/ajax/

13 Private information
14 http://www.dailymail.co.uk/news/article-3976390/Britain-left-fewer-tanks-Serbia-existing-war-machines-replaced-Ajax-armoured-vehicles-stand-Russian-attack.html
15 https://hansard.parliament.uk/Commons/2018-04-16/debates/1804164000008/MechanisedInfantryVehicle
16 Private information
17 https://www.chathamhouse.org/sites/files/chathamhouse/field/field_document/20150217QBritishArmy.pdf
18 Private information
19 https://www.chathamhouse.org/sites/files/chathamhouse/field/field_document/20150217QBritishArmy.pdf
20 Ibid.
21 Private information
22 https://publications.parliament.uk/pa/cm201314/cmselect/cmdfence/576/576.pdf
23 https://publications.parliament.uk/pa/cm201617/cmselect/cmdfence/108/10807.htm#footnote-162
24 Confidential source; serving personnel
25 https://www.ft.com/content/3e7e0c70-53a7-11e8-b3ee-41e0209208ec
26 https://www.army.mod.uk/deployments/
27 https://www.telegraph.co.uk/news/2017/03/18/british-troops-arrive-estonia-deter-russian-aggression-one-biggest/
28 2015 Strategic Defence and Security Review, para. 4.48
29 Private information
30 http://www.dailymail.co.uk/news/article-5772945/Western-air-forces-no-longer-rule-skies-rival-powers-develop-new-defences-say-RAF-boss.html
31 Confidential source; serving personnel
32 Confidential source; serving personnel
33 Confidential source; serving personnel
34 https://ukdefencejournal.org.uk/british-army-unveils-sky-sabre-air-defence-system/
35 https://assets.publishing.service.gov.uk/government/uploads/system/uploads/attachment_data/file/36720/20090210_MODAFDLODAnalysis_V1_0_U.pdf
36 Private information
37 Virgil, *The Aeneid*, Book II
38 Ibid.
39 https://www.ancient.eu/Trojan_War/
40 http://www.bbc.co.uk/ahistoryoftheworld/objects/rLY25R1hTjeZvge1ciN1ZA
41 https://www.bbc.co.uk/news/world-asia-35278451
42 http://www.newsweek.com/how-putin-uses-fake-news-wage-war-ukraine-577430
43 https://www.parliament.uk/business/publications/written-questions-answers-statements/written-question/Commons/2015-02-24/225283/
44 Interview with authors
45 Confidential source; interview with authors
46 Confidential source; interview with authors
47 https://www.theregister.co.uk/2017/01/03/77_brigade_struggling_recruit_40_pc_below_establishment/
48 http://www.bbc.co.uk/news/uk-31070114
49 Ibid.
50 Confidential source; interview with authors
51 Confidential source; interview with authors
52 Confidential source; interview with authors
53 Confidential source; interview with authors
54 Interview with authors
55 Interview with authors
56 Interview with authors
57 Interview with authors
58 Interview with authors

CONCRETE JUNGLES

1   Private information
2   https://www.thetimes.co.uk/article/anthony-loyd-dispatches-from-the-front-line-2kp0tm6sb
3   https://www.rand.org/content/dam/rand/pubs/research_reports/RR1600/RR1602/RAND_RR1602.pdf, p. 31
4   Ibid.
5   https://en.wikipedia.org/wiki/Battle_of_Grozny_(1994–95)#Summary
6   https://www.nytimes.com/1996/08/18/world/how-the-chechen-guerrillas-shocked-their-russian-foes.html
7   https://assets.publishing.service.gov.uk/government/uploads/system/uploads/attachment_data/file/348164/20140821_DCDC_GST_5_Web_Secured.pdf, p. 18
8   https://www.defensenews.com/digital-show-dailies/ausa/2016/10/05/army-chief-soldiers-must-be-ready-to-fight-in-megacities/
9   Private information
10 Interview with authors
11 Tim Ripley, *Operation Telic* (Herrick-Telic Publications, 2014), p. 176
12 https://www.bbc.co.uk/news/world-middle-east-39339373
13 https://edition.cnn.com/2016/10/24/middleeast/iraq-mosul-isis-tactics/
14 US Army Mosul Study Group Report
15 Interview with authors
16 https://www.rand.org/content/dam/rand/pubs/research_reports/RR1600/RR1602/RAND_RR1602.pdf, p. 34
17 https://web.archive.org/web/20070821154629/http://www.hrvc.net/htmls/references.htm
18 https://www.amnesty.org/en/latest/news/2009/04/no-avances-chechenia-sin-rendicion-cuentas-20090417/

BALACLAVAS

1   http://www.guardian.co.uk/politics/blog/2009/apr/24/gordon-brown-angry
2   https://www.telegraph.co.uk/news/uknews/defence/9835746/SAS-units-threatened-by-new-defence-cuts.html
3   http://news.bbc.co.uk/onthisday/hi/witness/may/5/newsid_2989000/2989749.stm
4   Interview with authors
5   https://www.mirror.co.uk/news/uk-news/red-arrows-face-axe-threat-1569983
6   https://www.mirror.co.uk/news/uk-news/red-arrows-not-axed-david-1718740
7   Interview with authors
8   Interview with authors
9   https://www.thetimes.co.uk/article/sas-in-iraq-gets-kill-list-of-british-jihadis-p9l9s6vr7
10 Confidential source
11 Interview with authors
12 Confidential source; interview with authors
13 Private information
14 Private information
15 https://www.bbc.co.uk/news/magazine-16573516
16 https://www.channel4.com/news/libya-antigaddafi-rebels-seize-sas-troops
17 Ibid.
18 Ibid.
19 Confidential source; interview with authors
20 https://www.telegraph.co.uk/news/worldnews/africaandindianocean/libya/8365590/British-ambassador-broadcast-on-Libyan-state-TV.html
21 https://www.thetimes.co.uk/article/sas-bunglers-had-secret-computer-codes-in-pockets-twpm2q7cw85
22 Confidential source
23 Interview with authors
24 Interview with authors
25 Interview with authors
26 Interview with authors

27 Interview with authors
28 Private information
29 Private information
30 Interview with authors
31 Private information
32 https://assets.publishing.service.gov.uk/government/uploads/system/uploads/attachment_data/file/652784/20170807_Brecon_SI_Report_V2_Unclassified_External_Release_Elements_Roundtripped.pdf
33 Interview with authors
34 Private information
35 https://www.westmidlands-pcc.gov.uk/media/58058/10_PServices_19April2012_Operation_Plato.pdf
36 Confidential Special Forces source
37 Private information
38 Confidential source
39 Interview with authors
40 https://www.thetimes.co.uk/article/rogue-sas-unit-accused-of-executing-civilians-in-afghanistan-f2bqlc897
41 Confidential source
42 https://www.telegraph.co.uk/news/worldnews/africaandindianocean/libya/8727076/How-the-special-forces-helped-bring-Gaddafi-to-his-knees.html
43 Interview with authors
44 Interview with authors
45 Interview with authors

ORCHESTRAS

1 https://www.telegraph.co.uk/news/worldnews/ebola/11158504/WHO-says-Ebola-is-most-severe-acute-health-emergency-in-modern-times.html
2 Private information
3 Interview with authors
4 Interview with authors
5 https://www.gov.uk/government/news/rfa-argus-honoured-as-she-completes-sierra-leone-deployment
6 https://www.forces.net/news/army/operation-gritrock-plan-tackle-ebola
7 Interview with authors
8 Interview with authors
9 Interview with authors
10 http://www.who.int/news-room/detail/07-11-2015-sierra-leone-stops-transmission-of-ebola-virus
11 https://www.nhs.uk/news/medical-practice/ebola-risk-remains-low-as-medic-flown-home/
12 Interview with authors
13 https://assets.publishing.service.gov.uk/government/uploads/system/uploads/attachment_data/file/661480/autumn_budget_2017_web.pdf, pp 23–4
14 Interview with authors
15 Interview with authors
16 Interview with authors
17 Interview with authors
18 Interview with authors
19 Interview with authors
20 Interview with authors
21 Interview with authors

READY OR NOT

1 https://api.parliament.uk/historic-hansard/lords/1980/nov/04/exercise-crusader
2 Interview with authors
3 https://assets.publishing.service.gov.uk/government/uploads/system/uploads/attachment_data/file/707538/20180401-_SPS.pdf, p. 7

4   http://hansard.millbanksystems.com/written_answers/2002/jul/01/armed-forces-exercises

5   https://www.bbc.co.uk/news/world-europe-44208921

6   https://www.vbs.admin.ch/fr/ddps/faits-chiffres/armee.html

7   https://www.cia.gov/library/publications/the-world-factbook/fields/2024.html

8   https://www.swissinfo.ch/eng/politics/swiss-military_army-reforms-given-green-light-by-parliament/42006598

9   T. Dodd and M. Oakes, *The Strategic Defence Review White Paper* (House of Commons Library, 1998), p. 38

10   Farrell, *Transforming Military Power since the Cold War: Britain, France, and the United States, 1991–2012* (Cambridge University Press, 2013), p. 173

11   https://www.thetimes.co.uk/article/army-reduced-to-just-single-tank-regiment-rqkt8cr0rln; https://www.thetimes.co.uk/article/britain-has-only-36-tanks-ready-to-fight-cskdlk7cql2

12   http://janes.ihs.com/InternationalDefenceReview/Display/1751772

13   https://news.sky.com/story/submarine-hunt-raf-plane-back-on-argentine-soil-for-first-time-since-falklands-11139053

14   https://www.gov.uk/government/news/mod-set-to-save-over-500m-and-sustain-hundreds-of-uk-jobs-with-new-typhoon-support-deal

15   Interview with authors

16   Confidential source; interview with authors

17   https://www.thetimes.co.uk/article/british-submarine-in-underwater-duel-with-kremlins-black-hole-hunter-killer-dhxhlpwc9

18   Confidential source; interview with authors

19   Confidential source

20   https://www.express.co.uk/news/uk/574556/Britain-only-one-nuclear-submarine-active-patrol-defects-defence-fleet

21   http://www.dailymail.co.uk/news/article-5850349/The-6-billion-Royal-Navy-fleet-hardly-went-sea.html

22   https://www.thesun.co.uk/news/2829355/uks-entire-fleet-of-attack-submarines-is-out-of-action-and-theresa-may-doesnt-know/

23   https://www.gov.uk/government/news/royal-navy-and-army-release-redundancy-scheme-details

24   https://www.savetheroyalnavy.org/the-hidden-crisis-royal-navy-manpower/

25   https://www.parliament.uk/written-questions-answers-statements/written-question/commons/2016-06-08/40030; https://www.royalnavy.mod.uk/our-organisation/the-fighting-arms/surface-fleet/frigates/type-23/hms-lancaster

26   https://www.bbc.com/news/uk-england-devon-34909649

27   *Securing Britain in an Age of Uncertainty: The Strategic Defence and Security Review*, HM Government, 2010, p. 20

28   Ibid., pp 22, 26

29   https://www.royalnavy.mod.uk/news-and-latest-activity/news/2014/august/28/140828-hms-illustrious-takes-final-bow

30   http://www.royalnavy.mod.uk/news-and-latest-activity/news/2016/september/20/160920-ocean-deploys

31   https://www.ft.com/content/744754b8-9137-11e5-bd82-c1fb87bef7af

32   'Divisional Warfighting – the impact on UK MoD's decision-making, acquisition and support processes and activities', *Ares&Athena*, November 2016, CHACR, p. 31

33   https://www.parliament.uk/business/publications/written-questions-answers-statements/written-statement/Commons/2016-12-15/HCWS367/

34   Interview with authors

35   'Divisional Warfighting – the impact on UK MoD's decision-making, acquisition and support processes and activities', *Ares&Athena*, November 2016, CHACR, p. 16

36   Interview with authors

THE MIGHTY O

1   https://www.standard.co.uk/news/politics/local-elections-2018-jubilant-tories-cling-on-to-win-crown-jewel-stakes-in-wandsworth-after-early-a3831381.html

ENDNOTES

2 https://www.plymouthherald.co.uk/news/news-opinion/moment-plymouths-tories-knew-over-1532345
3 https://www.plymouthherald.co.uk/news/plymouth-news/bulwark-albion-council-unites-campaign-1168128
4 http://www.bbc.co.uk/news/uk-england-devon-43541209
5 https://www.plymouthherald.co.uk/news/plymouth-news/full-story-behind-500-job-1314006
6 https://www.independent.co.uk/news/uk/politics/local-elections-2018-plymouth-labour-tories-johnny-mercer-a8335626.html

THE WAR BUSINESS

1 https://www.independent.co.uk/news/uk/politics/dsei-2017-london-arms-fair-weapons-saudi-arabia-excel-centre-sadiq-khan-cancel-a7853286.html
2 Research trip by project contributors
3 https://themoscowtimes.com/articles/britain-excludes-russia-from-london-arms-expo-rostec-manager-43960
4 http://people.defensenews.com/top-100/
5 Research trip by project contributors
6 Research trip by project contributors
7 Research trip by project contributors
8 Research trip by project contributors
9 Research trip by project contributors
10 Research trip by project contributors
11 https://www.telegraph.co.uk/finance/2941537/Twenty-years-of-smokescreen-over-Saudi-deal.html
12 https://www.theguardian.com/uk/2004/oct/05/saudiarabia.armstrade
13 https://www.theguardian.com/politics/2003/oct/13/uk.freedomofinformation
14 http://news.bbc.co.uk/1/hi/business/8500535.stm
15 https://www.adsgroup.org.uk/wp-content/uploads/sites/21/2017/06/ADS-Annual-Facts-2017.pdf
16 https://www.gov.uk/government/publications/uk-defence-and-security-export-figures-2016/uk-defence-and-security-export-statistics-for-2016
17 https://www.adsgroup.org.uk/wp-content/uploads/sites/21/2017/06/ADS-Annual-Facts-2017.pdf
18 Private information
19 https://www.gov.uk/government/speeches/why-defence-matters-in-the-scottish-independence-debate
20 Confidential source
21 http://www.dailymail.co.uk/news/article-1344760/MoD-accused-covering-controversial-BAE-aircraft-carrier-deal-worth-5-2billion.html; https://www.independent.co.uk/news/uk/home-news/mod-signs-pound3bn-contracts-for-aircraft-carriers-859248.html
22 Interview with authors
23 Private information
24 Research trip by project contributors
25 Confidential source
26 https://www.caat.org.uk/resources/publications/government/justice-comm-foi-2012.pdf
27 https://www.telegraph.co.uk/finance/markets/2785317/Ambassador-faces-questions-over-BAE-deal.html
28 https://www.hsbc.com/-/media/HSBC-com/InvestorRelationsAssets/StockExchange Announcements/2010/september/sea-100924-leadership-team-en.ashx
29 https://www.theguardian.com/business/2015/feb/09/ex-hsbc-boss-stephen-green-the-ethical-banker-with-questions-to-answer
30 Interview with authors
31 https://publications.parliament.uk/pa/cm201213/cmselect/cmdfence/419/41921.htm
32 Interview with authors
33 Interview with authors
34 Interview with authors
35 Interview with authors
36 https://twitter.com/andreas_krieg/status/970939190048419840
37 https://twitter.com/AbdirahimS/status/971368665177190400

38 https://www.independent.co.uk/news/uk/politics/theresa-may-saudi-arabia-mohammed-bin-salman-crown-prince-brexit-a8242701.html

39 https://www.bbc.co.uk/news/world-middle-east-43235643

40 https://www.aljazeera.com/news/2018/03/demonstrators-mbs-hands-yemen-rally-visit-180307151305625.html

41 http://www.kateosamor.co.uk/protesting_saudi_arabia_s_crown_prince

42 https://www.independent.co.uk/news/world/middle-east/vince-cable-ministry-defence-misled-over-saudi-arabia-arms-deals-yemen-a7399196.html

43 https://assets.publishing.service.gov.uk/government/uploads/system/uploads/attachment_data/file/327679/UKTI_DSO_Export_Statistics_for_2013_-_Slides.pdf

44 'HMS Sheffield was a floating fire trap', *New Scientist*, 22 July 1982, p. 211.

45 http://iafss.org/publications/fss/1/761/view/fss_1-761.pdf, p. 770

46 Interview with authors

47 https://www.gov.uk/guidance/standing-commitments#urgent-operational-requirements-uors

48 Interview with authors

49 https://www.nao.org.uk/wp-content/uploads/2016/10/Departmental-Overview-2015-16-Ministry-of-Defence.pdf, p.8

50 http://news.bbc.co.uk/1/hi/business/3752176.stm

51 'Main Estimates: Government spending plans for 2018–19', House of Commons Library, p. 5

52 http://www.cimaglobal.com/Documents/ImportedDocuments/tech_resrep_annuality_in_public_budgeting_oct2005.pdf, p. 2

53 Interview with authors

54 Interview with authors

55 Interview with authors

56 Interview with authors

RAINBOW WARRIORS

1 https://www.telegraph.co.uk/news/uknews/1563114/British-troops-let-down-by-disgraceful-housing.html

2 Private information

3 https://www.telegraph.co.uk/news/2018/02/19/would-be-soldiers-dropping-army-recruitment-process-takes-long/

4 https://www.youtube.com/watch?v=OiMmh8T8Aug

5 https://www.youtube.com/watch?v=IUcaM_0ztbM

6 https://www.reuters.com/article/us-britain-army-lgbt/uk-army-adverts-tell-recruits-they-can-be-gay-pray-and-cry-idUSKBN1EZ2K6

7 https://www.youtube.com/watch?v=Q1vCe3BAnws

8 https://news.sky.com/story/defence-secretary-halts-plan-to-scrap-be-the-best-slogan-11183651

9 Internal MoD document, *The Army Brand*

10 Private information

11 https://www.irishexaminer.com/breakingnews/ireland/growth-in-female-recruits-after-360k-recruitment-campaign-in-2017-823952.html

12 https://twitter.com/ArmySgtMajor/status/952255316011503621

13 Private information; serving personnel, 2017

14 Interview with authors

15 https://assets.publishing.service.gov.uk/government/uploads/system/uploads/attachment_data/file/707538/20180401-_SPS.pdf, p. 6

16 Ibid., p. 1

17 Mark Francois, *Filling the Ranks*, https://www.markfrancois.com/filling-ranks

18 Confidential source; interview with authors

19 https://www.independent.co.uk/news/uk/politics/pay-cap-armed-forces-public-sector-limit-labour-theresa-may-a7945741.html

20 Confidential interview

21 https://www.gov.uk/government/statistics/armed-forces-continuous-attitude-survey-2017

22 Francois, op. cit.

23 Confidential source, interview with authors
24 https://britisharmy.wordpress.com/2011/05/23/steely-eyed-dealers-in-death/
25 https://civilservice.blog.gov.uk/2017/11/23/creating-a-network-of-straight-allies-to-support-diversity-in-defence/
26 Confidential source; interview with authors
27 Confidential source; interview with authors
28 Confidential source; interview with authors
29 http://www.bbc.co.uk/news/uk-england-35458611
30 https://assets.publishing.service.gov.uk/government/uploads/system/uploads/attachment_data/file/272303/6851.pdf
31 https://www.theguardian.com/uk-news/2013/oct/01/royal-marine-drill-instructor-fined
32 Private information
33 https://assets.publishing.service.gov.uk/government/uploads/system/uploads/attachment_data/file/698884/2018-02760.pdf
34 Confidential source; interview with authors
35 http://www.bbc.co.uk/news/uk-43111121
36 https://sofrep.com/94786/careerism-cronyism-malfeasance-special-warfare-center-end-special-forces-capability/
37 https://www.vice.com/en_uk/article/gqdx44/full-v13n4
38 https://www.nytimes.com/2006/08/13/world/europe/13hazing.html
39 Private information
40 Serving personnel; pseudonyms
41 https://www.telegraph.co.uk/news/2017/10/27/nine-british-servicemen-removed hms-vigilant-testing-positive/
42 Eyewitness account; confidential source
43 https://www.gov.uk/government/news/ban-on-women-in-ground-close-combat-roles-lifted
44 https://www.theguardian.com/uk-news/2014/dec/19/women-combat-roles-british-army-infantry-armoured-units
45 https://www.gov.uk/government/news/ban-on-women-in-ground-close-combat-roles-lifted
46 Interview with authors
47 http://www.dailymail.co.uk/news/article-5025485/HMS-Sex-Cocaine.html
48 Confidential source; interview with authors
49 https://assets.publishing.service.gov.uk/government/uploads/system/uploads/attachment_data/file/664180/UK_Armed_Forces_Biannual_Diversity_Statistics_1_October_2017-b.pdf
50 Confidential source; interview with authors

LAWFARE

1   Mark de Rond, *Doctors at War* (ILR Press, 2017), p. 14
2   Ibid., p. 34
3   Ibid., p. 3
4   Ibid., p. 105
5   Ibid., p. 51
6   Ibid.
7   Ibid.
8   https://www.independent.co.uk/news/uk/home-news/sgt-alexander-blackman-the-case-for-and-against-the-royal-marine-who-murdered-a-wounded-unarmed-10508375.html
9   Confidential source; interview with authors
10 Private information
11 https://casebook.icrc.org/case-study/echr-al-skeini-et-al-v-uk
12 Ibid.
13 http://www.rulac.org/assets/downloads/CASE_OF_AL-SKEINI_AND_OTHERS_v._THE_UNITED_KINGDOM.pdf
14 https://www.theguardian.com/uk/2012/oct/12/inquiry-british-abuse-iraqi-prisoners
15 https://www.gov.uk/government/groups/iraq-historic-allegations-team-ihat
16 https://policyexchange.org.uk/wp-content/uploads/2016/09/the-fog-of-law.pdf, p. 10

17 https://policyexchange.org.uk/wp-content/uploads/2016/09/clearing-the-fog-of-law.pdf, p. 26
18 https://www.supremecourt.uk/decided-cases/docs/UKSC_2012_0249_Judgment.pdf
19 https://www.telegraph.co.uk/news/2017/09/23/will-nightmare-end-war-vet-tells-shock-fourth-inquiry-intosuspicious/
20 Interview with authors
21 https://policyexchange.org.uk/wp-content/uploads/2016/09/the-fog-of-law.pdf, p. 10
22 Johnny Mercer, *We Were Warriors* (Sidgwick & Jackson, 2017), p. 2
23 Ibid.
24 https://www.telegraph.co.uk/news/worldnews/asia/afghanistan/7874950/Courageous-restraint-putting-troops-lives-at-risk.html
25 Mercer, op. cit.
26 Interview with authors
27 Interview with authors
28 Interview with authors
29 Interview with authors
30 Interview with authors
31 Interview with authors
32 Interview with authors
33 Interview with authors
34 Interview with authors
35 Interview with authors
36 https://policyexchange.org.uk/wp-content/uploads/2016/09/the-fog-of-law.pdf, p. 18
37 https://policyexchange.org.uk/wp-content/uploads/2016/09/clearing-the-fog-of-law.pdf

SIXTH SENSE

1 https://assets.publishing.service.gov.uk/government/uploads/system/uploads/attachment_data/file/323440/Tornado_ZD743_ZD812_Part_1_4_1.pdf, p. 28
2 https://www.bbc.co.uk/news/uk-scotland-highlands-islands-28115813
3 https://www.theyworkforyou.com/wrans/?id=2015-01-14.220806.h&s=%28%28%28%28%28section%3Awrans%29+typhoon%29%29%29%29+speaker%3A11189#g220806.q0
4 1998 Strategic Defence Review, p. 43
5 https://assets.publishing.service.gov.uk/government/uploads/system/uploads/attachment_data/file/323440/Tornado_ZD743_ZD812_Part_1_4_1.pdf, p. 19
6 https://assets.publishing.service.gov.uk/government/uploads/system/uploads/attachment_data/file/323453/Tornado_ZD743_ZD812_Part_1_4_6_cont2.pdf, pp 257–8
7 Ibid., pp 258–9
8 Ibid., p. 259
9 Ibid., p. 265
10 Ibid.
11 Ibid., p. 260
12 Ibid., pp 130–38
13 https://www.bbc.co.uk/news/uk-scotland-highlands-islands-31859020
14 https://www.pressandjournal.co.uk/fp/news/highlands/1454818/near-misses-prompt-calls-for-highland-tornado-crash-public-inquiry/
15 https://www.airproxboard.org.uk/Reports-and-analysis/Monthly-summaries/Monthly-Airprox-reviews/
16 https://stories.swns.com/news/raf-typhoon-flights-over-lancashire-suspended-after-near-miss-with-passenger-jet-1565/
17 https://www.express.co.uk/news/uk/467524/Eurofighter-Typhoon-in-near-miss-with-passenger-plane-over-Scotland
18 Confidential source, interview with authors

ROBOTS

1 https://www.telegraph.co.uk/news/uknews/1316277/Calls-to-honour-inventor-of-bomb-disposal-device.html

ENDNOTES

2 https://www.thetimes.co.uk/article/lieutenant-colonel-peter-miller-t8t6hr3zxlm
3 https://www.bbc.com/news/technology-34066941
4 https://www2.deloitte.com/content/dam/Deloitte/uk/Documents/consumer-business/deloitte-uk-augmentation-through-automation.pdf
5 Industry Driven Development Session, DSEI, 11 September 2017
6 Seminar on Robotics, Shangri La Dialogue, June 2017
7 Transforming the British Army – Adaptation and Efficiency; Modernising Army Capability Session, DSEI, 12 September 2017
8 Ibid.
9 Ibid.
10 Essential Collaboration Session, DSEI, 11 September 2017
11 https://www.youtube.com/watch?v=xaGCkseMYyo
12 https://www.theguardian.com/world/2016/sep/05/royal-navy-tests-unmanned-speedboat-ahead-of-drone-exercises
13 http://www.bbc.com/future/story/20150715-killer-robots-the-soldiers-that-never-sleep
14 Interview with authors
15 https://news.sky.com/story/elon-musk-joins-100-tech-chiefs-warning-un-that-killer-robots-could-be-third-revolution-of-warfare-10998721
16 https://assets.publishing.service.gov.uk/government/uploads/system/uploads/attachment_data/file/348164/20140821_DCDC_GST_5_Web_Secured.pdf, p. 96
17 http://www.atimes.com/article/china-shows-off-drone-brigade-guangzhou-fortune-forum-gala/
18 Confidential source; interview with authors
19 https://podcasts.ox.ac.uk/artificial-intelligence-robotics-and-conflict
20 Keynote Speech, Future Force Design, DSEI, 11 September 2017
21 Ibid.
22 Ibid.
23 Confidential source; interview with authors
24 Interview with authors

SHOWDOWN

1 Private information
2 https://www.independent.co.uk/news/uk/politics/richard-madeley-interview-gavin-williamson-good-morning-britain-elephant-putin-a8375061.html
3 https://www.mirror.co.uk/news/uk-news/theresa-may-vicars-daughter-kitten-8399895
4 Interview with authors
5 https://www.independent.co.uk/news/uk/home-news/police-armed-routine-uk-terror-attacks-target-missed-recruitment-a8354926.html
6 https://www.nao.org.uk/report/the-equipment-plan-2016-2026, p. 4
7 https://www.gov.uk/government/uploads/system/uploads/attachment_data/file/629284/Major_Projects_MOD_Annual_Report_-_consolidated_data_and_narratives.xlsx
8 https://www.gov.uk/government/news/strategic-defence-and-security-review-implementation and https://www.gov.uk/government/publications/national-security-capability-review-nscr
9 https://janes.ihs.com/DefenceWeekly/Display/1813078
10 Original documents seen by authors
11 Original documents seen by authors
12 https://www.generaldynamics.uk.com/general-dynamics-uk-awarded-135-million-contract-to-provide-enhanced-communications-to-british-armed-forces/
13 Original documents seen by authors
14 https://www.thetimes.co.uk/article/merger-threat-to-elite-forces-royal-marines-and-paratroopers-hjf9rm2wr
15 Confidential source; interview with authors
16 https://www.independent.co.uk/news/uk/politics/nhs-funding-theresa-may-20-billion-2023-tax-brexit-a8402566.html
17 https://www.express.co.uk/news/uk/976168/nhs-funding-boost-government-theresa-may-tax-increase

18 https://www.newstatesman.com/2018/06/no-money-chancellor-philip-hammond-nhs-boost-police-schools-prisons-defence
19 https://www.politicshome.com/news/uk/defence/news/96459/us-defence-secretary-says-'special-relationship'-risk-unless-uk-boosts
20 https://www.independent.co.uk/news/uk/politics/uk-military-army-theresa-may-gavin-williamson-defence-secretary-tier-one-a8410781.html
21 https://www.telegraph.co.uk/politics/2018/06/21/theresa-may-refuses-say-britain-will-remain-tier-one-military/
22 http://www.dailymail.co.uk/news/article-5878221/Give-20billion-Ill-bring-Defence-Secretarys-astonishing-threat-PM.html

CONCLUSION

1 Original documents seen by authors
2 Interview with authors
3 https://www.bbc.co.uk/news/uk-43090206
4 https://www.standard.co.uk/news/world/raf-plane-lands-in-argentina-for-first-time-since-falklands-war-to-help-search-for-missing-submarine-a3699211.html
5 https://www.bbc.co.uk/news/uk-politics-44609494; https://www.ukpublicspending.co.uk/uk_national_defence_analysis
6 https://www.telegraph.co.uk/news/2017/07/17/government-departments-struggling-spend-foreign-aid-budgets/
7 https://www.bbc.co.uk/news/uk-politics-41266189
8 Full results are in the Appendix to this book

INDEX

425